Math Expressions

Volume 1

Developed by
The Children's Math Worlds Research Project

PROJECT DIRECTOR AND AUTHOR
Dr. Karen C. Fuson

This material is based upon work supported by the
National Science Foundation
under Grant Numbers
ESI-9816320, REC-9806020, and RED-935373.

Any opinions, findings, and conclusions, or recommendations expressed in this material are those of the author and do not necessarily reflect the views of the National Science Foundation.

HOUGHTON MIFFLIN HARCOURT

Teacher Reviewers

Kindergarten
Patricia Stroh Sugiyama
Wilmette, Illinois

Barbara Wahle
Evanston, Illinois

Grade 1
Sandra Budson
Newton, Massachusetts

Janet Pecci
Chicago, Illinois

Megan Rees
Chicago, Illinois

Grade 2
Molly Dunn
Danvers, Massachusetts

Agnes Lesnick
Hillside, Illinois

Rita Soto
Chicago, Illinois

Grade 3
Jane Curran
Honesdale, Pennsylvania

Sandra Tucker
Chicago, Illinois

Grade 4
Sara Stoneberg Llibre
Chicago, Illinois

Sheri Roedel
Chicago, Illinois

Grade 5
Todd Atler
Chicago, Illinois

Leah Barry
Norfolk, Massachusetts

Special Thanks

Special thanks to the many teachers, students, parents, principals, writers, researchers, and work-study students who participated in the Children's Math Worlds Research Project over the years.

Credits

© Kerstin Layer/Age Fotostock

Illustrative art: Robin Boyer/Deborah Wolfe, LTD; Dave Clegg, Geoff Smith, Ron Mahoney, Tim Johnson
Technical art: Nesbitt Graphics, Inc.
Photos: Nesbitt Graphics, Inc.; Page 93 © C Squared Studios/Photodisc/Getty Images; Page 455 © Nick Green/Jupiter Images.

Printed in the U.S.A.

ISBN: 978-0-547-05725-5

9 1421 17 16 15 14 13
4500407845

VOLUME 1 CONTENTS

Basic Facts Fluency Plan

Basic Addition and Subtraction Strategies

Unit 1 Place Value and Multi-Digit Addition and Subtraction

Understand Place Value

Grouping to Add

Ungrouping to Subtract

Mini Unit 2 Lines, Line Segments, and Quadrilaterals

Properties of Quadrilaterals

Unit 3 Addition and Subtraction Word Problems

Solve Word Problems

Solve Multi-Digit Word Problems

VOLUME 1 CONTENTS (CONTINUED)

Mini Unit 4 Figures, Angles, and Triangles

Properties of Quadrilaterals and Triangles

Unit 5 Use Addition and Subtraction

Round, Estimate, and Compare

Use Money

Tables

Complex Word Problems

Pictographs, Bar Graphs, and Line Plots

Mini Unit 6 Patterns

Patterns

Unit 7Multiplication and Division with 0–5, 9, and 10

Meanings of Multiplication and Division

Class Activity

Name ___ Date ___

► Check Up for Additions

Add.

1. 9 + 4 = ___	2. 6 + 3 = ___	3. 4 + 6 = ___	4. 7 + 7 = ___
5. 0 + 6 = ___	6. 7 + 1 = ___	7. 8 + 3 = ___	8. 8 + 9 = ___
9. 9 + 3 = ___	10. 6 + 4 = ___	11. 8 + 5 = ___	12. 5 + 4 = ___
13. 7 + 3 = ___	14. 5 + 6 = ___	15. 9 + 2 = ___	16. 5 + 5 = ___
17. 1 + 9 = ___	18. 8 + 2 = ___	19. 4 + 4 = ___	20. 3 + 6 = ___
21. 2 + 8 = ___	22. 9 + 1 = ___	23. 2 + 7 = ___	24. 3 + 8 = ___
25. 7 + 4 = ___	26. 4 + 5 = ___	27. 9 + 8 = ___	28. 6 + 8 = ___
29. 6 + 6 = ___	30. 9 + 5 = ___	31. 8 + 4 = ___	32. 1 + 6 = ___
33. 8 + 6 = ___	34. 6 + 7 = ___	35. 7 + 5 = ___	36. 8 + 8 = ___
37. 4 + 8 = ___	38. 7 + 9 = ___	39. 6 + 5 = ___	40. 9 + 6 = ___
41. 9 + 9 = ___	42. 3 + 7 = ___	43. 7 + 8 = ___	44. 4 + 7 = ___
45. 3 + 9 = ___	46. 7 + 6 = ___	47. 5 + 9 = ___	48. 7 + 8 = ___
49. 2 + 9 = ___	50. 5 + 7 = ___	51. 9 + 0 = ___	52. 5 + 8 = ___
53. 9 + 7 = ___	54. 6 + 0 = ___	55. 4 + 9 = ___	56. 6 + 9 = ___

Class Activity

Name ______________________ Date ______________

▶ Check Up for Subtractions

Subtract.

1. $13 - 9 =$ ___
2. $9 - 0 =$ ___
3. $6 - 4 =$ ___
4. $7 - 5 =$ ___
5. $11 - 4 =$ ___
6. $15 - 6 =$ ___
7. $11 - 6 =$ ___
8. $8 - 1 =$ ___
9. $10 - 5 =$ ___
10. $12 - 7 =$ ___
11. $8 - 4 =$ ___
12. $7 - 6 =$ ___
13. $5 - 4 =$ ___
14. $6 - 5 =$ ___
15. $12 - 8 =$ ___
16. $8 - 5 =$ ___
17. $10 - 8 =$ ___
18. $18 - 9 =$ ___
19. $14 - 5 =$ ___
20. $9 - 9 =$ ___
21. $13 - 5 =$ ___
22. $9 - 6 =$ ___
23. $10 - 7 =$ ___
24. $8 - 6 =$ ___
25. $15 - 8 =$ ___
26. $16 - 9 =$ ___
27. $9 - 8 =$ ___
28. $14 - 7 =$ ___
29. $9 - 5 =$ ___
30. $11 - 9 =$ ___
31. $12 - 5 =$ ___
32. $10 - 4 =$ ___
33. $13 - 8 =$ ___
34. $9 - 7 =$ ___
35. $14 - 8 =$ ___
36. $13 - 6 =$ ___
37. $14 - 9 =$ ___
38. $13 - 4 =$ ___
39. $10 - 6 =$ ___
40. $16 - 8 =$ ___
41. $6 - 3 =$ ___
42. $11 - 7 =$ ___
43. $12 - 4 =$ ___
44. $10 - 9 =$ ___
45. $13 - 7 =$ ___
46. $15 - 9 =$ ___
47. $11 - 5 =$ ___
48. $14 - 6 =$ ___
49. $12 - 6 =$ ___
50. $9 - 4 =$ ___
51. $7 - 4 =$ ___
52. $12 - 9 =$ ___
53. $16 - 7 =$ ___
54. $11 - 8 =$ ___
55. $17 - 9 =$ ___
56. $15 - 7 =$ ___

Name ______________________ Date ____________

Vocabulary
place value

► Practice Place Value Drawings to 999

Write the number for each dot drawing.

1. 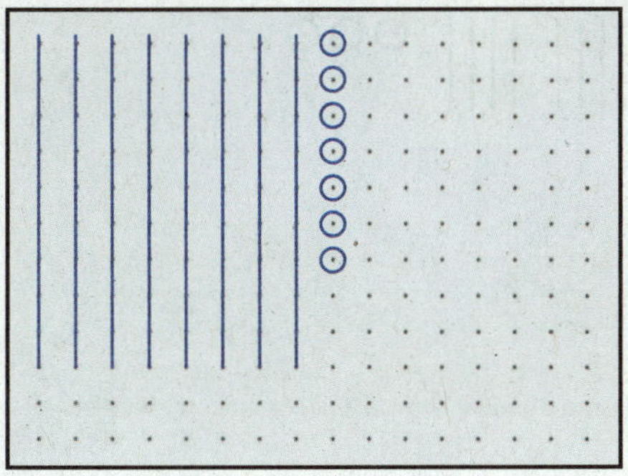

____

2. 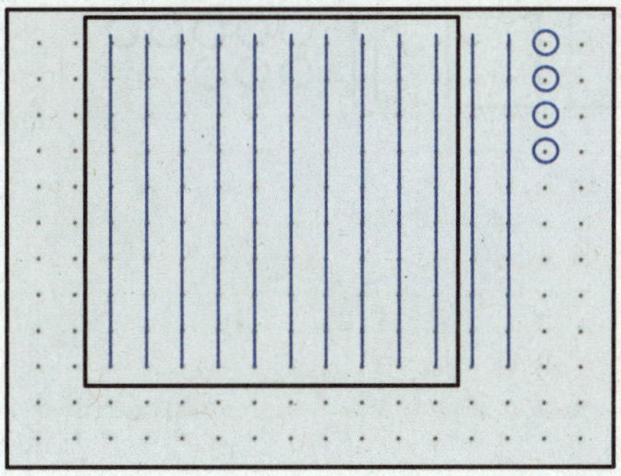

____

Write the number for each place value drawing.

3. 

____

4. 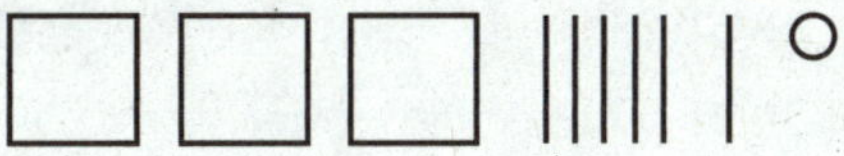

____

5. 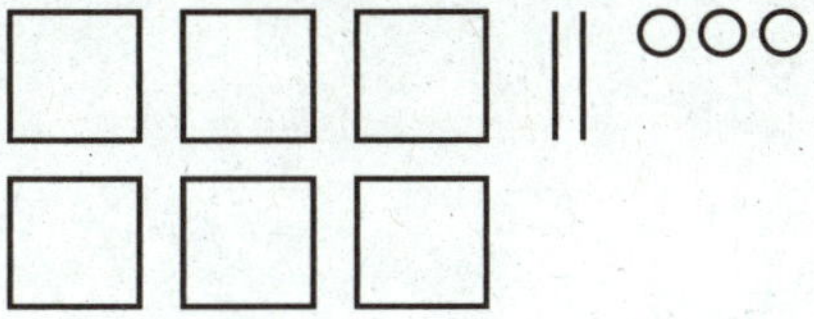

____

6. 

____

Make a place value drawing for each number.

7. 86

8. 587

1–1 Class Activity

Name ____________________ Date ____________

▶ Practice with the Thousand Model

Write the number for each place value drawing.

9. 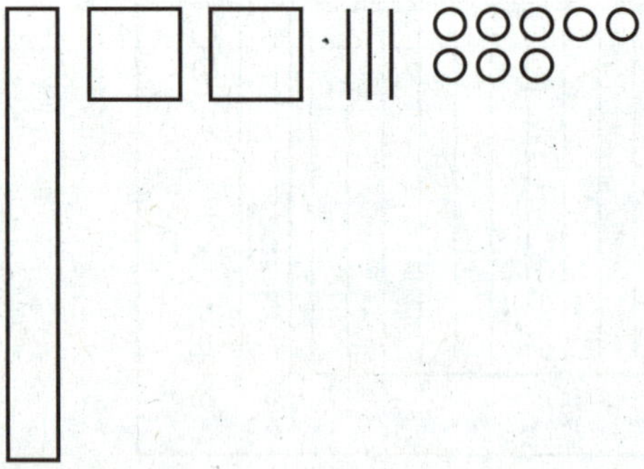

____

10. 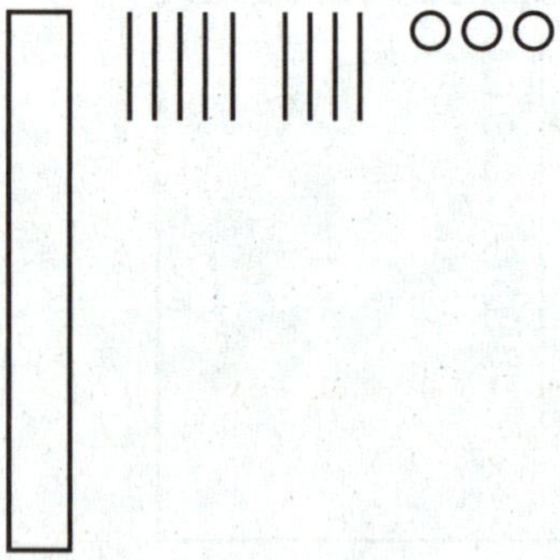

____

Make a drawing for each number.

11. 2,368

12. 5,017

▶ Write Numbers for Word Names

Write the number for the words.

13. eighty-two _______________

14. ninety-nine _______________

15. four hundred sixty-seven _______________

16. nine hundred six _______________

17. one thousand, fifteen _______________

18. eight thousand, one hundred twenty _______________

Family Letter

Dear Family,

Your child is learning math in an innovative program called *Math Expressions.* This program interweaves abstract mathematical concepts with everyday experiences of children. This approach helps children to understand math better.

In *Math Expressions* your child will learn math and have fun by:

- working with objects and making drawings of math situations
- working with other students and sharing problem-solving strategies with them
- writing and solving problems and connecting math to daily life
- helping classmates learn

Your child will have math homework almost every day. He or she needs a Homework Helper. The helper may be anyone — you, an older brother or sister (or other family member), a neighbor, or a friend.

Please decide who the main Homework Helper will be and ask your child to tell the teacher tomorrow.

Make a specific time for homework and provide your child with a quiet place to work. Encourage your child to talk about what he or she is doing in math class. If your child is having problems with math, please talk to me to see how you might help.

To make the concepts clearer, the *Math Expressions* program uses some special methods and activities. Two are described on the back of this letter.

Thank you. You are vital to your child's learning.

Sincerely,
Your child's teacher

continued ►

- **Place Value Drawings:** Students learn to represent numbers with drawings that show how many hundreds, tens, and ones are in the numbers. Hundreds are represented by boxes. Tens are represented by vertical line segments. Ones are represented by small circles. The drawings are also used to help students understand regrouping in addition and subtraction. Here is a place value drawing for the number 178.

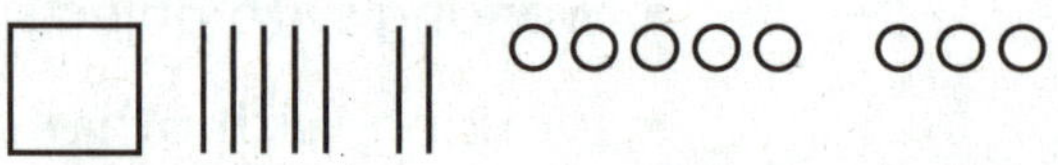

1 hundred 7 tens 8 ones

The 7 ten sticks and 8 circles are grouped in 5s so you can see the quantities easily and avoid errors.

- **Secret Code Cards:** Secret Code Cards are a set of cards for hundreds, tens, and ones. Students learn about place value by assembling the cards to show two- and three-digit numbers. Here is how the number 148 would be assembled.

Hundreds card Tens card Ones card Assembled cards

Carta a la familia

Estimada familia:

Su niño está aprendiendo matemáticas por medio de un programa innovador llamado *Math Expressions.* Este programa relaciona conceptos matemáticos abstractos con la experiencia diaria de los niños. Esto ayuda a los niños a entender mejor las matemáticas.

Con *Math Expressions* su niño aprenderá matemáticas y se divertirá mientras:

- trabaja con objetos y hace dibujos de problemas matemáticos
- trabaja con otros estudiantes y comparte con ellos estrategias para resolver problemas
- escribe y resuelve problemas, y relaciona las matemáticas con su vida diaria
- ayuda a sus compañeros a aprender.

Su niño tendrá tarea de matemáticas casi todos los días. Le hará falta una persona que le ayude con la tarea. Esa persona puede ser usted, un hermano mayor (u otro familiar), un vecino o un amigo.

Por favor, decida quién será el ayudante principal y dígale a su niño que se lo informe al maestro mañana.

Establezca una hora para hacer la tarea y ofrezca a su niño un lugar tranquilo donde trabajar. Anime a su niño a comentar lo qué está aprendiendo en la clase de matemáticas. Si su niño tiene problemas con las matemáticas, por favor comuníquese conmigo para ver cómo puede ayudarlo.

Para presentar los conceptos de manera más clara, el programa *Math Expressions* usa métodos y actividades especiales. Dos de ellos se describen en el reverso de esta carta.

Gracias. Su ayuda es muy importante en el aprendizaje de su niño.

Atentamente,
El maestro de su niño

continúa ►

Carta a la familia

- **Dibujos de valor posicional:** Los estudiantes aprenden a representar números por medio de dibujos que muestran cuántas centenas, decenas y unidades contienen. Las centenas están representadas con casillas, las decenas con segmentos de recta verticales y las unidades con círculos pequeños. Los dibujos también se usan para ayudar a los estudiantes a que comprendan cómo se reagrupa en la suma y en la resta. Éste es un dibujo de valor posicional para el número 178.

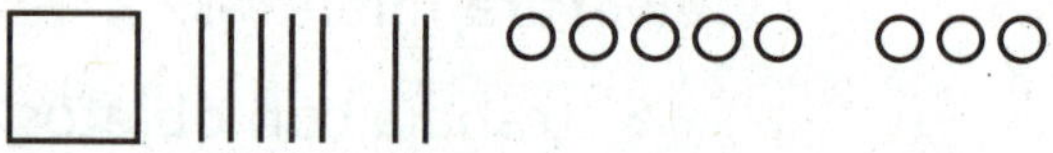

1 centena 7 decenas 8 unidades

Los palitos de decenas y los círculos se agrupan en grupos de 5 para que puedan ver las cantidades más fácilmente y eviten errores.

- **Tarjetas de código secreto:** Las tarjetas de código secreto son un conjunto de tarjetas con centenas, decenas y unidades. Los estudiantes aprenden acerca del valor posicional organizando las tarjetas de manera que muestren números de dos y de tres dígitos. Así es como se puede armar el número 148.

Tarjeta de centenas | Tarjeta de decenas | Tarjeta de unidades | Tarjetas organizadas

1 1	2 2	10 1 0	20 2 0
3 3	4 4	30 3 0	40 4 0
5 5	6 6	50 5 0	60 6 0
7 7	8 8	70 7 0	80 8 0
9 9	90 9 0	100 1 0 0	

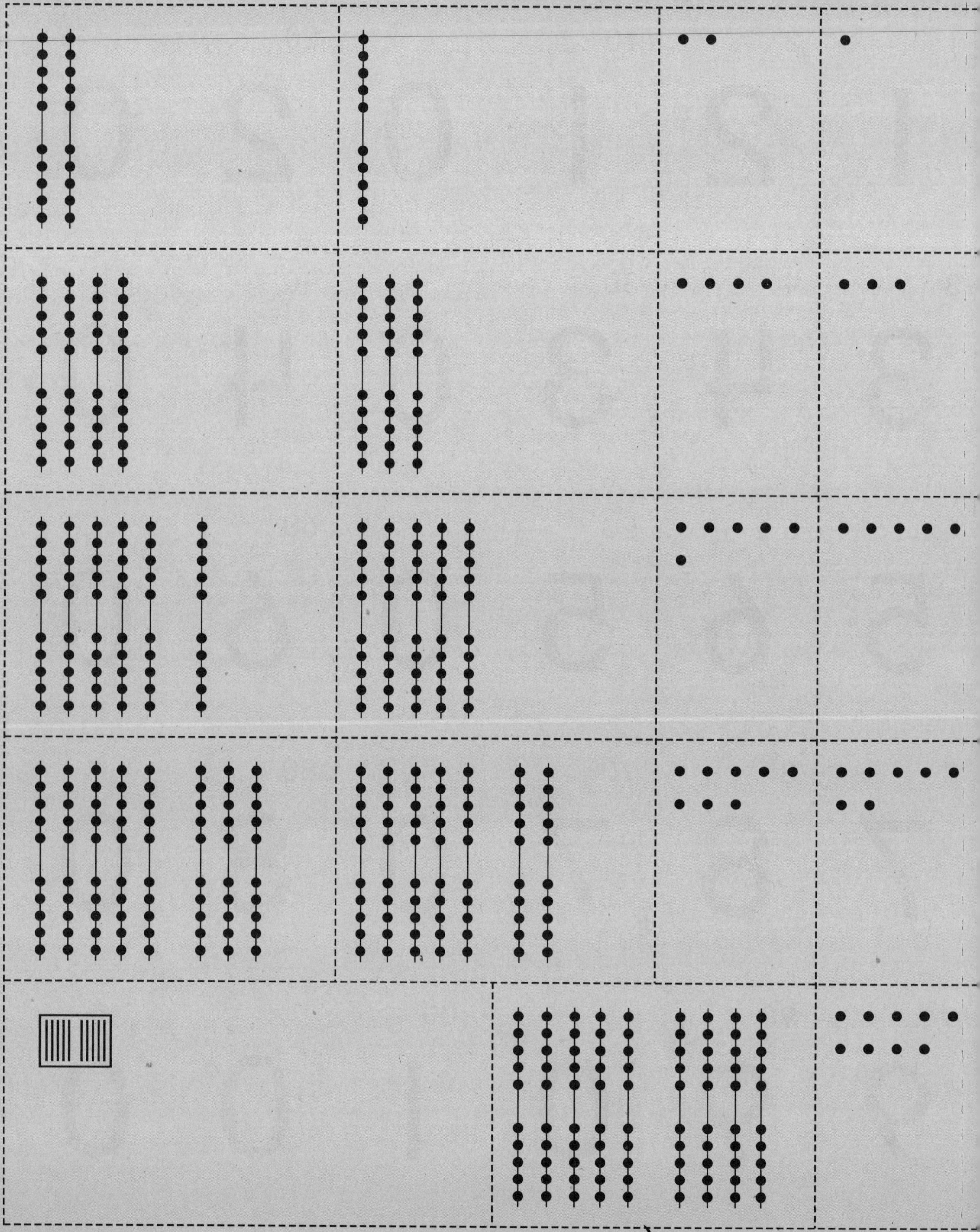

200

2 0 0

300

3 0 0

400

4 0 0

500

5 0 0

600

6 0 0

700

7 0 0

800

8 0 0

900

9 0 0

1000

1 0 0 0

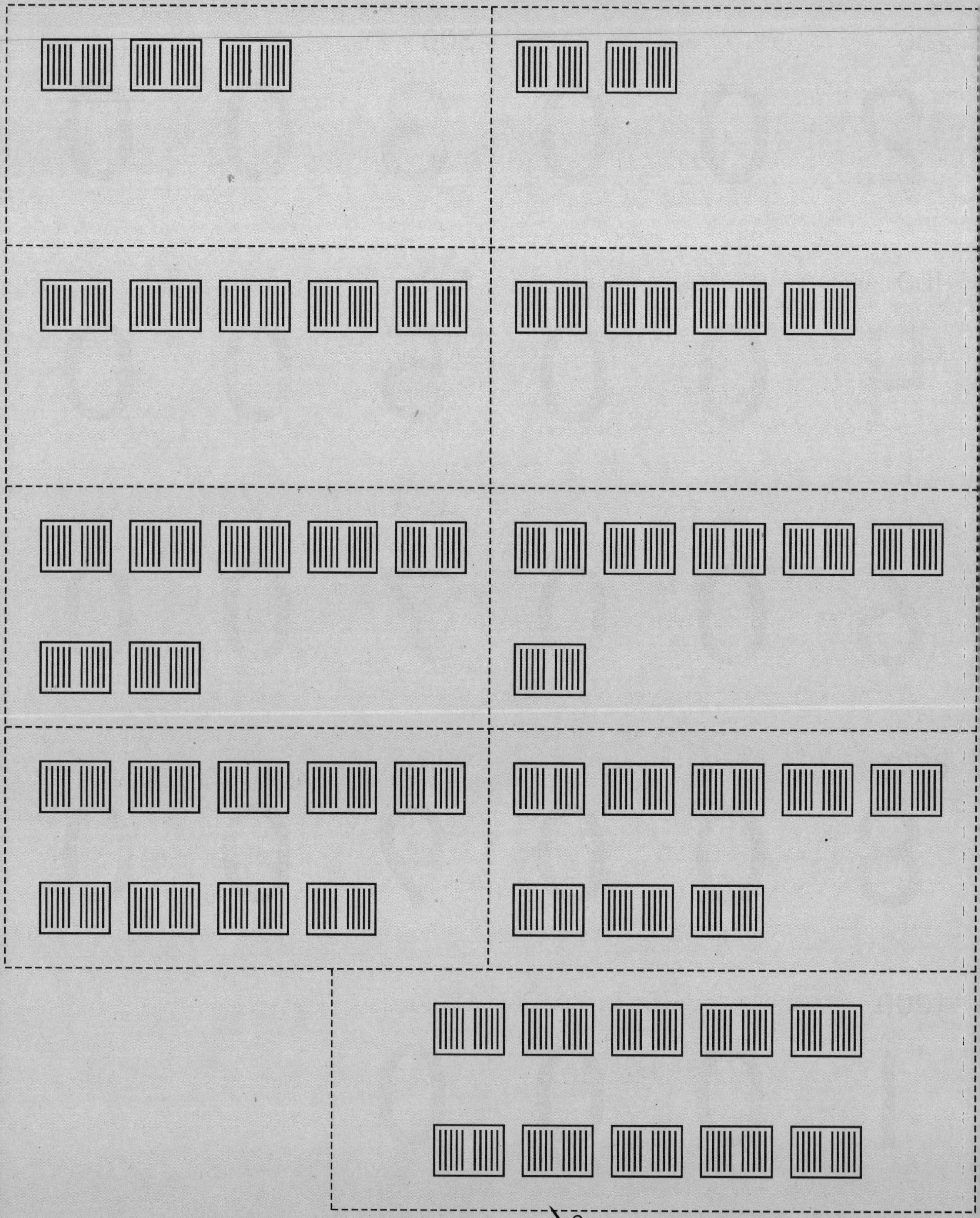

1–2 Class Activity

Name ______________________ Date ______________

▶ Money Drawings on the Dot Array

On the dot side of your MathBoard, make a drawing to represent each money amount.

1. $1.84 **2.** $4.17 **3.** $3.03

▶ Money Drawings Without Dots

On the blank side of your MathBoard, make a drawing to represent each money amount.

4. $3.58 **5.** $6.29 **6.** $16.17

Write the money value for each drawing.

7.

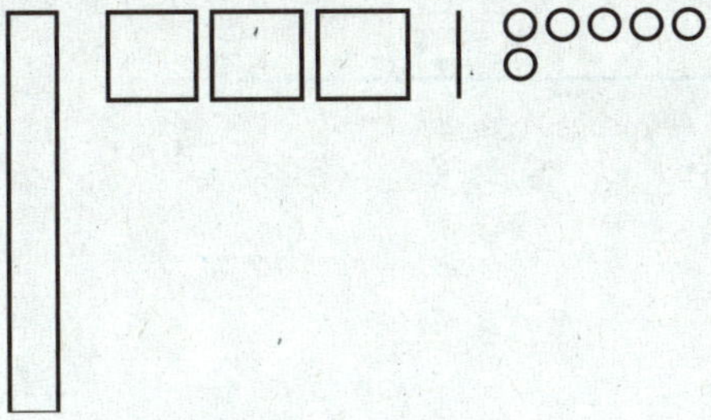

____

8.

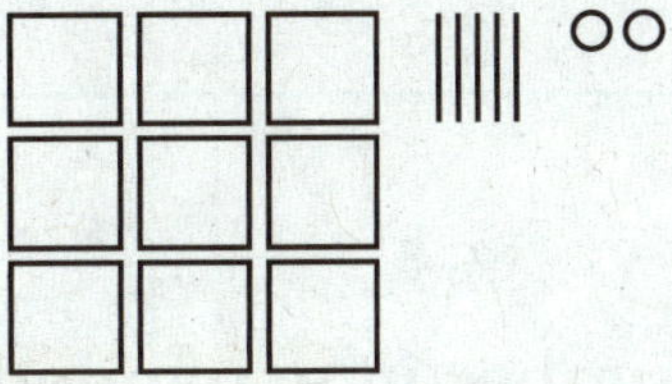

____

9.

____

10.

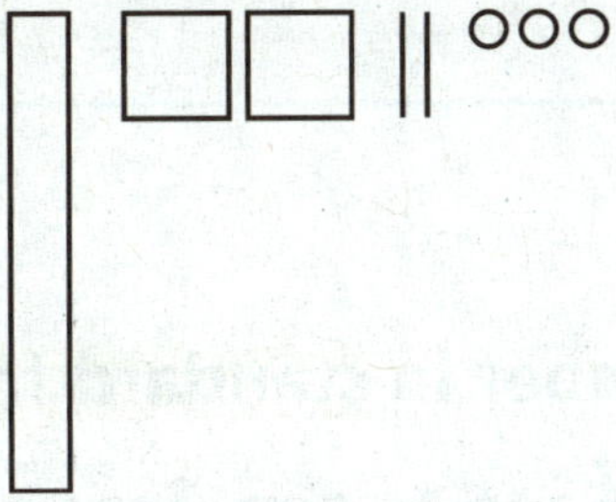

____

11.

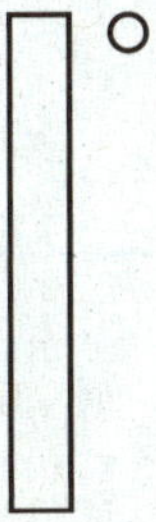

____

12.

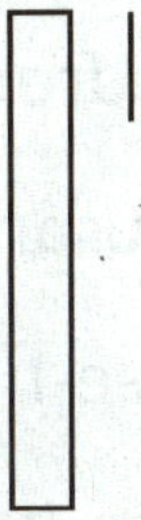

____

1–2 Going Further

Name ______ Date ______

Vocabulary
expanded form
standard form

► Numbers Through Ten Thousands

Write the place of the underlined digit. Then write its value.

1. 12,3̲45 ______
2. 35,74̲0 ______
3. 5̲8,436 ______
4. 89̲,782 ______

Write the word name for each number.

5. 43,875 ______
6. 75,086 ______
7. 98,502 ______

Write each number in expanded form.

8. 14,762 ______
9. 27,013 ______
10. 79,874 ______

Write the number in standard form.

11. 40,000 + 3,000 + 500 + 20 + 7 ______
12. 50,000 + 4,000 + 300 + 8 ______
13. 7 ten thousands + 6 hundreds + 5 ones ______
14. 9 ten thousands + 8 thousands + 4 hundreds + 7 tens ______
15. seventeen thousand, three-hundred ninety-five ______
16. eighty nine thousand, one hundred five ______

Name ______________________ Date ______________

▶ Read and Write Numbers

Write the number for the words.

1. two hundred twelve ______
2. two thousand, eight ______
3. nine hundred ninety-one ______
4. six thousand, fifty-one ______
5. four hundred sixteen ______
6. six hundred nine ______
7. nine hundred eighty-seven ______
8. two thousand, eight ______
9. four thousand, seventeen ______
10. eight thousand, six hundred ______

Write the word name for each number.

11. 783 ______
12. 907 ______
13. 3,001 ______
14. 8,043 ______

Write each number in expanded form.

15. 314 ______
16. 2,148 ______
17. 7,089 ______
18. 8,305 ______

Write each number in standard form.

19. 5 thousands + 8 tens + 7 ones ______
20. 6 thousands + 4 hundreds + 5 ones ______

Name ____________________ Date ____________

► Solve and Discuss

Show your work.

Use a place value drawing to help you solve each problem. Label your answers.

21. Scott baked a batch of rolls. He gave a bag of 10 rolls to each of 7 friends. He kept 1 roll for himself. How many rolls did he bake in all?

____

22. Sixty-two bags of hotdog buns were delivered to the school cafeteria. Each bag had 10 buns. How many buns were delivered?

____

Mario and Rosa baked 89 corn muffins. They put the muffins in boxes of 10.

23. How many boxes did they fill?

____

24. How many muffins were left over?

____

Zoe's scout troop collected 743 cans of food to donate to a shelter. They put the cans in boxes of 10.

25. How many boxes did they fill?

____

26. How many cans were left over

____

27. **Math Journal** Write your own place value word problem. Make a drawing to show how to solve your problem.

1–4

Class Activity

Name ______ Date ______

Vocabulary

place value

► Scrambled Place Value Names

Unscramble the place values and write the number.

1. 8 ones + 6 hundreds + 4 tens

______

2. 9 hundreds + 7 tens + 1 one

______

3. 5 ones + 0 tens + 7 hundreds

______

4. 5 tens + 4 ones + 3 hundreds

______

5. 2 tens + 2 hundreds + 2 ones

______

6. 8 hundreds + 3 ones + 6 tens

______

Unscramble the place values and write the number.
Then, make a place value drawing for the number.

7. 6 hundreds + 9 ones + 3 tens

______

8. 9 ones + 3 tens + 8 hundreds

______

9. 8 ones + 3 hundreds + 4 tens

______

10. 2 hundreds + 9 tens + 1 one

______

Name ____________________ Date ____________

▶ Solve and Discuss

Solve each problem. Label your answer.

11. The bookstore received 35 boxes of books. Each box held 10 books. How many books did the store receive?

____

Maya's family picked 376 apples and put them in baskets. Each basket holds 10 apples.

12. How many baskets did they fill?

____

13. How many apples were left over?

____

Aidee had 672 buttons. She put them in bags with 100 buttons each.

14. How many bags did Aidee fill?

____

15. How many buttons were left over?

____

When Joseph broke open his piggy bank, there were 543 pennies inside. He grouped the pennies into piles of 100.

16. How many piles of 100 did Joseph make?

____

17. How many extra pennies did he have?

____

1–5 Class Activity

Name ______________________ Date ______________

▶ Solve and Discuss

Solve each problem. Label your answer. Use your Mathboard or a separate sheet of paper.

1. Elena made necklaces for her friends. She used 586 green beads and 749 red beads. How many beads did Elena use in all?

____

2. Fabrice has a collection of 485 basketball cards and 217 baseball cards. How many sports cards does Fabrice have in all?

____

▶ Introduce Addition Methods

Tonya and Mark collect seashells. Tonya has 249 shells, and Mark has 386 shells. How many shells do they have in all?

Here are three ways to find the answer:

Show all totals Method	New Groups Below Method	New Groups Above Method
249 + 386 500 120 + 15 635	249 + 386 1 1 635	1 1 249 + 386 635

Proof Drawing:

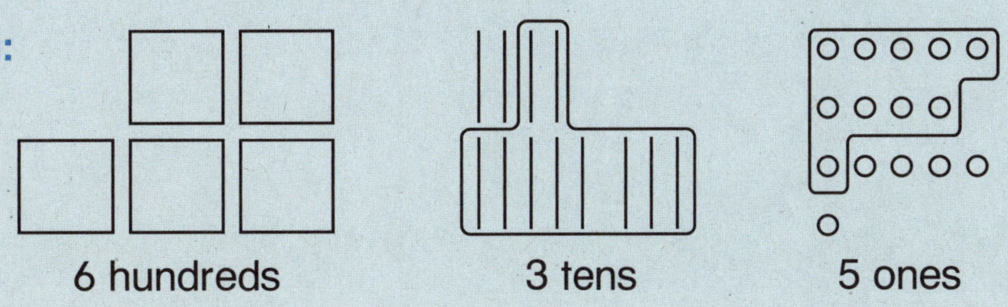

Name ____________________ Date ____________

► Practice Addition Methods

Solve each problem. Make proof drawings to show your answers are correct.

3. Ryan has two stamp albums. One album has 554 stamps, and the other has 428 stamps. How many stamps does Ryan have in all?

   ____

4. One week Ashley read 269 pages. The next week she read 236 pages. What is the total number of pages she read in the two weeks?

   ____

5. The video store has 445 comedy videos and 615 drama videos. How many comedy and drama videos does the store have altogether?

   ____

6. Ali has 128 photos of her pets and 255 photos of her family. How many photos does Ali have altogether?

   ____

Family Letter

Dear Family,

Your child is currently participating in math activities that help him or her to understand addition and subtraction of 2- and 3-digit numbers.

Addition Methods: Students may use the common U.S. method, referred to as the New Groups Above Method, as well as two alternative methods. In the New Groups Below Method, students add from right to left and write the new ten and new hundred on the line. In the Show All Totals method, students add in either direction, write partial sums and then add the partial sums to get the total. Students also use proof drawings to demonstrate grouping 10 ones to make a new ten and grouping 10 tens to make a new hundred.

The New Groups Below Method shows the teen number 13 better than does the New Groups Above Method, where the 1 and 3 are separated. Also, addition is easier in New Groups Below, where you add the 2 numbers you see and just add 1.

New Groups Above:

```
 1  ← the new ten
 46
+37
 83
```

New Groups Below:

```
 46
+37
 1   ← the new ten
 83
```

Add right to left.

Show All Totals:

```
 46
+37
 70
 13
 83
```

Add left to right.

Proof Drawing:

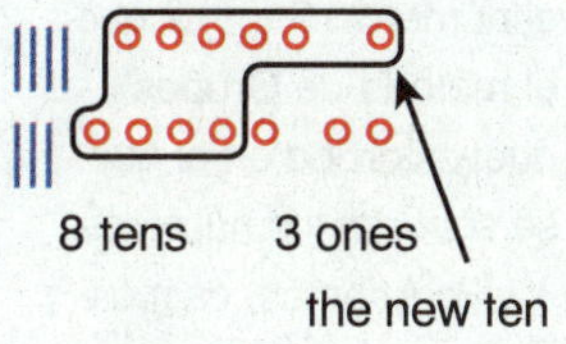

Subtraction Methods: Students may use the common U.S. method in which the subtraction is done right to left, with the ungrouping done before each column is subtracted. They also learn an alternative method in which all the ungrouping is done *before* the subtracting. If they do all the ungrouping first, students can subtract either from left to right or from right to left.

The Ungroup First Method helps students avoid the common error of subtracting a smaller top number from a larger bottom number.

1. Ungroup first
2. Subtract (from left to right or from right to left).

```
   15
  3 5 13
  4̶ 6̶ 3̶
- 2 7 5
  1 8 8
```

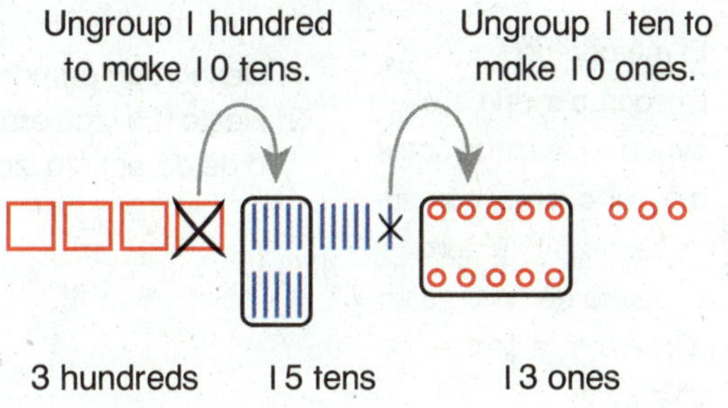

Please call if you have any questions or comments.

Thank you.

Sincerely,
Your child's teacher

Carta a la familia

Estimada familia:

En estos momentos, su niño está participando en actividades matemáticas que le ayudan a comprender la suma y la resta de números de 2 y de 3 dígitos.

Métodos de suma: Los estudiantes pueden usar el método común de los EE. UU., conocido como método de grupos nuevos arriba, y dos métodos alternativos. En el método de grupos nuevos abajo, los estudiantes suman de derecha a izquierda y escriben la nueva decena y la nueva centena en el renglón. En el método de mostrar todos los totales, los estudiantes suman en cualquier dirección, escriben sumas parciales y luego las suman para obtener el total. Los estudiantes también usan dibujos de prueba para demostrar cómo se agrupan 10 unidades para hacer una nueva decena, y 10 decenas para hacer una nueva centena.

El método de Grupos nuevos abajo muestra el número 13 mejor que el método de Grupos nuevos arriba en el que se separan los números 1 y 3. Además, es más fácil sumar con Grupos nuevos abajo, donde se suma los dos números que se ven y simplemente se añade 1.

Grupos nuevos arriba:

1 ← la decena nueva
46
+ 37
83

Grupos nuevos abajo:

46
+ 37
1 ← la decena nueva
83

← Sumar de derecha a izquierda.

Mostrar todos los totales:

46
+ 37
70
13 (la decena nueva)
83

→ Sumar de izquierda a derecha.

Dibujo de prueba:

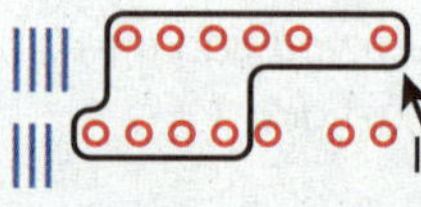

Métodos de resta: Los estudiantes pueden usar el método común de los EE. UU., en el cual la resta se hace de derecha a izquierda, desagrupando antes de restar cada columna. También aprenden un método alternativo en el que desagrupan todo *antes* de restar. Si los estudiantes desagrupan todo primero, pueden restar de izquierda a derecha o de derecha a izquierda.

El método de Desagrupar primero ayuda a los estudiantes a evitar el error común de restar un número pequeño de arriba a un número más grande de abajo.

1. Desagrupa primero.
2. Resta (de izquierda a derecha o de derecha a izquierda).

15
3 5 13
~~463~~
− 275
188

Desagrupar 1 centena para formar 10 decenas. Desagrupar 1 decena para formar 10 unidades.

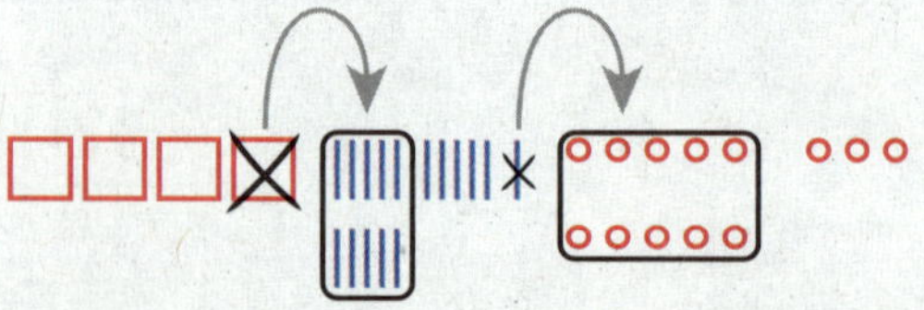

Si tiene alguna pregunta o comentario, por favor comuníquese conmigo. Gracias.

Atentamente,
El maestro de su niño

Name ________ Date ________

▶ Solve and Discuss

Solve each problem using a numerical method and a proof drawing.

1. There are 359 cars and 245 trucks in the parking garage. How many vehicles are in the garage?

   ____

2. The Creepy Crawler exhibit at the science museum has 693 spiders and 1,592 centipedes. How many spiders and centipedes are there in all?

   ____

3. On Saturday, 1,590 people went to the art fair. On Sunday, it rained, and only 355 went to the fair. How many people went to the fair altogether?

   ____

4. There were 1,120 people on the ferry yesterday. Today the ferry had 967 people. How many people did the ferry have in all during the past two days?

   ____

Name ______________________________ Date ______________

► The Puzzled Penguin

Dear Math Students:

Today I found the answer to 168 + 78, but I don't know if I added correctly. Please look at my work. Is my answer right? If not, please correct my work and tell what I did wrong.

$$\begin{array}{r} 168 \\ +78 \\ \hline 948 \end{array}$$

Thank you,

The Puzzled Penguin

► Line Up the Places to Add

Write each addition vertically. Line up the places correctly. Then add and make a proof drawing.

5. 179 + 38 = ______

6. 1,250 + 345 = ______

7. 907 + 877 = ______

Name ______________________ Date ______________

▶ Add Money

$3.49

$1.89

$0.75

$4.20

$0.99

$2.35

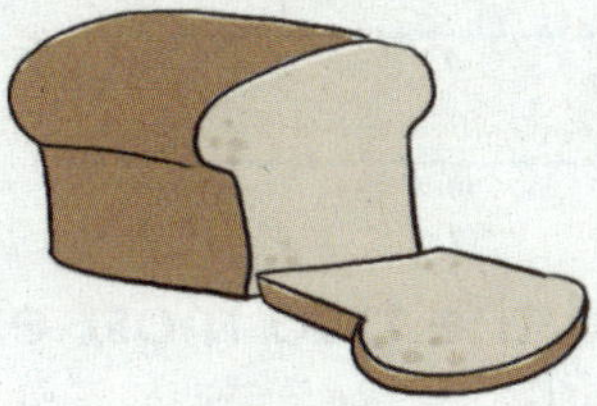

$1.49

$0.40

Use the pictures above to solve. Use a MathBoard or a separate sheet of paper to show your work.

1. Maria wants to buy milk and cheese. How much will the two items cost?

   ____

2. Arturo wants to buy a tomato and a steak. How much will Arturo's groceries cost?

   ____

3. Tamika wants to buy bananas and a watermelon. How much will she spend?

   ____

4. Choose two items. Which items did you choose? How much do they cost together?

   ____

   ____

   ____

1–7 Class Activity

Name ______________________ Date ____________

▶ Add Money Amounts from a Grocery Store Ad

Use an ad from a grocery store. List the names and prices of five or six items you would like to buy. Then answer the questions below. Use a MathBoard or a separate sheet of paper to show your work.

______________________ ______________________

______________________ ______________________

______________________ ______________________

5. How much would the two most expensive items on your list cost altogether?

____

6. How much would the two least expensive items cost in all?

____

7. What would be the total cost of your two favorite items?

____

8. Which items would you buy if you had $5.00 to spend?

____

9. Use the grocery ad to write and solve a word problem involving money.

____

____

____

____

Name ____________________ Date ____________

Lunchtime Diner

Sandwiches

Grilled Cheese $2.39
Tuna $2.57
Chicken $3.84

Sides

Veggies $0.74
Salad $0.98
Fruit $0.66

Drinks

Iced Tea $1.12
Lemonade $1.09
Bottled Water $0.99

▶ Solve and Discuss

Use the menu above to solve. Use a MathBoard or a separate sheet of paper to show your work.

1. Mr. Jackson ordered a grilled cheese sandwich and an iced tea. How much did his order cost?

   ____

2. Mrs. Lin ordered a glass of lemonade and a chicken sandwich. How much did she spend?

   ____

3. **Choose a Method** Kurt and Ana ordered two salads. Think of a fast way to find the total cost. Describe your method.

   ____

   ____

4. **Number Sense** Anne-Marie has only $1.50. Which two items could she buy?

   ____

Name ____________________ Date ____________

▶ Use the Guess and Check Strategy

Use the pictures above to solve.

1. José bought two items. He paid with a $5 bill and two $1 bills, and got $0.50 change. Which items did he buy?

____

____

2. Explain how you found your answer.

____

____

____

____

____

____

Name Date

Carmen's Café

Lunches

Black-Eyed Peas and Rice	$3.72
Chili and Cornbread	$4.38
Ham and Bean Delight	$4.23
Peanut Butter and Jelly Sandwich	$2.65

Desserts

Mango Shake	$2.41
Cinnamon Apple Rings	$2.16
Melon Bowl	$1.99
Raspberry Ice Cream	$1.84

► Solve and Discuss

You and your partner can take turns being a customer and a server at Carmen's Café. Follow these steps:

- The **customer** chooses two items from the menu.
- The **server** writes down the names and prices of the two items and figures out the total cost.
- The **customer** checks to make sure the total is correct.

Show your work on your paper.

Name ____________________ Date ____________

▶ Add Larger Money Amounts

Use the pictures above to solve. Use your MathBoard or a separate sheet of paper to show your work.

1. Jeremy bought a dog and a cat. How much did he spend in all?

 ____

2. Keisha bought a horse. Juan bought a pig. How much did they spend together?

 ____

3. Chan bought a cat, a duck, and a horse. What was the total cost?

 ____

4. **Choose a Method** Rani wants to buy two rabbits. Think of a fast way to find the total cost. Describe your method.

 ____

 ____

5. **Number Sense** Betty has $20.00. Is that enough money for her to buy a cow and a horse? Explain why or why not.

 ____

 ____

 ____

1–10 Class Activity

Name ______________________ Date ______________

▶ Discuss Subtraction Methods

Solve this word problem.

Mr. Kim had 134 jazz CDs. He sold 58 of them at his garage sale. How many jazz CDs does he have now?

1. Write a subtraction that you could do to answer this question.

   ____

2. Make a place value drawing for 134. Take away 58. How many are left?

3. Write a numerical solution method for what you did in the drawing.

4. Describe how you ungrouped to subtract.

   ____

   ____

   ____

   ____

   ____

1–10 **Class Activity**

Name ______________________ Date ______________

Vocabulary
ungrouping
subtract

► The Puzzled Penguin

Dear Math Students:

Today I found the answer to 134 – 58, but I don't know if I did it correctly. Please look at my work. Is my answer right? If not, please correct my work and tell what I did wrong.

$$\begin{array}{r} 134 \\ -\ 58 \\ \hline 124 \end{array}$$

Thank you,

The Puzzled Penguin

► Subtraction Detective

To avoid making subtraction mistakes, look at the top number closely. Do all the **ungrouping** you need to *before* you **subtract**. The magnifying glass around the top number helps you remember to be a "subtraction detective."

Subtract. Show your ungroupings numerically and with proof drawings.

5. $\begin{array}{r} 371 \\ -\ 86 \\ \hline \end{array}$

6. $\begin{array}{r} 163 \\ -\ 47 \\ \hline \end{array}$

7. $\begin{array}{r} 459 \\ -175 \\ \hline \end{array}$

8. $\begin{array}{r} 277 \\ -\ 68 \\ \hline \end{array}$

1–11 Class Activity

Name ______________________ Date ______________

► Ungroup to Subtract

Solve each problem. Show your work numerically and with proof drawings.

1. Lakesha bought a box of 500 paper clips. So far, she has used 138 of them. How many are left?

   ____

2. A movie theater has 400 seats. At the noon show, 329 seats were filled. How many seats were empty?

   ____

3. At the start of the school year, Seiko had a brand new box of 300 crayons. Now 79 crayons are broken. How many unbroken crayons does Seiko have?

   ____

1–11 Class Activity

Name ______________________ Date ______________

► Subtract from Whole-Dollar Amounts

Solve each problem. Show your work numerically and with proof drawings.

4. Armando brought $9.00 to the store. He bought a game for $3.42. How much money did he have left?

____

5. Shelby's neighbor gave her $5 for pulling the weeds in his garden. She spent $1.79 on a jump rope. How much money does she have left?

____

6. Harold got $4.00 for his allowance. He spent $2.68 for an ice cream cone. How much money does he have left?

____

Name Date

▶ Practice Subtracting Across Zeros

Subtract. Make proof drawings for exercises 7–10 on MathBoards or a separate sheet of paper.

7. $\begin{array}{r} 800 \\ -391 \\ \hline \end{array}$

8. $\begin{array}{r} 500 \\ -333 \\ \hline \end{array}$

9. $\begin{array}{r} 400 \\ -217 \\ \hline \end{array}$

10. $\begin{array}{r} 900 \\ -818 \\ \hline \end{array}$

11. $\begin{array}{r} 600 \\ -575 \\ \hline \end{array}$

12. $\begin{array}{r} 1,000 \\ -\ \ 356 \\ \hline \end{array}$

13. $\begin{array}{r} 2,000 \\ -\ \ 176 \\ \hline \end{array}$

14. $\begin{array}{r} 3,000 \\ -\ \ 654 \\ \hline \end{array}$

15. **Math Journal** Write a word problem that is solved by subtracting a 3-digit number from a number of thousands. Then solve the problem.

1–11 Class Activity

Name Date

▶ Practice Deciding When to Ungroup

Subtract. Make proof drawings if you need to on MathBoards or on a separate sheet of paper.

16. 912 − 265

17. 323 − 147

18. 280 − 136

19. 489 − 263

20. 1,754 − 589

21. 2,567 − 956

22. 8,215 − 1,265

23. 5,725 − 3,214

1–12 Class Activity

Name ______________________ Date ______________

▶ Ungroup from Left or Right

Tony and Maria each solved this problem:

On Tuesday morning, a music store had 463 copies of the new School Daze CD. By the end of the day, they had sold 275 copies. How many copies were left?

Tony

Tony started ungrouping from the left.

1. He has enough hundreds.
2. He does not have enough tens. He ungroups 1 hundred to make 10 more tens.

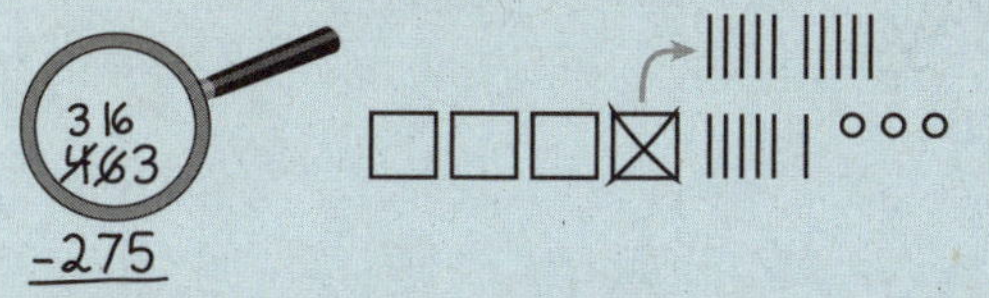

3. He does not have enough ones. He ungroups 1 ten to make 10 more ones.

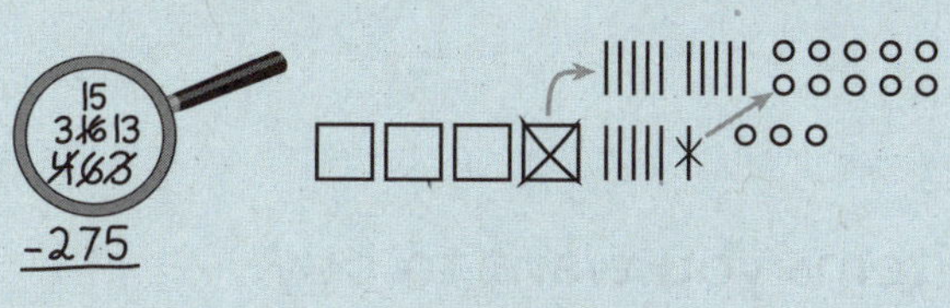

4. Complete the subtraction.

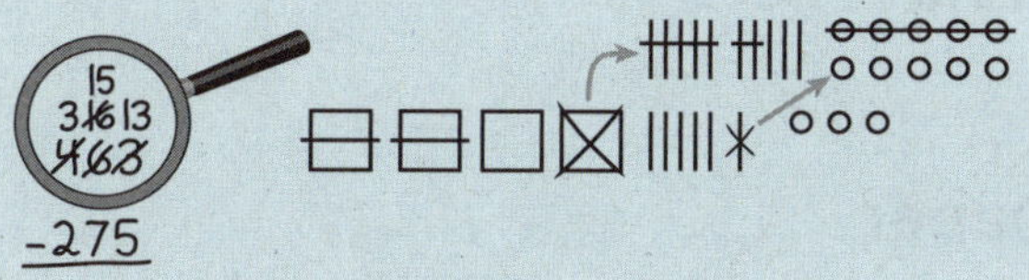

Maria

Maria started ungrouping from the right.

1. She does not have enough ones. She ungroups 1 ten to make 10 more ones.

2. She does not have enough tens. She ungroups 1 hundred to get 10 more tens.

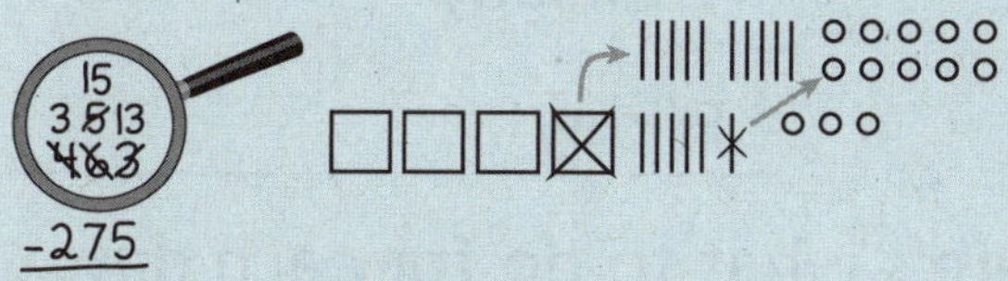

3. She has enough hundreds.
4. Complete the subtraction.

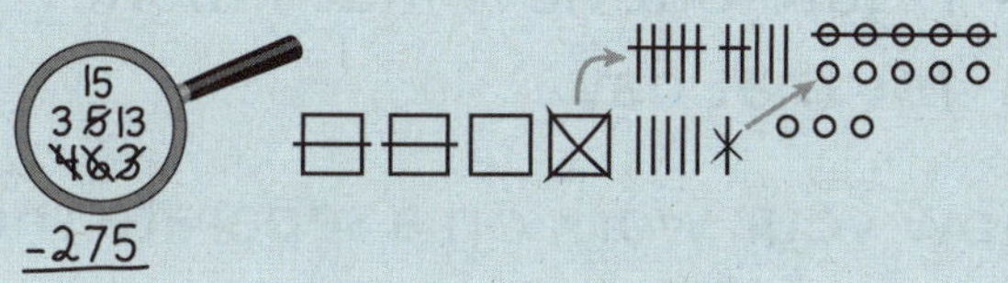

Name ____________________ Date ____________

ANDY'S ARTS AND CRAFTS STORE

SALE!

TOOLS

Paintbrush $0.29
Set of Cookie Cutters $2.42
Roller $1.17
Set of Stampers $2.89

PAINTS, INKS, AND CLAY

Set of Paints $2.37
Ink Pad $0.68
Clay $1.75

OTHER SUPPLIES

Marker $0.83
Glue $1.45
Construction Paper $1.25
Posterboard $1.26
Set of Large Blank Buttons $1.57

▶ Solve and Discuss

Imagine that you have the amount of money shown to spend at Andy's Arts and Crafts Store each day.

Monday	$8.00
Tuesday	$7.25
Wednesday	$6.50
Thursday	$6.95
Friday	$6.20

Here's what to do for each day:

- Choose two, three, or four different items you want to buy.
- Find the total cost for the items.
- Figure out how much money you will have left for that day.

Show your work on a separate sheet of paper

Name _______________ Date _______________

► Relate Addition and Subtraction

Solve each problem. Make a proof drawing if you need to.

1. There were 138 students in the gym for the assembly. Then, 86 more students came in. How many students were in the gym altogether?

____

2. There were 224 students in the gym for the assembly. Then, 86 students left. How many students were left in the gym?

____

3. Look at your addition, subtraction, and proof drawings from Exercises 1 and 2. How are addition and subtraction related?

____

____

____

1–13 Class Activity

Name ______________________ Date ______________

▶ Solve and Discuss

Show your work.

Solve. Label your answers.

4. Marly had 275 baseball cards. Her brother gave her a collection of 448 baseball cards. How many baseball cards does Marly have now?

____

5. Write a subtraction word problem related to the addition word problem in problem 4. Then find the answer without doing any calculations.

____

____

____

____

6. Brian spent $5.17. He spent $3.29 on drawing pencils and the rest on paper. How much money did he spend on paper?

____

7. Write an addition word problem related to the subtraction word problem in problem 6. Then find the answer without doing any calculations.

____

____

____

____

1–14 Class Activity

Name ________________ Date ________________

▶ Subtract and Check

Solve each problem.

1. Zane had $4.00. He bought a book for $3.76. How much money does he have left? Check by making a proof drawing. ________________

2. Jasmine bought a cap. She paid with a $5.00 bill and got $1.62 in change. How much did the cap cost? Check by adding. ________________

3. At the diner, Rita ordered the breakfast special for $2.91. She had $3.25 when she arrived at the diner. How much did she have after she paid her bill? Check by adding. ________________

4. Bill bought a CD for $5.98. He paid with a $10.00 bill. What will his change be? Check by adding. ________________

Name Date

Vocabulary
ungroup

► Practice Deciding When to Ungroup

Answer each question.

Adair subtracted 595 from 834.

5. Did she have to **ungroup** to make more tens? Explain.

6. Did she have to ungroup to make more ones? Explain.

Beatrice subtracted 441 from 950.

7. Did she have to ungroup to make more tens? Explain.

8. Did she have to ungroup to make more ones? Explain.

Wan subtracted 236 from 546.

9. Did he have to ungroup to make more tens? Explain.

10. Did he have to ungroup to make more ones? Explain.

Name ______ Date ______

Vocabulary
method
calculator
mental math

▶ Choose Mental Math, Pencil and Paper, or Calculator

Add or subtract. Then write what computation method you used. Write (p) for paper-and-pencil, (c) for calculator, or (m) for mental math.

1. $8.00 − 7.50

   Method: ______

2. 79 + 87

   Method: ______

3. 537 − 91

   Method: ______

4. 495 + 938

   Method: ______

5. $9.25 − 4.01

   Method: ______

6. 2,000 + 5,700

   Method: ______

7. $9,743 − 5,221

   Method: ______

8. 12,534 + 29,798

   Method: ______

9. $23,000 − 14,000

   Method: ______

Solve each problem. Write whether you used paper-and-pencil, a calculator, or mental math.

10. Liz scores 20,000 points in her first turn. She scores 19,000 points on her second turn. How many points did she score altogether?

    ______

11. There were 17,948 people at the basketball game on Friday night. There were 16,777 people at the game on Saturday night. How many more people were there on Friday night than on Saturday night?

    ______

12. **On the Back** Play the *Method Show-Down* game.

Name Date

▶ Method Show-Down Game

Work in groups of three. Write the following methods on three separate index cards.

paper and pencil	mental math	calculator

To play the game.

1. Each student writes an addition or subtraction exercise using numbers up to 5 digits on an index card. Put the cards in a paper bag.

2. One student mixes the three method cards and distributes them to the group, while another student picks an exercise card from the paper bag. Each student then uses the method on his or her card to solve the problem. The first student to get the correct answer scores 1 point. Mental math may be really difficult for problems with large numbers.

3. Mix the method cards and repeat the activity. The first student to earn 5 points wins the game.

1–16 Class Activity

Name ______________________ Date ______________

▶ Math and Literature

Step 1: Make two spinners.

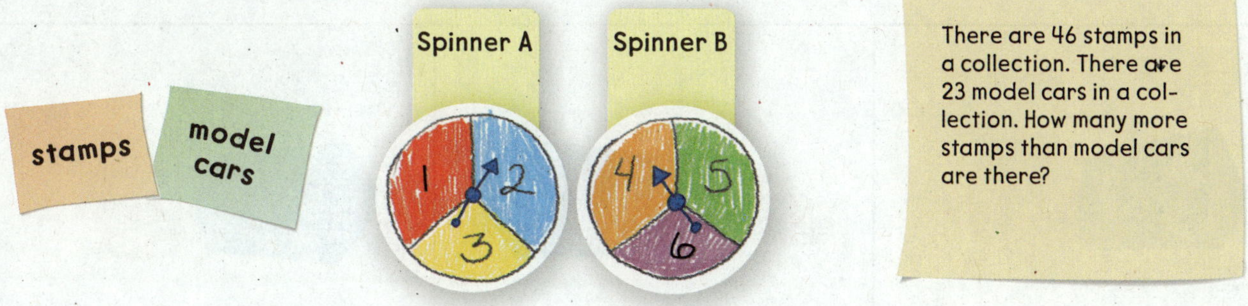

Step 2: Write names of collections on pieces of paper and put in a bag.

Step 3: Spin Spinner A twice to write a 2 or 3-digit number. Spin Spinner B twice to write a 2 or 3-digit number. Draw 1 or 2 collection names out of the bag.

Step 4: Use the numbers and collection names to write a word problem.

Act out the problems by modeling them on the MathBoard or with base ten blocks.

1. Write and solve a word problem using the rules above.

____

____

____

2. Sarah has 143 buttons. How many more buttons does she need to have 199 buttons?

____

3. Math Journal Write and solve more word problems about collections using the rules above.

____

Name ______________________ Date ______________

► Rock, Paper, Scissors

Rock, Paper, Scissors is a game. The players show a rock, paper, or scissors with their hands.

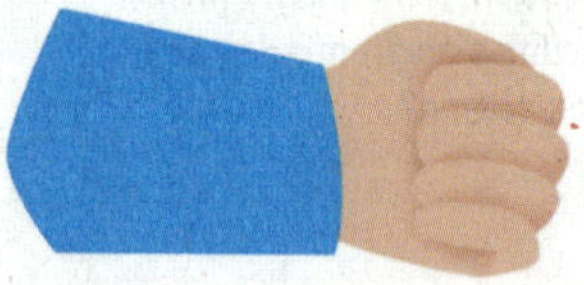

Rock

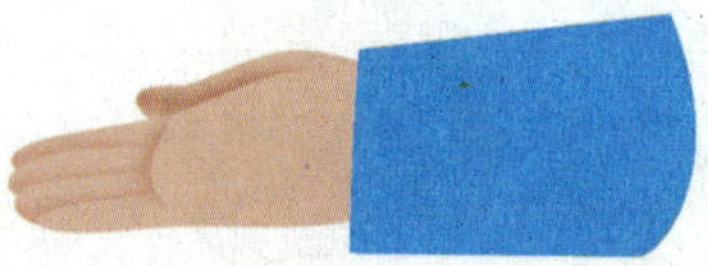

Paper

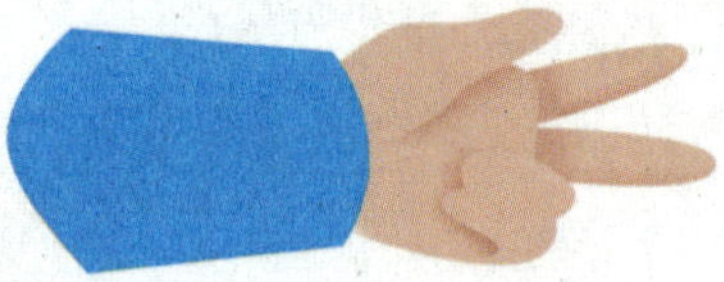

Scissors

Game Rules

1. The players throw their hand at the same time to show rock, paper, or scissors.
2. Rock crushes scissors and wins.
3. Scissors cuts paper and wins.
4. Paper covers rock and wins.
5. The player who scores a win gets 1 point.
6. If two players make the same throw with their hand, they must throw again.
7. The player with the most points wins.

4. List all of the different possibilities for one round if 2 players play the game?

____

5. How many different possibilities are there?

____

6. Play the game 10 times with a partner. Keep track of your results in a table. ______________________

Name ____________________ Date ____________

Make a place value drawing for each number.

1. 57

2. 392

Unscramble the place values and write the number.

3. 9 ones + 6 hundreds + 4 tens ____________

4. 5 hundreds + 2 ones + 3 tens ____________

5. 5 ones + 7 hundreds + 1 thousand + 6 tens ____________

6. 8 tens + 4 ones + 0 hundreds + 1 thousand ____________

Write the number for the words.

7. eight hundred seventy-two ____________

8. five hundred four ____________

9. one thousand fifty ____________

Add or subtract.

10. 435 + 283 = ____________

11. 962 − 87 = ____________

1 Unit Test

Name ____________________ Date ____________

Add or subtract.

12.
```
  972
+ 129
```

13.
```
  617
− 549
```

14.
```
  800
− 684
```

15.
```
  $3.29
+  5.98
```

16.
```
  $5.31
−  0.32
```

17.
```
  $10.00
−   7.54
```

18. Gordon baked 346 blueberry muffins and 287 bran muffins. How many muffins did he bake in all?

____

19. Write a subtraction word problem related to the addition word problem in problem 18. Then find the answer without doing any calculations.

____

____

____

____

20. **Extended Response** Veronica has 423 baseball cards. She put them in piles of 10 cards each.

How many piles of 10 cards did she make? __________

How many extra cards did she have? __________

Explain your reasoning. ______________________________

____

____

____

2–1 Class Activity

Name ________________ Date ________

Vocabulary
line segment
centimeter

► Measure Line Segments

Measure each line segment to the nearest centimeter.

1. ______ cm

2. ______ cm

3. ______ cm

4. ______ cm

5. ______ cm

6. ______ cm

2–1 Class Activity

Name Date

Vocabulary
horizontal
vertical

▶ Draw Line Segments of Given Lengths

Draw each line segment.

7. a **horizontal** line segment about 7 cm long

8. a **vertical** line segment about 4 cm long

9. a slanted line segment about 13 cm long

10. a vertical line segment that is a little more than 2 cm long

11. a horizontal line segment that is a little less than 9 cm long

2–1 Class Activity

Name ______________________ Date ______________

Vocabulary
perimeter

▶ Measure the Perimeter of a Triangle

Find the perimeter of each triangle to the nearest centimeter.

12.

____

13.

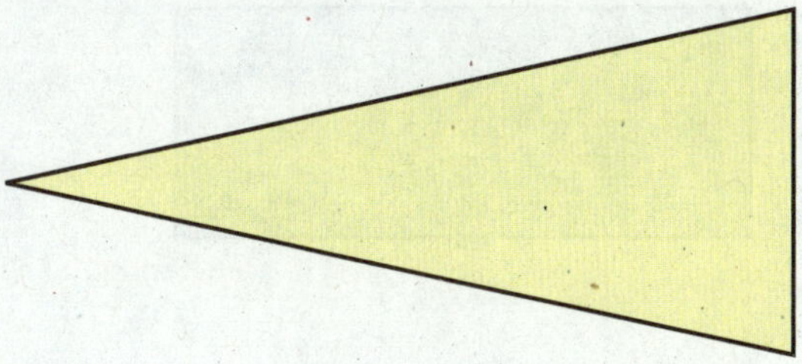

____

14.

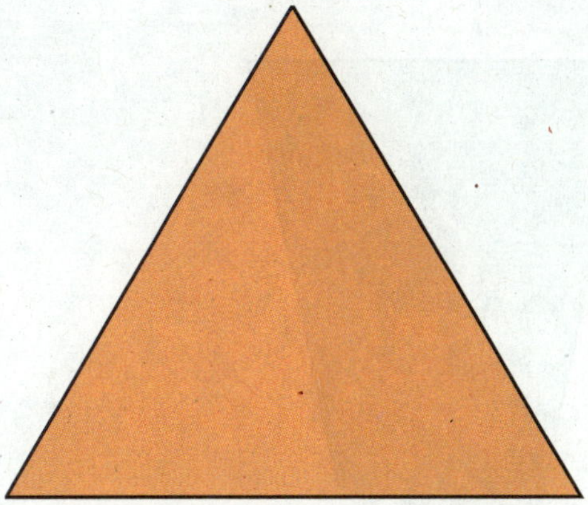

____

15.

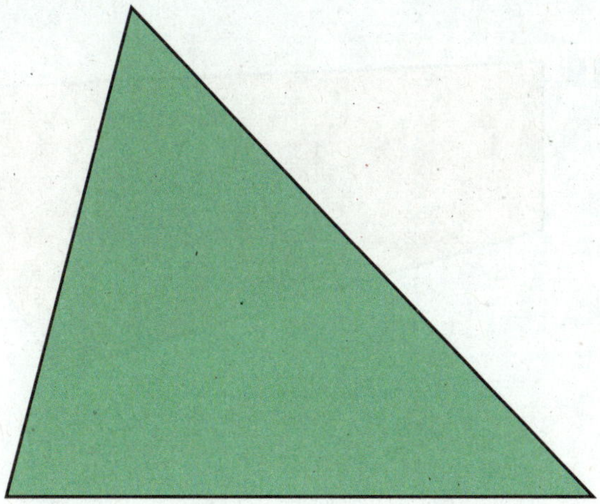

____

16. Join the points to make a triangle. Find its perimeter.

____

2–1 Class Activity

Name ______________________ Date ______________

Vocabulary
quadrilateral

▶ Measure the Perimeter of a Quadrilateral

Find the perimeter of each quadrilateral to the nearest centimeter.

17.

____

18.

____

19.

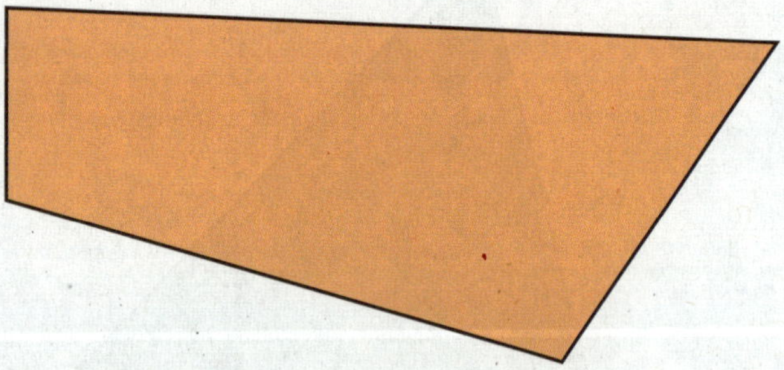

____

20.

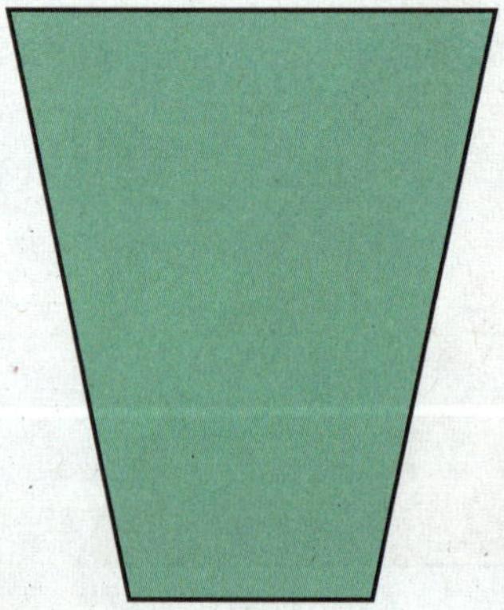

____

21. Join the points to make a rectangle. Find its perimeter.

____

Family Letter

Dear Family,

Your child will be learning about geometry during this school year. This first unit is about the geometric figures called quadrilaterals. These get their name because they have four (*quad-*) sides (*-lateral*).

Students will learn about four different kinds of quadrilaterals in this unit.

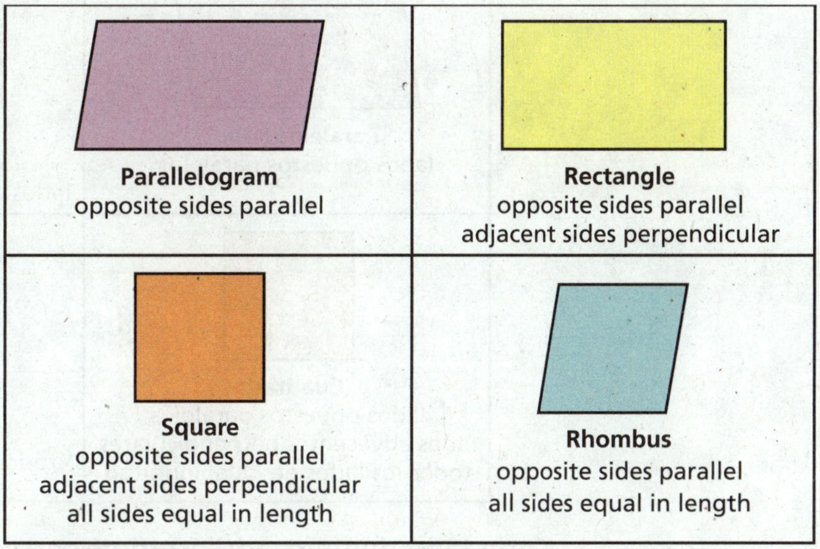

Each side of a quadrilateral is a part or a segment of a straight line. Your student will practice making careful measurements of line segments.

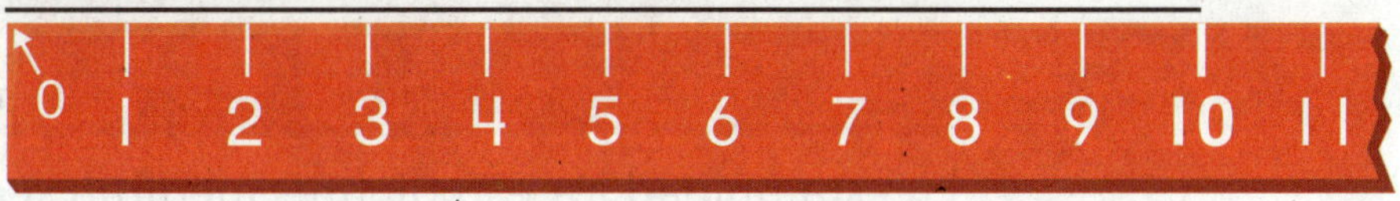

Students will measure line segments in centimeters in this unit. Centimeters are a convenient size for measuring and they are closely linked to the base 10 numeration system we use.

Your student will be able to recognize and describe different quadrilaterals by their sides. Some sides may be of equal length. Some sides may be parallel: they do not meet no matter how far they are extended. Some sides may be perpendicular: where they meet is like the corner of a square.

If you have any questions, please call or write to me.
Thank you.

Sincerely,
Your child's teacher

Carta a la familia

Estimada familia:

Durante este año escolar, su niño aprenderá geometría. La primera unidad se ocupa de figuras geométricas llamadas cuadriláteros. Éstas se llaman así porque tienen cuatro lados.

En esta unidad los estudiantes aprenderán acerca de cuatro tipos diferentes de cuadriláteros.

 **Paralelogramo** lados opuestos paralelos	 **Rectángulo** lados opuestos paralelos lados adyacentes perpendiculares
 **Cuadrado** lados opuestos paralelos lados adyacentes perpendiculares todos los lados de igual longitud	 **Rombo** lados opuestos paralelos todos los lados de igual longitud

Cada lado de un cuadrilátero es parte de un segmento de recta. Su niño practicará cómo medir segmentos de recta cuidadosamente.

En esta unidad los estudiantes medirán segmentos de recta en centímetros. Los centímetros son una medida apropiada y están directamente relacionados con el sistema numérico de base 10 que usamos.

Su niño podrá reconocer y describir diferentes cuadriláteros según sus lados. Algunos lados pueden tener la misma longitud. Algunos lados pueden ser paralelos: nunca se encuentran a pesar de lo largos que sean. Algunos lados pueden ser perpendiculares: cuando se encuentran, forman lo que podría ser el vértice de un cuadrado.

Si tiene alguna pregunta o comentario, por favor comuníquese conmigo. Gracias.

Atentamente,
El maestro de su niño

2–2 Class Activity

Name ____________________ Date ____________

Vocabulary
line
line segment
endpoint

▶ Define Lines and Line Segments

A **line** is a straight path that goes on forever in both directions. When we draw a line, we put arrows on the ends to show that it goes on and on. Here are some lines.

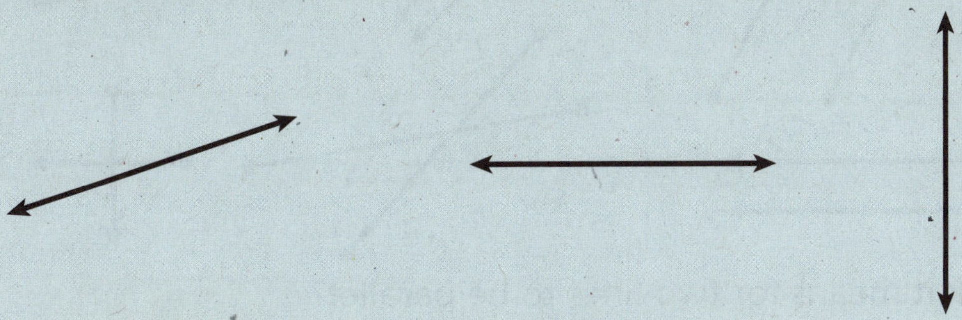

A **line segment** is part of a line. It has two ends, which are called **endpoints**. Here are some line segments.

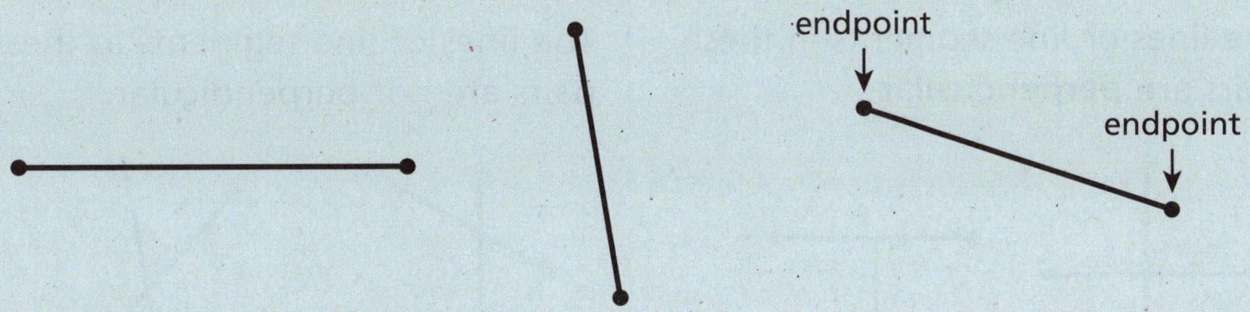

1. You can measure to find the length of a line segment, but you cannot measure to find the length of a line. Explain why.

____

____

____

____

____

2–2 Class Activity

Name ______________________ Date ______________

Vocabulary
parallel
perpendicular

▶ Define Parallel Lines

The lines or line segments in these pairs are **parallel**.

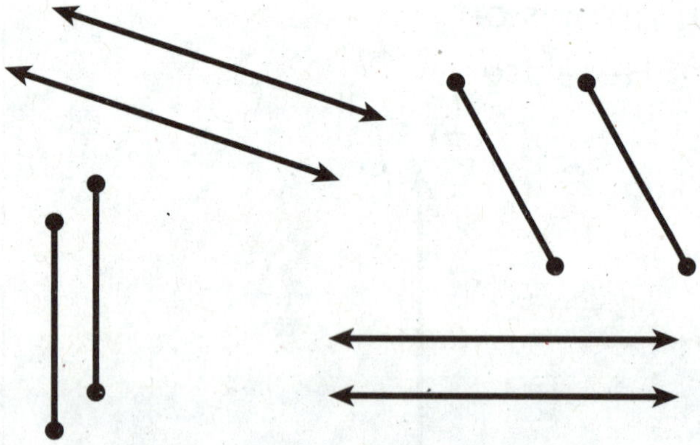

The lines or line segments in these pairs are not parallel.

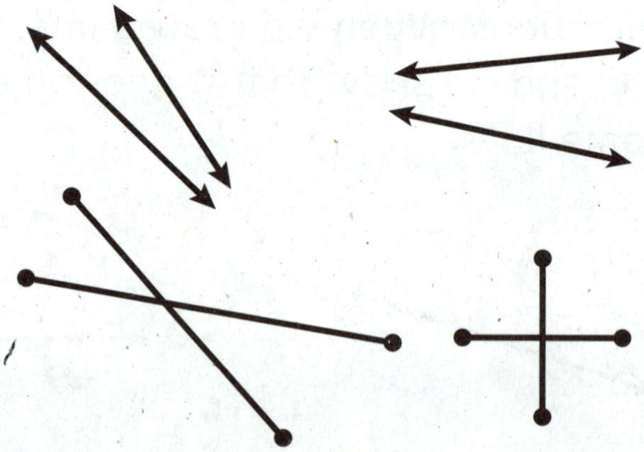

2. What do you think it means for two lines to be parallel?

____

____

▶ Define Perpendicular Lines

The lines or line segments in these pairs are **perpendicular**.

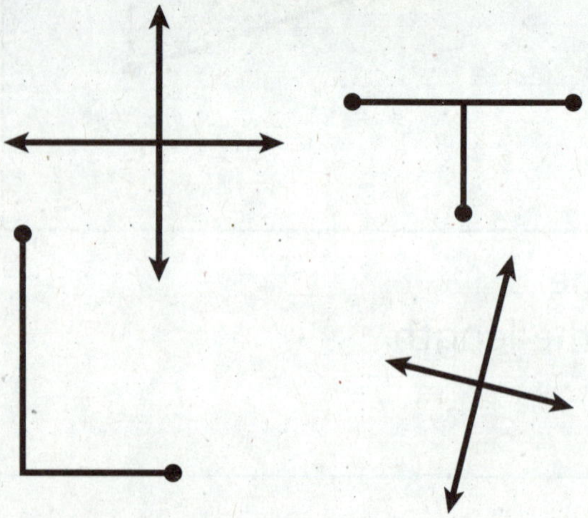

The lines or line segments in these pairs are not perpendicular.

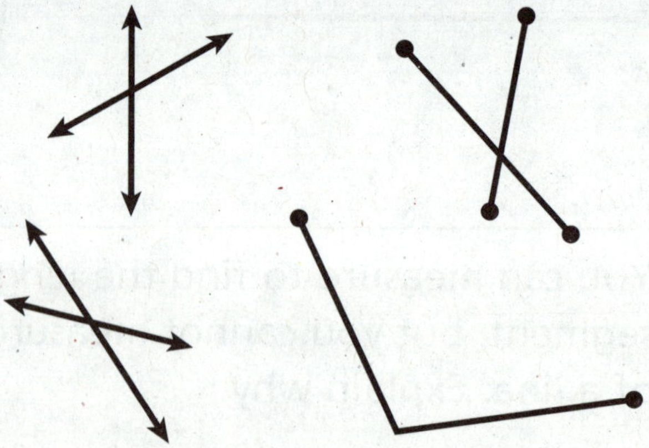

3. What do you think it means for two lines to be perpendicular?

____

____

2–2 **Class Activity**

Name ____________________ Date ____________

Vocabulary
adjacent opposite

▶ Identify Opposite and Adjacent Sides

Look at these quadrilaterals.

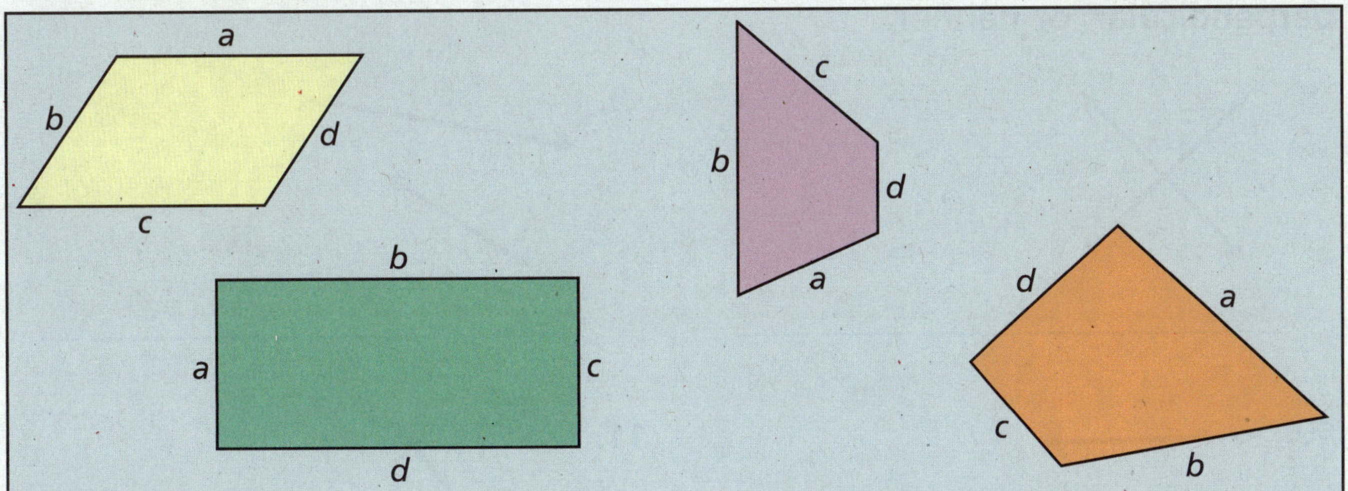

In all of the quadrilaterals, the sides labeled *a* and *b* are **adjacent** to each other. The sides labeled *b* and *c* are also adjacent to each other.

4. What do you think it means for two sides to be adjacent?

____

____

5. Which other sides are adjacent to each other?

____

In all of the quadrilaterals, the sides labeled *a* and *c* are **opposite** each other.

6. What do you think it means for two sides to be opposite each other?

____

____

7. Which other sides are opposite each other?

____

2–2 Class Activity

Name ____________________ Date ____________

▶ Identify Types of Lines

Tell whether each pair of lines is parallel, perpendicular, or neither.

8.

____

9.

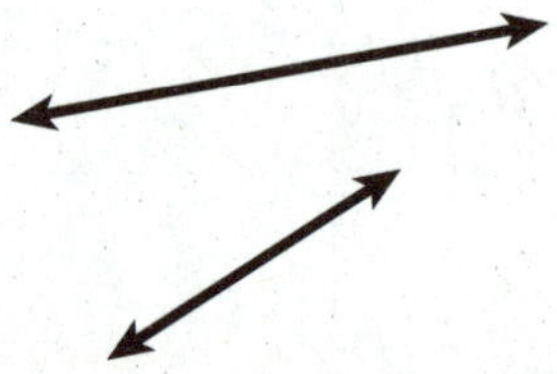

____

10.

____

11.

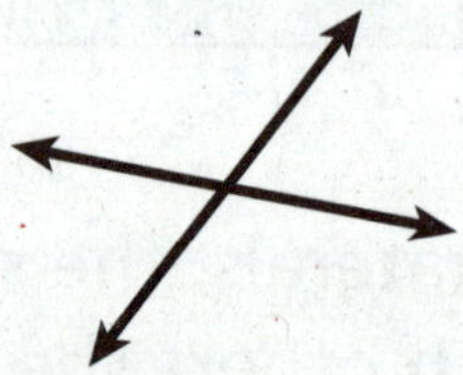

____

12. Draw a pair of parallel line segments.

13. First, draw a line segment 3 cm long. Then, draw a line segment 6 cm long that looks perpendicular to your first line segment.

14. Name two perpendicular adjacent sides in this figure.

____

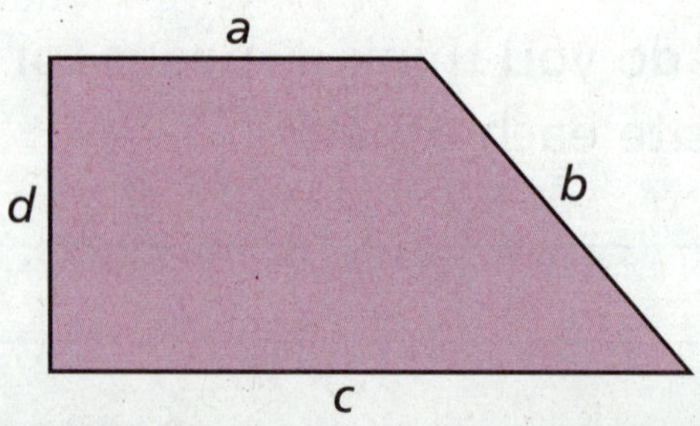

15. Name two parallel opposite sides in the figure.

____

2–3 Class Activity

Name ____________________ Date ____________

Vocabulary
parallelogram
quadrilateral

▶ Define a Parallelogram

All of these figures are **parallelograms**.

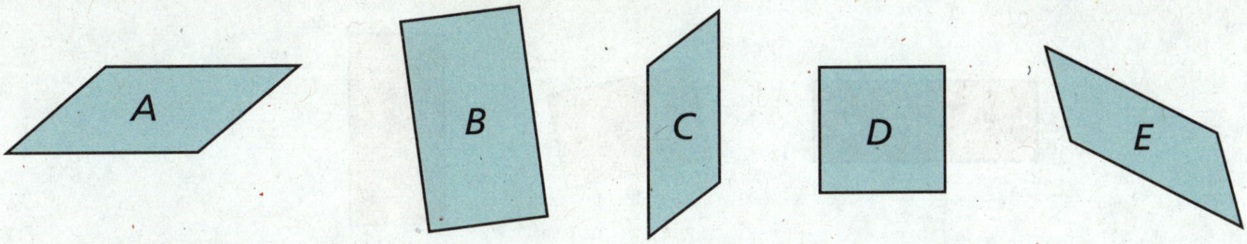

These figures are not parallelograms.

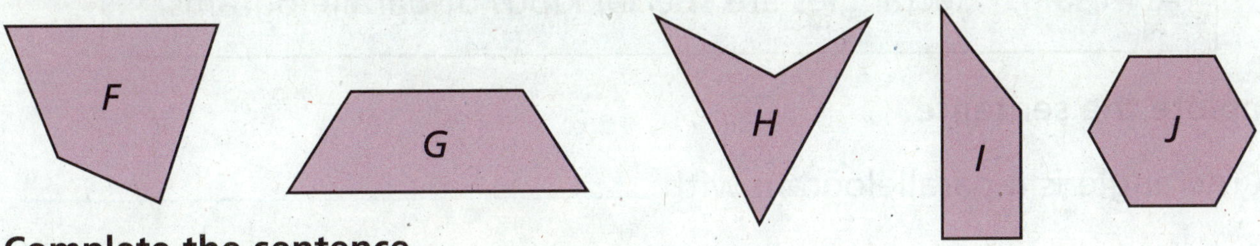

Complete the sentence.

1. A parallelogram is a **quadrilateral** with ______________________________

____

▶ Measure Parallelograms

For each parallelogram, measure the sides and label them with their lengths. Then, find the perimeter.

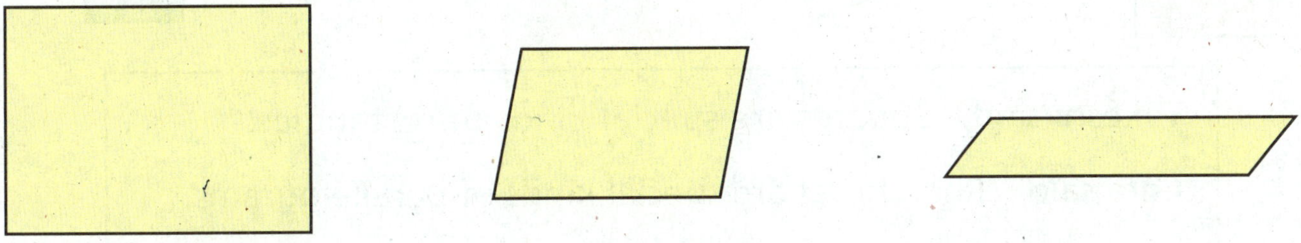

2. __________ cm 3. __________ cm 4. __________ cm

5. Look at the lengths of the sides. What patterns do you notice? ______________________________

____

____

Name ____________________ Date ____________

Vocabulary
rectangle
square
rhombus

▶ Define a Rectangle

All of these figures are **rectangles**.

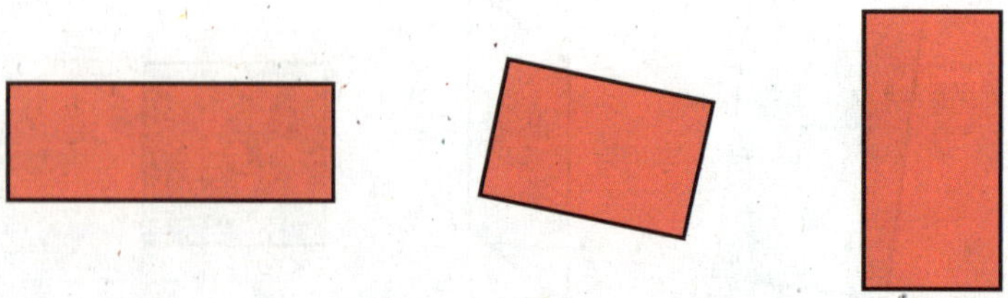

Adel said, "Rectangles are special kinds of parallelograms."

Complete the sentence.

6. A rectangle is a parallelogram with ______________________________

____

▶ Explore Squares and Rhombuses

These figures are **squares**.

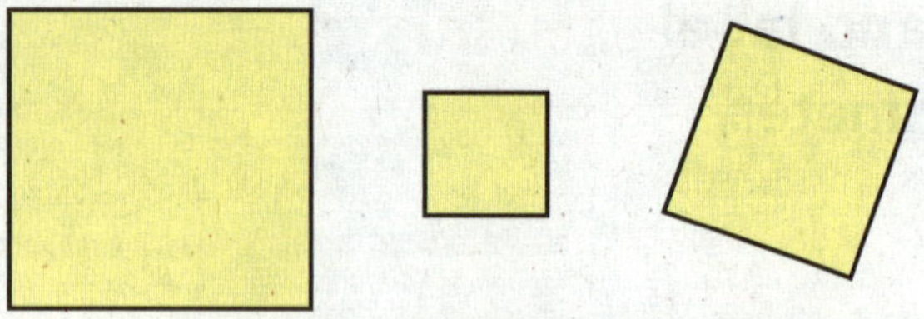

These figures are **rhombuses**.

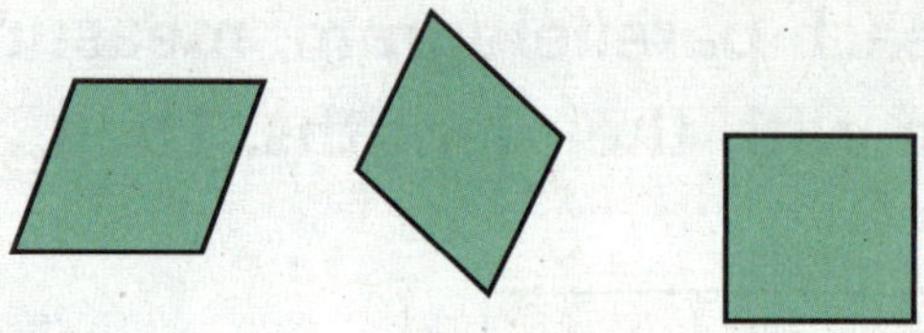

Takeshi said, "Squares are special kinds of rectangles."

Cora said, "Rhombuses are special kinds of parallelograms."

Complete each sentence.

7. A square is a rectangle with ______________________________

____

8. A rhombus is a parallelogram with ______________________________

____

2–3 Class Activity

Name ____________________ Date ____________

Vocabulary
rectangle
square

▶ Find the Perimeters of Rectangles and Squares

Find the perimeter of each figure in centimeters *without* measuring all four sides.

These figures are **rectangles**.

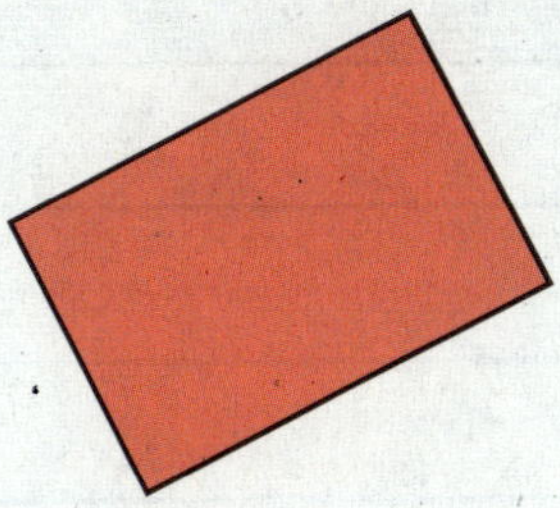

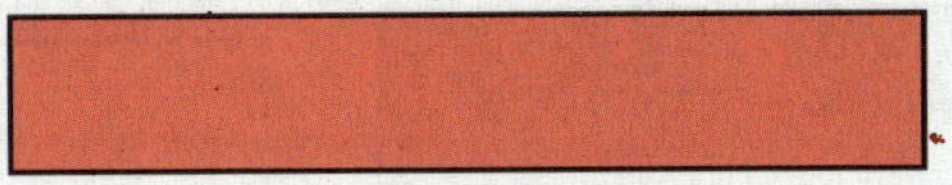

9. ________ cm

10. ________ cm

These figures are **squares**.

11. ________ cm

12. ________ cm

13. Write About It How are rectangles and squares the same? How are they different?

____

____

____

____

____

2–3 Class Activity

Name ____________________ Date ____________

Vocabulary
quadrilateral
parallelogram
rectangle
square

▶ Describe Quadrilaterals

Use as many words below as possible to describe each figure.

quadrilateral	parallelogram	rectangle	square

14. 

____
____
____
____

15. 

____
____
____
____

16. 

____
____
____
____

17. 

____
____
____
____

Name ____________________ Date ____________________

▶ Tangram Figures

Carefully cut out each figure along the dotted lines. Make sure you cut as carefully and straight as you can.

Use your figures to create the patterns on Student Activity Book page 63.

2–3 Going Further

Name ______________________ Date __________

Use your tangram figures from page 58A to make this cat. When you finish, draw lines to show how you placed the figures.

Try to create as many of these patterns as you can.

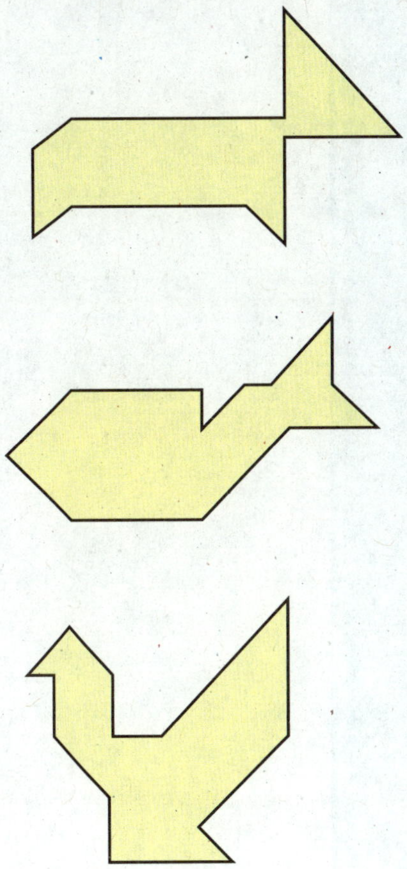

On the Back Create your own pattern with tangrams and make a drawing of it.

Name _______________________________ Date _______________

2–4 Class Activity

Name ______________________________ Date ____________

Vocabulary
opposite
parallelogram

▶ Explore Parallelograms

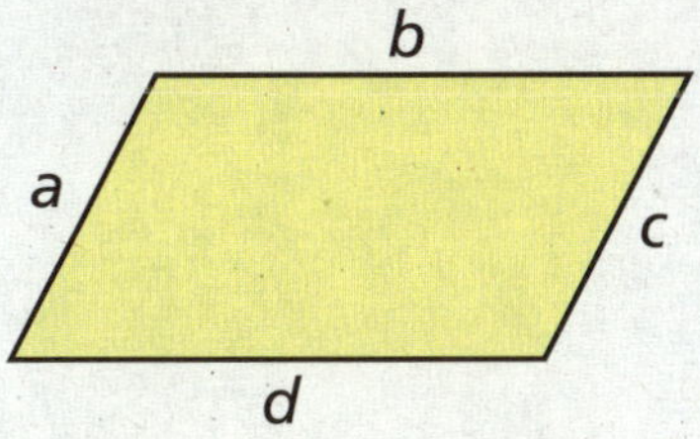

1. Write what you know about the **opposite** sides of a **parallelogram**.

____

____

2. Draw three different parallelograms.

Name ______________________ Date ____________

Vocabulary
rectangle
adjacent

▶ Review Rectangles

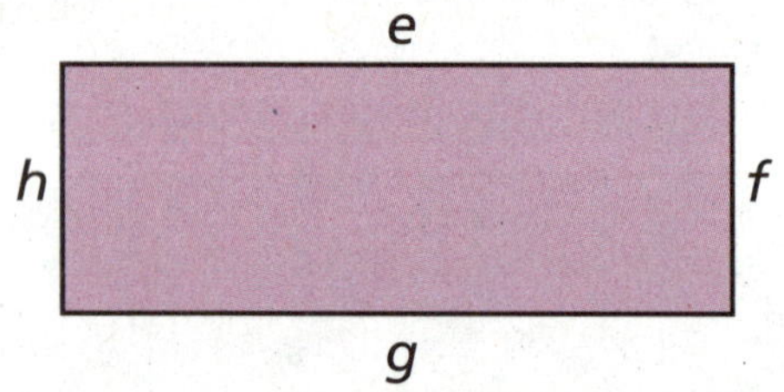

3. Write everything you know about the opposite sides of a **rectangle**.

____

4. What do you know about the **adjacent** sides of a rectangle?

____

5. Draw three different rectangles on the grid.

Name ____________________ Date __________

▶ Describe Quadrilaterals

Place a check mark beside every name that describes the figure.

1.

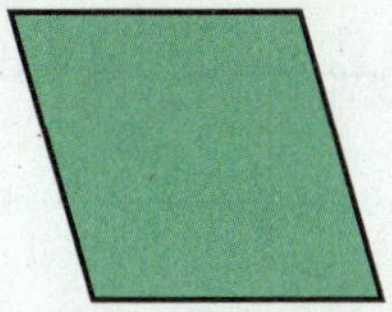

☐ quadrilateral
☐ parallelogram
☐ rhombus
☐ rectangle
☐ square

2.

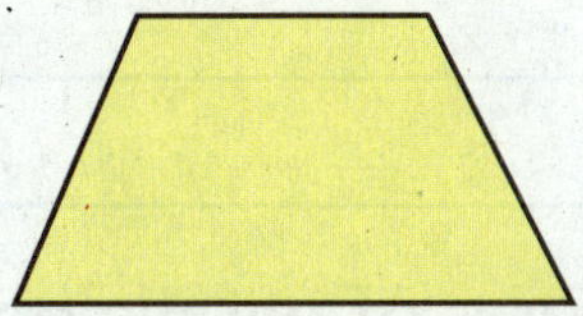

☐ quadrilateral
☐ parallelogram
☐ rhombus
☐ rectangle
☐ square

3.

☐ quadrilateral
☐ parallelogram
☐ rhombus
☐ rectangle
☐ square

4.

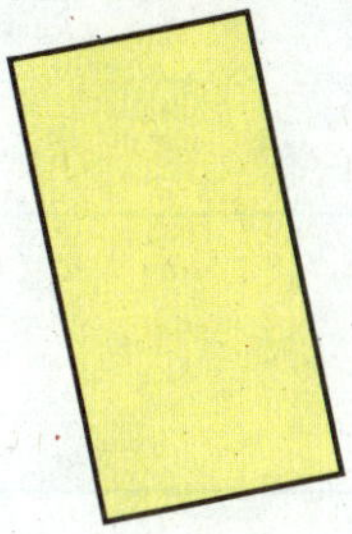

☐ quadrilateral
☐ parallelogram
☐ rhombus
☐ rectangle
☐ square

5.

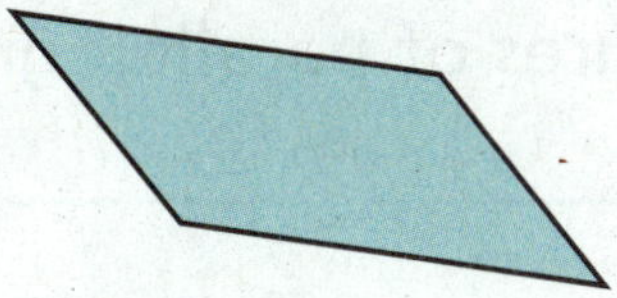

☐ quadrilateral
☐ parallelogram
☐ rhombus
☐ rectangle
☐ square

6.

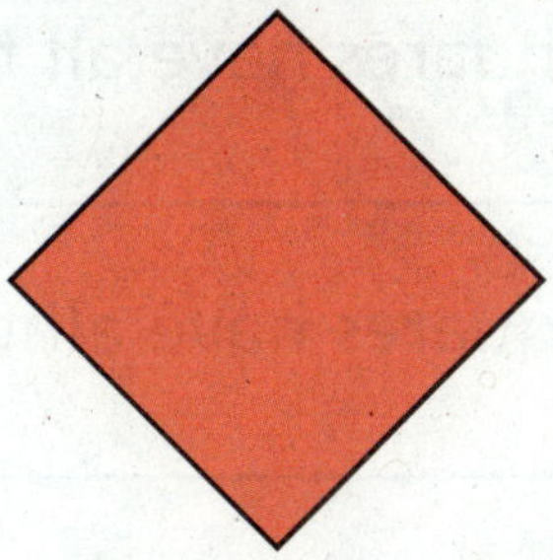

☐ quadrilateral
☐ parallelogram
☐ rhombus
☐ rectangle
☐ square

7. For each figure, put Xs under the descriptions that are always true.

	Four sides	Both pairs of opposite sides parallel	Both pairs of opposite sides the same length	Four square corners	All sides the same length
Quadrilateral					
Parallelogram					
Rhombus					
Rectangle					
Square					

Name ______________________ Date ______

Use the finished chart on page 63 to complete each statement.

8. Parallelograms have all the features of quadrilaterals *plus*

9. Rectangles have all the features of parallelograms *plus*

10. Squares have all the features of quadrilaterals *plus*

11. Squares have all the features of parallelograms *plus*

12. Squares have all the features of rectangles *plus*

▶ Draw Quadrilaterals if Possible

Draw each figure if you can. If it is impossible, explain why.

13. Draw a quadrilateral that is *not* a parallelogram.

14. Draw a square that is *not* a rectangle.

15. Draw a parallelogram that is *not* a rectangle.

16. Draw a rectangle that is *not* a square.

17. Draw a rhombus that is *not* a parallelogram.

Name ______________________ Date ______________

Find the perimeter of each figure. Use a centimeter ruler.

1.

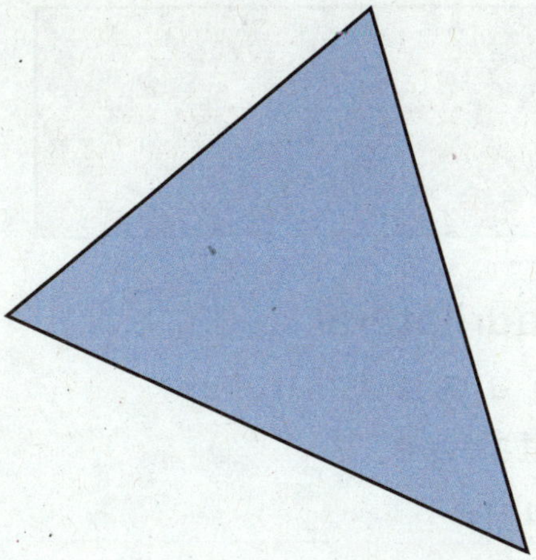

____

2.

____

Name each figure.

3.

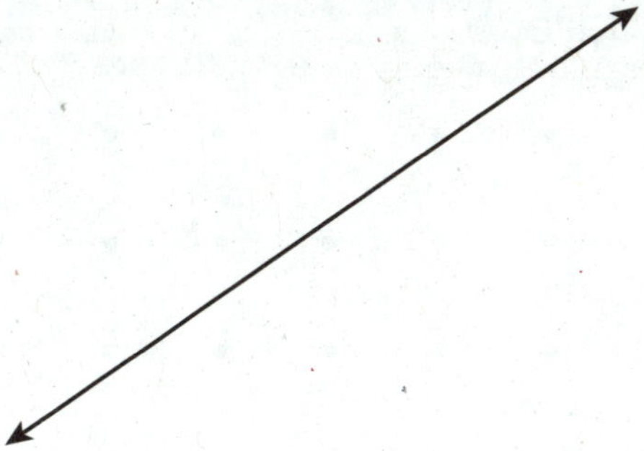

____

4.

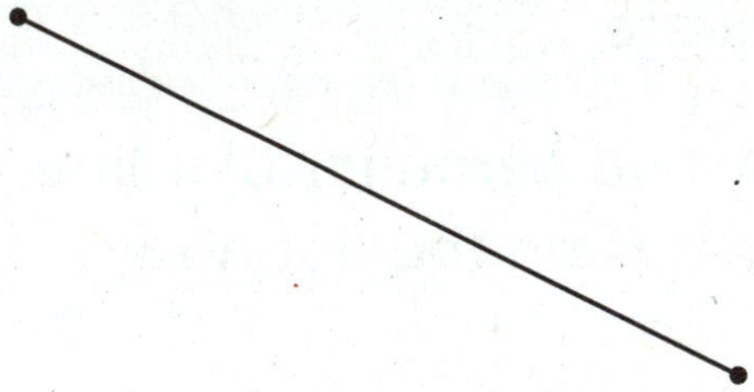

____

Name ____________________ Date ____________

Put a check mark beside every name that describes the figure.

5.

☐ quadrilateral
☐ not a quadrilateral
☐ rectangle
☐ square

6.

☐ quadrilateral
☐ not a quadrilateral
☐ rectangle
☐ square

7.

☐ quadrilateral
☐ not a quadrilateral
☐ rectangle
☐ square

8.

☐ quadrilateral
☐ not a quadrilateral
☐ rectangle
☐ square

9. Draw two perpendicular line segments on the dot array.

10. Extended Response Explain what it means for two line segments to be parallel. Draw an example.

____

____

____

Name ______________________ Date ______________

Vocabulary

partner	total
addend	sum
equation	

► Math Mountains and Equations

Complete.

1. Look at the Math Mountain and the 8 **equations**. What relationships do you see? In each equation, label each number as a **partner** (*P*) or the **total** (*T*).

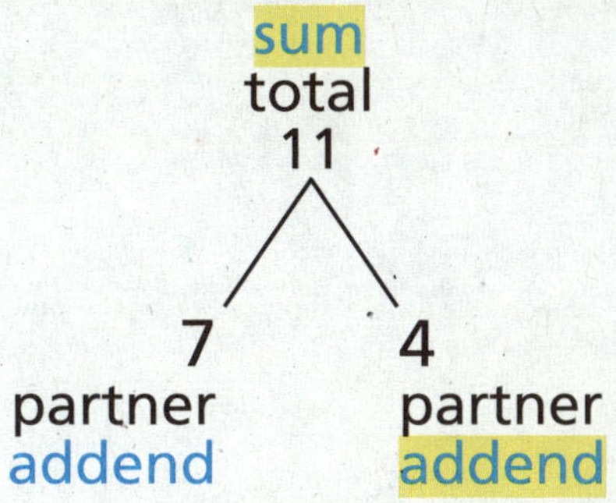

11 = 7 + 4	7 + 4 = 11
___ ___ ___	___ ___ ___
11 = 4 + 7	4 + 7 = 11
___ ___ ___	___ ___ ___
4 = 11 − 7	11 − 7 = 4
___ ___ ___	___ ___ ___
7 = 11 − 4	11 − 4 = 7
___ ___ ___	___ ___ ___

2. Write the 8 equations for this Math Mountain. Label each number as the total (*T*) or a partner (*P*).

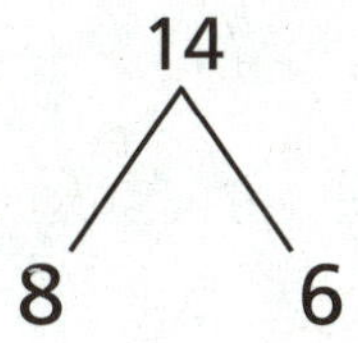

______________________ ______________________

______________________ ______________________

______________________ ______________________

______________________ ______________________

Name ______________________ Date ____________

► Solve and Discuss

Solve each problem. Label your answers.

Show your work.

3. **Change Plus** Chris picked 8 apples. His mother picked 6 more. How many apples do they have now?

____

4. **Change Minus** Chris had 14 apples. He ate 8 of them. How many apples does he have now?

____

5. **Put Together** Alison has 7 juice boxes. Taylor has 5 juice boxes. How many juice boxes do they have altogether?

____

6. **Take Apart** There are 12 juice boxes at the picnic. Alison puts 7 on the table and leaves the rest in the cooler. How many juice boxes are in the cooler?

____

Name ______________________ Date __________

►Represent Word Problems with Math Tools

The equations and Math Mountains below show the word problems on page 68.

Change Plus

8	+	6	=	□
Chris		Mom		total

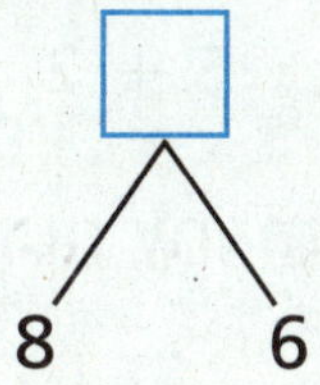

Change Minus

14	−	8	=	□
total		ate		now

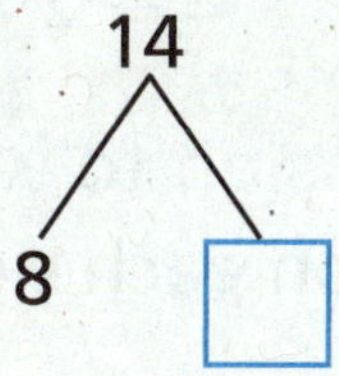

Put Together

7	+	5	=	□
Alison		Taylor		total

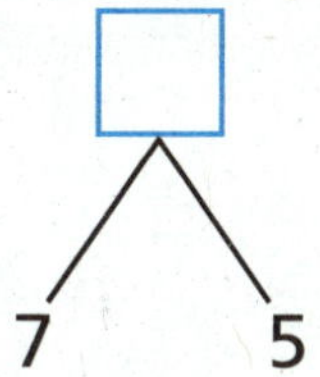

Take Apart

12	−	7	=	□
total		table		cooler

7	+	□	=	12
table		cooler		total

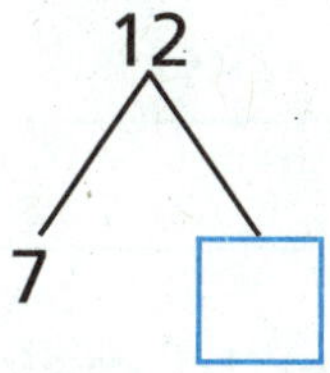

7. Write the unknown numbers in the boxes.

8. How are these math tools the same? How are they different?

____

9. Math Journal Write a word problem for this equation: $11 - 4 = \square$. Then solve it.

3–1 Class Activity

Name ______________________ Date ______________

Vocabulary
expression
equation

▶ Discuss the = and ≠ Signs

An **expression** is a combination of numbers, variables, and/or operation signs. Expressions do not have an equal sign.

An **equation** is made up of two equal quantities or expressions. An equal sign (=) is used to show that the two sides are equal.

$8 = 5 + 3$ $4 + 2 = 6$ $7 = 7$ $3 + 2 = 2 + 3$ $6 - 2 = 1 + 1 + 2$

The "is not equal to" sign (≠) shows that two quantities are not equal.

$7 \neq 5 + 3$ $4 + 2 \neq 8$ $7 \neq 6$ $6 - 2 \neq 2 + 3$ $5 + 2 \neq 1 + 1 + 3$

10. Use the = sign to write four equations. Vary how many numbers you have on each side.

____

____

____

____

11. Use the ≠ sign to write four "is not equal to" statements. Vary how many numbers you have on each side.

____

____

____

____

Write a number to make the number sentence true.

12. $16 = \square + 9$ **13.** $3 + \square \neq 12$ **14.** $7 + 2 = 2 + \square$

15. $15 - \square = 7$ **16.** $\square \neq 14 - 7$ **17.** $6 - 2 \neq 1 + 1 + \square$

Write = or ≠ to make a true number sentence.

18. 8 + 2 + 4 ___ 9 + 5 **19.** 8 ___ 6 − 2 **20.** 7 ___ 4 + 3

Dear Family,

In this unit, your child will solve addition and subtraction word problems involving a total and two partners.

- If one of the partners is unknown, it can be found by subtracting the known partner from the total or by counting on from the known partner to the total.
- If the total is unknown, it can be found by adding the partners.

Math Mountains are used to show a total and two partners. Students can use the Math Mountain to write an equation and then solve the equation to find the unknown.

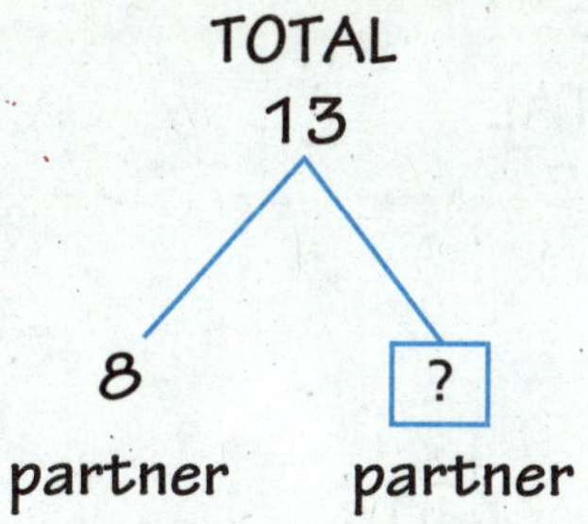

$8 + \boxed{?} = 13$

partner partner total

$5 + 8 = 13$

$13 = 8 + 5$

$13 = 5 + 8$

$13 - 5 = 8$

$13 - \boxed{8} = 5$

$8 = 13 - 5$

$5 = 13 - 8$

Equations with numbers alone on the left are also emphasized to help with the understanding of algebra.

Comparison Bars are used to solve problems that involve one amount that is more than or less than another amount. Making Comparison Bars can help a student organize the information in the problem in order to find the unknown smaller amount, larger amount, or the difference.

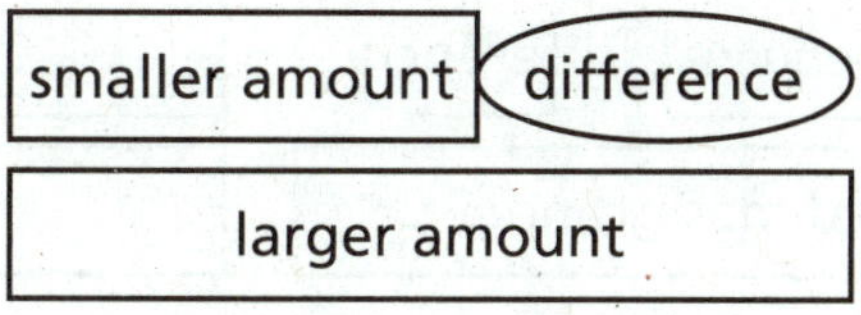

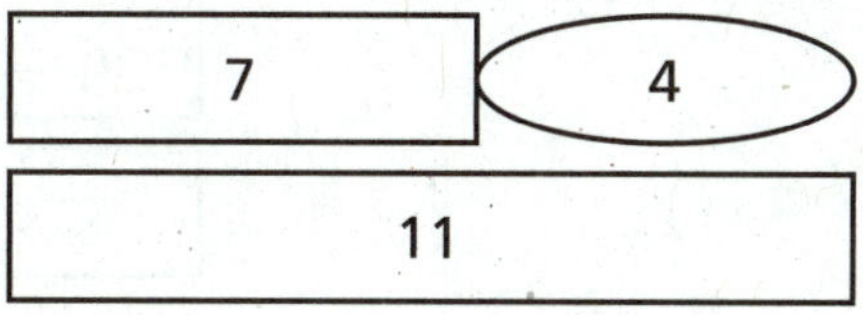

Please call or write if you have any questions or comments.

Sincerely,
Your child's teacher

Carta a la familia

Estimada familia:

En esta unidad, su niño resolverá problemas verbales de suma y resta que contienen un total y dos partes.

- Si no se conoce una de las partes, se la puede hallar restando la parte conocida del total o contando hacia adelante desde la parte conocida hasta el total.
- Si no se sabe el total, se lo puede hallar sumando las partes.

Para mostrar un total y dos partes se usan **montañas matemáticas**. Los estudiantes pueden usar *montañas matemáticas* para escribir una ecuación y luego resolverla para hallar el número desconocido.

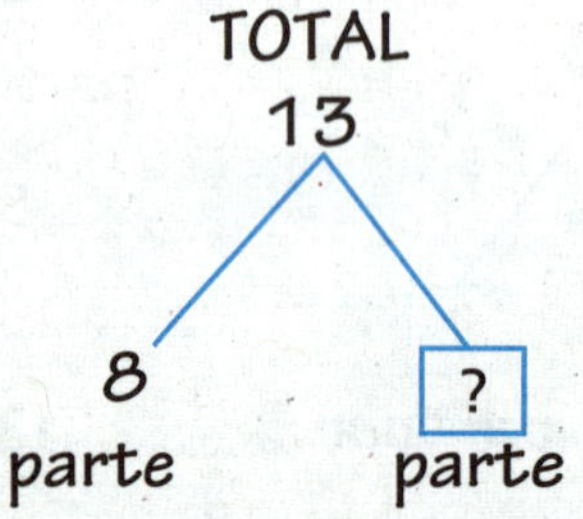

$8 + \boxed{?} = 13$

parte — parte — total

$13 = 8 + 5$

$13 = 5 + 8$

$5 + 8 = 13$

$13 - 5 = 8$

$13 - \boxed{8} = 5$

$8 = 13 - 5$

$5 = 13 - 8$

Se les da enfasis a las ecuaciones que tienen los números solos en el lado izquierdo, para facilitar la comprensión del álgebra.

Para resolver problemas que contengan una cantidad mayor o menor que otra se pueden usar **barras de comparación**. Estas *barras de comparación* pueden ayudar al estudiante a organizar la información que se presenta en el problema para hallar la cantidad más pequeña desconocida, la más grande o la diferencia.

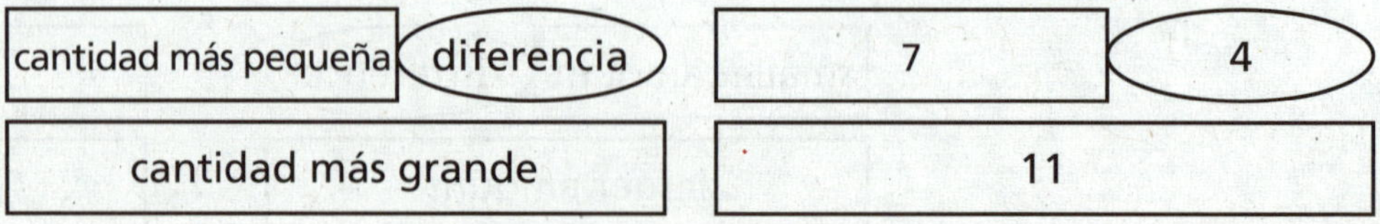

Si tiene alguna pregunta o comentario, por favor comuníquese conmigo.

Atentamente,
El maestro de su niño

Name Date

►Solve Unknown Partner Word Problems

Draw a Math Mountain and write and label an equation to solve each problem.

Show your work.

1. **Put Together: Unknown Partner** Stacy invited 9 girls and some boys to her party. 16 children were invited in all. How many boys were invited?

____

2. **Take Apart: Unknown Partner** There were 15 people at the park. 7 were playing soccer. The others were playing softball. How many people were playing softball?

____

3. **Change Plus: Unknown Partner** Jan planted 8 tulips last week. Today she planted some lilies. Now she has 17 flowers. How many lilies did she plant?

____

4. **Change Minus: Unknown Partner** Tim had 14 tennis balls. Then his brother borrowed some. Now Tim has 6 tennis balls. How many did his brother borrow?

____

Name ____________________ Date ____________

▶ Represent Unknown Partners with Math Tools

The equations and Math Mountains below show the word problems on page 73.

Put Together: Unknown Partner

9 + [ ] = 16
girls, boys, children

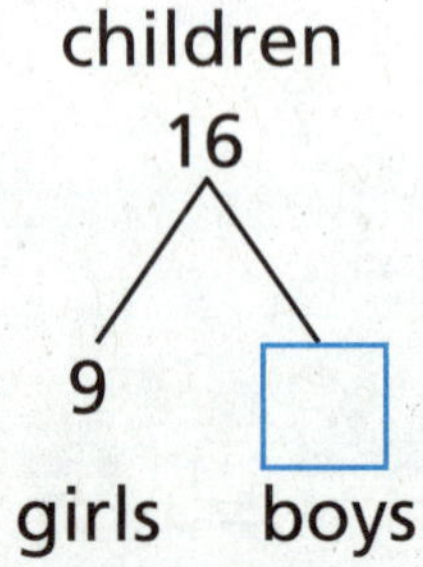

Take Apart: Unknown Partner

15 − [ ] = 7
park, softball, soccer

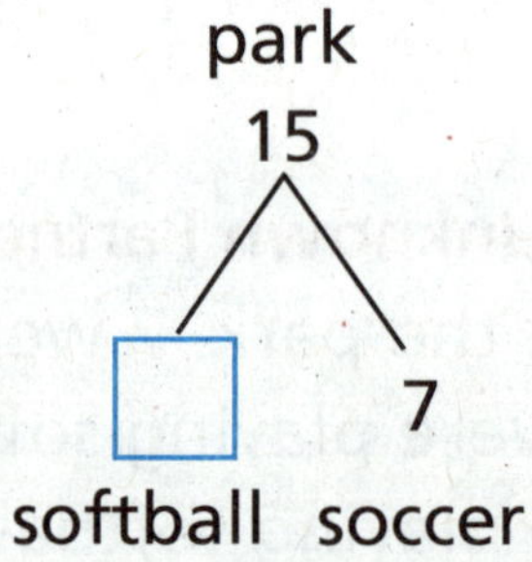

Change Plus: Unknown Partner

8 + [ ] = 17
tulips, lilies, flowers

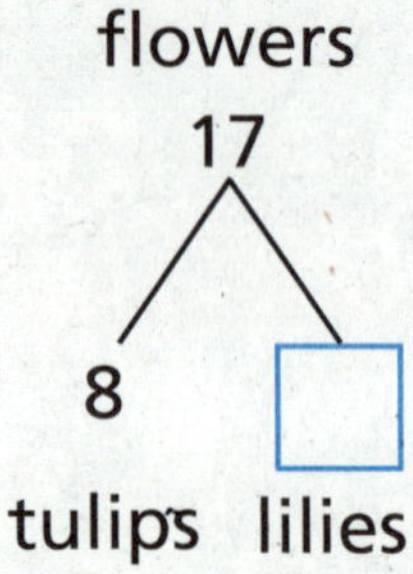

Change Minus: Unknown Partner

14 − [ ] = 6
all, some, now

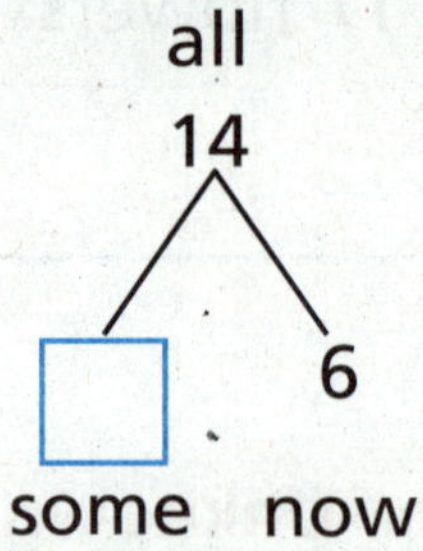

5. Write the unknown numbers in the boxes.

6. How are these math tools alike? How are they different?

____

____

3–3 Class Activity

Name ______________________ Date ______

► Solve Unknown Start Problems

Solve each problem. Label your answers.

Show your work.

1. **Change Plus: Unknown Start** Greta puts some beads on a string. Then she puts on 7 more beads. Now there are 13 beads on the string. How many beads did she put on the string to start?

____

2. **Change Minus: Unknown Start** Greta puts some beads on a string. Seven of the beads fell off the string. Six beads are still on the string. How many beads were there at first?

____

3. **Change Plus: Unknown Start** Patrick was carrying some books. His teacher asked him to carry 3 more books. Now he has 11 books. How many books did he start with?

____

4. **Change Minus: Unknown Start** Patricia was carrying some books. Her friend took 3 of them. Patricia has 8 books left. How many books was she carrying at first?

____

Name ______________________ Date ____________

▶ Represent Unknown Start Problems with Math Tools

The equations and Math Mountains below show the word problems on page 75.

Change Plus: Unknown Start

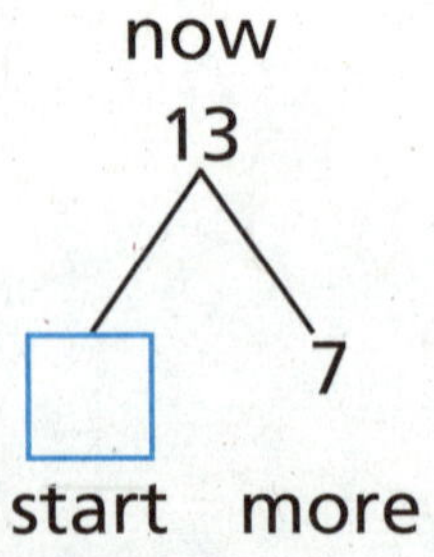

situation equation:

$\square + 7 = 13$

start more now

solution equations:

$7 + \square = 13$

$13 - 7 = \square$

Change Minus: Unknown Start

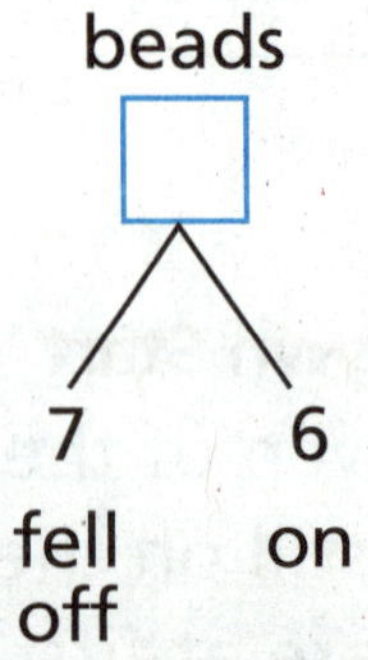

situation equation:

$\square - 7 = 6$

beads fell off on

solution equation:

$6 + 7 = \square$

Change Plus: Unknown Start

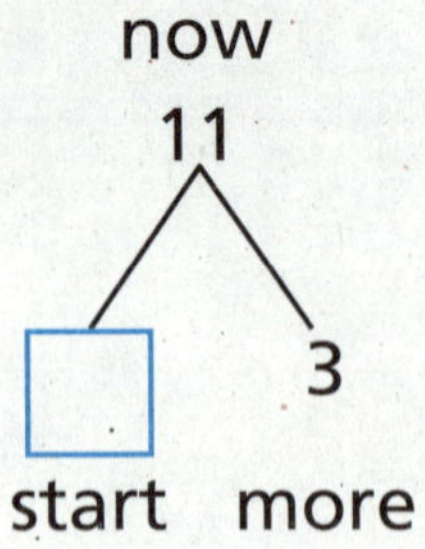

situation equation:

$\square + 3 = 11$

start more now

solution equations:

$3 + \square = 11$

$11 - 3 = \square$

Change Minus: Unknown Start

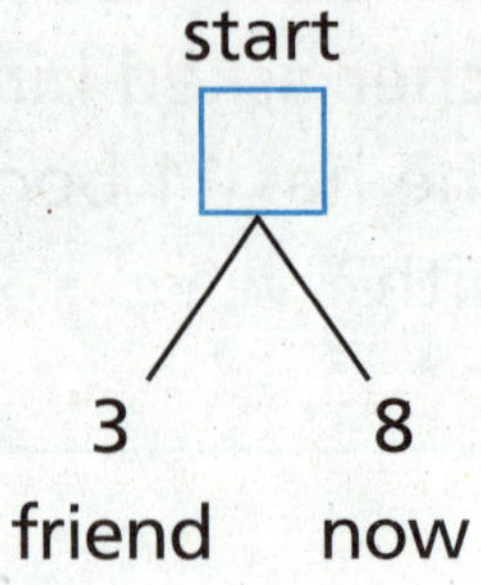

situation equation:

$\square - 3 = 8$

start friend now

solution equation:

$8 + 3 = \square$

5. Write the unknown numbers in the boxes.

6. How are these math tools alike? How are they different?

____

____

Name ______________________ Date ____________

▶ Discuss Comparison Problems

Solve each problem. Label your answers.

David has 5 marbles. Ana has 8 marbles.

1. How many more marbles does Ana have than David? ____________

2. How many fewer marbles does David have than Ana? ____________

Here are two ways to represent the comparison situation.

Comparison Drawing

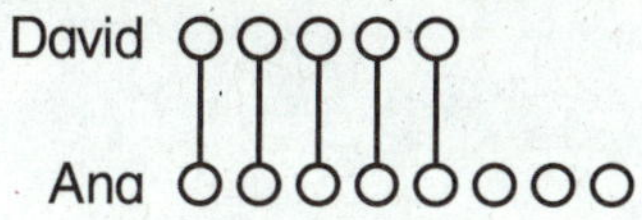

Comparison Bars

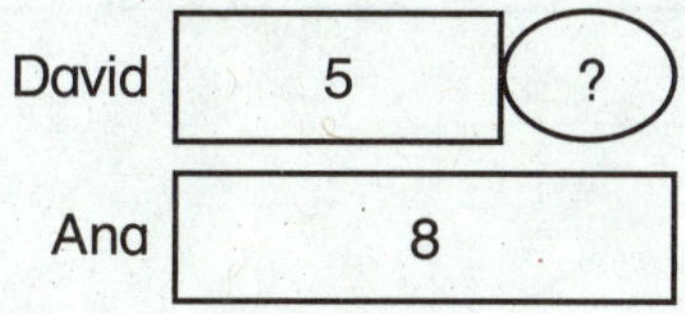

Claire has 8 marbles. Sasha has 15 marbles.

Show your work.

3. How many more marbles does Sasha have than Claire? ____________

4. How many fewer marbles does Claire have than Sasha? ____________

Rocky has 7 fishing lures. Megan has 12 fishing lures.

5. How many fewer fishing lures does Rocky have than Megan? ____________

3–4 Class Activity

Name ______________________ Date ______________

▶ Find an Unknown Larger or Smaller Amount

Solve each problem. Label your answers.

Show your work.

6. **Unknown Larger Amount** Maribel has 8 stickers. Arnon has 3 more stickers than Maribel. How many stickers does Arnon have?

   ____

7. **Unknown Smaller Amount** Arnon has 11 stickers. Maribel has 3 fewer stickers than Arnon. How many stickers does Maribel have?

   ____

8. **Unknown Larger Amount** Ivan has 9 goldfish. Milo has 5 more goldfish than Ivan. How many goldfish does Milo have?

   ____

9. **Unknown Smaller Amount** Milo has 14 goldfish. Ivan has 5 fewer goldfish than Milo. How many goldfish does Ivan have?

   ____

Name ______________________ Date ____________

▶ The Puzzled Penguin

Dear Math Students,

As part of my math homework, I solved this problem:

Carlos has 9 fish. He has 4 fewer fish than Daniel. How many fish does Daniel have?

Here is what I did: $9 - 4 = 5$ Daniel has 5 fish.

Is my answer right? If not, please correct my work, and tell what I did wrong.

Sincerely,
The Puzzled Penguin

▶ Solve Comparison Problems with Misleading Language

Solve each problem on a separate piece of paper.

1. **Unknown Smaller Amount** Daniel has 13 fish. Daniel has 4 more fish than Carlos. How many fish does Carlos have?

   ____

2. **Unknown Larger Amount** Gina ran 8 laps. She ran 6 fewer laps than Bettina. How many laps did Bettina run?

   ____

3. **Unknown Smaller Amount** Bettina ran 14 laps. Bettina ran 6 more laps than Gina. How many laps did Gina run?

   ____

4. Sara read 8 books this month. She read 6 fewer books than Lupe. How many books did Lupe read this month?

   ____

Name ________________ Date ________

► Solve Comparison Problems Without the Words *More* or *Fewer*

Solve each problem. Label your answers.

Show your work.

5. The coach brought 8 hockey sticks to practice. There were 13 players at practice. How many players didn't get sticks?

____

6. At a meeting, 5 people had to stand because there were not enough chairs. There were 12 chairs. How many people came to the meeting?

____

7. Jess had 16 apples. After he gave one to each of his cousins, he had 3 apples left. How many cousins does Jess have?

____

8. At the park, 4 of the children could not swing because there were not enough swings. There were 10 children at the park. How many swings were on the swing set?

____

9. Maile took one step on each tile along the garden path. After she took 14 steps, there were 3 more tiles left to go. How many tiles were there along the path?

____

3–6 Class Activity

Name _______________ Date _______________

► Solve Multi-Digit Problems with Unknown Partners

Solve each problem. Label your answers. Use your MathBoard or another sheet of paper.

1. Amanda had 783 seashells in her collection. She found some more seashells at the beach. Now she has 912 seashells. How many seashells did she find at the beach?

   ____

2. Michelle and Sanjay are playing pinball. Together they have scored 1,509 points. Michelle has scored 718 points. How many points has Sanjay scored?

   ____

3. Beth and Olivia are driving across the country. Beth drove 923 miles. Together they drove 1,586 miles. How many miles did Olivia drive?

   ____

4. There were 1,936 people at a baseball game. A number of people left during the sixth inning. There were 856 people at the game after the sixth inning. How many people left during the sixth inning?

   ____

Name ______________________ Date ______________

▶ Solve Multi-Digit Problems with Unknown Starts

Solve each problem. Label your answers.

Show your work.

5. The students at Oakdale School collected some cans of food in May. They collected 978 cans of food in June. They collected 1,729 cans of food in all in those two months. How many cans of food did they collect in May?

____

6. Mrs. Perez ordered some sheets of colored paper for her art class. Her students used 831 sheets of colored paper. There are 369 sheets left over. How many sheets of colored paper did Mrs. Perez order?

____

7. Today a grocer sold 682 melons. At the end of the day, 756 melons were left over. How many melons did the grocer have at the beginning of the day?

____

8. Mr. Chung's class earned some money selling pizzas last month. This month, Mr. Chung's class earned $562 more. Now they have $986. How much money did the class earn last month?

____

Name _______________ Date _______________

▶ Solve Mixed Problems

Solve each problem. Label your answers.

Show your work.

9. A book has 876 pages. Maria has read 456 pages of the book. How many more pages must Maria read to finish the book?

____

10. Natalie polished some rocks in March. She polished 418 more rocks in April. She now has 682 polished rocks. How many rocks did Natalie polish in March?

____

11. Today the visitors at the library checked out a total of 1,326 books. Of these books, 679 did not come from the children's section. How many books did come from the children's section?

____

12. Jeff collects nickels. He puts 368 of his nickels in the bank. He now has 283 nickels left. How many nickels did Jeff start with?

____

13. **Math Journal** Write a problem that can be solved using this equation: $\square + 156 = 215$. Then solve it.

3–6 **Class Activity**

Name ____________________ Date ____________

Vocabulary
inequality

▶ Discuss Equations and Inequalities

An equation shows that two quantities or expressions are equal. An equal sign (=) is used to show that the two sides are equal.

$8 = 5 + 3$ $4 + 2 = 6$ $7 = 7$ $3 + 2 = 2 + 3$ $6 - 2 = 1 + 1 + 2$

An **inequality** shows that two quantities or expressions are not equal. The signs less than ($<$), greater than ($>$), and not equal ($\neq$) show that the two sides are not equal.

$7 < 5 + 3$ $9 + 2 > 8$ $7 \neq 6$ $6 - 2 < 2 + 3$ $5 + 2 > 1 + 1 + 3$

1. Use the $>$ sign to write four inequalities. Vary how many numbers you have on each side.

______________________ ______________________

______________________ ______________________

2. Use the $<$ sign to write four inequalities. Vary how many numbers you have on each side.

______________________ ______________________

______________________ ______________________

Write a number to make the inequality true.

3. $16 > \square + 9$ **4.** $3 + \square > 12$ **5.** $7 + 2 > 2 + \square$

6. $18 - \square > 9$ **7.** $\square < 15 - 7$ **8.** $5 - 2 < 1 + 1 + \square$

Write $>$, $<$, or $=$ to make a true number sentence.

9. $5 + 2 + 4$ ___ $9 + 5$ **10.** 9 ___ $8 - 2$ **11.** 12 ___ $7 + 5$

3–7 Class Activity

Name ______________________ Date ______________

▶ Solve Multi-Digit Comparison Problems

Solve each problem. Label your answers.

Show your work.

1. The Sunnytown Library has 1,052 history books. The Judson Library has 863 history books. How many more history books does the Sunnytown Library have than the Judson Library?

____

2. Today the Daisy Café used 465 plates. They used 197 fewer plates yesterday than they used today. How many plates did the Daisy Café use yesterday?

____

3. José received 749 votes in the school election. Cora received 126 more votes than José. How many votes did Cora receive?

____

4. Marco earned $428 doing yard work. Troy earned $186. How much less money did Troy earn than Marco?

____

3–7 Class Activity

Name ______ Date ______

▶ Solve Multi-Digit Comparison Problems with Misleading Language

Solve each problem. Draw comparison bars to help you. Label your answers.

5. Billy has 679 pennies. He has 278 more pennies than Lee. How many pennies does Lee have?

______

6. Rebecca drove 362 miles. She drove 439 fewer miles than Fiona. How many miles did Fiona drive? ______

7. The baseball team gave 250 caps to people who came to the game today. There were 569 people at the game. How many people did not get a cap? ______

8. The principal bought 975 pencils at the beginning of the school year. Each student in the school received one pencil. The principal had 123 pencils left over. How many students are in the school? ______

Name Date

▶ Use Logical Reasoning to Solve Problems

Solve.

Show your work.

1. Darnell, Rita, and Mark each bought a CD. Mark spent $3 less than Darnell. Rita spent $7 more than Mark. Darnell spent $11. How much did Rita spend?

2. Helmer, Lily, and Pete live on Maple Street. Pete's house number is twice Helmer's. Lily's house number is 251. Helmer's house number is 45 less than Lily's. What is Pete's house number?

3. Luisa, Sally, and Tran each have a coin collection. Sally has 72 more coins than Luisa. Luisa has 126 fewer coins than Tran. Sally has 429 coins. How many coins does each have?

4. Tonya, Seth, Ann, and Len were in a walk-a-thon. They walked 14 mi, 26 mi, 19 mi, and 10 mi. Seth walked the farthest. Tonya walked farther than Len. Ann walked 10 mi. How far did each walk?

5. Dave, Shawna, Liz, and Matt are friends. Liz is taller than Shawna. Dave is the tallest. Matt is taller than Liz. What is their order from shortest to tallest?

6. **Math Journal** Explain the strategy you used to solve problem 5.

Name ______________________ Date __________

Going Further

▶ Choose the Equation

Circle the equation that represents the problem. Then solve.

7. Trinh had 9 pennies. Then he found some more pennies. Trinh has 17 pennies in all. How many pennies did Trinh find?

$17 - \square = 9$ $\quad$ $9 + 8 = \square$ $\quad$ $9 + \square = 17$

____

8. There are 13 boys and girls at the park. 6 of the children are girls. How many boys are at the park?

$6 - 13 = \square$ $\quad$ $6 + \square = 13$ $\quad$ $13 + 6 = \square$

____

9. Taci found some shells. Then she found 8 more shells. Taci has 14 shells. How many shells did Taci find at the beginning?

$\square + 8 = 14$ $\quad$ $8 + 6 = \square$ $\quad$ $14 - \square = 8$

____

10. Miguel made some paper airplanes. He gave 5 of the paper airplanes to a friend. Miguel has 7 left. How many paper airplanes did he make?

$7 - 5 = \square$ $\quad$ $\square - 5 = 7$ $\quad$ $5 + 7 = \square$

____

Name _______________ Date _______________

► Solve Mixed Multi-Digit Word Problems

Show your work.

Solve each problem. Label your answers.

1. Jacob had 219 bottle caps in his collection. Then he found some more. Now he has 347 bottle caps. How many bottle caps did Jacob find?

____

2. Yesterday Tamara stamped some invitations. Today she stamped 239 invitations. She stamped 427 invitations in all. How many invitations did she stamp yesterday? _______________

3. Batai made 122 calls in the phone-a-thon. Gina made 261 calls. How many more calls did Gina make than Batai? _______________

4. Greta has 449 feet of fencing for her dog run. Mitch has 110 fewer feet of fencing for his dog run. How many feet of fencing does Mitch have? _______________

3–8

Class Activity

Name ____________________ Date ____________

Solve each problem. Label your answers.

Show your work.

5. The Grove Street bus carried 798 passengers today. The Elm Street bus carried 298 more passengers today than the Grove Street bus. How many passengers did the Elm Street bus carry today?

____

6. Park City Cycle has 876 bicycles in stock. This is 134 more bicycles than Bentley's Bike Shop has in stock. How many bicycles does Bentley's Bike Shop have in stock?

____

7. At Sunflower Bakery's grand opening, the first 250 customers received a free bagel. There were 682 customers at the grand opening. How many customers did not get a free bagel?

____

8. There were some chairs set up for a concert. Then Shantel set up 256 more chairs. Now 610 chairs are set up. How many chairs were set up to start with?

____

3–8 **Going Further**

Name ____________________________ Date ____________

▶ Find the Missing Digits

In each box, write the digit that makes a correct addition or subtraction.

1.
$$\begin{array}{r} \square\,9 \\ +\ 8\,\square \\ \hline 1\,2\,6 \end{array}$$

2.
$$\begin{array}{r} 8\,\square \\ -\ \square\,4 \\ \hline 5\,7 \end{array}$$

3.
$$\begin{array}{r} 7\,\square \\ +\ \square\,8 \\ \hline 1\,3\,0 \end{array}$$

4.
$$\begin{array}{r} 1\,\square\,5 \\ -\ 4\,\square \\ \hline 8\,6 \end{array}$$

5.
$$\begin{array}{r} 3\,\square\,9 \\ +\ \square\,7\,\square \\ \hline 1\,1\,8\,5 \end{array}$$

6.
$$\begin{array}{r} \square\,\square\,5 \\ +\ 3\,9\,\square \\ \hline \square\,0\,2\,3 \end{array}$$

7.
$$\begin{array}{r} 5\,8\,\square \\ -\ \square\,\square\,6 \\ \hline 4\,3\,6 \end{array}$$

8.
$$\begin{array}{r} 5\,\square\,7 \\ -\ 2\,6\,\square \\ \hline \square\,4\,9 \end{array}$$

9.
$$\begin{array}{r} \square\,6\,4 \\ +\ 3\,\square\,8 \\ \hline 9\,5\,\square \end{array}$$

10.
$$\begin{array}{r} 9\,\square\,2\,8 \\ -\ \square\,1\,\square\,3 \\ \hline 4\,8\,5\,\square \end{array}$$

11.
$$\begin{array}{r} \square\,7\,\square\,6 \\ +\ 2\,3\,8\,\square \\ \hline 4\,\square\,4\,0 \end{array}$$

12.
$$\begin{array}{r} 6\,\square\,2\,\square \\ -\ \square\,1\,\square\,8 \\ \hline 3\,8\,2\,2 \end{array}$$

13. On the Back Write your own missing digit addition and missing digit subtraction.

Name Date

Name ______________________ Date ______________

▶ Math and Social Studies

1. Find the difference between the height of the Statue of Liberty and the height of your teacher.

____

2. The table shows the length of different parts of the Statue of Liberty. Fill in the table. Then find each difference.

Length	Statue of Liberty	You	Difference
Pointing Finger	about 96 inches		
Left Hand	about 128 inches		
Right Arm	about 504 inches		

3. **Use a Calculator** There are 168 steps to climb in the Statue of Liberty. Measure how long it takes you to climb a stairway. Use that information to find out how about how long it would take you to climb to the top of the Statue of Liberty. Explain what you did.

____

____

____

____

____

3–9 Class Activity

Name ____________________ Date ____________

▶A Day at the Amusement Park

Pedro's class is going to the amusement park.

The timeline shows how the students will spend their day.

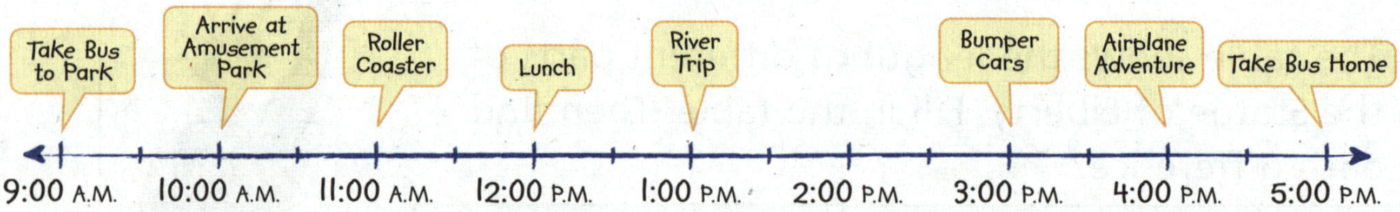

1. What time will Pedro's class go on the Airplane Adventure?

____

2. How long is the trip on the bus to the amusement park?

____

3. The students went on the Ferris wheel at 3:30 P.M. Mark that on the timeline.

4. Put these events in order starting with the earliest: Airplane Adventure, Roller Coaster, River Trip.

____

____

5. **Math Journal** Make a timeline that shows how you would like to spend the day at an amusement park. Then write two sentences about your timeline.

Name ______________________ Date ______________

Solve each problem. Label your answer.

Show your work.

1. Helga is a dog walker. Today she walked 8 beagles and some terriers. Altogether she walked 14 dogs. How many terriers did she walk?

____

2. Li Wei had some apples. She gave 9 of the apples to her friends. She has 5 apples left. How many apples did she start with?

____

3. Luis received 6 cards. He received 7 fewer cards than Carlos received. How many cards did Carlos receive?

____

4. On Tuesday, Rashid polished 143 rocks. He polished some more rocks on Wednesday. He polished 228 rocks altogether. How many rocks did Rashid polish on Wednesday?

____

5. Some students were playing in the schoolyard. Then 119 students went into the school. Now there are 286 students in the schoolyard. How many students were in the schoolyard to start with?

____

6. Pat has 425 pennies in his collection. Miguel has 201 fewer pennies. How many pennies does Miguel have?

____

Name ______________________ Date ______________

7. Write a number to make the number sentence true.

a. $10 = \square + 3$ b. $8 - \square \neq 3$

c. $5 + \square = 11$ d. $15 > \square + 8$

e. $9 - 2 < \square + 5$

Write an equation and then solve each problem. Label your answer.

Show your work.

8. On Monday and Tuesday, Franco spent 5 hours doing homework altogether. He did homework for 2 hours on Tuesday. How many hours did Franco spend doing homework on Monday?

____

9. Tony had some baseball cards. Jeremy gave him 8 more. Then he had 19 baseball cards. How many did he have to start?

____

10. **Extended Response** Elsa read 13 books this month. She read 6 fewer books than Cliff read. Draw Comparison Bars to represent the problem.

How many books did Cliff read? __________

Explain how you know who read more books, Elsa or Cliff.

____

____

____

4–1 Class Activity

Name ______________________ Date ____________

▶ **Review Quadrilaterals and Types of Lines**

Place the letter Q on each quadrilateral. Then label each quadrilateral with the names that describe it using the letters from the Key.

Key
Parallelogram **(P)**
Rectangle **(R)**
Square **(S)**
Rhombus **(Rh)**

1. 

2. 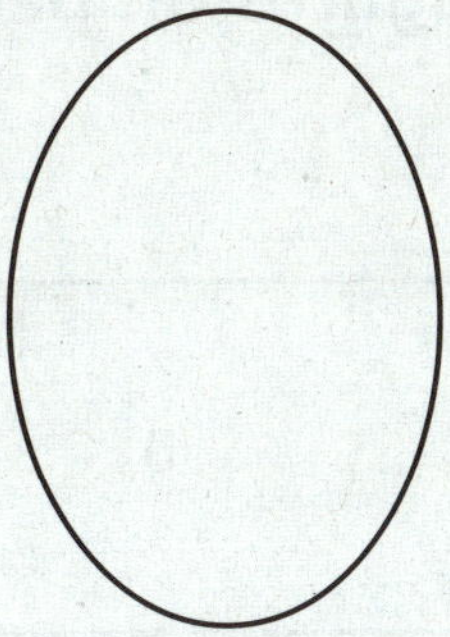

3. 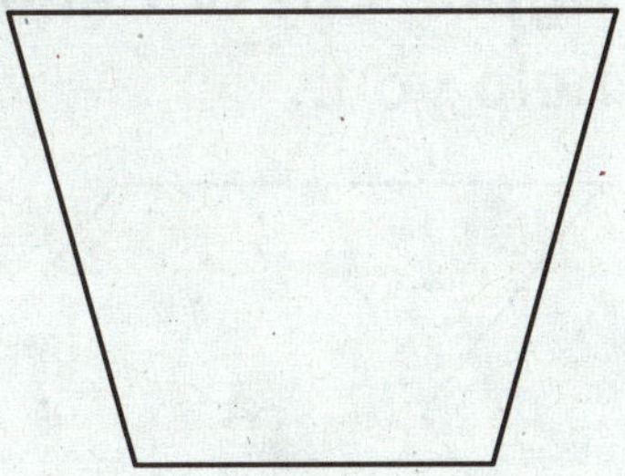

4. 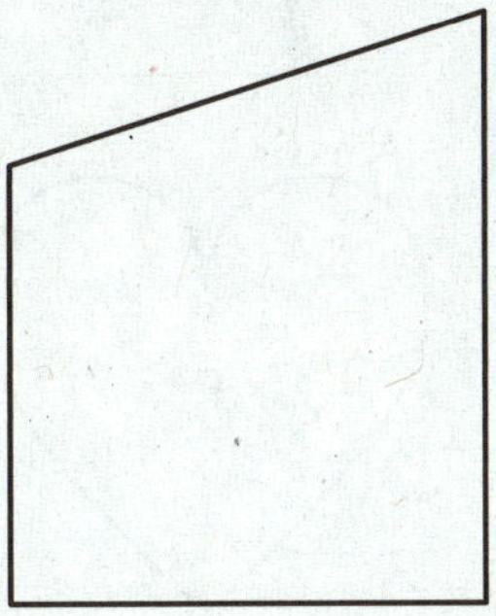

5. 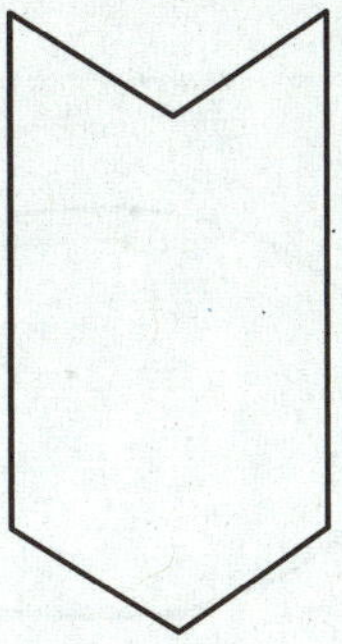

6. 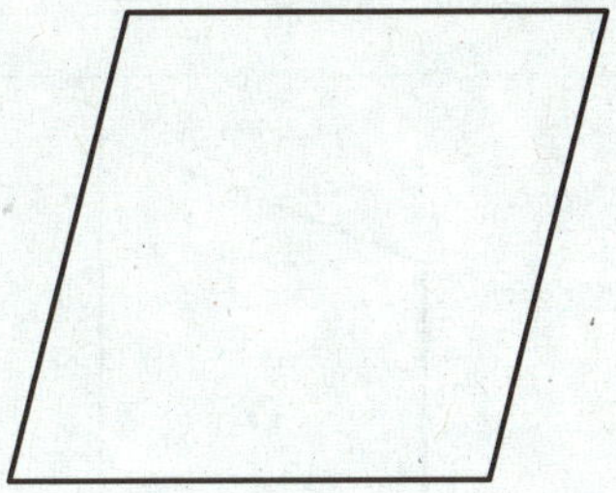

7. 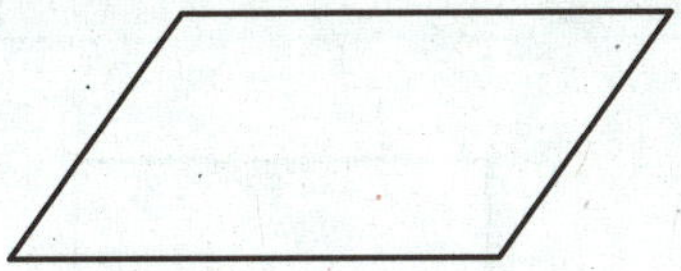

8. 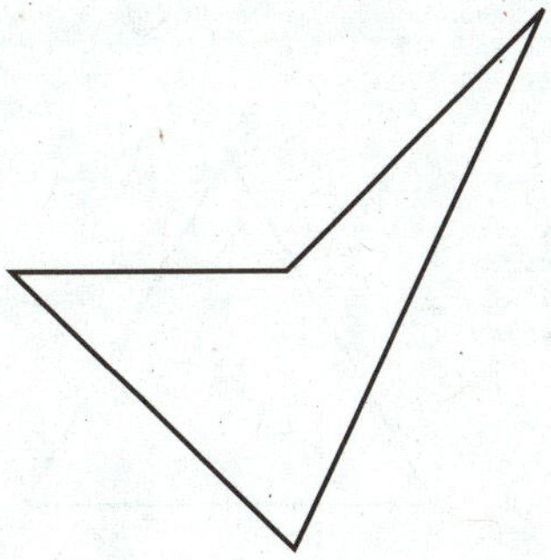

9. 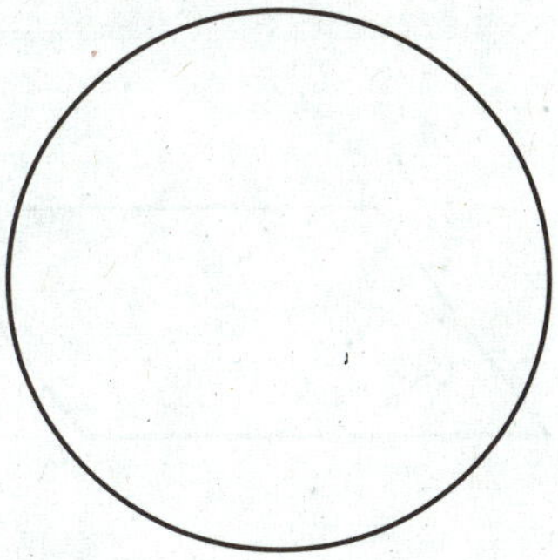

10. 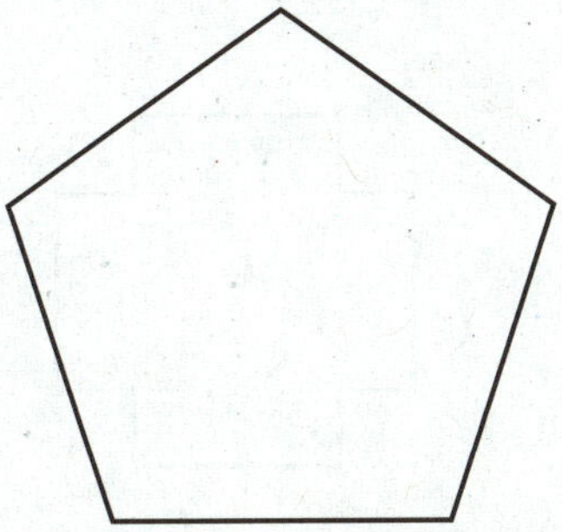

11. 

12. 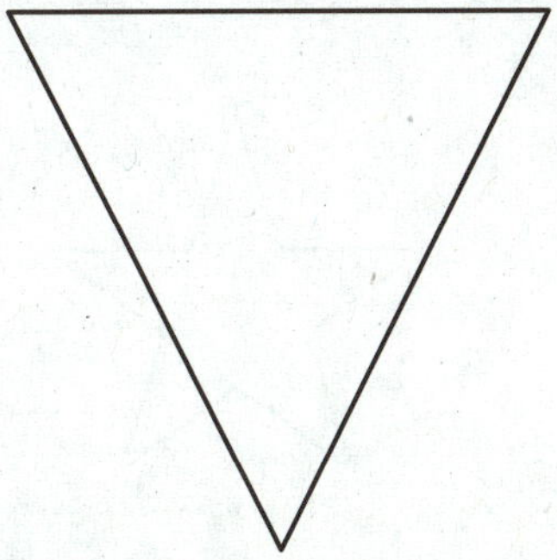

4–1 Class Activity

Name ______________________ Date ____________

Vocabulary
line of symmetry

▶ Draw Lines of Symmetry

A line of symmetry divides a figure in half so that if you fold along the line, the two halves match each other exactly.

Draw all of the possible lines of symmetry on each figure. Cut out and fold the figures on page 101 to help you.

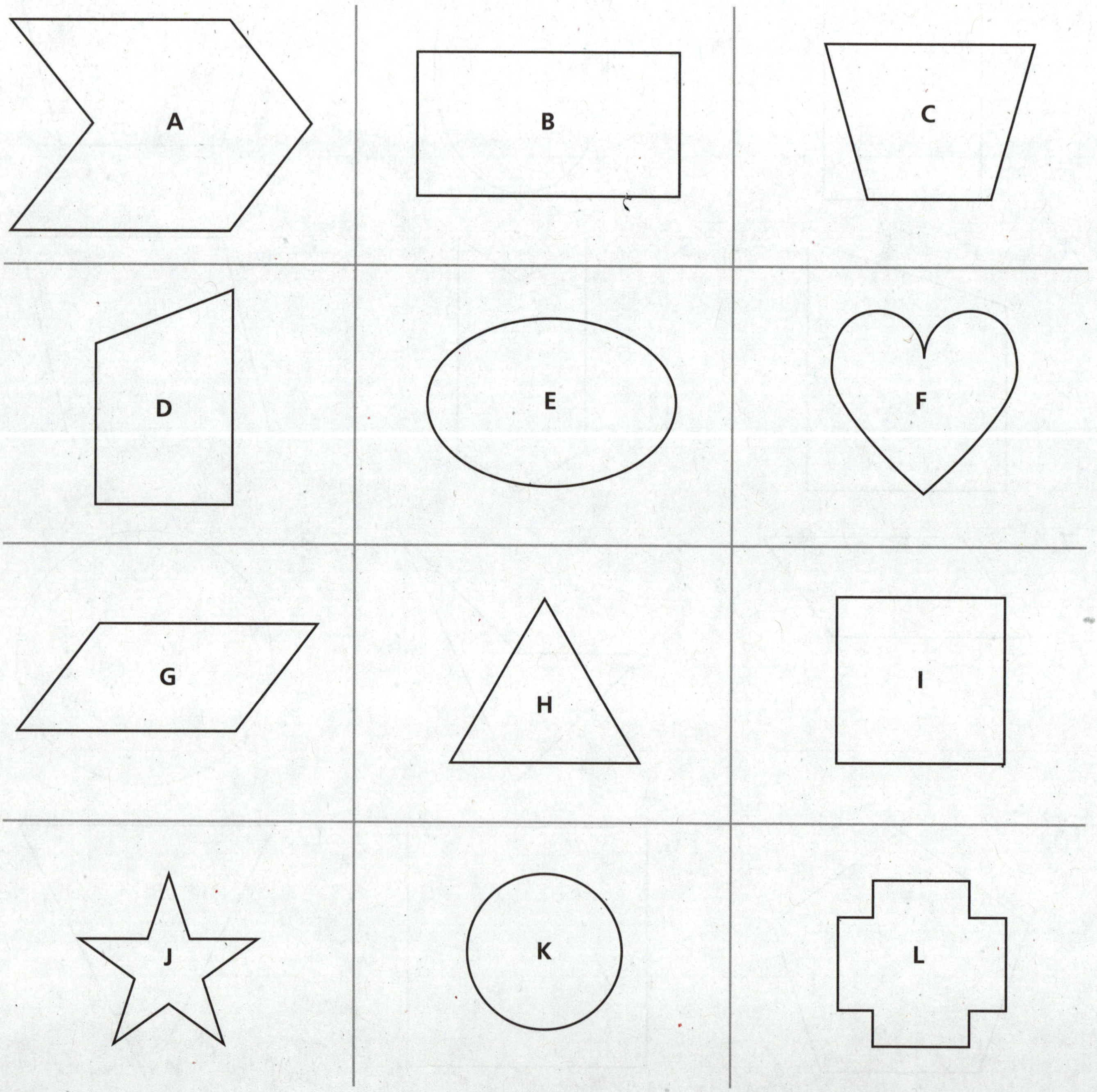

Name ______________________ Date ______________

▶ Draw Lines of Symmetry

Cut out these figures to help you with Student Activity Book page 98.

4–1 Class Activity

Name ____________ Date ____________

Vocabulary
congruent

▶ Identify Congruent Halves of Figures

Two halves of a figure are **congruent** if they are the same size and shape.

Does the dashed line divide the figure into congruent halves? Write *yes* or *no.*

1.

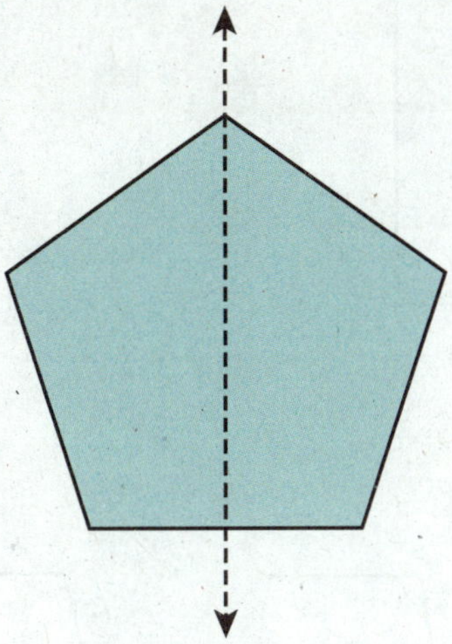

____

2.

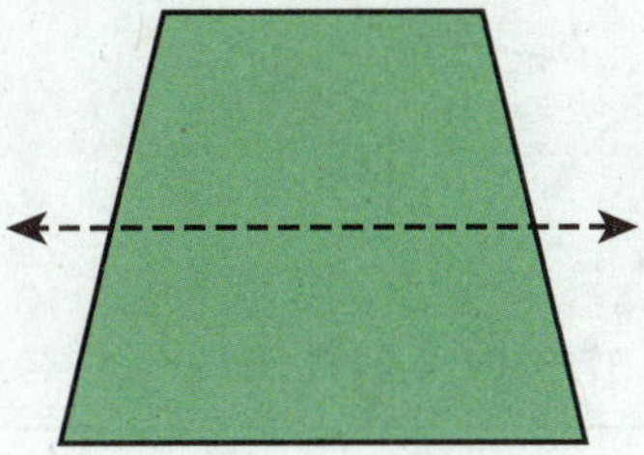

____

3.

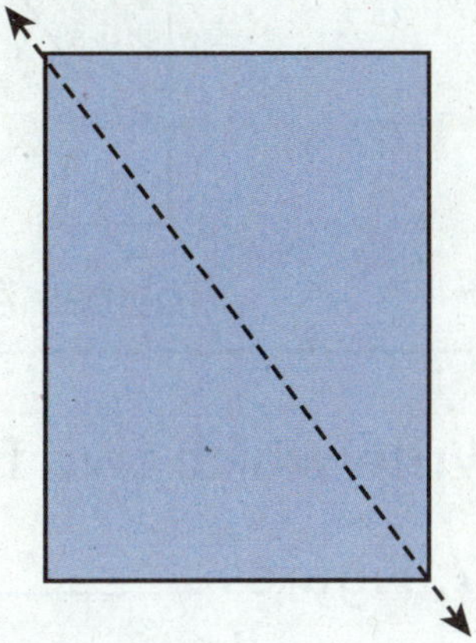

____

4.

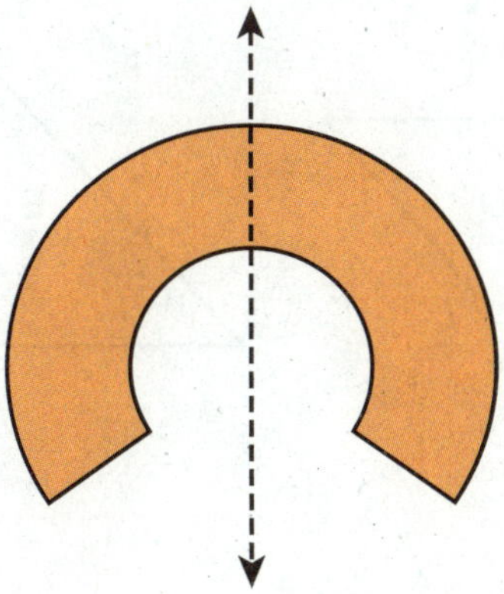

____

5.

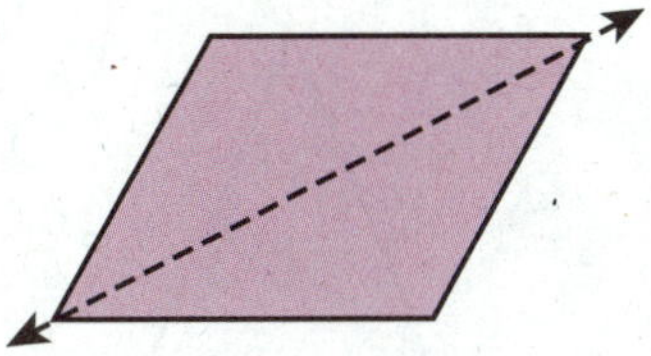

____

6.

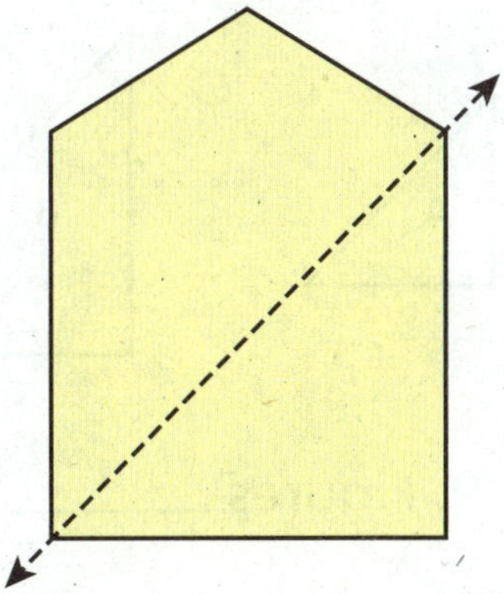

____

Name ____________________ Date ____________

Vocabulary
congruent

▶ Identify Congruent Figures

Two figures are **congruent** if they are the same size and shape. If you can slide, flip, or turn one figure so that it fits exactly on top of the other, the figures are congruent.

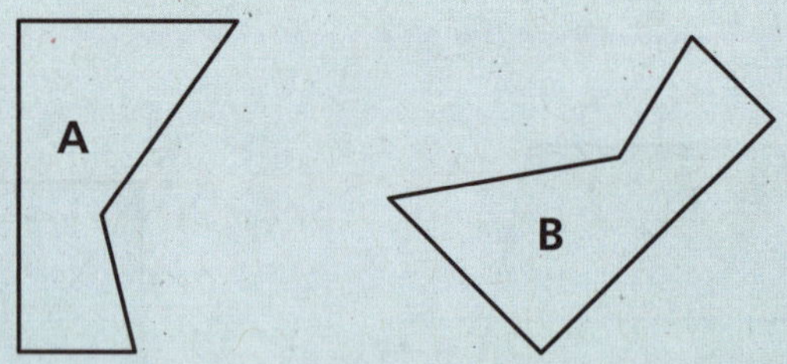

Figures A and B are congruent.

Write which two figures in each row are congruent.

7. Figures __________ and __________ are congruent.

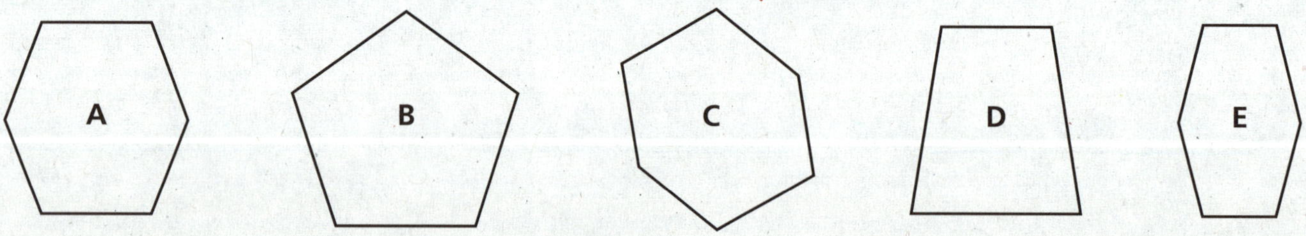

8. Figures __________ and __________ are congruent.

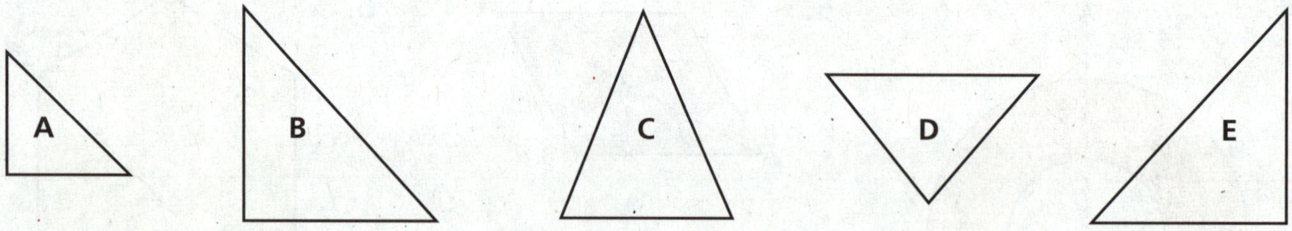

9. Figures __________ and __________ are congruent.

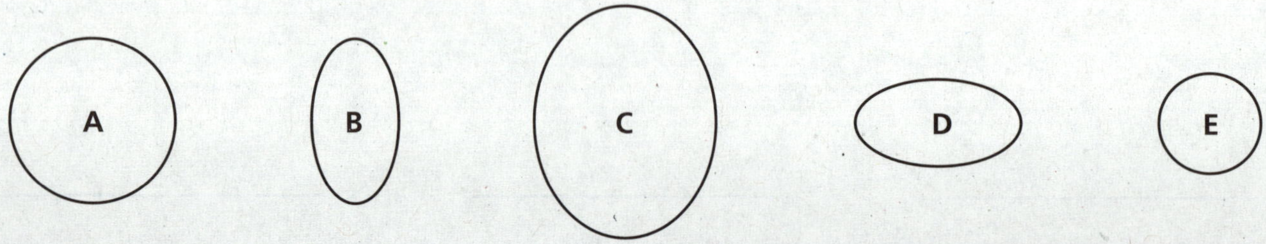

4-1 Going Further

Name ______ Date ______

▶ Use Congruence and Symmetry

Solve.

1. The triangles at the right are congruent. Find the missing measure.

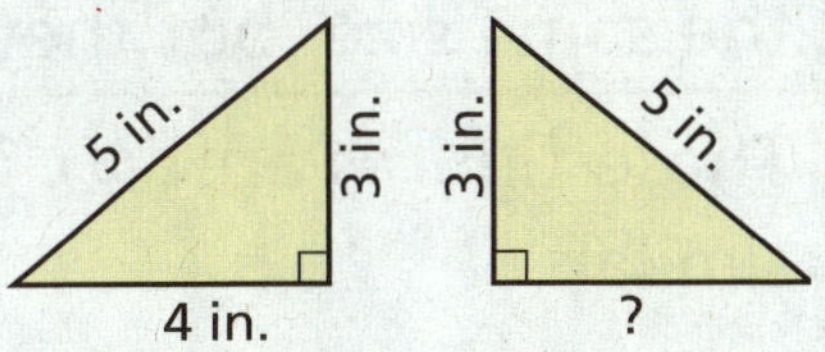

______

2. Complete the figure so it has the line of symmetry shown.

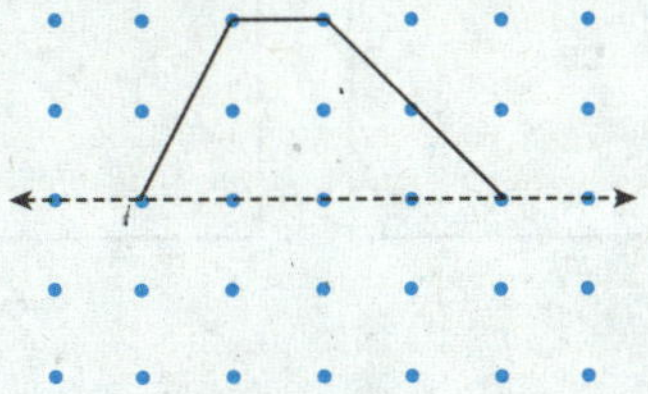

3. All parts of the two dog houses are congruent. How tall is Fido's dog house?

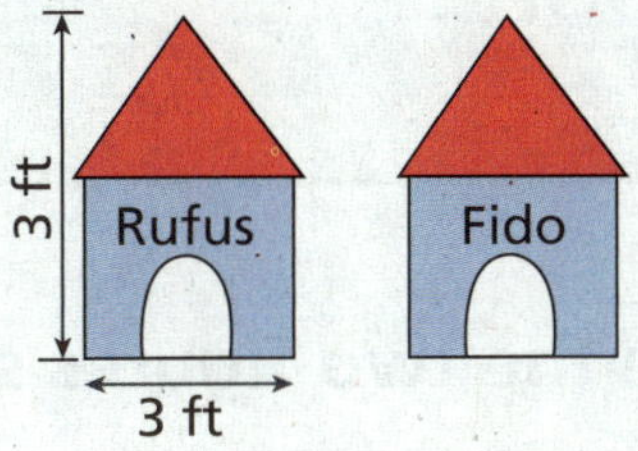

______

4. The lines of symmetry shown in the figure at the right divide the figure into congruent triangles. The base (short side) of one triangle measures 10 inches. What is the perimeter of the figure?

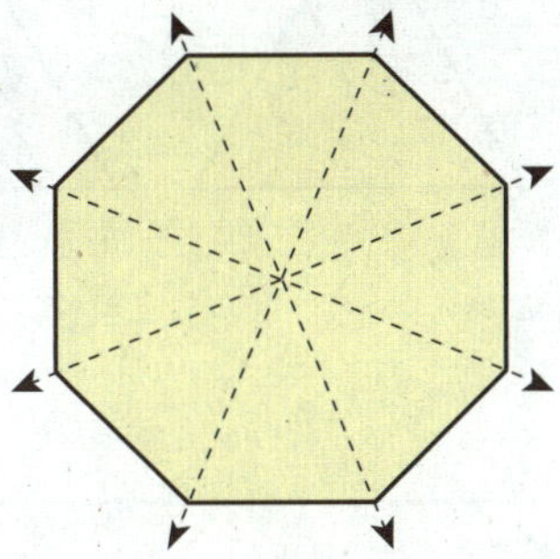

______

5. The rectangular field at the right has the lines of symmetry shown. How many feet of fencing are needed?

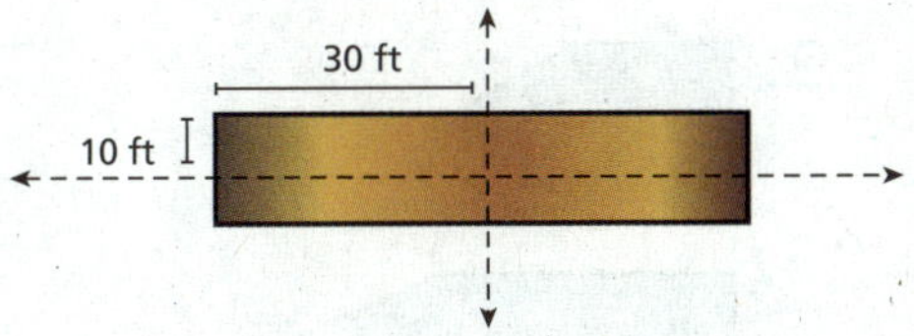

______

6. **Math Journal** Draw a design that has at least one line of symmetry and that uses at least two congruent figures.

Name ______________________ Date ______________

Vocabulary
similar

▶ Identify Similar Figures

Similar figures are the same shape. They may also be the same size, but they don't have to be.

These figures are similar.

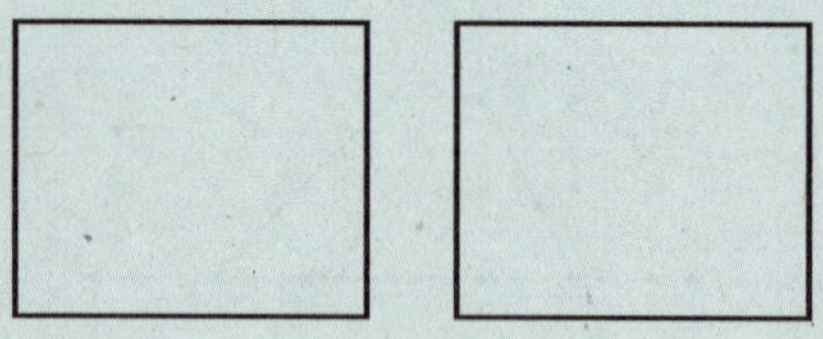

These figures are similar.

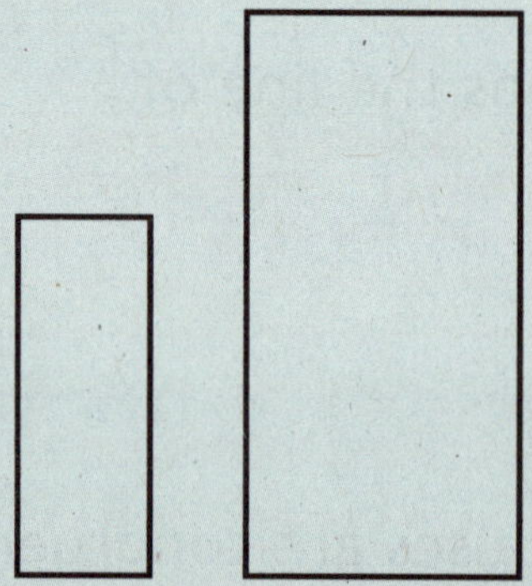

These figures are not similar.

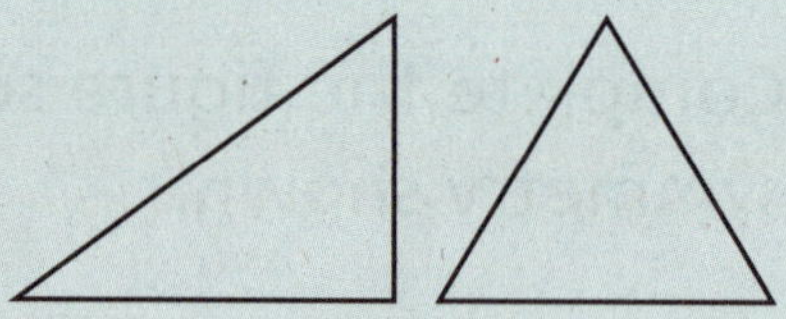

Are the two figures similar? Write similar or not similar.

1. 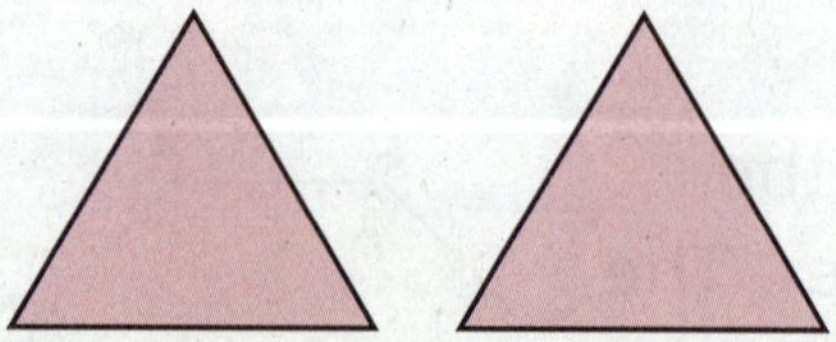

____

2. 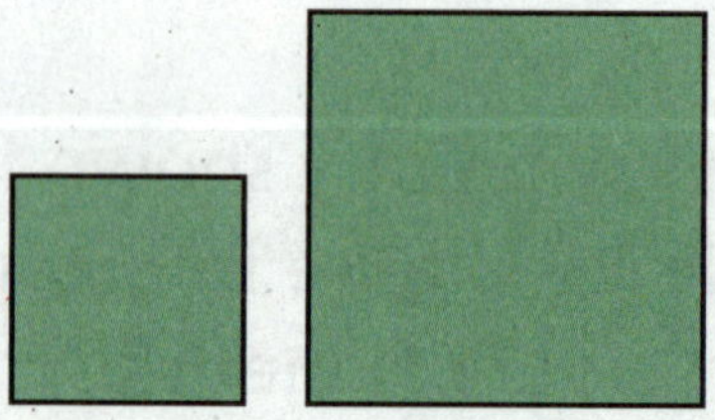

____

3. 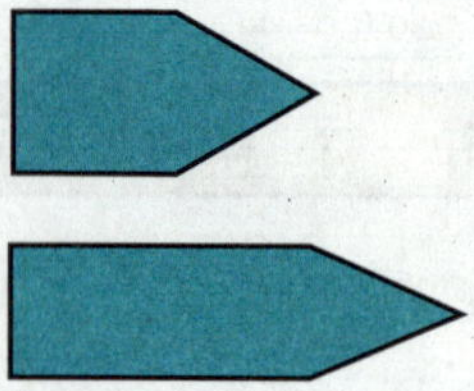

____

4. 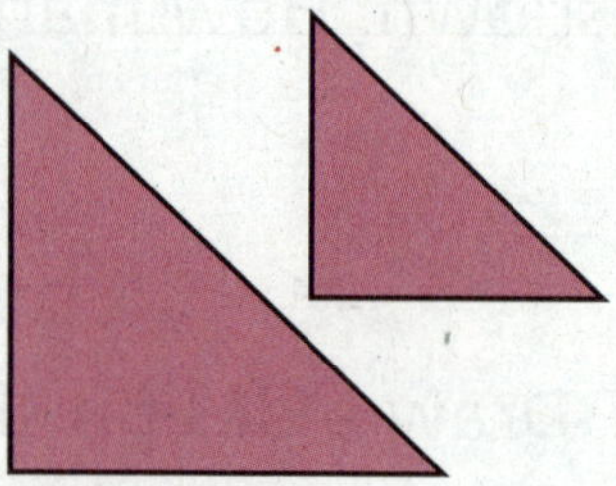

____

Family Letter

Dear Family,

Your child is currently participating in math activities that help him or her understand basic geometry in two dimensions.

Your child will be looking for **lines of symmetry**. If you fold a figure along a line of symmetry, the two halves will match each other exactly.

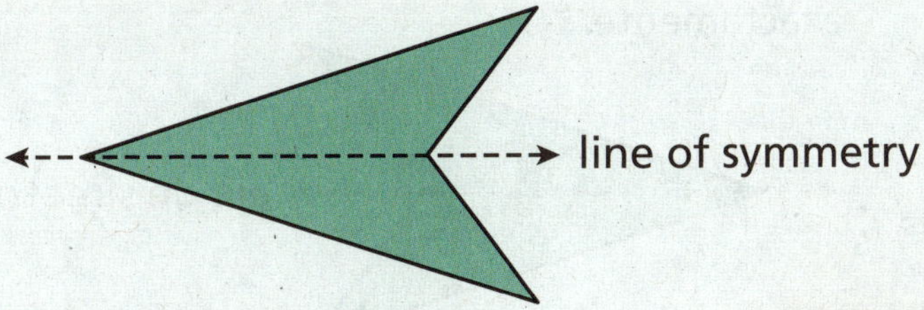

Your child will also be identifying **congruent** figures. Congruent figures are the same size and shape.

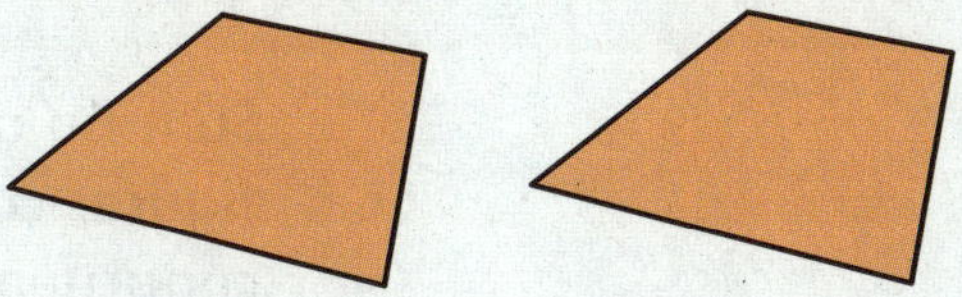

Encourage your child to look for congruent figures in your home or neighborhood and to identify lines of symmetry in various two-dimensional figures.

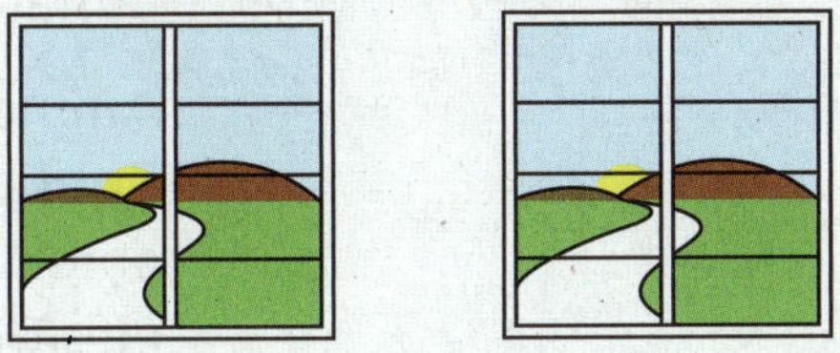

Your child will be learning how to label, name, and describe geometric figures. For example, the line segment *AC* is a **diagonal** of the square *ABCD*.

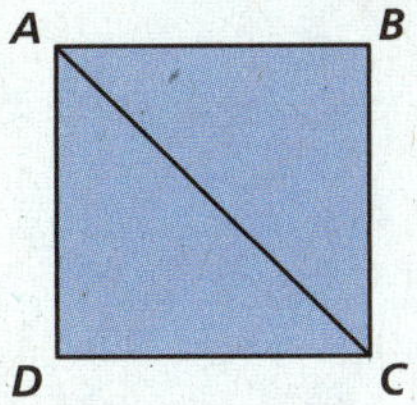

Your child will learn that angles are measured in **degrees** and discover that the sum of the measures of the angles in a triangle is always 180 degrees (180°).

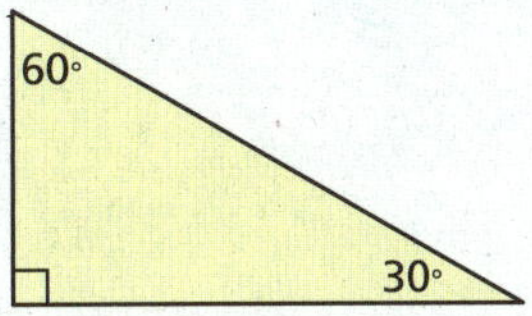

$60° + 30° + 90° = 180°$

If you have any questions or comments, please call or write to me.

Thank you.

Sincerely,
Your child's teacher

Carta a la familia

Estimada familia:

En estos momentos su niño o niña está participando en actividades matemáticas que le ayudan a entender la geometria básica en dos dimensiones.

Su niño o niña buscará **ejes de simetría**. Si se pliega una figura a lo largo de su eje de simetría, las dos mitades coincidirán exactamente.

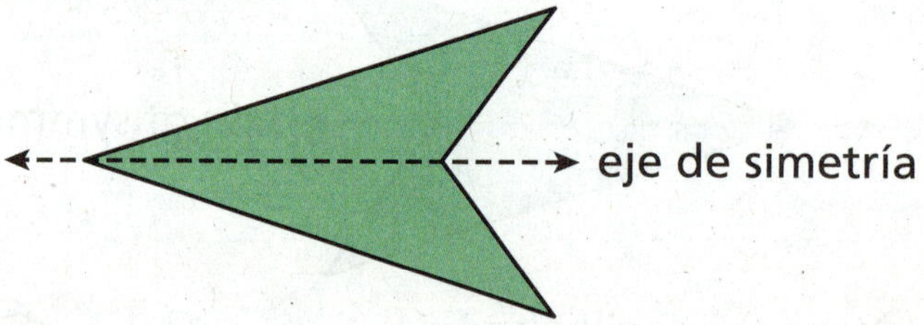

Su niño o niña también identificará figuras **congruentes**. Las figuras congruentes tienen el mismo tamaño y forma.

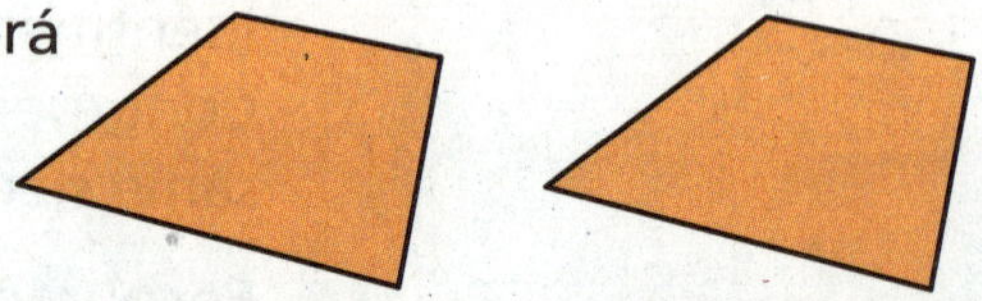

Anime a su niño o niña a buscar figuras congruentes en la casa o en el vecindarioh y a identificar los ejes de simetría de varias figuras bidimensionales.

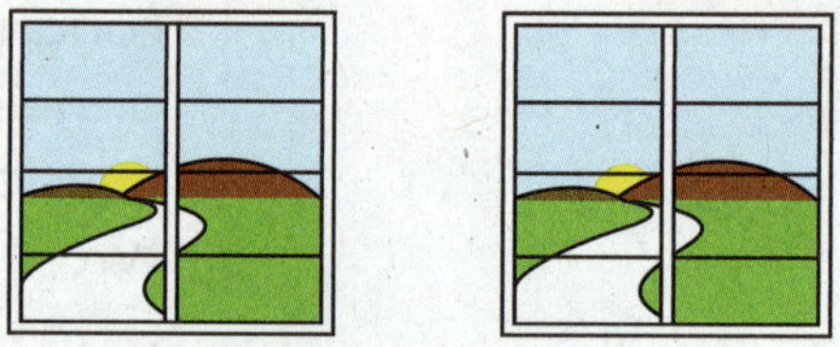

Su niño o niña aprenderá a rotular, nombrar y describir figuras geométricas. Por ejemplo, el segmento *AC* es una **diagonal** del cuadrado *ABCD*.

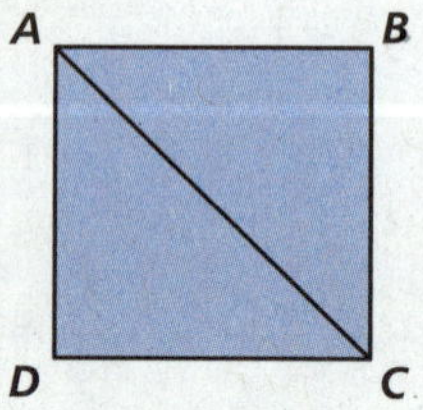

Su niño o niña aprenderá que los ángulos se miden en **grados** y descubrirá que la suma de las medidas de los ángulos de un triángulo es siempre 180 grados (180°).

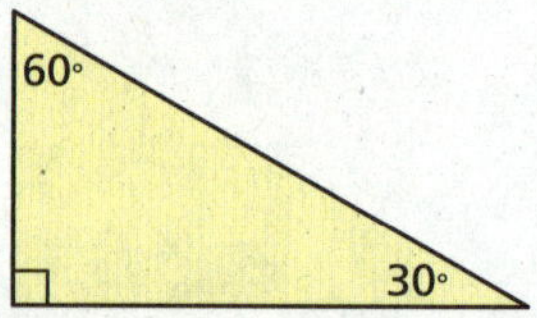

$60° + 30° + 90° = 180°$

Si tiene alguna pregunta o comentario, por favor comuníquese conmigo.

Gracias.

Atentamente,

El maestro de su niño

4–2 Class Activity

Name ____________________ Date ____________

▶ Label Corners with Letters

You can name figures by labeling their corners with letters.

Give two possible names for each figure.

1.

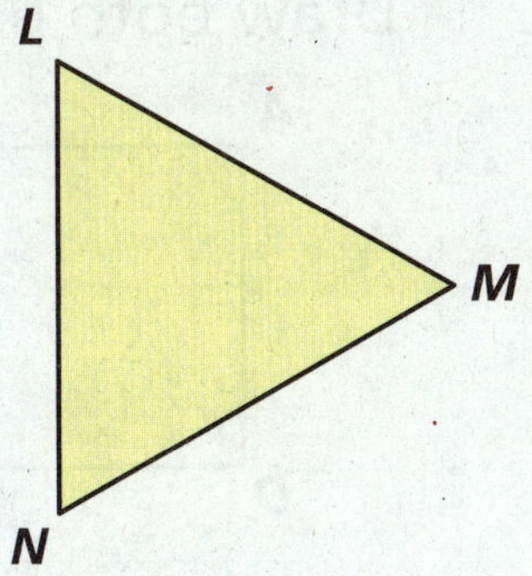

____

____

2.

____

____

3. Draw a triangle. Name it *ABC*.

4. Draw a rectangle. Name it *MNOP*.

4–2 Class Activity

Name ____________________ Date ____________

Vocabulary
diagonal

▶ Diagonals

A line segment that connects two corners of a figure and is not a side is called a **diagonal**.

5. Draw the diagonals in the square.

Draw diagonal *AC*.

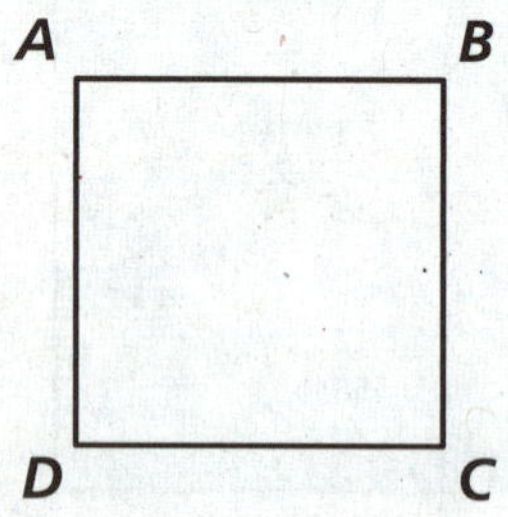

Draw diagonal *BD*.

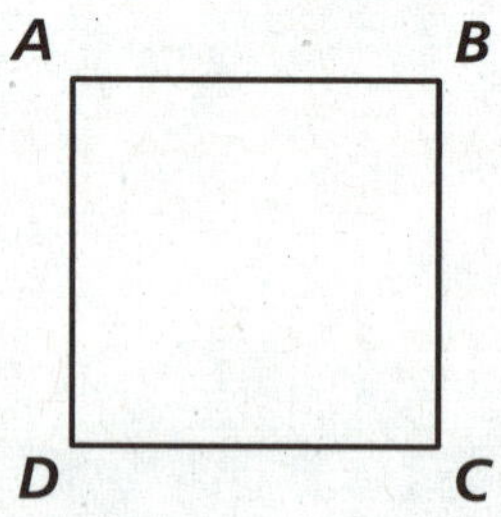

Draw both diagonals.

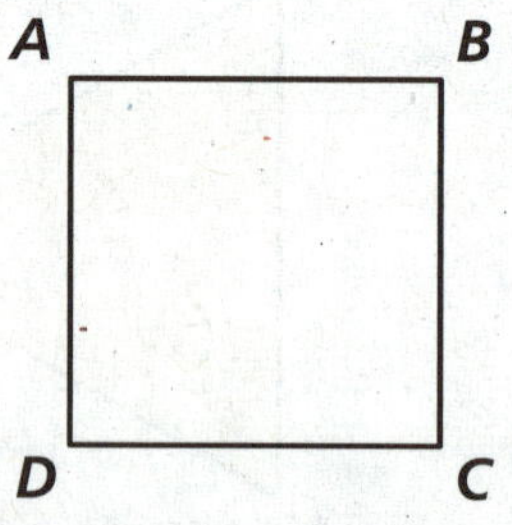

6. What do you notice about the diagonals you drew?

____

7. What do you notice about the triangles that were formed by the diagonals you drew?

____

8. Draw the diagonals in the rectangle.

Draw diagonal *FH*.

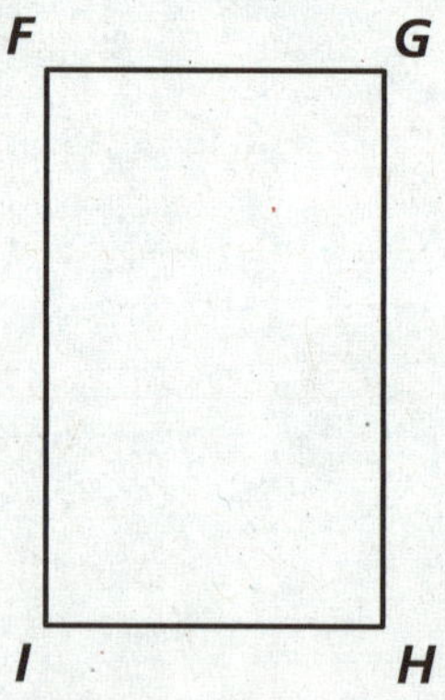

Draw diagonal *GI*.

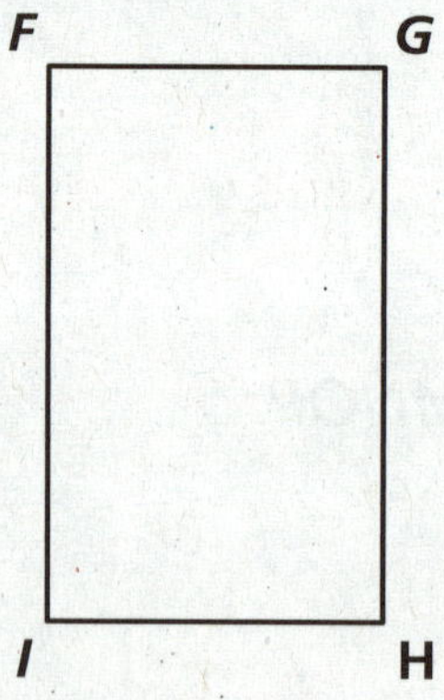

Draw both diagonals.

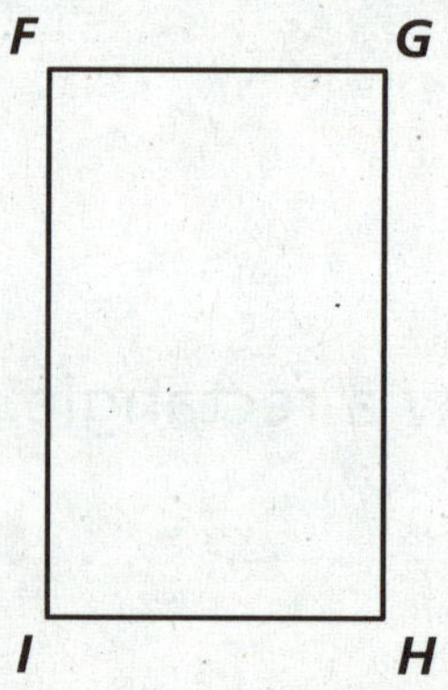

9. What do you notice about the diagonals and the triangles they formed?

____

____

Name ______________________ Date ____________

10. Draw the diagonals in the quadrilateral.

Draw diagonal *WY*.

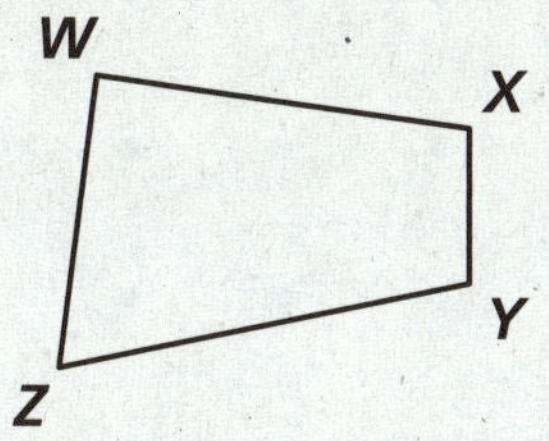

Draw diagonal *ZX*.

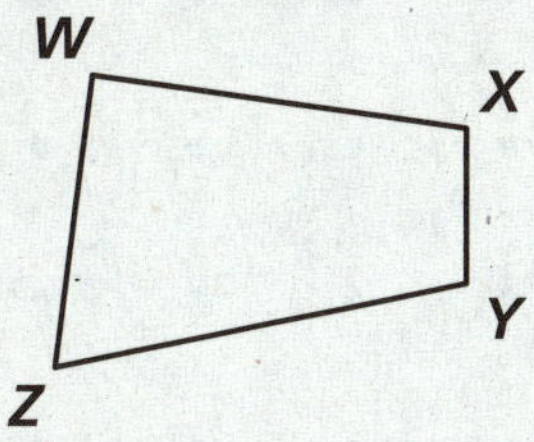

Draw both diagonals.

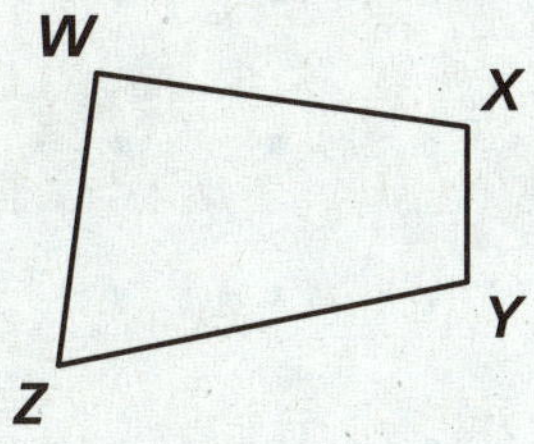

11. What do you notice about the diagonals you drew and the triangles they formed?

____

____

12. Draw the diagonals in the parallelogram.

Draw diagonal *KM*.

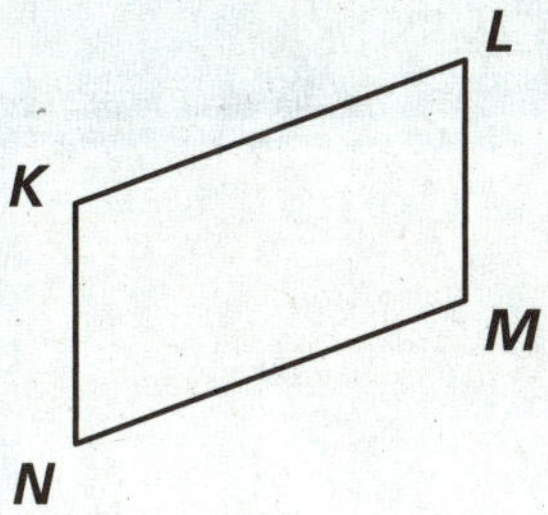

Draw diagonal *LN*.

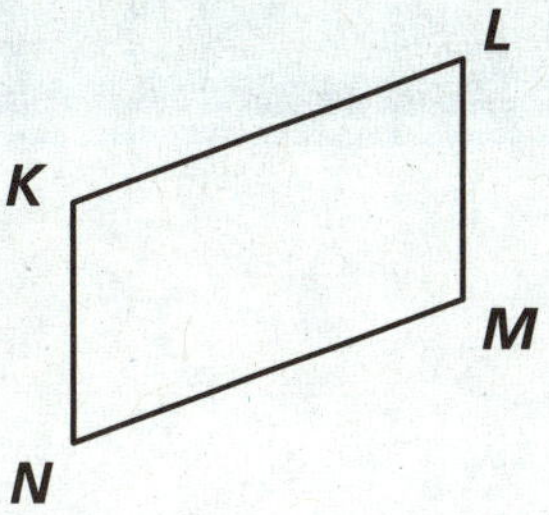

Draw both diagonals.

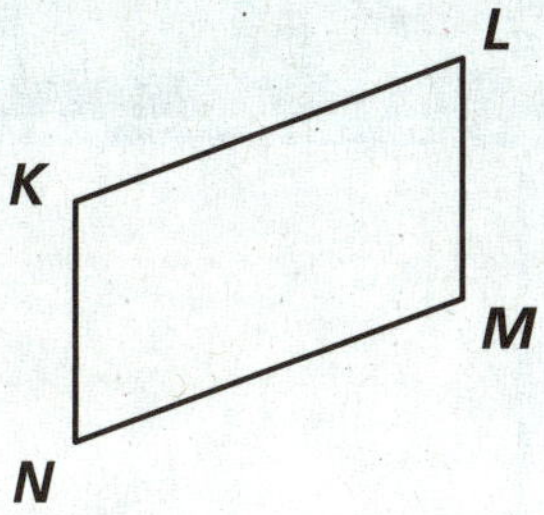

13. What do you notice about the diagonals you drew and the triangles they formed?

____

____

14. On the Back Draw a quadrilateral, label it, and draw all the diagonals. Name all of the sides and diagonals of your quadrilateral.

Name _______________________________ Date _______________

4–3 Class Activity

Name ____________________ Date ____________

Vocabulary

ray
angle
right angle
acute angle
obtuse angle

▶ Types of Angles

A **ray** is part of a line that has one endpoint and continues forever in one direction. To draw a ray, make an arrow to show that it goes on forever.

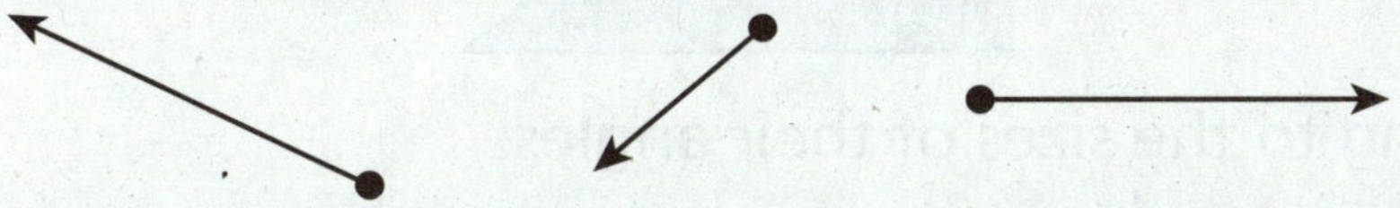

Two line segments or two rays that meet at an endpoint form an **angle**.

An angle that forms a square corner is called a **right angle**.

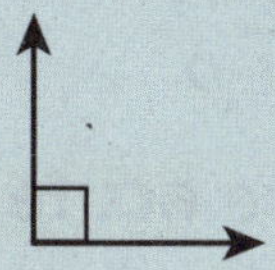

right angle

An angle that is smaller than a right angle is called an **acute angle**.

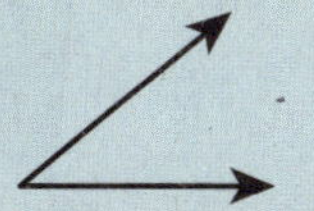

acute angle

An angle that is larger than a right angle is called an **obtuse angle**.

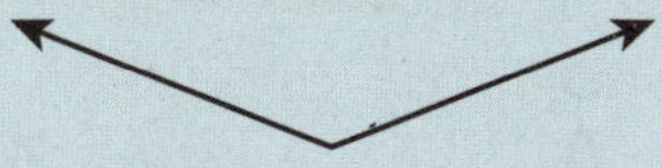

obtuse angle

These angles are named with a letter in the corner.

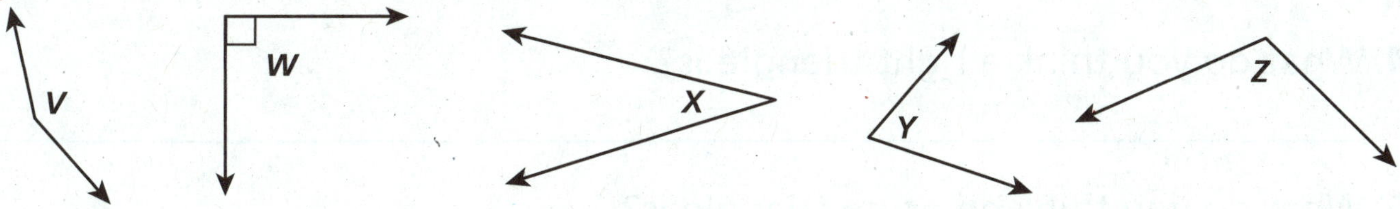

1. Which of the angles are right angles? ____________

2. Which of the angles are acute angles? ____________

3. Which of the angles are obtuse angles? ____________

4-3 Class Activity

Name ______________________ Date ____________

Vocabulary
right triangle
acute triangle
obtuse triangle

▶ Name Triangles by Sizes of Angles

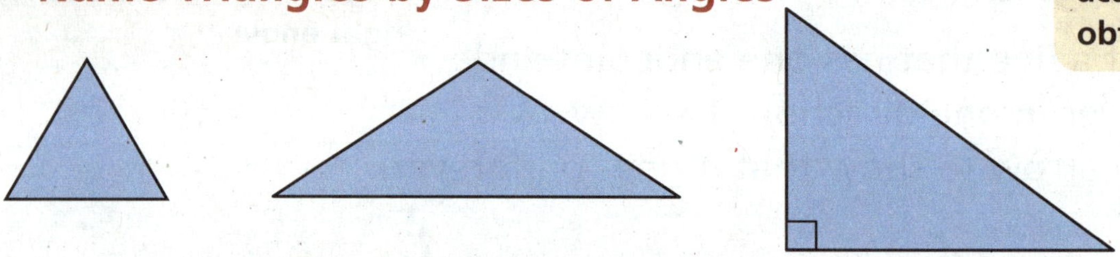

You can name triangles according to the sizes of their angles.

These are **right triangles**.

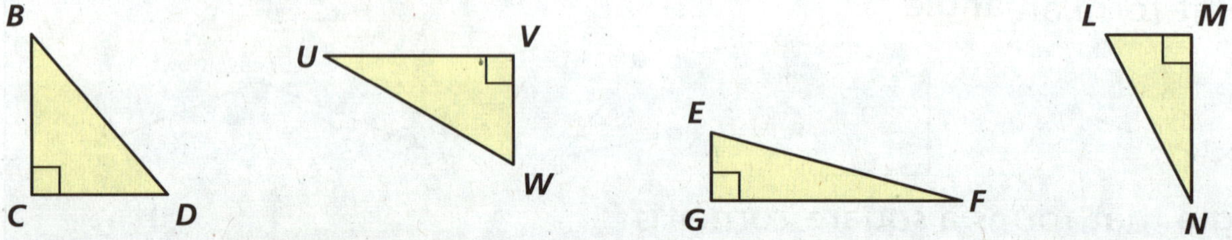

These are **acute triangles**.

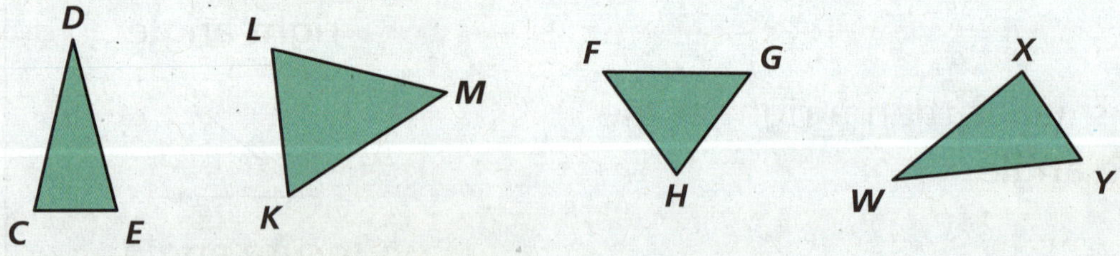

These are **obtuse triangles**.

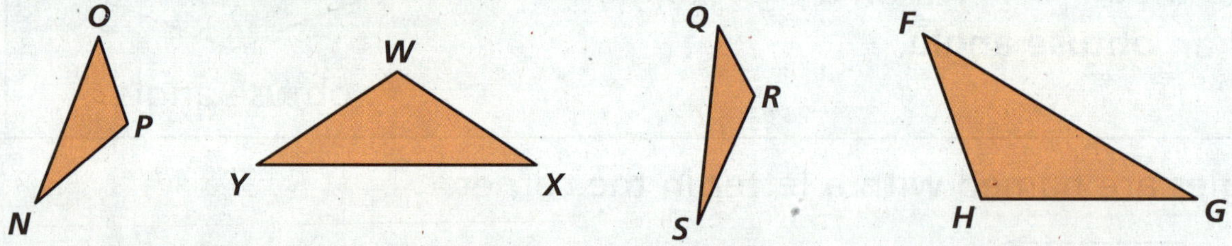

4. What do you think a right triangle is?

____

5. What do you think an acute triangle is?

____

6. What do you think an obtuse triangle is?

____

4–3 Class Activity

Name ______________________ Date ______________

Vocabulary
equilateral triangle
isosceles triangle
scalene triangle

▶ Name Triangles by Lengths of Sides

You can also name triangles according to the lengths of their sides.

These are **equilateral triangles**.

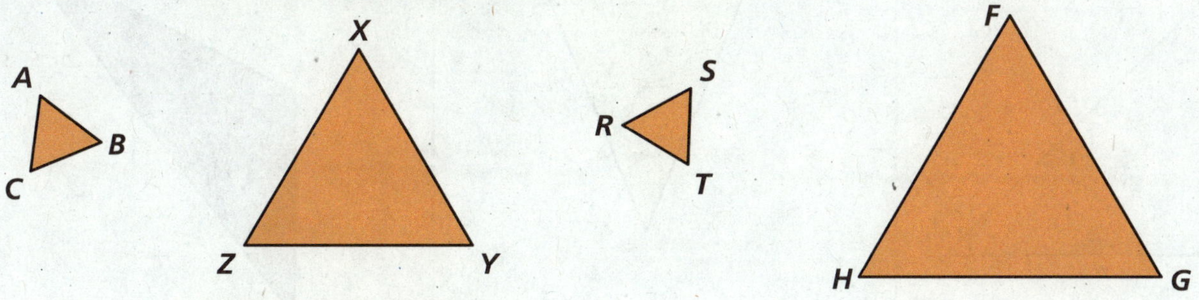

These are **isosceles triangles**.

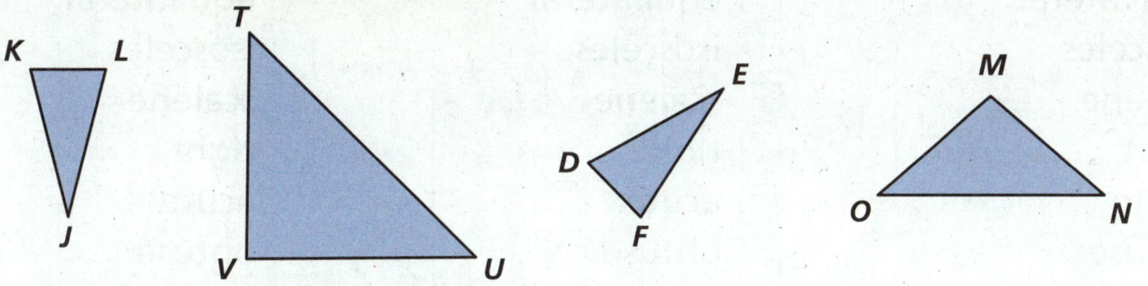

These are **scalene triangles**

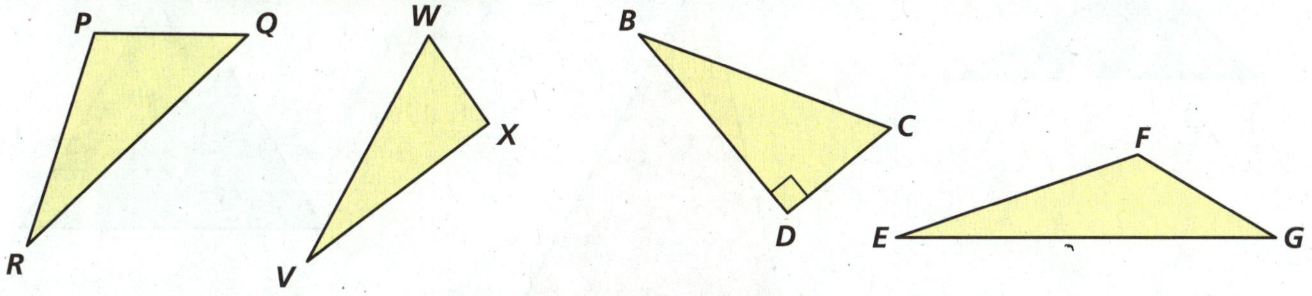

7. What do you think an equilateral triangle is?

____

8. What do you think an isosceles triangle is?

____

9. What do you think a scalene triangle is?

____

Name ______________________ Date __________

► Name Triangles by Sizes of Angles and Lengths of Sides

Mark all the words that describe each triangle.

10.

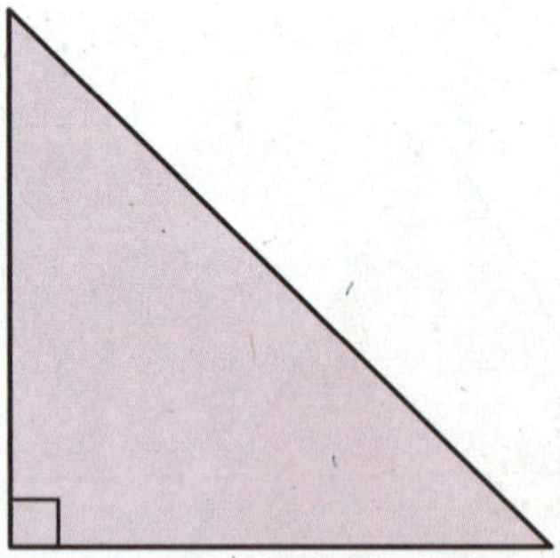

- ☐ equilateral
- ☐ isosceles
- ☐ scalene
- ☐ right
- ☐ acute
- ☐ obtuse

11.

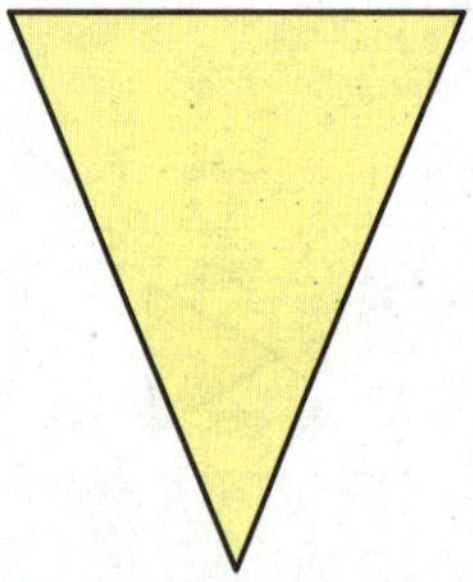

- ☐ equilateral
- ☐ isosceles
- ☐ scalene
- ☐ right
- ☐ acute
- ☐ obtuse

12.

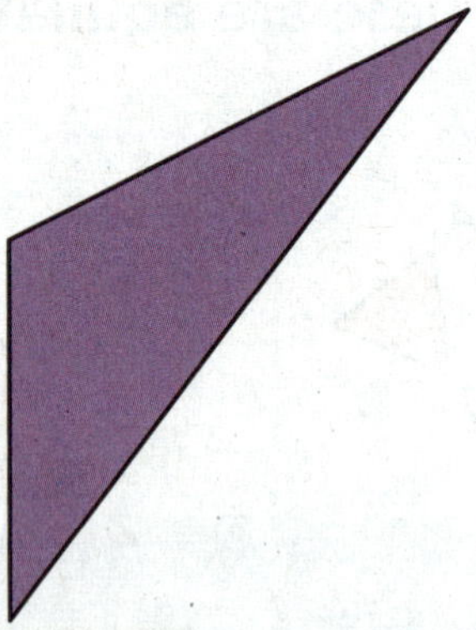

- ☐ equilateral
- ☐ isosceles
- ☐ scalene
- ☐ right
- ☐ acute
- ☐ obtuse

13.

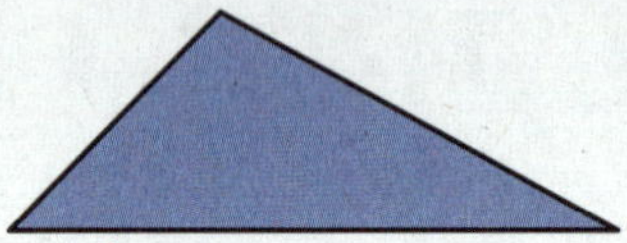

- ☐ equilateral
- ☐ isosceles
- ☐ scalene
- ☐ right
- ☐ acute
- ☐ obtuse

14.

- ☐ equilateral
- ☐ isosceles
- ☐ scalene
- ☐ right
- ☐ acute
- ☐ obtuse

15.

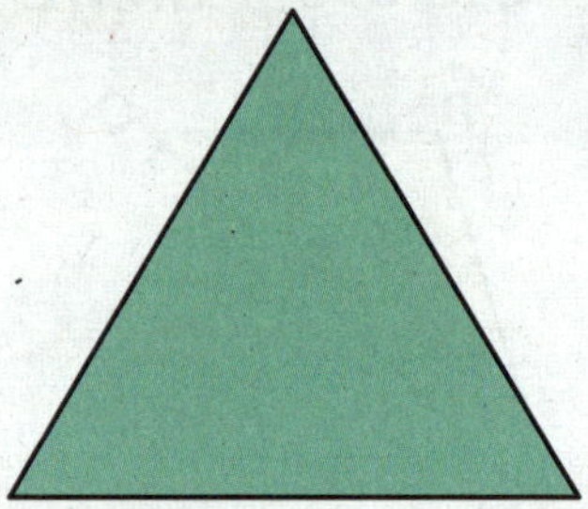

- ☐ equilateral
- ☐ isosceles
- ☐ scalene
- ☐ right
- ☐ acute
- ☐ obtuse

4–3 Class Activity

Name Date

▶ Build Quadrilaterals from Triangles

Cut out each pair of triangles. Use each pair to make as many different quadrilaterals as you can. (You may flip a triangle and use the back.) On a separate piece of paper, trace each quadrilateral that you make.

Obtuse Triangles

Acute Triangles

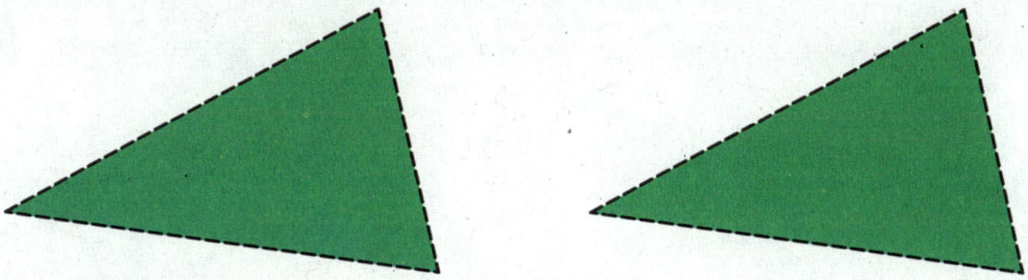

Right Triangles

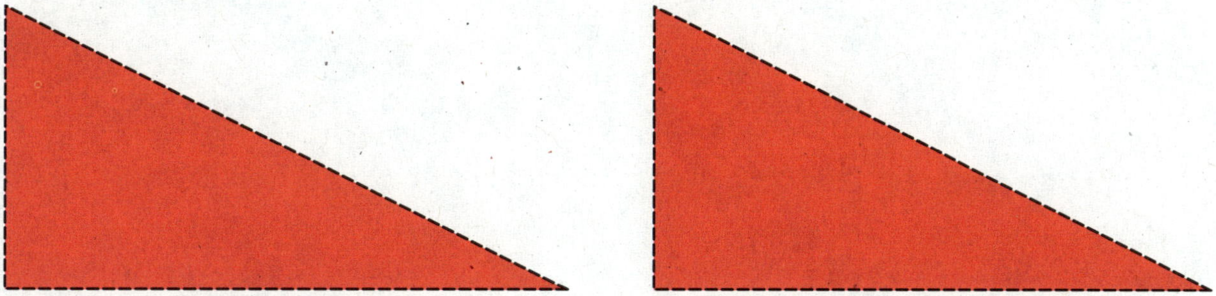

4–3 Class Activity

Name ______________________________ Date ______________

Vocabulary
polygon
concave
convex

▶ Polygons

A **polygon** is a flat, closed figure made up of line segments that do not cross each other.

Circle the figures that are polygons.

1. 

2. 

3. 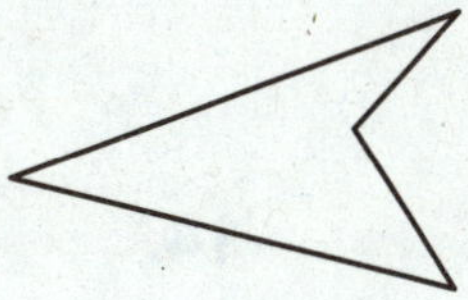

4. 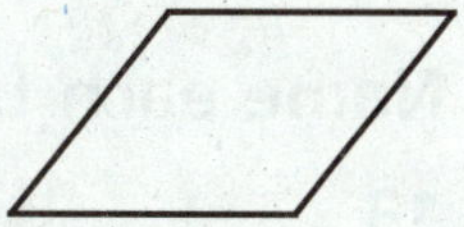

5. 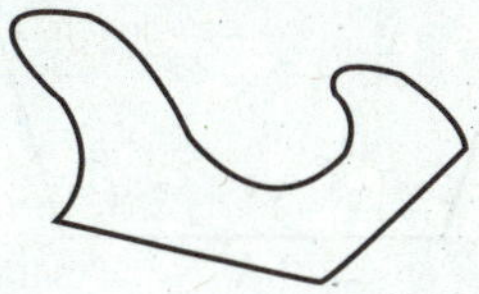

6. 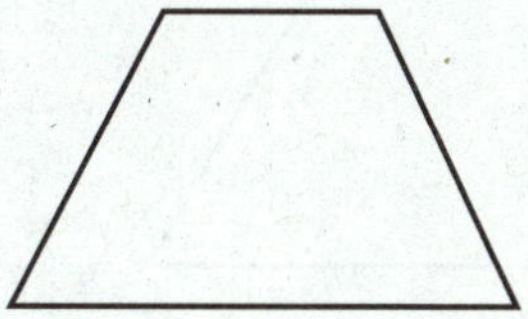

7. 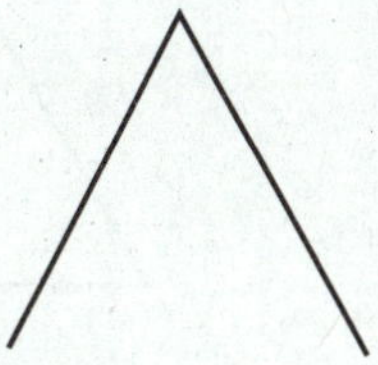

8. 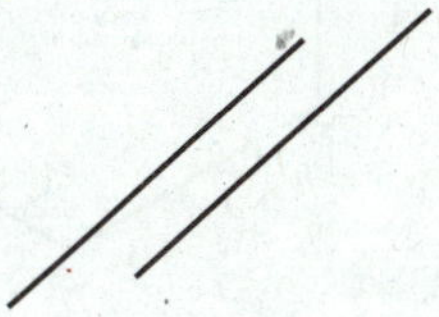

A figure can be **concave** or **convex**. In concave polygons, there exists a line segment with endpoints inside the polygon and a point on the line segment that is outside the polygon. A convex figure has no such line segment.

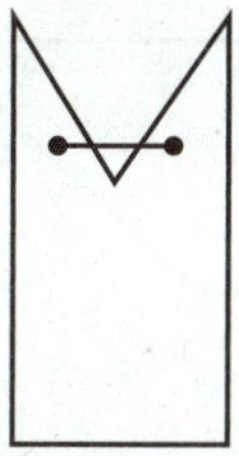

concave

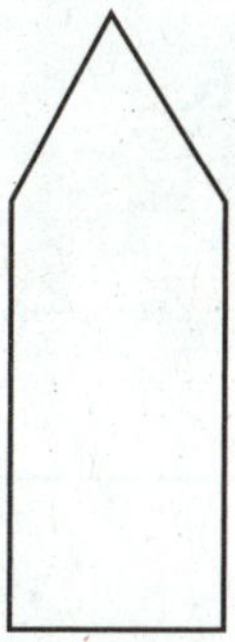

convex

Which figures are convex and which are concave?

9. 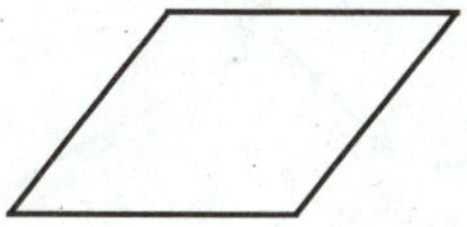
____

10. 
____

11. 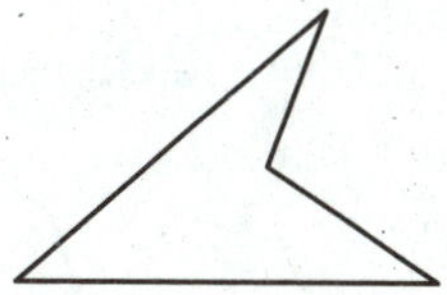
____

12. 
____

4–3 Class Activity

Name ________________________ Date ____________

Vocabulary

pentagon hexagon
octagon decagon

▶ Name Polygons

Polygons are named according to how many sides they have.

3 sides – **tri**angle 4 sides – **quadri**lateral 5 sides – **penta**gon

6 sides – **hexa**gon 8 sides – **octa**gon 10 sides – **deca**gon

Name each figure.

13.

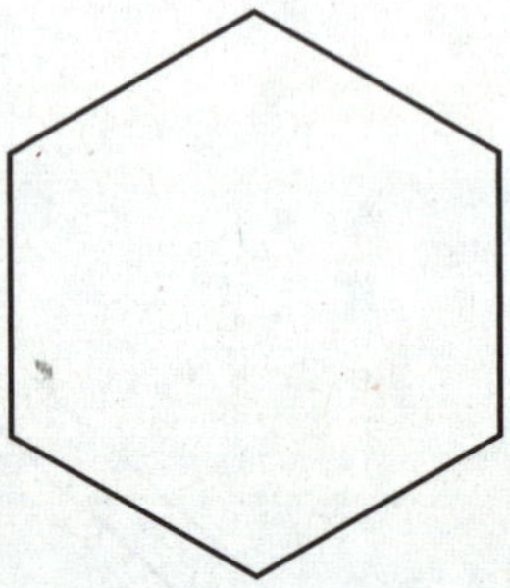

____

14.

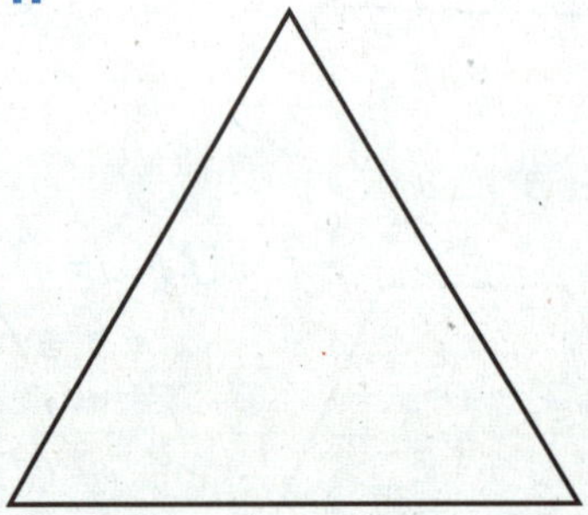

____

15.

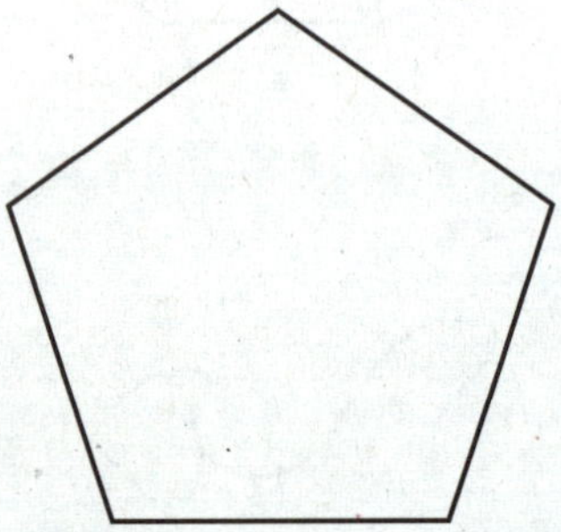

____

16.

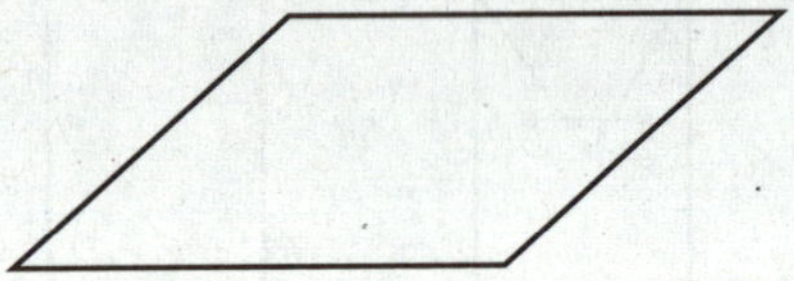

____

17.

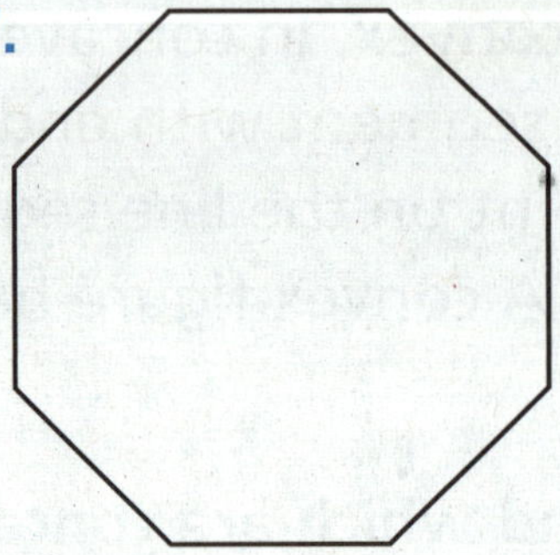

____

18.

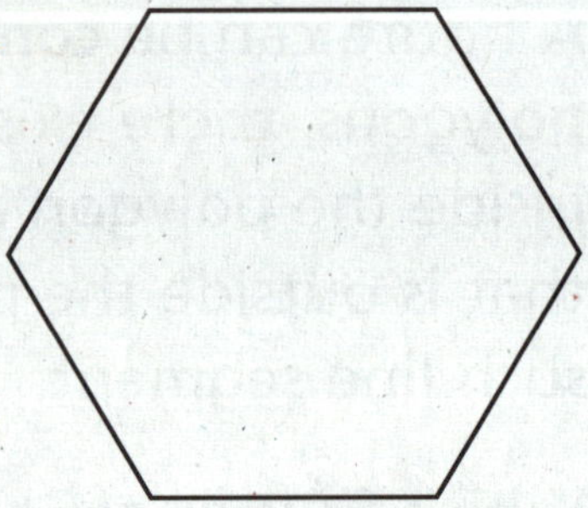

____

19.

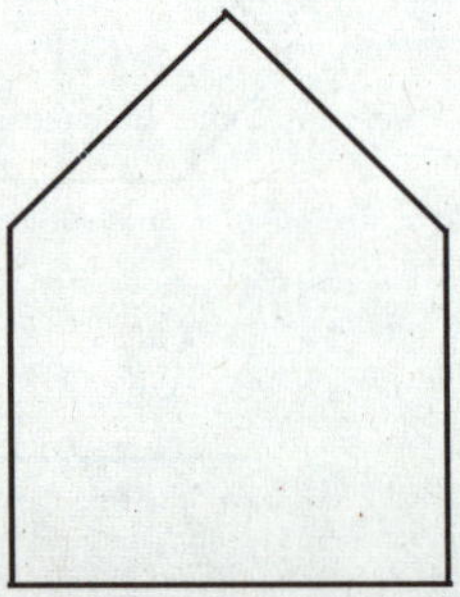

____

20.

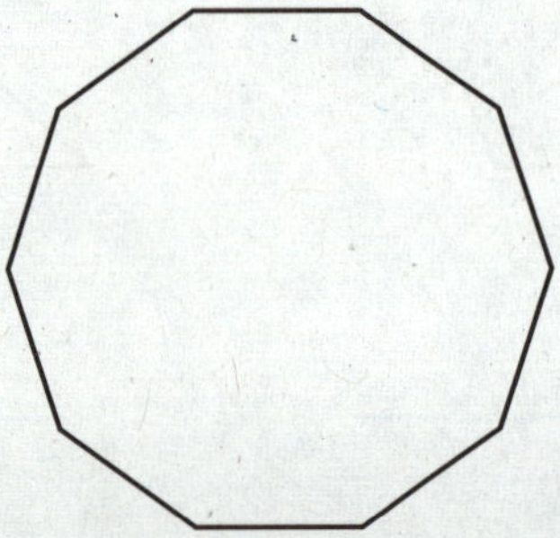

____

21.

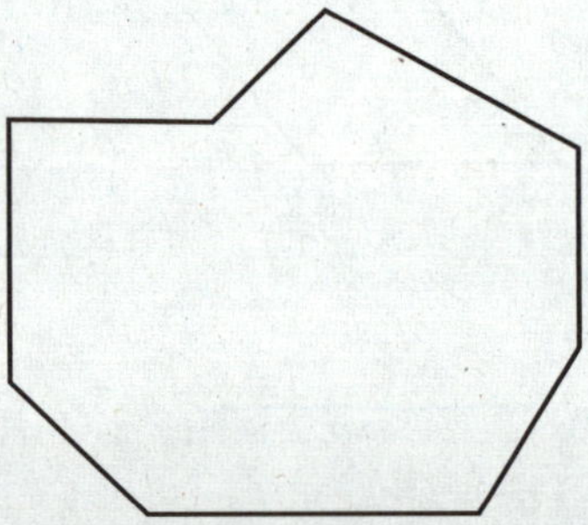

____

Name Date

▶ Build Polygons from Triangles

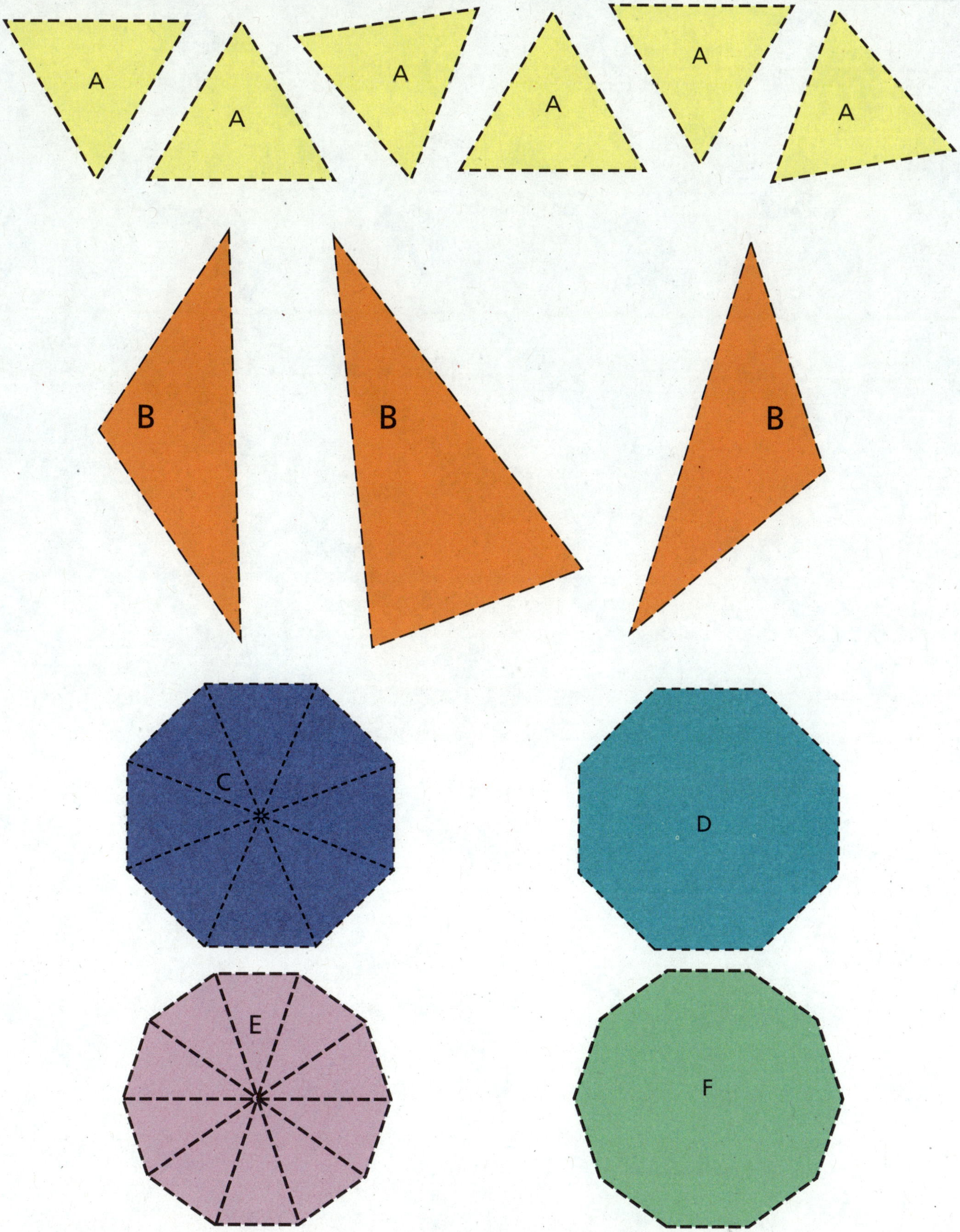

4–4 Class Activity

Name Date

Vocabulary
degree
straight angle
right angle

▶ Introduce Degrees

Angles are measured in units called **degrees**.
One degree is the measure of one very small rotation.

This angle has a measure of 1 degree.

The measure of an angle is the total number of 1-degree angles that fit inside it.

This angle measures 5 degrees.

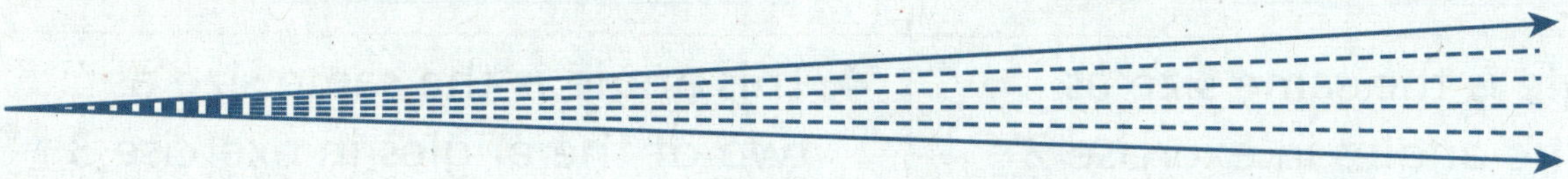

The symbol for degrees is a small raised circle (°). You can write the measure of the angle above as 5°.

A **right angle** has a measure of 90°.
A 90°-rotation traces one quarter of a circle.

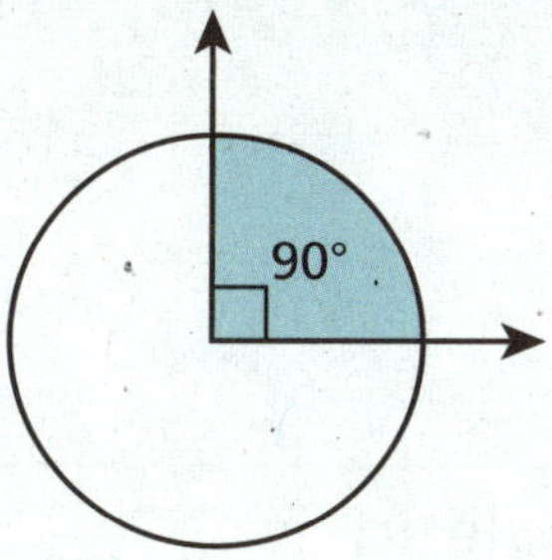

A **straight angle** measures 180°.
A 180°-rotation traces one half of a circle.

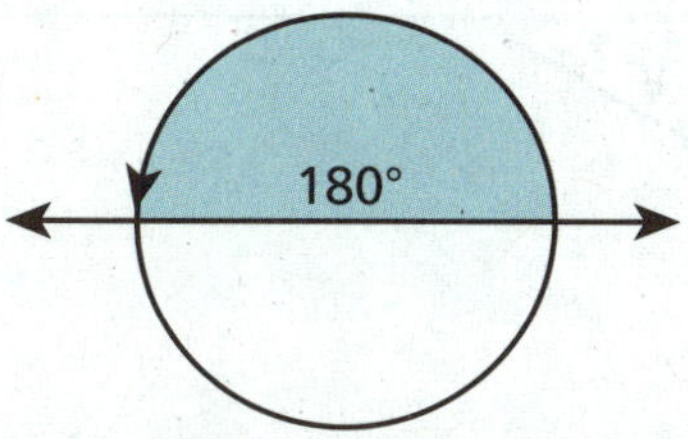

This angle measures 360°.
A 360°-rotation traces a complete circle.

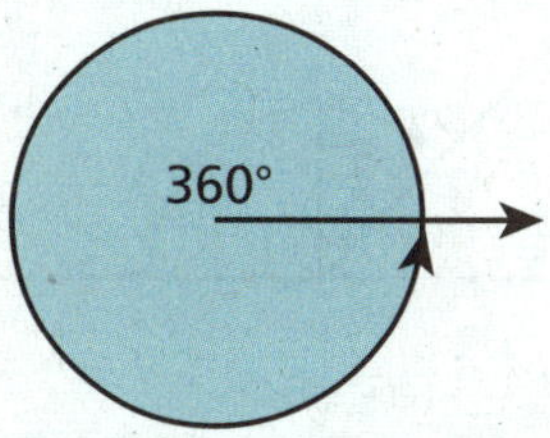

4–4 Class Activity

Name ____________________ Date ____________

► Angle Measures

Find the size of each angle.

1. This angle is half the size of a right angle.

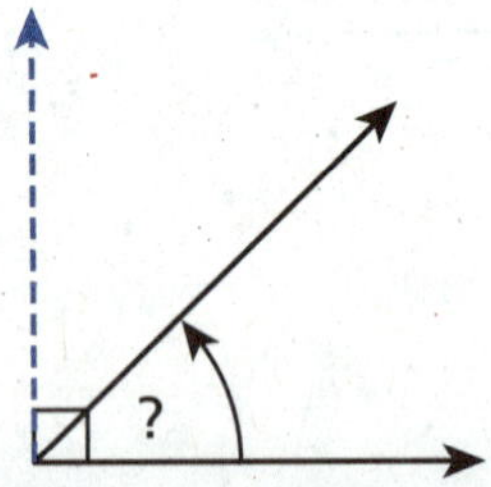

____

2. If you put three of these angles together, you will get a right angle.

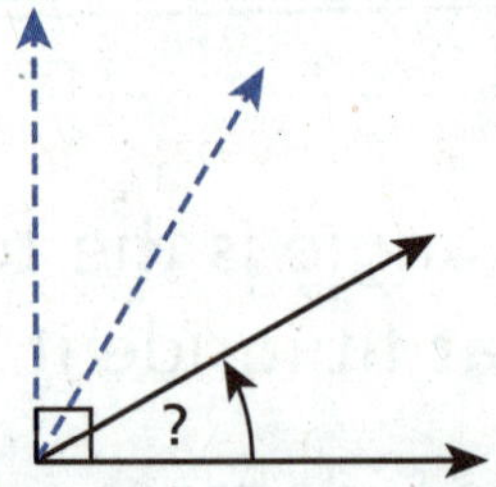

____

3. This angle is the same size as two of the angles in exercise 2 put together.

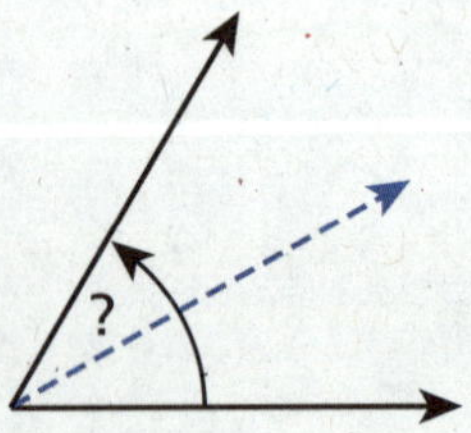

____

4. This angle is the same size as two of the angles in exercise 3 put together.

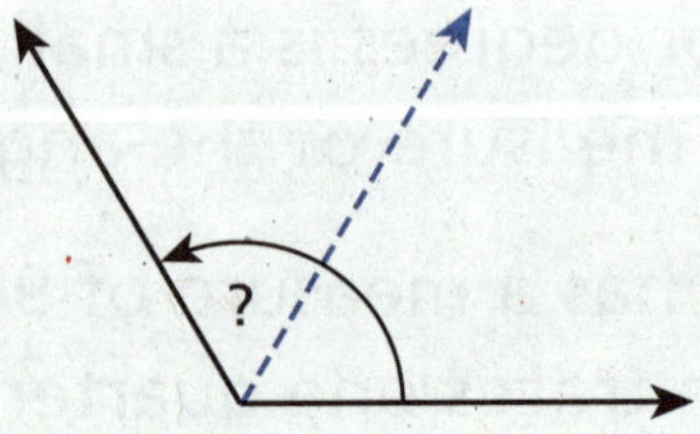

____

5. This angle is the angle in exercise 1 added to a right angle.

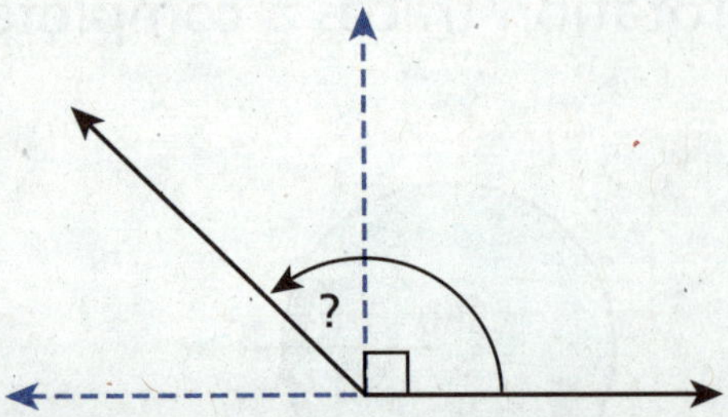

____

6. This angle is the angle in exercise 2 added to a straight angle.

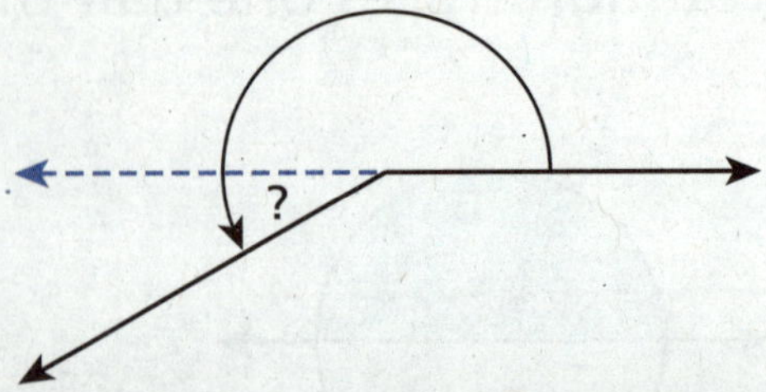

____

4–4 Class Activity

Name _______________ Date _______________

► Join Angles of a Triangle

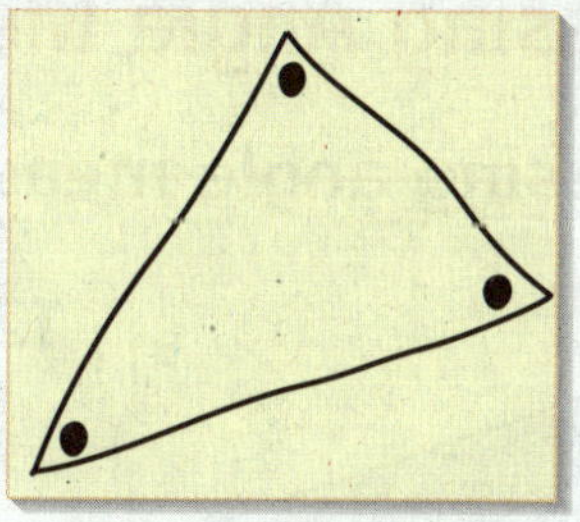

Draw a large triangle on a sheet of unlined paper. You can draw any type of triangle. Mark each corner with a dot and then cut out the triangle.

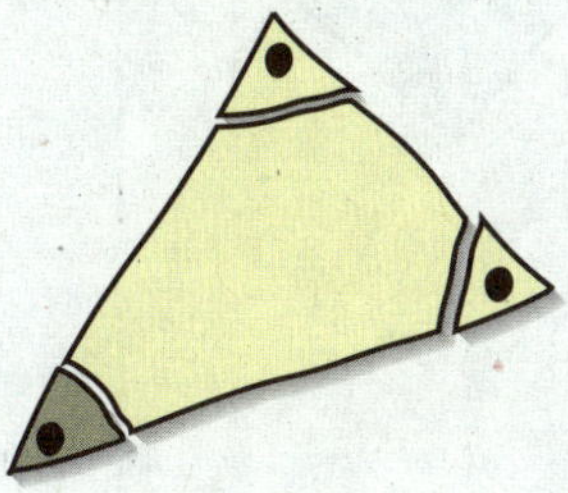

Tear each angle off the triangle, and place the three angles together so that the dotted corners are touching.

7. Sketch your three angles joined at the dotted corners.

8. What kind of angle is formed when you put together the three angles of your triangle?

____

Compare your sketch with those of your classmates.

9. Is the sum of the measures of the three angles the same for every triangle?

____

Complete this statement.

10. The sum of the measures of the three angles in a triangle is _______________.

Name ______________________ Date ______________________

▶ Find Missing Angle Measures

Find the missing angle measure in each triangle.

11.

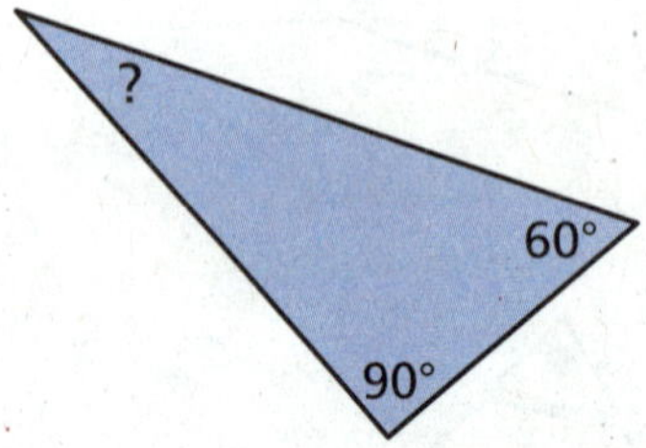

____

12.

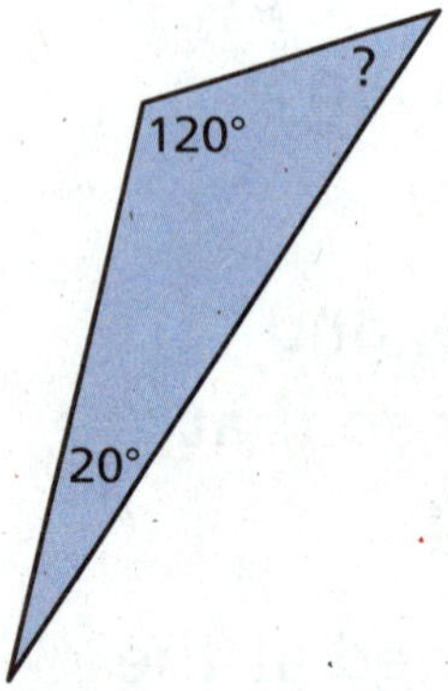

____

13.

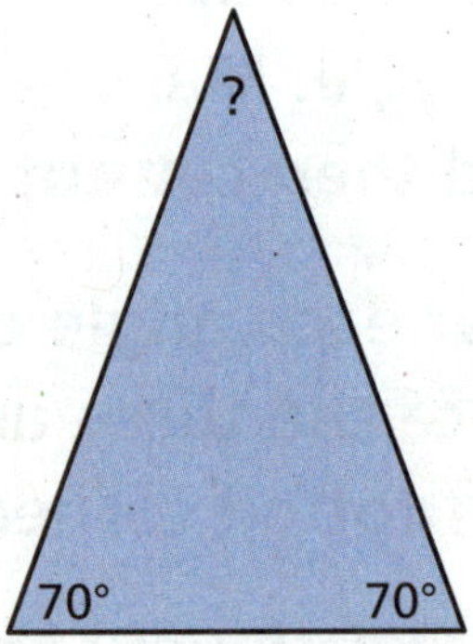

____

14.

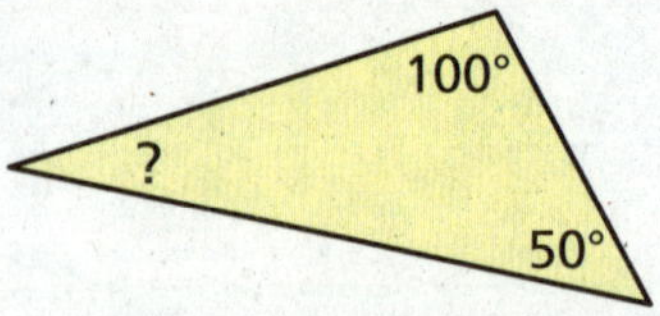

____

15.

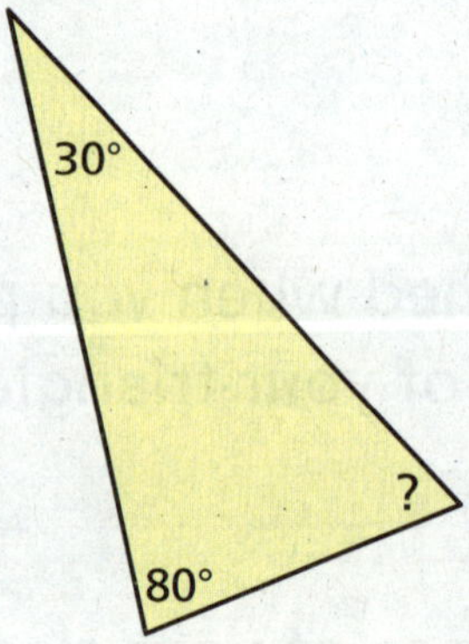

____

16.

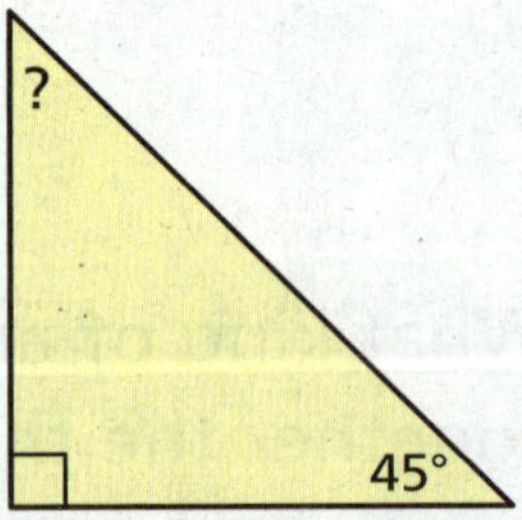

____

17. In an equilateral triangle, each angle has the same measure. What is the measure of each angle in this equilateral triangle? _______________

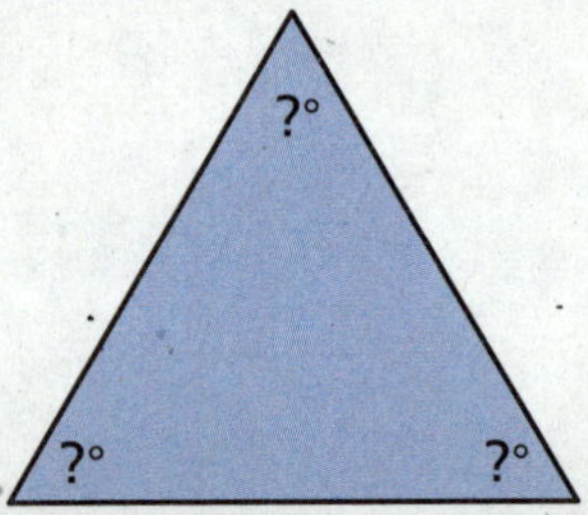

Name ______________________ Date ______________

1. Which two figures below are congruent?

Figures __________ and __________ are congruent.

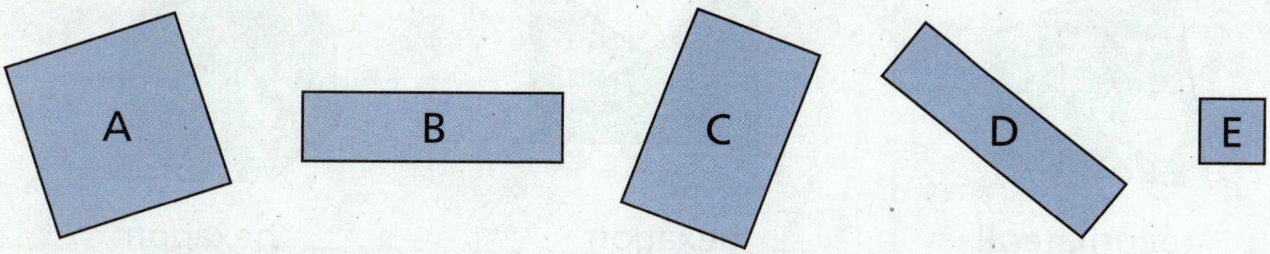

2. Draw all the lines of symmetry on the figure.

3. Draw diagonal *AC* in the rectangle.

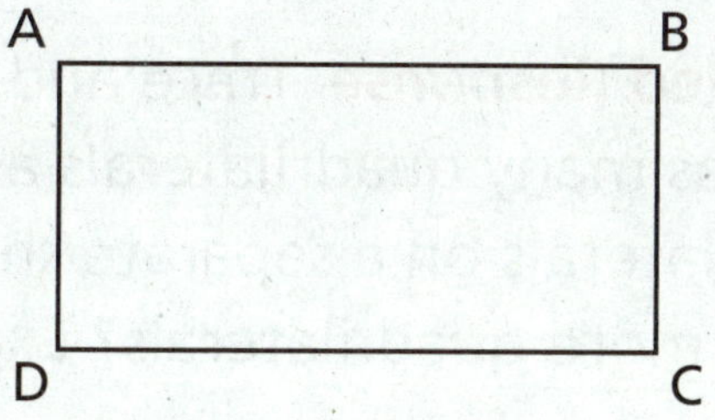

Place a check mark next to all of the words that describe the triangle.

4.

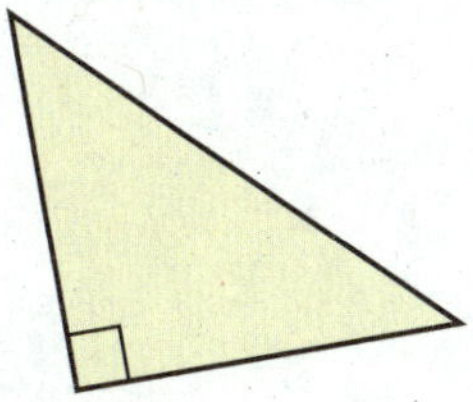

- ☐ equilateral
- ☐ isosceles
- ☐ scalene
- ☐ right
- ☐ acute
- ☐ obtuse

5.

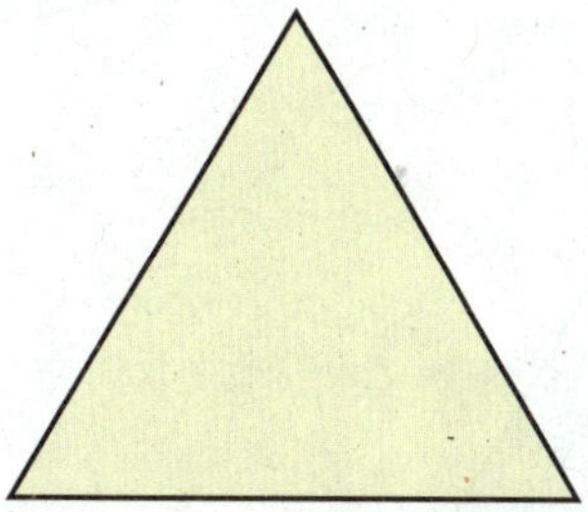

- ☐ equilateral
- ☐ isosceles
- ☐ scalene
- ☐ right
- ☐ acute
- ☐ obtuse

6.

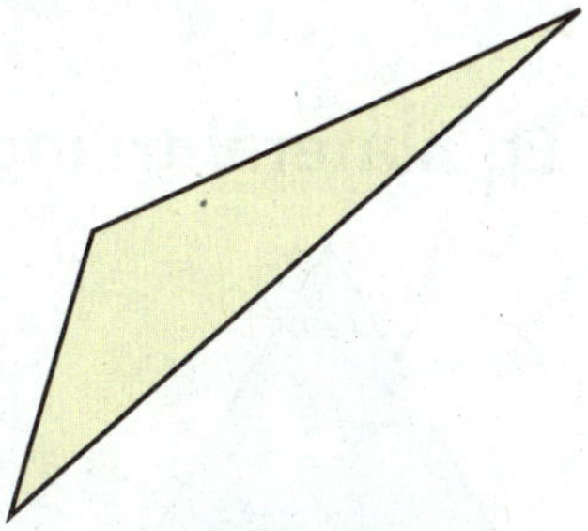

- ☐ equilateral
- ☐ isosceles
- ☐ scalene
- ☐ right
- ☐ acute
- ☐ obtuse

Name ______________________ Date ______________

Place a check mark beside the words that describe the figure.

7.

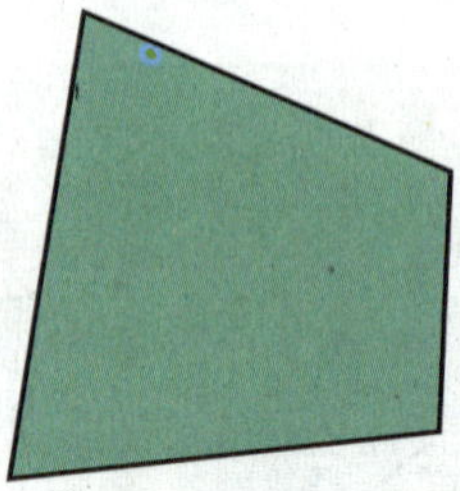

☐ quadrilateral
☐ parallelogram
☐ concave
☐ polygon

8.

☐ hexagon
☐ pentagon
☐ concave
☐ convex

9.

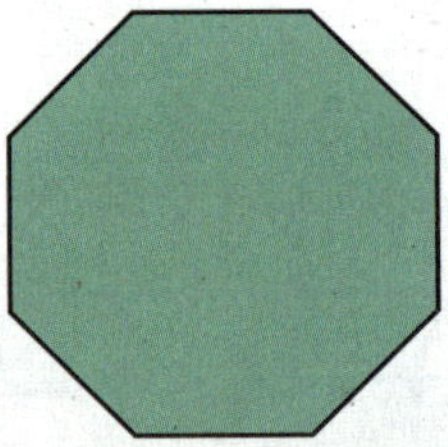

☐ hexagon
☐ convex
☐ polygon
☐ octagon

10. Extended Response Trace and cut out each pair of congruent triangles. Make as many quadrilaterals as you can from each pair. Trace the quadrilaterals on a separate sheet of paper. Which pair of triangles makes more quadrilaterals? Explain why.

Isosceles triangles

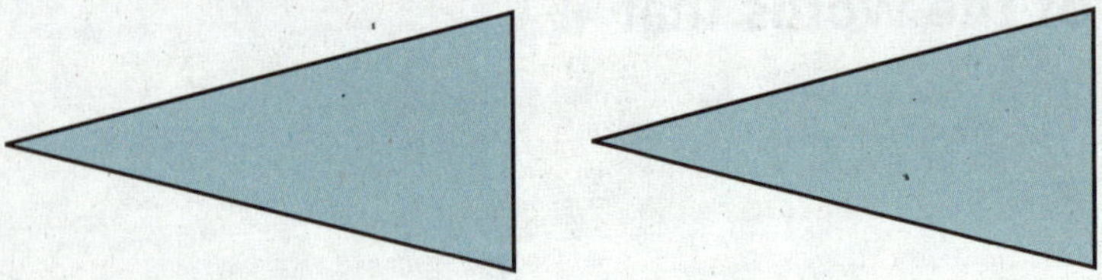

Equilateral triangles

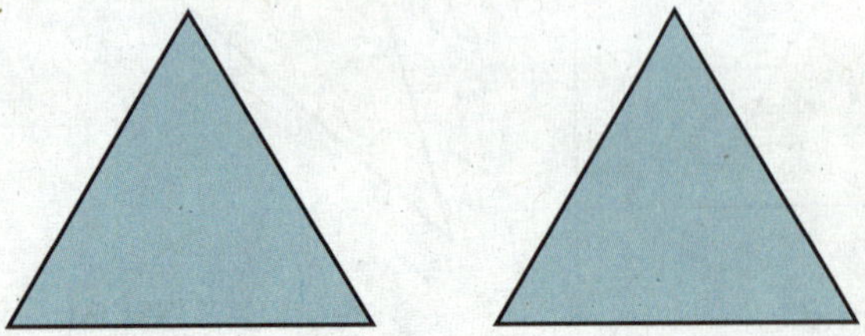

____

____

____

5–1 Class Activity

Name ____________________ Date ____________

Vocabulary
estimate
round

▶ Estimate

Solve the problem.

1. Tasha read three books over the summer. Here is the number of pages in each book:

Watership Down	494 pages
Sounder	128 pages
The Secret Garden	368 pages

About how many pages did Tasha read? Explain how you made your **estimate**.

____

____

▶ Practice Rounding

Round each number to the nearest hundred. Use drawings or Secret Code Cards if they help you.

2. 128 ________
3. 271 ________
4. 376 ________
5. 649 ________
6. 415 ________
7. 550 ________
8. 62 ________
9. 1,481 ________
10. 2,615 ________

11. **Explain Your Thinking** When you round a number to the nearest hundred, how do you know whether to round up or round down?

____

____

____

____

____

Name ____________________ Date ____________

▶ Solve Problems by Estimating

Show your work.

Solve by rounding to the nearest hundred.

12. At the Lakeside School, there are 286 second graders, 341 third graders, and 377 fourth graders. About how many students are there at the Lakeside School?

____

13. Last week, Mrs. Larson drove 191 miles on Monday, 225 miles on Wednesday, and 107 miles on Friday. About how many miles did she drive altogether?

____

14. Of the 1,432 people at the hockey game, 292 sat on the visiting team side. The rest sat on the home team side. About how many people sat on the home team side?

____

▶ Reasonable Answers

Use rounding to decide if the answer is reasonable. Then find the answer to see if you were right.

15. 604 − 180 = 586

____

16. 377 + 191 = 568

____

17. 268 − 17 = 107

____

18. 1,041 + 395 = 646

____

19. 407 − 379 = 28

____

20. 535 + 287 = 642

____

Family Letter

Dear Family,

Your child has started a new unit on using addition and subtraction. These are important math operations that we use almost every day.

At the beginning of the unit, students learn to estimate sums and differences by rounding numbers. They also use estimates to check that actual answers are reasonable, and compare numbers using the symbols for greater than (>), less than (<), or equal to (=).

$$78 > 35 \qquad 114 < 25 + 175 \qquad 14 + 16 = 15 + 15$$

Students also identify and compare the values of a collection of U.S. coins and bills, act out making purchases by counting out the exact amounts, and find out how much change they should receive when giving more than the exact amount for a purchase.

66¢ > 41¢

Later in the unit, students learn to recognize word problems that contain hidden, extra, and not enough information. They solve problems with two or more steps and learn to analyze information when it is presented in tables and graphs.

Your child is learning how math is used in the world around us. You can help your child learn by sharing shopping situations with them and pointing out graphs and tables in the newspaper or magazines. Encourage your child to spend time acting out shopping situations with coins and bills at home.

Thank you for helping your child learn important math skills.

Sincerely,
Your child's teacher

Carta a la familia

Estimada familia:

Su niño ha comenzado una nueva unidad sobre suma y resta. Éstas son operaciones matemáticas importantes que usamos casi todos los días.

Al principio de esta unidad los estudiantes aprenden a estimar sumas y diferencias redondeando números. También usan la estimación para comprobar que las respuestas que dieron son razonables y comparan números usando los símbolos *mayor que* ($>$), *menor que* ($<$) o *igual* ($=$).

$$78 > 35 \qquad 114 < 25 + 175 \qquad 14 + 16 = 15 + 15$$

Los estudiantes también identifican y comparan los valores de una colección de monedas y billetes de los EE.UU., representan compras contando las cantidades exactas y aprenden cuánto cambio deben recibir cuando dan más de la cantidad exacta durante una compra.

66¢ $>$ 41¢

Más adelante en esta unidad, los estudiantes aprenden a reconocer problemas verbales que contienen información implícita, exceso o falta de información. Resuelven problemas de dos o más pasos y aprenden a analizar la información presentada en tablas y gráficas.

Su niño está aprendiendo cómo se usan las matemáticas en la vida diaria. Usted puede ayudar a su niño compartiendo situaciones de compra y señalando gráficas y tablas en periódicos o revistas. Anime a su niño a representar en casa situaciones de compra con monedas y billetes.

Gracias por ayudar a su niño a aprender destrezas matemáticas importantes.

Atentamente,
El maestro de su niño

5–2 Class Activity

Name ______ Date ______

►Round 2-Digit Numbers to the Nearest Ten

Round each number to the nearest ten.

1. 63 ______
2. 34 ______
3. 78 ______
4. 25 ______
5. 57 ______
6. 89 ______
7. 42 ______
8. 92 ______

►Round 3-Digit Numbers to the Nearest Ten

Round each number to the nearest ten.

9. 162 ______
10. 741 ______
11. 309 ______
12. 255 ______
13. 118 ______
14. 197 ______
15. 503 ______
16. 246 ______

17. **Explain Your Thinking** When you round a number to the nearest ten, how do you know whether to round up or round down?

______

______

______

______

Name ____________________ Date ____________

▶Estimate the Answer

Solve each problem.

18. The chart at the right shows how many smoothies the Juice Hut sold yesterday. By rounding each number to the nearest ten, estimate how many smoothies the Juice Hut sold in all.

____

Smoothies Sold at Juice Hut
13 raspberry-peach smoothies
38 strawberry-banana smoothies
44 guava-mango smoothies
61 peach-blueberry smoothies

19. Ms. Singh has 52 rock CDs, 75 jazz CDs, 36 classical CDs, and 23 hip-hop CDs. Round each number to the nearest ten, to find *about* how many CDs she has.

____

20. Roz rented a video that is 123 minutes long. She watched 48 minutes of it. Round each number to the nearest ten to estimate how many more minutes she has to watch.

____

Use the table at the right to solve problems 21–23.

21. Estimate the total number of books the school received by rounding each number to the nearest hundred.

____

Jefferson Elementary School Books Received	
Math	436
Reading	352

22. Estimate the total number of books the school received by rounding each number to the nearest ten.

____

23. Find the total number of books. Which of your estimates is closer to the actual total?

____

____

5–2

Class Activity

Name _______________ Date _______________

▶ Reasonable Answers

Use rounding to decide if the answer is reasonable. Write *yes* or *no*. Then find the answer to see if you were correct.

24. 58 + 37 = 131 _______________

25. 122 − 67 = 55 _______________

26. 28 + 45 = 53 _______________

27. 93 − 29 = 64 _______________

28. 113 + 57 = 140 _______________

29. 83 + 19 = 102 _______________

▶ Estimate the Number of Objects

Jar D has 100 Beans. Estimate how many beans are in the other jars.

30. Jar A _______________

31. Jar B _______________

32. Jar C _______________

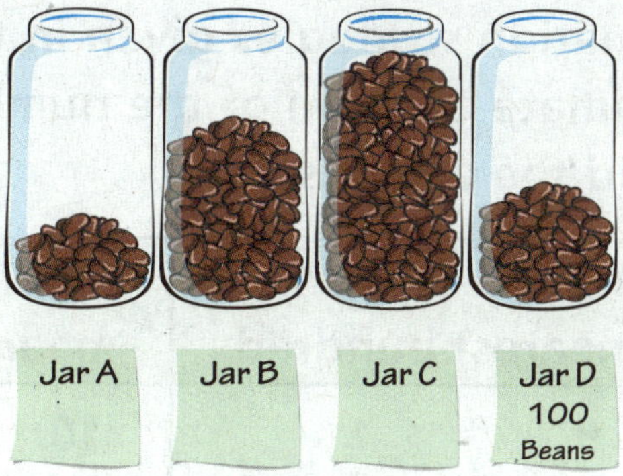

33. Explain how you estimated to find the number of beans in Jars A, B, and C.

____

____

____

____

____

34. Explain how you would estimate the number of oranges in an orange tree.

____

____

____

____

____

5–2 Going Further

Name ________ Date ________

▶ Different Ways to Estimate

Use clustering to estimate each sum.

1. 62 + 58 + 59 ________

2. 227 + 198 + 212 ________

3. 375 + 402 + 412 ________

4. 498 + 512 + 475 ________

Use front-end estimation to estimate each sum or difference.

5. 4,327 − 1,340

6. 1,806 + 3,110

7. 625 + 462

8. 321 − 130

Use the estimation strategies given in the table below to estimate the sum of the numbers on the left. Then find the actual sum.

329
28
776
+ 408

Round to the nearest hundred	Round to the nearest ten	Front-end estimation
9.	10.	11.

12. Which estimation strategy above gave you the closest estimate?

____

5–3 Class Activity

Name ____________________ Date ________

▶ Compare Numbers

Compare the numbers. Write >, < or = in each ◯.

1. 34 ◯ 86
2. 97 ◯ 67
3. 653 ◯ 663
4. 875 ◯ 587
5. 1,752 ◯ 1,572
6. 1,572 ◯ 1,527
7. 1,932 ◯ 1,951
8. 2,633 ◯ 2,487
9. 3,478 ◯ 3,478
10. 4,786 ◯ 4,876

▶ Order Numbers

Write the numbers in order from greatest to least.

11. 69; 20; 81

____

12. 381; 124; 197

____

Write the numbers in order from least to greatest.

13. 2,245; 1,642; 1,787

____

14. 1,982; 1,892; 1,782

____

5–3 Class Activity

Name   Date

▶ Multi-Step Comparisons

Compare. Write >, <, or = in each ◯.

Show your work.

15. 35 + 28 ◯ 23 + 39

16. 864 + 29 ◯ 699 + 265

17. 273 + 641 ◯ 850 + 57

18. 84 + 148 ◯ 151 + 71

19. 38 + 165 ◯ 572 − 365

20. 419 − 109 ◯ 160 + 150

21. 241 − 157 ◯ 175 − 86

22. 525 − 231 ◯ 146 + 173

▶ Compare Using Number Sense

Compare without calculating. Write >, <, or = in each ◯.

23. 888 + 5 ◯ 888 − 5

24. 510 + 0 ◯ 510 − 0

25. 145 + 17 ◯ 17 + 145

26. 1,250 − 300 ◯ 900 + 150

27. 143 + 68 ◯ 96 + 71

28. 421 − 103 ◯ 347 − 98

29. 267 − 138 ◯ 279 − 199

30. 257 + 259 ◯ 702 − 219

Name ____________________ Date ____________

►Coin Equivalents

What relationships do you see in this coin chart?

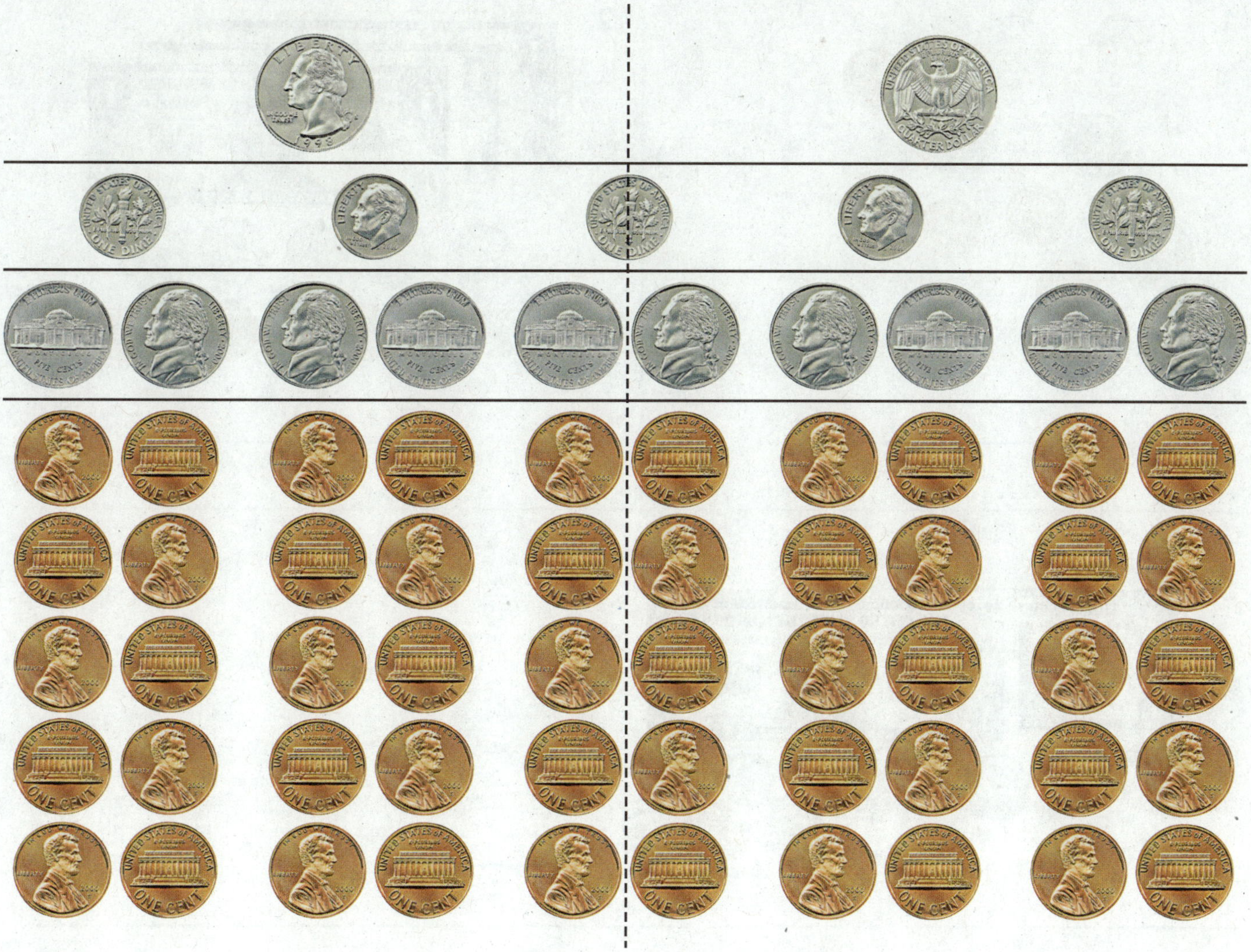

____

____

____

____

____

Name ______________________ Date ____________

▶ Count Coins and Bills

Find the value of each collection of coins and bills.

1.

____

2.

____

3.

____

4.

____

5–4 Class Activity

Name ______________________ Date __________

►Compare Amounts of Money

Compare the two collections of coins and bills. Write >, <, or = in the answer box.

5. 

☐

6. 

☐

7. 

☐

►Solve Problems Involving Money

Solve each problem.

8. Kevin wants to buy a book that costs $1.50. He has 3 quarters, 6 nickels, and 4 pennies. Does he have enough money to buy the book?

____

9. Jade has 7 nickels, 2 dimes, and 5 quarters. Elias has 8 dimes, 6 pennies, 2 quarters, and 3 nickels. Who has more money?

____

10. **On the Back** Explain how you solved problem 8.

Name Date

Name Date

▶ Coins that Make a Dollar

Look at the two different combinations of coins that make a dollar. Can you think of some other coin combinations that make a dollar?

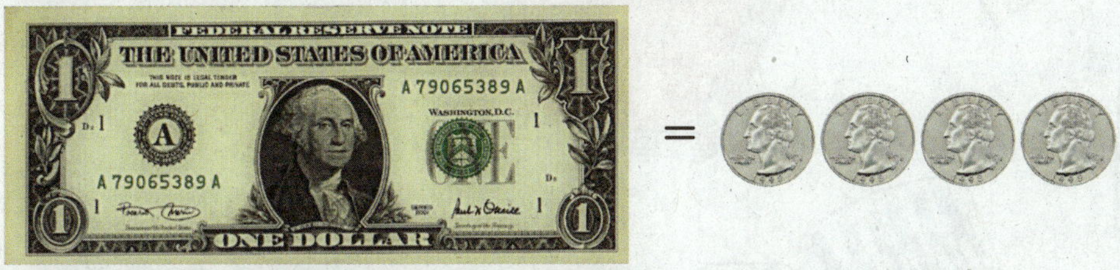

▶ Coin Combinations

Draw two different coin combinations for each amount.

1. 37¢

2. $0.75

Draw each amount with the *fewest* coins. Use quarters, dimes, nickels, or pennies.

3. $0.88

4. $0.43

5. 71¢

6. $.95

Name ______________________ Date ______________

These items are for sale at Snappy School Supplies:

▶Act It Out

You and your partner can take turns being the customer and the shopkeeper. Here's what to do:

Step 1: The customer chooses two or three items to buy.

Step 2: The shopkeeper writes down the prices and finds the total cost.

Step 3: The customer pays the exact amount of money for the items.

Step 4: The shopkeeper counts the money to make sure it is the right amount and draws the coins and bill used.

Show your work on a separate sheet of paper.

Name ______________________ Date ______________

▶ Count On to Make Change

Imagine you are working at a sandwich shop. A customer pays for a sandwich that costs $2.78 with a $5 bill. Your cash register is broken and you don't have a pencil. How can you figure out how much change to give the customer?

Start with $2.78. Count on until you get a whole-dollar amount, and then count on by whole dollars until you get to $5.00.

$2.78

$2.79 $2.80 $2.90 $3.00 $4.00 $5.00

Add the coins and bills to find the total amount of change, $2.22.

▶ Practice Making Change

Find the amount of change by counting on to the amount paid. Draw the coins and bills you counted.

1. Fernando paid for a $1.39 bottle of juice with two $1 bills. How much change did he get? ____________

2. At a garage sale, Ana bought a $3.53 CD with a $5 bill. How much change did she get? ____________

3. Valerie bought a $2.12 magazine with three $1 bills. How much change did she get? ____________

Name ____________________ Date ____________

The following items are for sale at the Beach Snack Shop:

►Act It Out

You and your partner can take turns being the customer and the shopkeeper. Here's what to do:

Step 1: The customer chooses two items to buy.

Step 2: The shopkeeper writes down the prices and finds the total cost.

Step 3: The customer pays with bills only.

Step 4: The shopkeeper counts on to find the change. Then the shopkeeper writes down the bills used to pay and the amount of change.

Show your work on a separate sheet of paper.

5–7 Class Activity

Name ______________________ Date ______________

▶ Round Amounts of Money

Round each amount first to the nearest dime and then to the nearest dollar.

	Rounded to the nearest dime	Rounded to the nearest dollar
1. \$3.62	______	______
2. \$5.09	______	______
3. \$1.25	______	______
4. \$2.99	______	______
5. \$7.50	______	______

Solve each problem.

Show your work.

6. Carl spent \$3.35 on a sandwich and \$1.85 on a drink. Estimate the total amount he spent by rounding the prices to the nearest dollar and adding.

____

7. Rose spent 85¢ on a pen, 32¢ on an eraser, and 78¢ on a pencil sharpener. Estimate the total amount she spent by rounding the prices to the nearest dime and adding.

____

8. Aisha spent \$4.12 on a book, \$3.65 on a magazine, and \$1.75 on a greeting card. Estimate the total amount she spent by rounding the prices to the nearest dollar and adding.

____

5–7 **Class Activity**

Name ______________________ Date ______________________

▶ Estimate with Money

Jess brought $5.00 to the store. She wants to buy the items shown at the right. She needs to make an estimate to see if she has enough money.

9. Estimate the total cost of the items by rounding each price to the nearest dollar and adding. Is your estimate $5.00 or less?

____

10. Find the actual cost of the items. Does Jess have enough money to buy the items?

____

11. How could Jess make an estimate to be sure she has enough money?

____

____

Ben has $3.28. Faiz has $1.63. They want to combine their money to buy a model car that costs $5.00.

12. Estimate the total amount the boys have by rounding each amount to the nearest dollar and adding. Is your estimate $5.00 or more?

____

13. Find the actual total amount the boys have. Do they have enough to buy the model?

____

14. How could the boys make an estimate to be sure they have enough money?

____

____

____

Name _______________ Date _______________

Solve each problem.

Tang has $1.20. He wants to buy the items shown at the right. He wants to estimate the total cost of the items to make sure he has enough money.

Tom's Toy Store

15. How do you think Tang should make his estimate? What estimate do you get if you use your method?

____

____

____

16. Can Tang be sure he has enough money to buy the toys?

____

Lidia is selling the items shown at the right at a garage sale. She wants to estimate how much money she will make to be sure she will have enough to buy a video game that costs $10.

Lidia's Garage Sale

17. How do you think Lidia should make her estimate? What estimate do you get if you use your method?

____

____

____

18. Can Lidia be sure she will have enough money?

____

Going Further

▶ Different Ways to Estimate with Money

Estimate the total cost of the notebook, marker, and baseball cap using the strategies given below.

Round to the nearest dollar	Use Mental Math
1.	2.

Complete.

3. What is the actual cost of the notebook, marker, and baseball cap? Use your estimates above to check that your answer is reasonable.

____

4. What estimation strategy would you use to estimate the cost of several items when shopping? Explain.

____

____

____

5–8 Class Activity

Name ______________________ Date ______________

Vocabulary
- table
- row
- cell
- column

▶ Read a Table

The Riverside School is taking orders for pizzas to raise money for field trips. This **table** shows the number of orders the third graders took for each type of pizza.

Third Graders' Pizza Orders

	Cheese	Supreme	Vegetable
Saturday	37	26	5
Sunday	19	28	15

A **row** goes across.

A **cell** is where a column and row meet.

A **column** goes up and down.

Use the table above to answer the questions.

Show your work.

1. How many cheese pizzas were ordered on Sunday?

   ____

2. How many vegetable pizzas were ordered on Saturday?

   ____

3. How many supreme pizzas were ordered altogether?

   ____

4. How many pizzas were ordered on Sunday?

   ____

5–8 **Class Activity**

Name ____________________ Date __________

▶ Use a Table

This table shows the number of animals a veterinarian treated over three months.

Animals Treated

	Dogs	Cats	Birds	Reptiles	All Animals
January	68	118	25	11	
February	94	106	8	19	
March	122	77	19	26	
3-Month Total					

5. Fill in the total for each column and row.
6. Write two addition questions about this table.

____

____

____

____

____

7. Write two subtraction questions about this table.

____

____

____

____

____

5–8 Going Further

Name Date

▶ Find a Pattern in a Table

Complete the tables and answer the questions.

Blocks in a Tower

Row 1	Row 2	Row 3	Row 4	Row 5	Row 6	Row 7
8 Blocks		6 Blocks	5 Blocks	4 Blocks		

1. What pattern did you use to complete the table?

Money in Savings Account

Week 1	Week 2	Week 3	Week 4	Week 5	Week 6	Week 7
$300	$285		$255	$240		

2. If the pattern continues, how much money do you predict will be in the savings account in week 8? Explain.

Water Level in Tank

	Hour 1	Hour 2	Hour 3	Hour 4	Hour 5	Hour 6
Tank A	4 in.	5 in.		7 in.	8 in.	
Tank B	6 in.	8 in.	10 in.		14 in.	

3. How would you describe the pattern for each tank?

4. **Math Journal** Create your own table with a pattern. Describe the pattern.

5–8 Going Further

Name ______________________ Date ______________

► Function Tables

Vocabulary
function table
rule

Complete each **function table**.

5.

Rule: Add 7	
Input	Output
12	19
25	
32	
54	
68	
73	

6.

Rule: Add 45	
Input	Output
45	90
15	
80	
100	
125	
255	

7.

Rule: Subtract 16	
Input	Output
36	20
48	
88	
100	
126	
159	

Write the **rule** for each function table.

8.

Rule: ______	
Input	Output
20	40
35	55
50	70
65	85
100	120
250	270

9.

Rule: ______	
Input	Output
15	5
20	10
38	28
57	47
110	100
212	202

10.

Rule: ______	
Input	Output
1	16
15	30
40	55
65	80
90	105
120	135

11.

Rule: ______						
Input	100	85	70	65	52	43
Output	95	80	65	60	47	38

5–9 Class Activity

Name ____________________ Date ____________

▶ Analyze Tables

This table shows the number of people who went on different rides at an amusement park.

Number of People Who Went on Rides

	Roller Coaster	Ferris Wheel	Bumper Cars
Monday	383	237	185
Tuesday	459	84	348
Wednesday	106	671	215

Use the table above to answer the questions.

1. What do the numbers in the row for Tuesday stand for?

____

____

____

2. What do the numbers in the column for bumper cars stand for?

____

____

____

3. Find the cell with 106 in it. What does this number stand for?

____

____

____

Name ____________________ Date ____________

►Fill in the Tables

4. This table shows the number of loaves of bread baked and sold last week at the Lotsa Dough Bakery. Fill in the empty cells.

Bread Sales at Lotsa Dough Bakery

	Loaves Baked	Loaves Sold	Loaves Left
Monday	122	38	
Tuesday	113	47	
Wednesday	145		89
Thursday		96	38
Friday	91		44

5. This table shows the number of CDs and videotapes sold at the Sound Out Music Store last week. Fill in the empty cells.

Sound Out Music Sales

	CDs	Videotapes	Total
Monday	62	19	81
Tuesday	73	32	
Wednesday	88		133
Thursday		26	120
Friday	155		223
Saturday		66	294

Name ____________________ Date ____________

▶ Use Deductive Reasoning

Solve each problem.

1. Jan, Bev, Luis, and Alex are wearing different color caps. The colors are red, blue, green, and yellow. Jan's cap is not red or green. Alex's cap is red. Bev's cap is not green or yellow. What color cap is each wearing?

____

____

	Red	Blue	Green	Yellow
Jan				
Bev				
Luis				
Alex				

2. Ty, Sal, Amy, and Lea were in a race. Amy did not finish either first or second. Lea finished last. Sal finished before Ty. In what order did they finish the race?

____

	First	Second	Third	Fourth
Ty				
Sal				
Amy				
Lea				

3. Mai, Abdul, Bill, and Rita each play different instruments. The instruments are violin, flute, harp, and guitar. Mai's instrument does not have strings. Bill plays the violin. Abdul does not play the harp. What does each person play?

____

____

	violin	flute	harp	guitar
Mai				
Abdul				
Bill				
Rita				

4. **Math Journal** Create your own problem like the ones above.

Name ______________________ Date ______________

▶ Use Inductive Reasoning

5. Look for a pattern in the lines of symmetry inside the squares below and the number of triangles formed by them. How many triangles will there be in a square with three lines of symmetry? four lines of symmetry? ________

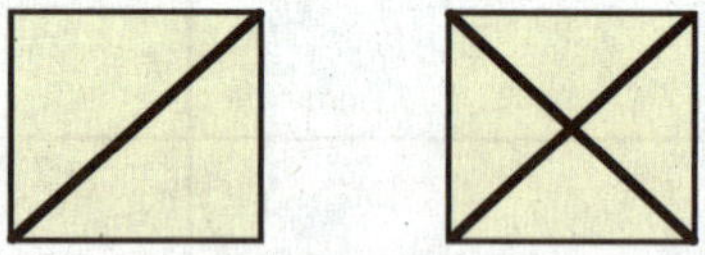

6. Eight baseball teams will play each of the other teams once. Use a pattern to find how many games will take place? ________

2 teams   3 teams   4 teams   5 teams

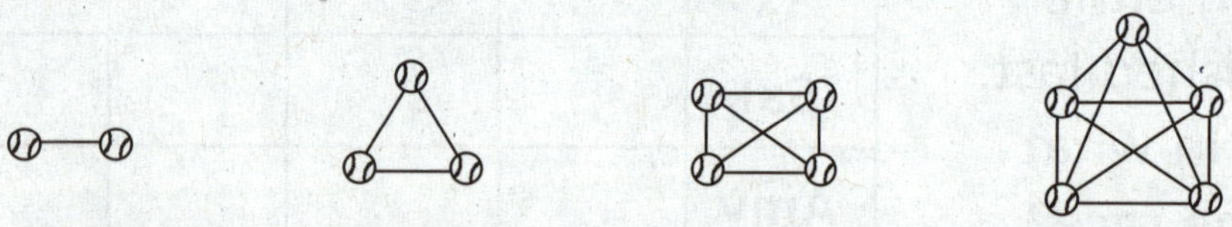

1 game   3 games   6 games   10 games

7. Describe the pattern you used to find the answer to Problem 6.

____

8. Connect the six dots using just three line segments. Do not lift your pencil from the paper or retrace any line segment. The dashed line segments show you a way to start.

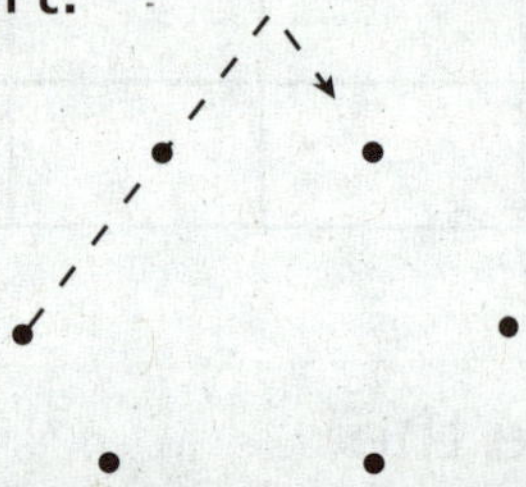

9. Connect all nine dots using just four line segments. Do not lift your pencil from the paper or retrace any line segment.

10. Is there a pattern that you could use to solve Problems 8 and 9? ________

5–10 Class Activity

Name ____________________ Date __________

▶ Make a Table

Use the data the class collected to fill in the table.

____

▶ Use a Table

1. Write a comparison question using data from the table above and the word *more.* Answer your question.

____

____

2. Write a comparison question using data from the table above and the word *fewer.* Answer your question.

____

____

3. Write a question using data from the table and the word *altogether.* Answer your question.

____

____

Name _______________ Date _______________

▶ Analyze Data

Fill in the missing information in the tables and answer the questions.

This table shows the number of souvenirs the Wildcats baseball team sold last weekend.

Souvenir Sales for Wildcats Baseball Team

	White	Red	Total
Caps	134		211
T-shirts	64	109	
Pennants	59		151

4. Which item above had the most total sales? _______________

5. Which color T-shirt had the most sales? _______________

This table shows the number of items the Green Thumb Garden Shop sold at their Spring sale.

Spring Sale at Green Thumb Garden Shop

	Number Before the Sale	Number Sold	Number Left
Spades	232	185	
Straw Hats		68	76
Small Pots	412		70
Big Pots		227	98

6. Which item had the most sales? _______________

7. Which item has the least number left? _______________

5–11

Class Activity

Name ____________________ Date ____________

▶ Solve Problems with Extra Information

Read each problem. Cross out any extra information. Then solve.

1. Emma solved 9 math problems and answered 7 reading questions. Her sister solved 8 math problems. How many math problems did they solve in all?

   ____

2. Mark had 6 shirts and 5 pairs of pants. Today his aunt gave him 4 more shirts and another pair of pants. How many shirts does he have now?

   ____

3. A parking lot had 179 cars and 95 trucks. Then 85 cars left the lot. How many cars are in the parking lot now?

   ____

4. Laura had some roses in a vase. From her garden, she picked 7 more roses and 6 daisies. Now she has 12 roses in all. How many roses did she have at first?

   ____

5. Nikko had 245 pennies and 123 nickels. His brother gave him 89 more pennies and 25 more nickels. How many pennies does Nikko have now?

   ____

Name ______________________________ Date ______________

►Solve Problems with Hidden Information

Read each problem. Circle the hidden information. Then solve.

6. Samuel had 16 horseshoes in the shed yesterday. Today he put a new set of horseshoes on his horse Betsy. How many horseshoes are left in the shed?

____

7. Maya is going on a vacation with her family for a week and 3 days. How many days will she be on vacation?

____

8. Julie bought a dozen eggs at the market. She gave 3 of them to Serge. How many eggs does Julie have left?

____

9. Lisa had 3 quarters and 2 dimes. Then she found 3 nickels and 12 pennies. How many cents does she have now?

____

10. Marissa is moving away. She is going to move back in a year and 21 days. How many days will she be gone?

____

Name _______________ Date _______________

▶ Solve Word Problems with Not Enough Information

Read each problem. Is there a way to solve it? Explain.

1. Sara bought 8 bananas at the fruit market. She put them in a bowl with some oranges. How many pieces of fruit are in the bowl?

____

____

2. Josh had some money in his pocket. He spent $1.25 on a bottle of juice. How much money does he have left?

____

____

Tell what information is needed to solve each problem.

3. Meg bought 3 mystery books and put them on the shelf with her other mystery books. How many mystery books are now on the shelf?

____

____

4. Our school has 5 soccer balls, 6 basketballs, and 4 footballs. Today, some of the footballs were lost. How many balls does the school have now?

____

____

5–12

Class Activity

Name _______________ Date _______________

Tell what information is needed to solve each problem.

5. A stepladder is 8 feet tall. Two of the steps are broken. How many steps are not broken?

____

____

6. Rebecca did 112 dives in competition last summer. This summer, she did many more dives in competition. How many competition dives did she do in the two summers?

____

____

7. Today, Maggie's Café sold more hot chocolate than yesterday. Yesterday, Maggie's Café sold 237 cups of hot chocolate. How many more cups were sold today than yesterday?

____

____

8. A living room couch is 6 feet long. There are 4 blue pillows and several gray pillows on the couch. How many pillows are on the couch altogether?

____

____

5–12 **Class Activity**

Name ____________________ Date ____________

► Practice

Solve each problem if possible. If more information is needed, rewrite the problem to include the necessary information and then solve it.

9. Leah began fishing at 2 o'clock in the afternoon. She stopped at dinnertime. How many hours did Leah fish?

10. On Saturday, Maria handed out 646 flyers in the morning and the same number of flyers in the afternoon. How many flyers did Maria hand out on Saturday?

11. The Kitchen Store sold 532 pans and 294 pots. Then some pans were returned. How many pans were not returned?

12. There are 3 tables in the room with 4 legs each. One has a broken leg. How many table legs in the room are not broken?

5–12 Class Activity

Name ______ Date ______

► Extra Practice

Solve each problem if possible. If more information is needed, rewrite the problem to include the necessary information and then solve it.

13. The train traveled 476 miles on Tuesday. It traveled even more miles on Wednesday. How many miles did the train travel on Tuesday and Wednesday?

______

______

14. The hikers walked 12 miles on Tuesday and camped overnight. On Wednesday, they walked back along the same route. How many miles did they hike altogether?

______

______

15. One week, Rene cooked meals for 235 people. The next week, she cooked meals for 413 people. How many people did Rene cook meals for in those two weeks?

______

______

16. Julio and Scott played 6 card games and 4 computer games today. How many hours did they play games?

______

______

5–13 Class Activity

Name Date

►Solve Two-Step Word Problems

Show your work.

Solve each problem. Label your answers.

1. The Hillside bus had 14 passengers. When it stopped, 5 people got off and 8 people got on. How many people are riding the Hillside bus now?

   ____

2. There are 15 fish in a tank. 12 are goldfish, and the others are angelfish. How many more goldfish are there than angelfish?

   ____

3. Luther had 11 sheets of colored paper. 6 were orange, and the rest were blue. Today he used 2 sheets of blue paper. How many sheets of blue paper does Luther have now?

   ____

4. Sun Mi picked 14 apricots. Celia picked 5 fewer apricots than Sun Mi. How many apricots did Sun Mi and Celia pick altogether?

   ____

5. Annie took 8 photographs at home and 7 photographs at school. Her sister Amanda took 6 fewer photographs than Annie. How many photographs did Amanda take?

   ____

5–13

Class Activity

Name ______ Date ______

Show your work.

▶Solve and Discuss

Solve each problem. Label your answers.

6. There are 5 mice, 3 gerbils, and some hamsters in a cage. Altogether there are 15 animals in the cage. How many hamsters are there?

______

7. A new library opened on Saturday. The library lent out 234 books on Saturday. On Sunday, they lent out 138 books. That day, 78 books were returned. How many books were not returned?

______

8. Katie had 8 dimes and some nickels in her duck bank. She had 4 more nickels than dimes. She took out 5 nickels to buy a newspaper. How many nickels are in her duck bank now?

______

9. Tony had 14 colored pencils. 9 of them needed sharpening, and the rest were sharp. Yesterday, his uncle gave him some new colored pencils. Now Tony has 12 sharp colored pencils. How many colored pencils did his uncle give him?

______

10. José ate 6 strawberries. Then he ate 7 more. Lori ate 9 strawberries. How many fewer strawberries did Lori eat than José?

______

5–14 Class Activity

Name _______________ Date _______________

► Solve Multi-Step Word Problems

Show your work.

Solve each problem. Label your answers.

1. Isabel has 14 pieces of fruit. 6 are apples, 2 are bananas, and the rest are pears. Then she buys more pears. Now she has 9 pears. How many pears does she buy?

____

2. Four jugglers were practicing. Ted was juggling 3 balls, Ruby was juggling 6 balls, and Mai was juggling 4 balls. 5 of their balls fell. Then Toby started juggling 7 balls. What total number of balls were they juggling then?

____

3. Travis had \$3.06 and Marie had \$1.42. Then Travis earned \$1.74 more and Marie earned \$2.86 more. Who has more money now? How much more?

____

4. Finn delivered 3 pizzas. Then he delivered 5 more pizzas. He delivered 6 fewer pizzas than Liz. How many pizzas did Liz deliver?

____

5. Majeed built 7 car models and 14 airplane models. Jasmine built 9 more car models than Majeed and 6 fewer airplane models. How many models did Jasmine build in all?

____

5–14 **Class Activity**

Name ______________________ Date ______________

▶ Use a Strategy

Read the problem below and answer the questions.

Marika wants to teach her dog Rufus some tricks. She will reward Rufus with a treat each time he practices a trick. She has a book that lists how many times a dog usually has to practice each trick in order to learn it. The list is shown below.

Trick	Practice Needed
Sit	3 times
Stay	6 times
Fetch	5 times
Come	2 times
Lie down	4 times
Roll over	7 times

6. Marika has 12 treats. She would like to teach Rufus 4 tricks. Can she do it? Explain why or why not.

____

____

____

____

7. What are all the possible combinations of tricks she can teach with *exactly* 12 treats?

____

____

____

Name ____________________ Date ____________

►Use the Work Backward Strategy

Show your work.

Solve each problem. Label your answers.

1. Marvin cut some new line for his fishing pole. Then he cut the new line into 2 equal pieces. Next he cut 8 inches off one piece of line. That gave him a piece of line that was 42 inches long. How long was the original piece of new line?

   ____

2. Sam weighed a bag of peanuts. Then he added 2 more pounds of peanuts to the bag. After taking 5 pounds of peanuts out, the bag weighed 6 pounds. How much did the bag of peanuts weigh in the beginning?

   ____

3. Tim has a collection of trading cards. His brother gave him 4 more cards. Tim gave 6 cards to his neighbor. Then Tim bought 24 cards. Tim now has 42 cards. How many cards did he have to start with?

   ____

4. Jack had an amount of money. He spent $7 for a model car kit and $4 for paint. His mother gave him $5. Jack now has $11. How much money did he have to begin with?

   ____

5. **On the Back** Write a word problem that needs to be solved by working backward.

Name ______________________ Date __________

Name ____________________ Date ____________________

Vocabulary
pictograph

▶ Read a Pictograph

A **pictograph** is a graph that uses pictures or symbols to represent data. The pictograph below shows the number of votes for favorite ice cream flavors.

Use the pictograph above to answer the questions.

1. How many votes were there for chocolate?

   ____

2. How many votes were there for Cherry Vanilla?

   ____

3. How many people voted in all for their favorite ice cream flavor?

   ____

4. How many fewer votes were there for Peanut Butter Crunch than Chocolate?

   ____

▶ Make a Pictograph

5. **Use the data about Kanye's CDs to make your own pictograph.**

Kanye's CDs	
Type	**Number of CDs**
Jazz	12
Rap	16
Classical	4

Name ______________________ Date __________

Vocabulary
horizontal bar graph
vertical bar graph

▶ Read a Horizontal Bar Graph

Look at this horizontal bar graph and answer the question.

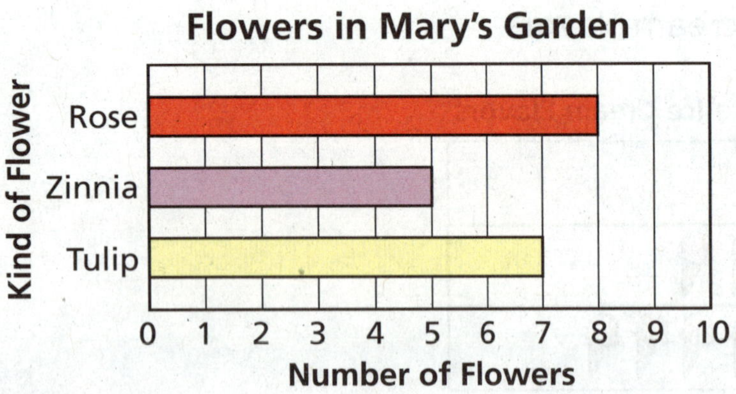

6. What do the bars represent?

____

____

____

▶ Read a Vertical Bar Graph

Look at this vertical bar graph and answer the question.

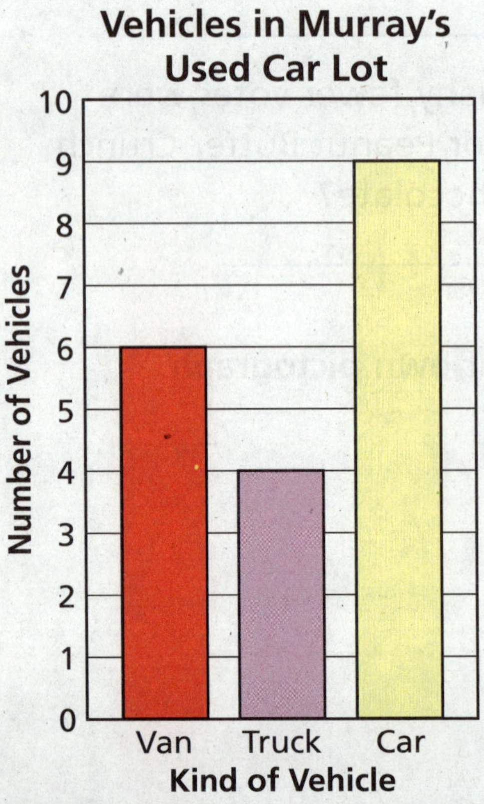

7. What do the bars represent?

____

____

____

Name ______________________ Date ______________

► Create a Horizontal Bar Graph

Use the information in this table to complete the horizontal bar graph.

Balls in the Gym

Type of Ball	Number of Balls
Soccer ball	4
Basketball	6
Softball	9

8.

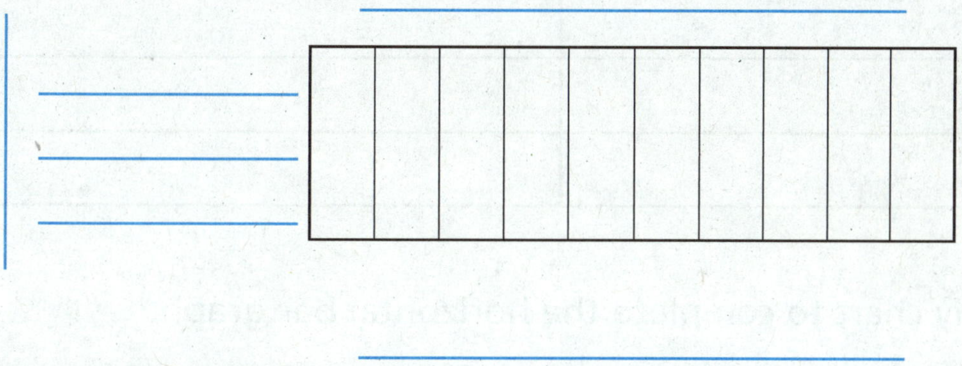

► Create a Vertical Bar Graph

Use the information in this table to complete the vertical bar graph.

Favorite Fruits

Type of Fruit	Number Who Chose It
Apple	5
Banana	6
Orange	4

9.

5–15 Going Further

Name ______________________ Date ____________

▶ Take a Survey and Record Results

Topics
Sports
Animals
Colors
School Subjects
Snacks

10. Choose a survey topic from the box or make up one of your own. Then take a survey to find the favorite.

Which ______________ is your favorite?	
Answer Choice	**Tally**

11. Use the tally chart to complete the horizontal bar graph.

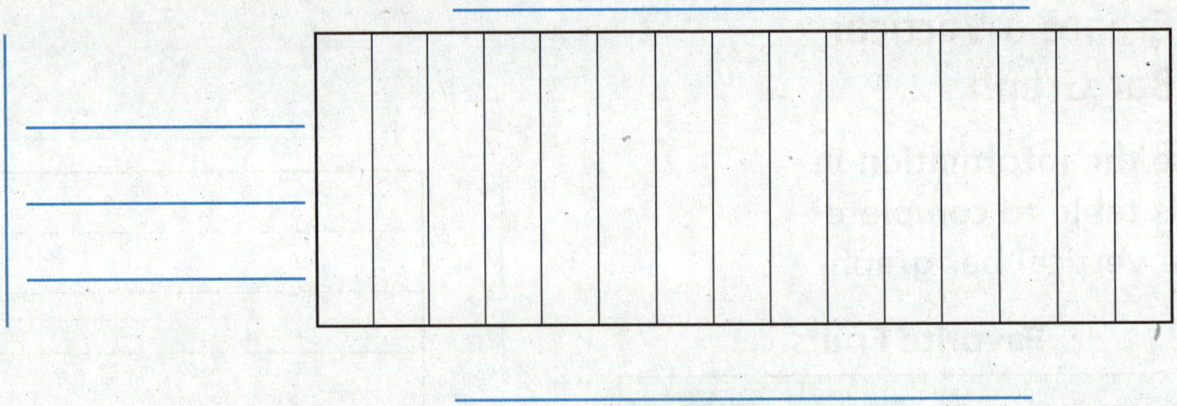

12. Math Journal Write two questions that can be answered using the bar graph. Then answer them.

Name ______________________ Date ______________

▶Horizontal Bar Graphs with Multi-Digit Numbers

Use this horizontal bar graph to answer the questions below.

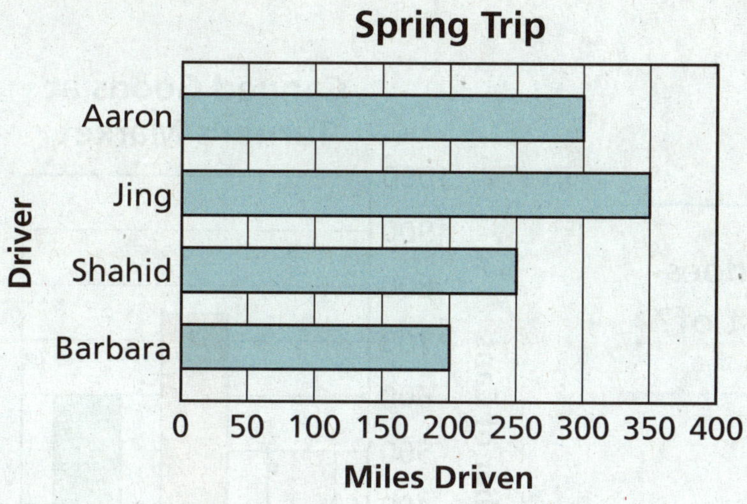

1. How many miles did Shahid drive?

____

2. Who drove the most miles?

____

3. How many miles did Aaron and Barbara drive altogether?

____

4. How many more miles did Jing drive than Shahid?

____

5. How many fewer miles did Barbara drive than Jing?

____

6. Write two more questions that can be answered by using the graph.

____

____

Name ________________ Date ________

►Vertical Bar Graphs with Multi-Digit Numbers

Use the vertical bar graph at the right to answer the questions below.

7. How many cans of peas are at Turner's Market?

____

8. Which type of canned goods does Turner's Market have the least of?

____

9. How many cans of beans and peaches are there altogether?

____

10. How many more cans of beans are there than peas?

____

11. How many fewer cans of peaches are there than peas?

____

12. Write two more questions that can be answered by using the graph.

____

____

____

____

____

____

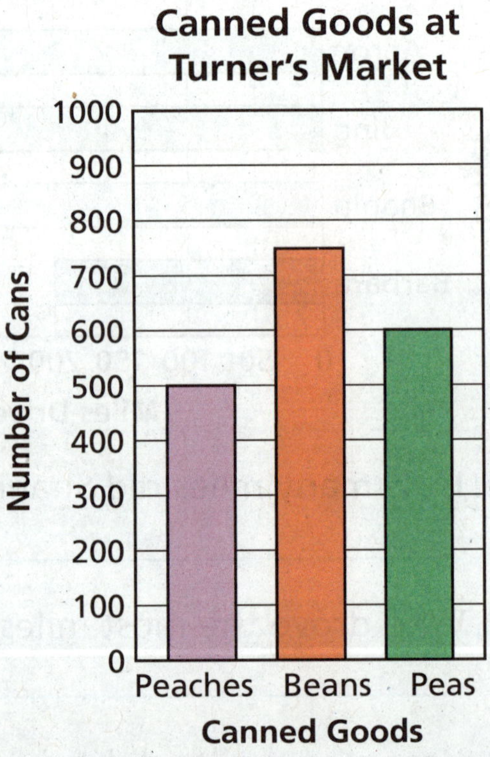

5–16 Class Activity

Name ______________________ Date ______________

►Create a Horizontal Bar Graph with Multi-Digit Numbers

13. Use the information in this table to make a horizontal bar graph.

Joe's Video Collection	
Type	**Videos**
Comedy	60
Action	35
Drama	20

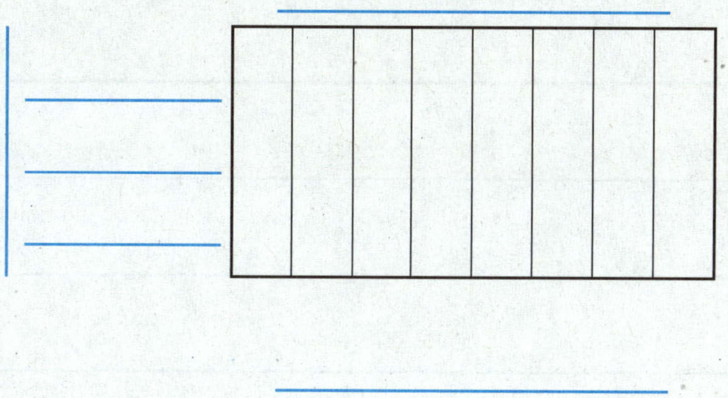

►Create a Vertical Bar Graph with Multi-Digit Numbers

14. Use the information in this table to make a vertical bar graph.

Summer Bike Sales	
Type of Bike	**Number Sold**
Road Bike	200
Mountain Bike	600
Hybrid Bike	450

15. On the Back Write two questions that can be answered using one of the graphs.

Name Date

5–17 Class Activity

Name ______________________________ Date ____________

Vocabulary
- tally chart
- frequency table
- line plot
- mode
- range

► Introduce Frequency Tables and Line Plots

The ages of some players on a basketball team can be shown in different ways.

A **tally chart** can be used to record and organize data.

A **frequency table** shows how many times events occur.

A **line plot** shows the frequency of data on a number line.

Tally Chart

Age	Tally
7	I
8	III
9	~~IIII~~I
10	IIII
11	II

Frequency Table

Age	Tally
7	1
8	3
9	5
10	4
11	2

Line Plot

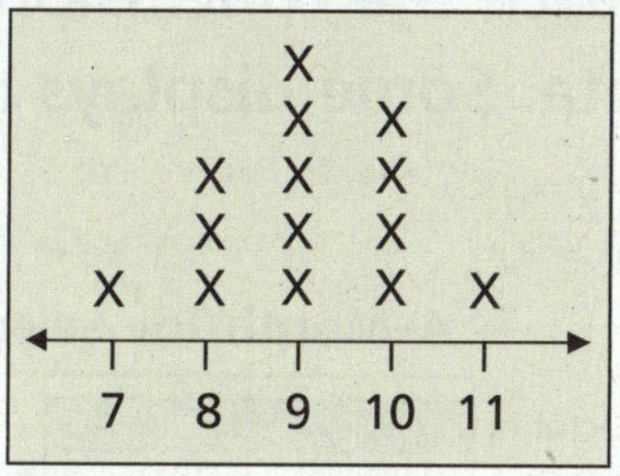

Ages of Basketball Players

► Review Mode and Range

The **mode** is the value that appears most frequently in a set of data.

The **range** is the difference between the greatest value and the least value in a set of data.

Use the line plot above to complete exercises 1 and 2.

1. What is the mode for the set of data? ____________
2. What is the range for the set of data? ____________

5–17 Class Activity

Name ______________________ Date ______________

▶Match Conclusions to Data

Suppose that you work at a toy store. You show information in different displays. Below are conclusions made from displays about toy sales in three stores.

A. Store A sold more items than Store B and Store C.

B. More toys were bought in October than in January.

C. More stuffed animals were sold than any other items.

D. Most dolls purchased cost $10.

Match the conclusions above to the display that represents that data. Some displays may not match a conclusion.

3. **4–Month Toy Sales**

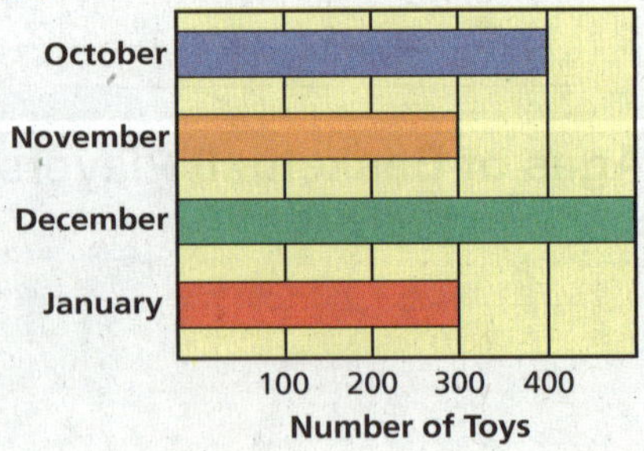

4. **2008 Toy Sales**

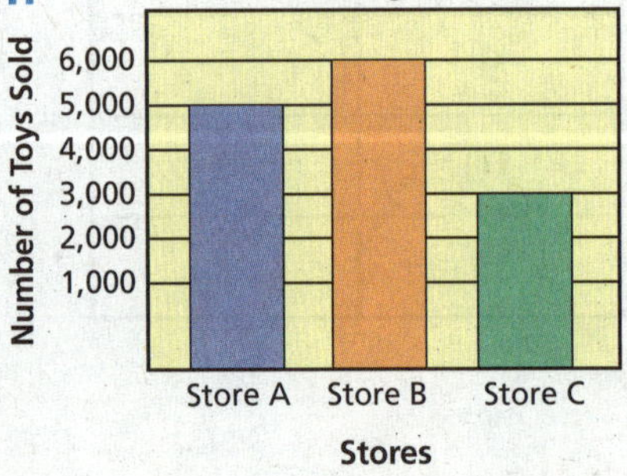

5. **Prices of Dolls Purchased**

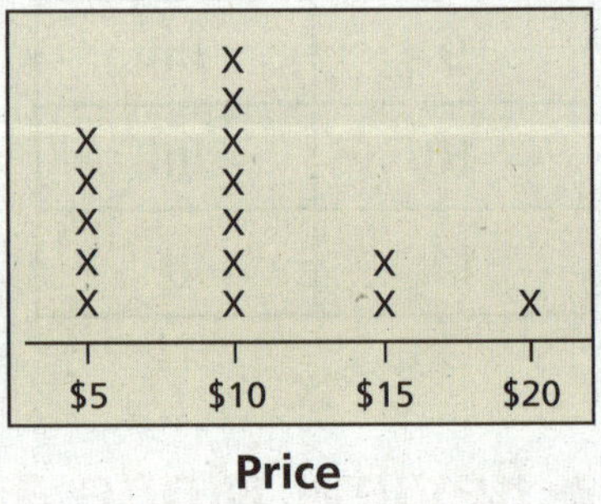

6.

7.

Weekly Doll Purchases	
Sunday	0
Monday	3
Tuesday	2
Wednesday	3
Thursday	1
Friday	4
Saturday	5

8.

2008 Toy Sales for stores A, B, and C	
Board Games	10,863
Video Games	15,829
Stuffed Animals	29,362
Books	13,256

5–18 Class Activity

Name ______________________ Date ______________________

▶ Math and Science

Three frogs are having a Frog Jumping Contest.
The length of the race is 1,000 cm.
The table shows how far each frog goes in 1 jump.

Name of Frog	Length of Jump
Freddie	about 200 cm
Flora	about 315 cm
Frankie	about 144 cm

Use a Calculator.

1. Bena says it will take Flora about 3 jumps to cross the finish line? Is she right?

____

____

2. What conclusions can you make about how many jumps it will take the other frogs to cross the finish line?

____

____

3. What conclusion can you make about how many of his body lengths Freddie the Frog can jump?

____

____

Freddie's Body Length

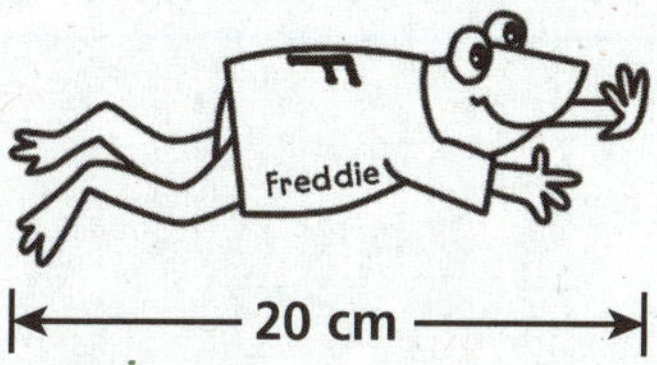

Name ____________________ Date __________

▶ How Far Can You Jump?

4. Ask 10 students to jump. Measure the length of each jump. Record the names of the students and the length of the jumps in a table.

5. Make a bar graph on grid paper that shows the length of each jump. Put the data in order from shortest jump to longest jump.

6. Look at the graph you made. What is the shape of the data?

____

7. What is the mode and range?

____

8. What is your prediction for the jump of another student who has not jumped yet? Why do you think that is a good prediction?

____

9. What conclusion can you make about how far the 10 students can jump?

____

____

5 **Unit Test**

Name ______________________ Date ______________

Compare the numbers. Write >, <, or = in each ◯.

1. 742 ◯ 724

2. 2,329 ◯ 2,319

Write the numbers in order from least to greatest.

3. 598, 678, 590

____

4. 6,543, 7,585, 6,585

____

Round each number to the given place.

5. 567 (nearest hundred) ______________________

6. $7.89 (nearest dime) ______________________

7. $6.29 (nearest dollar) ______________________

Use the line plot to answer question 8.

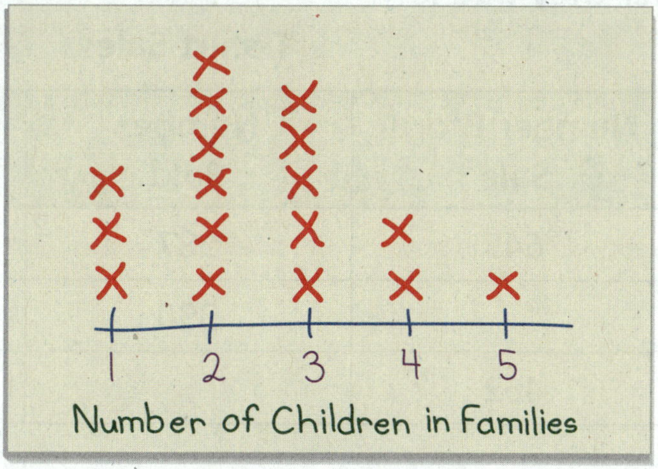

8. What is the mode and range of the data?

mode: ____________ range: ____________

Name ____________________ Date ____________________

Use the bar graph to answer questions 9 and 10.

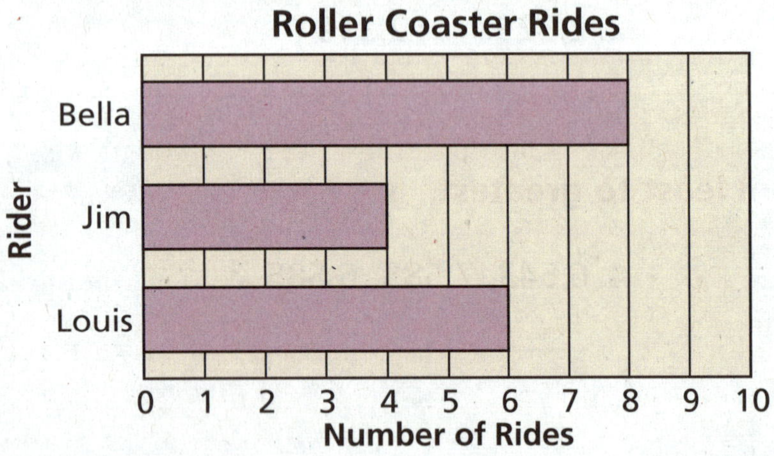

9. How many more rides did Louis take than Jim? ____________________

10. How many rides did Bella and Louis take altogether? ____________________

This table shows the numbers of T-shirts of different sizes a store had before a big sale, the number they sold, and the number they had left.

T-shirt Sales

	Number Bfore Sale	Number Sold	Number Left After Sale
Small	645	587	
Medium		390	45
Large	462		29

11. Fill in the blank cells.

12. How many more small T-shirts than large T-shirts did the store have before the sale?

____

Name ______________________ Date ______________

Solve. Cross out any extra information. Circle any hidden information.

Show your work.

13. Becky has 20 fish and 2 hamsters. There are 8 angelfish and the rest of the fish are goldfish. She gets 7 more goldfish. How many goldfish does she have now?

____

14. Raj is going on vacation for a week and 5 days. How many days will Raj be gone?

____

Solve. Label your answer.

15. Jason has 485 toy dinosaurs in his collection. He plans to sell 243 toy dinosaurs. Round each number to the nearest ten to estimate how many he will have left.

____

Solve the problem if possible. If more information is needed, rewrite the problem to include the necessary information and then solve it.

16. Julie and Sam grew tomato plants. Julie's plant grew 16 inches. How much taller did Sam's plant grow?

____

____

____

____

Name ______________________ Date ______________

Compare the two collections of coins and bills.
Write >, <, or = in the ◯.

17.  ◯ 

18. Draw two different coin combinations for 78¢.

Solve.

19. Uri bought a tube of toothpaste for $2.58. He paid with a $5.00 bill. Find the amount of change by counting on. Draw the coins and bills you counted. How much change did he get?

Show your work.

____

20. **Extended Response** Alexa has $5.00. She wants to order a sandwich for $3.65 and a drink for $1.48. How can she estimate to be sure she has enough money? ______________________________

____

____

____

What estimate do you get using your method? Can Alexa be sure she has enough money to buy the sandwich and the drink?

____

6–1 Class Activity

Name ____________________ Date ____________

Vocabulary
flip

▶ Draw Flips

When you **flip** a figure over a line, you get a mirror image.

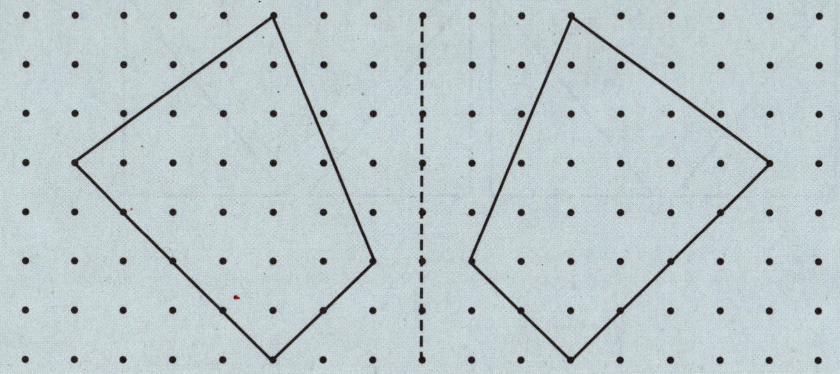

Draw the flipped image of each figure.

1.
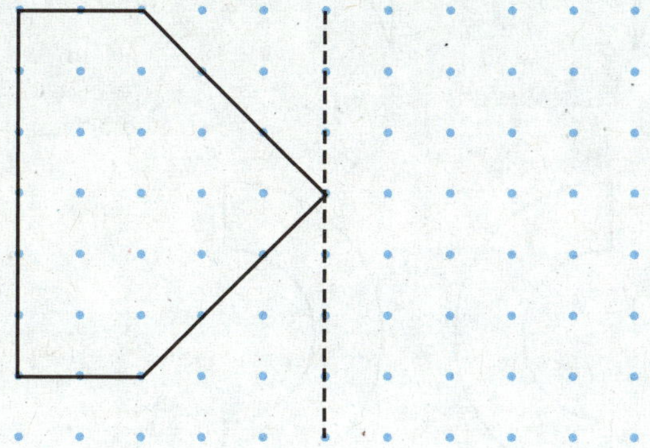

2.
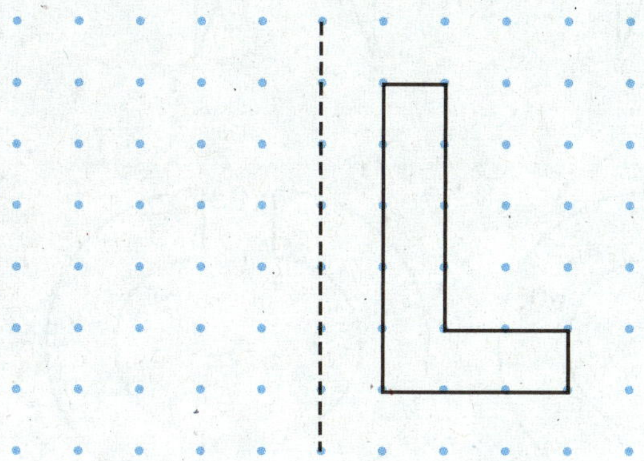

3.
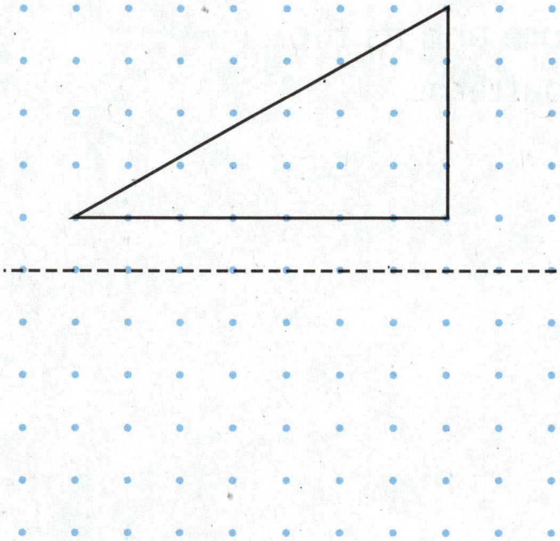

4.
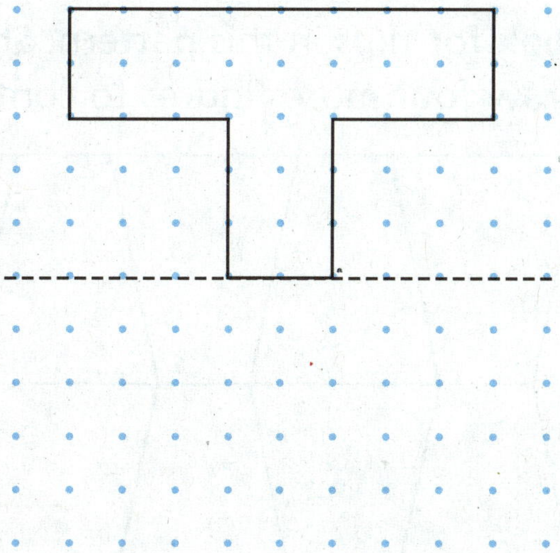

Name ______________________ Date __________

►Use Flips in Patterns

Draw the next figure in each pattern.

5.

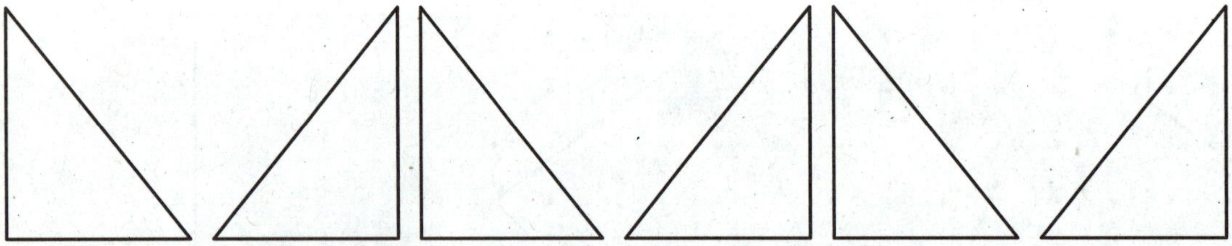

6.

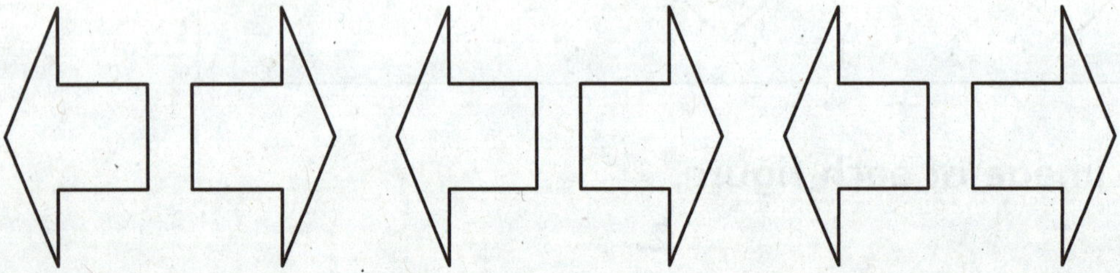

7.

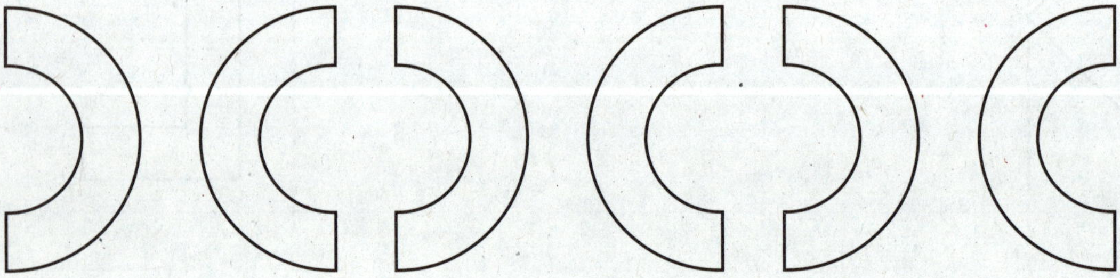

8. Look for flips in this pattern. Shade a figure and its flip. Draw four more figures to continue the pattern.

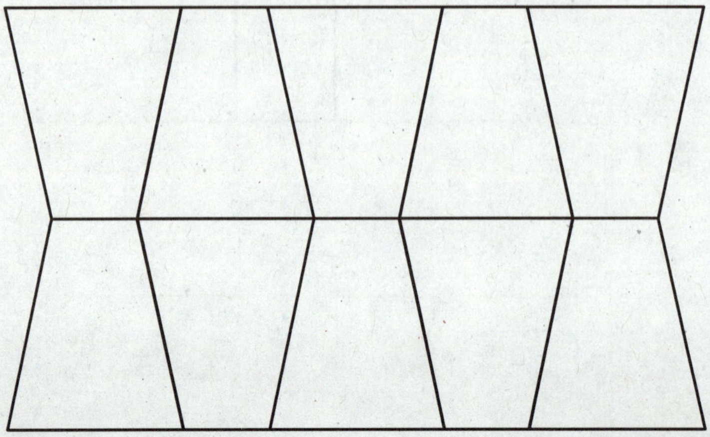

6–1 Class Activity

Name ______________________ Date ______________________

Vocabulary
slide

►Describe and Draw Slides

You can **slide** a figure along a line.

This slide moves the figure to the right and down.

This slide moves the figure up and to the right.

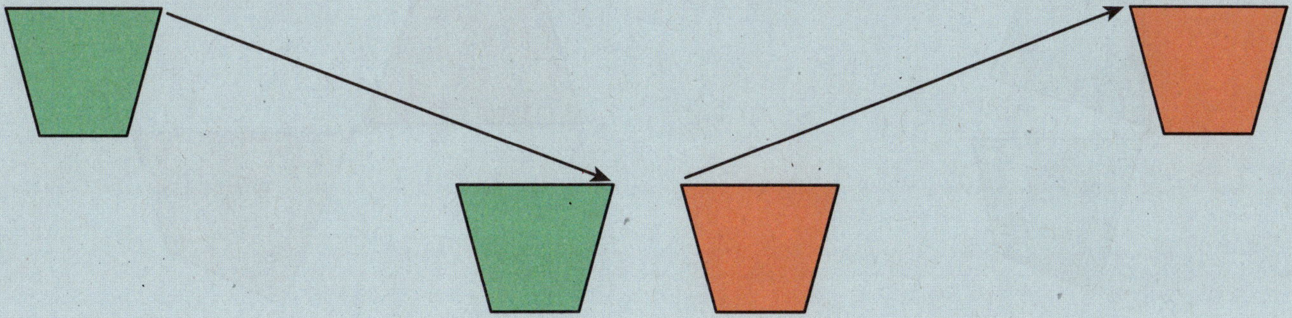

Describe each slide. Draw the new figure.

9.

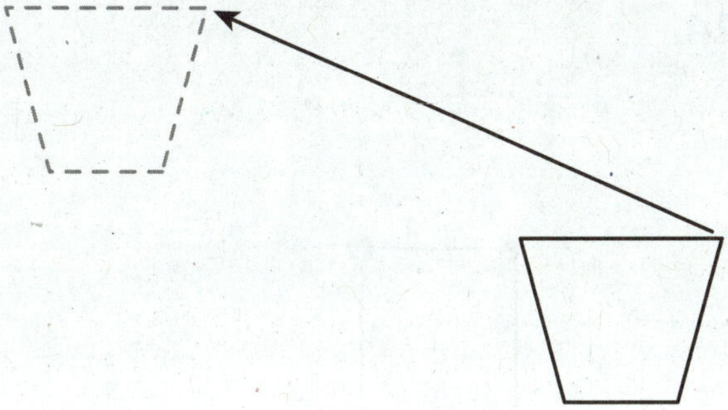

____

10.

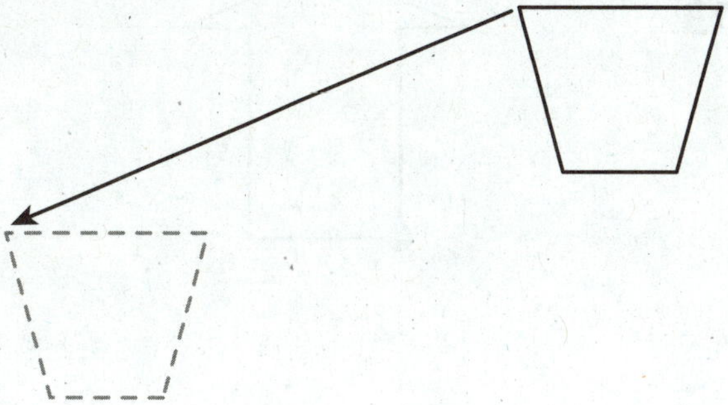

____

11.

____

12.

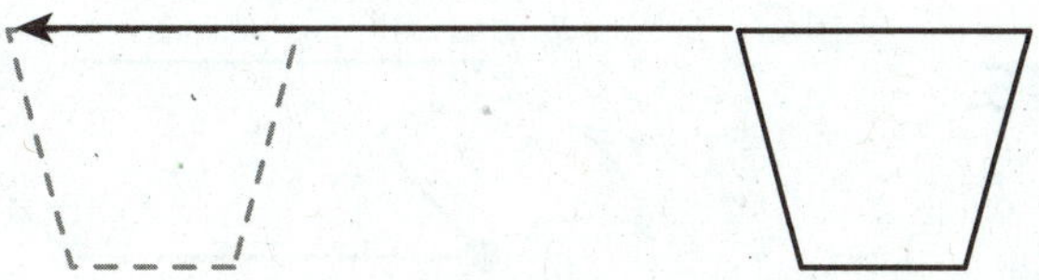

____

Name ______________________ Date ______________

Vocabulary
turn

▶ Describe and Draw Turns

You can **turn** a figure around a point.

This is a quarter turn.

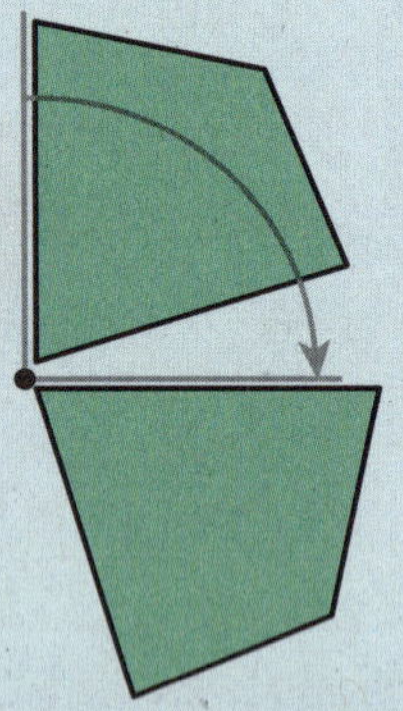

This is a half turn.

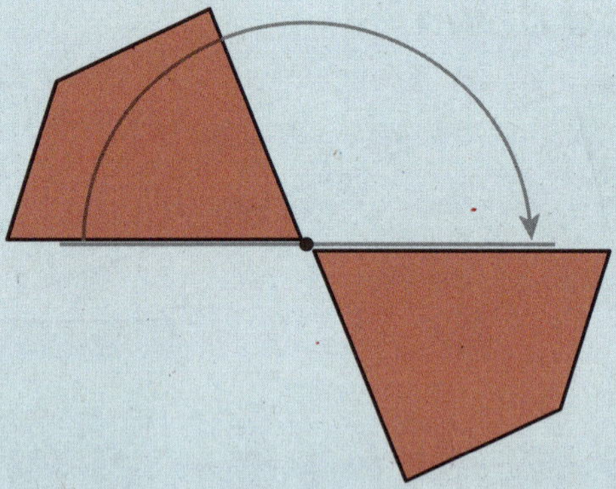

Describe each turn. Draw the new figure.

13.

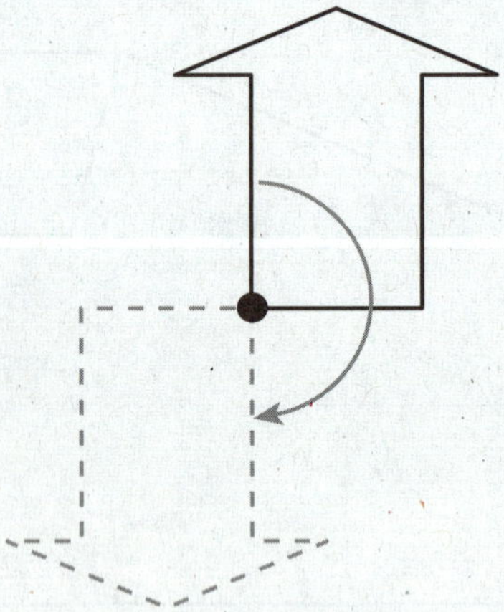

____

14.

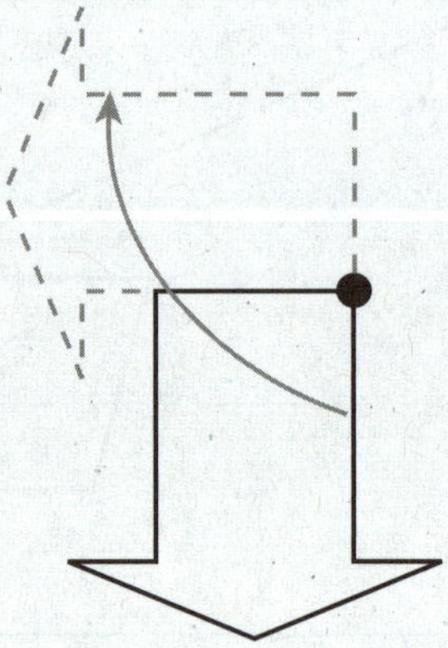

____

15.

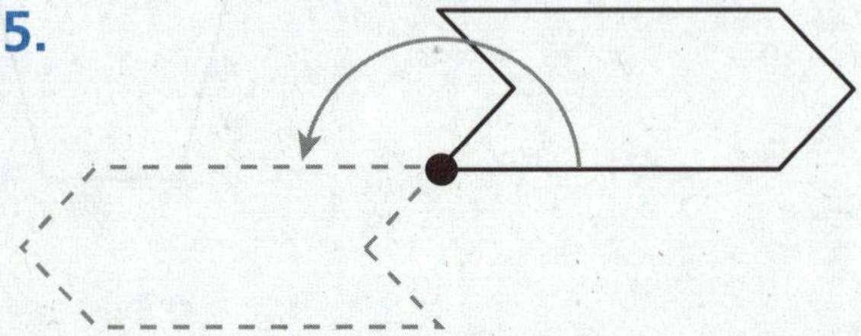

____

16.

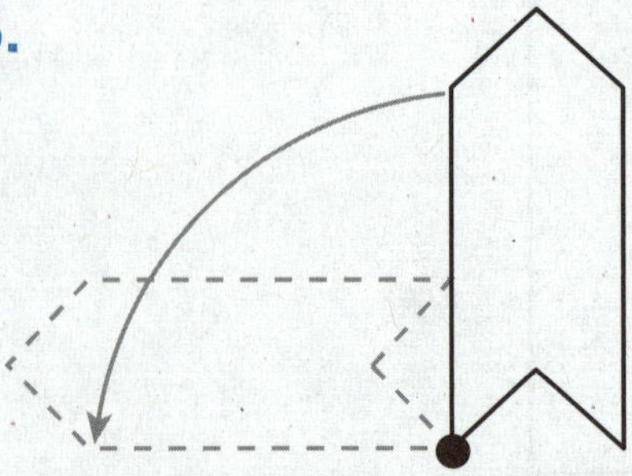

____

Family Letter

Dear Family,

Your child is studying patterns that grow, patterns that shrink, and patterns that repeat. Students will find pattern rules and continue patterns for both number and geometric patterns. Students will also use patterns to solve real-world problems. Repeating patterns from geometry are used everywhere: in art, tiling designs, quilts, and clothing. Slides (translations), flips (reflections), and turns (rotations) can be used to make tiling patterns.

This diagram shows how copies of this geometric figure can fit together to make a tiling pattern.

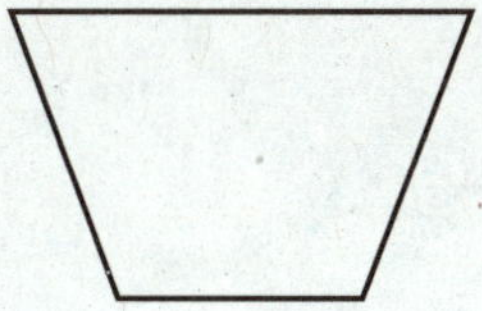

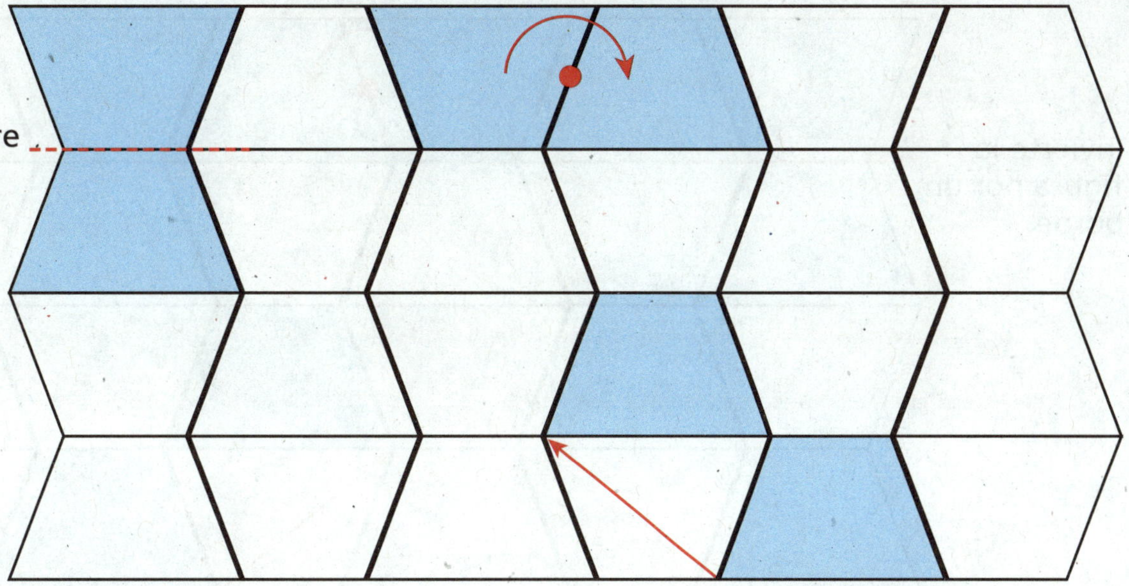

If you have any questions or comments, please call or write to me.

Thank you.

Sincerely,
Your child's teacher

Estimada familia:

La unidad que su niño está estudiando trata de patrones: patrones que aumentan, patrones que disminuyen, patrones que se repiten. Los patrones geométricos que se repiten se usan en todas partes: en arte, en diseños de azulejos, en colchas y en ropa. Los deslizamientos (traslaciones), las inversiones (reflexiones) y los giros (rotaciones), servirán para hacer patrones de azulejos.

Este diagrama muestra de qué manera pueden combinarse las copias de esta figura geométrica para formar un patrón de azulejos.

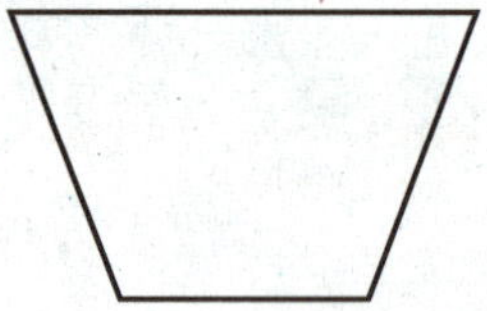

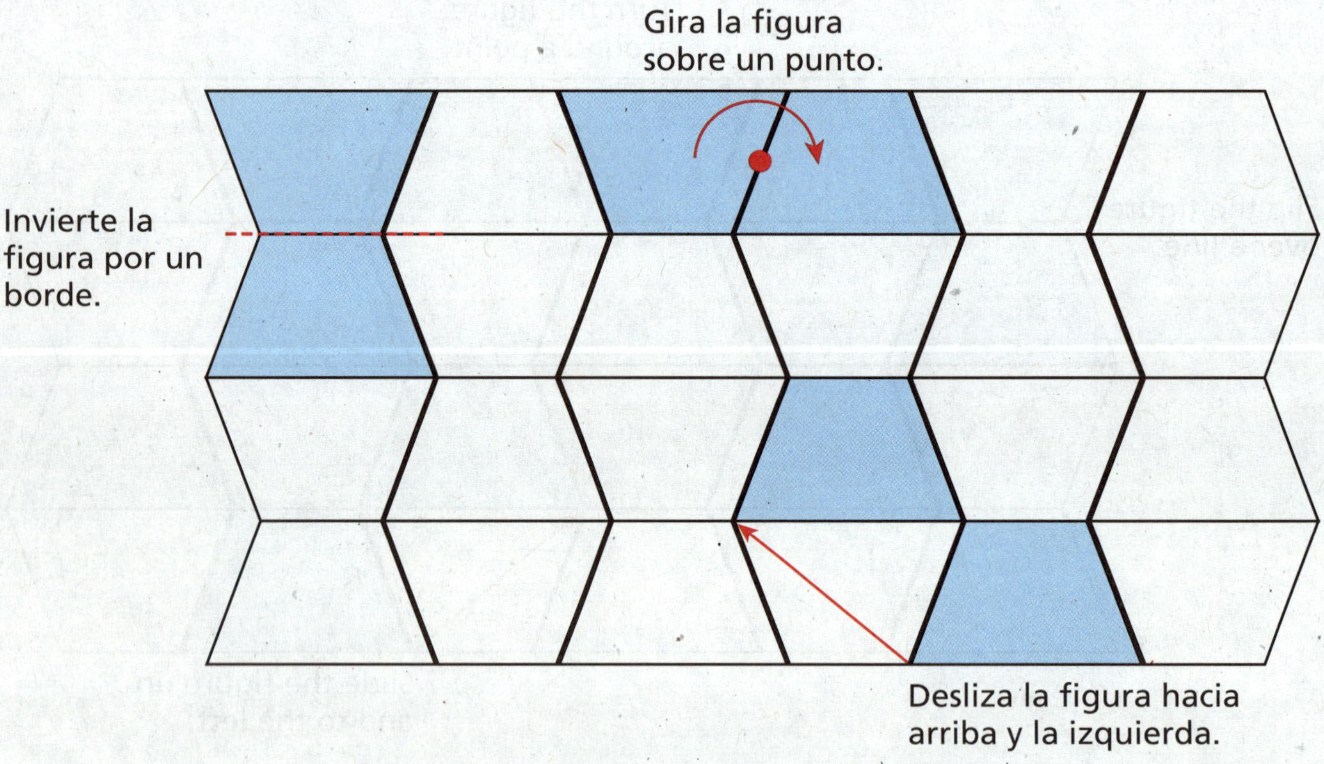

Si tiene alguna pregunta o comentario, por favor comuníquese conmigo. Gracias.

Atentamente,
El maestro de su niño.

6–2 **Class Activity**

Name ____________________ Date ____________

Vocabulary
repeating pattern

▶ Explore Repeating Number Patterns

Sometimes a number pattern continues by repeating the same digits.

Continue each number pattern.

1. 2 7 2 7 2 7 ____________________

2. 1 2 2 1 2 2 1 2 2 ____________________

3. 1 3 2 1 3 2 1 3 2 ____________________

4. 1 0 0 1 1 0 0 1 1 0 0 1 ____________________

▶ Explore Repeating Patterns in Skip Counting

Complete.

5. Skip count by 2s.

2, 4, 6, 8, 10, ____, ____, ____, ____, ____, ____, ____, ____

6. Show the pattern in the ones digits when you skip count by 2s, starting at 2.

____, ____, ____, ____, ____, ____, ____, ____, ____, ____

7. Start at 1 and count by 2s.

1, 3, 5, ____, ____, ____, ____, ____, ____, ____

8. Show the pattern in the ones digits in exercise 7.

____, ____, ____, ____, ____, ____, ____, ____, ____, ____

9. Skip count by 5s.

5, 10, 15, ____, ____, ____, ____, ____, ____, ____, ____, ____

10. Show the pattern in the ones digits when you skip count by 5s, starting at 5.

____, ____, ____, ____, ____, ____, ____, ____

6–2 Class Activity

Name ____________________ Date ____________

► Explore Repeating Shape Patterns

This pattern repeats the same figures over and over. You can describe it as a triangle, flipped triangle, square, repeat.

Draw the next figure in each pattern.

11. 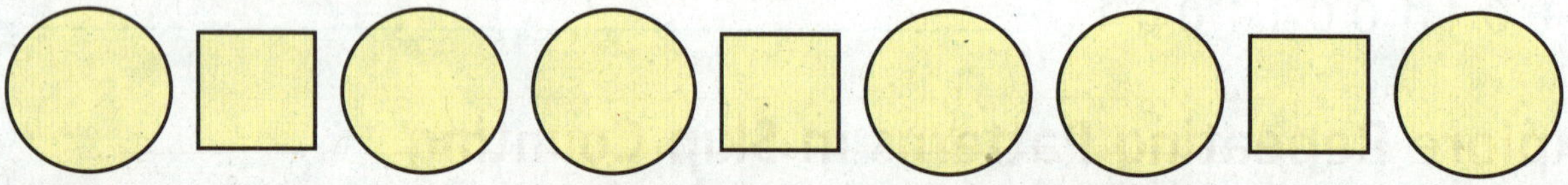

12. 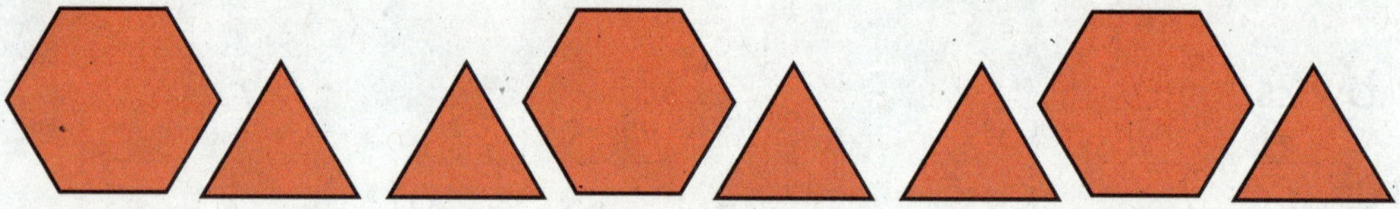

13. 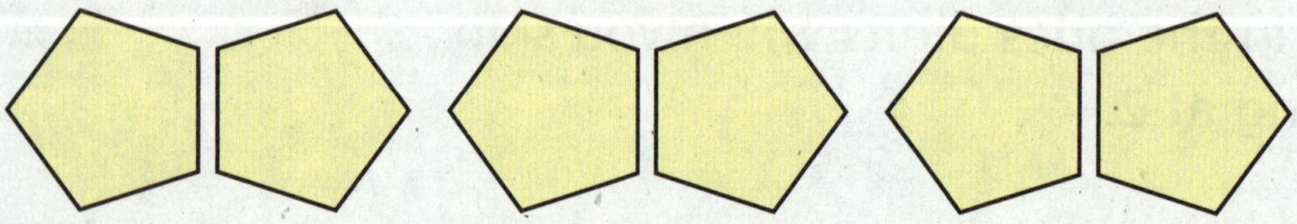

14. Show two ways to make a repeating pattern with these starting figures.

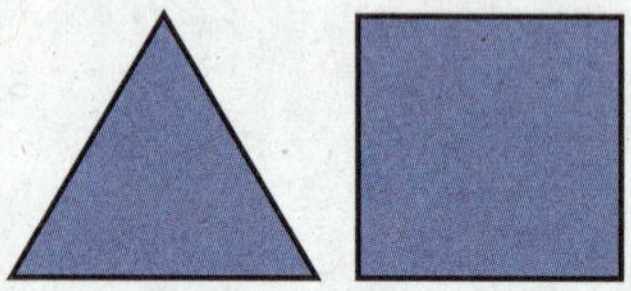

6–3 Class Activity

Name ____________________ Date __________

Vocabulary
growing pattern
shrinking pattern

► Continue a Growing or Shrinking Number Pattern

A number pattern can grow or shrink by the same amount.

Continue the pattern and write the rule.

1. 5, 8, 11, 14, 17, ____ , ____ , ____ , ____ , ____ , ____ , ____

____

2. 30, 27, 24, 21, ____ , ____ , ____ , ____ , ____ , ____

____

A number pattern can grow or shrink by a changing amount. When this happens, look for a pattern in the changes.

Continue the pattern and write the rule.

3. 6, 7, 9, 12, 16, ____ , ____ , ____ , ____ , ____ , ____ , ____

____

4. 2, 6, 11, 15, 20, 24, 29, ____ , ____ , ____ , ____ , ____ , ____

____

Make two patterns with these starting numbers.
Write the rule.

5. 2, 4, ____ , ____ , ____ ____________________

   2, 4, ____ , ____ , ____ ____________________

6. 50, 45, ____ , ____ , ____ ____________________

   50, 45, ____ , ____ , ____ ____________________

► Number Patterns on a Calculator

7. Use a calculator to check your pattern and rule in exercises 1 and 2.

Name ____________________ Date ____________

► Continue a Growing or Shrinking Shape Pattern

The figures in this pattern grow larger and larger.

8. How does the pattern grow?

____

____

Draw the next figure in each pattern.

9. 

10. 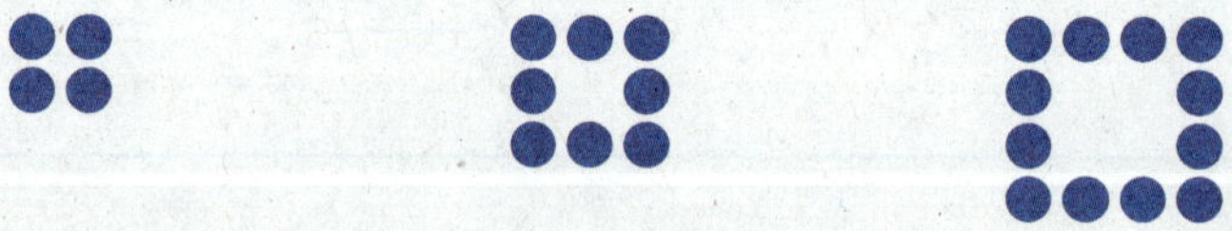

11. 

12. 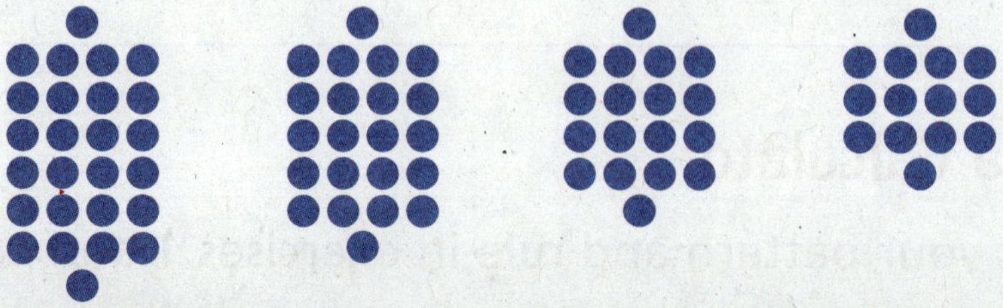

Name ______________________ Date ______________

▶ Solve a Simpler Problem

How many small triangles will be in triangle number 10? One way to solve problems like this one is to solve a simpler problem and look for a pattern.

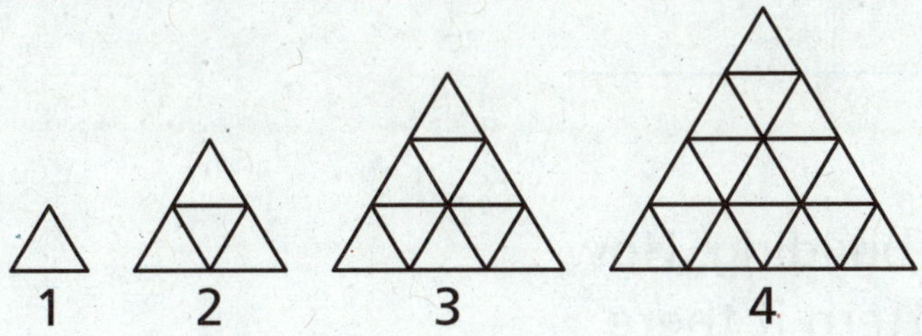

13. Complete the table to show how the number of small triangles grows.

14. Draw figure 5 in the pattern above. In the table, record the number of triangles it has.

Triangle Number	Number of Small Triangles
1	
2	
3	
4	
5	

15. Describe how the pattern grows.

____

____

____

____

16. Use this pattern to find how many small triangles are in triangle number 10. ______________________

Solve.

17. If 8 friends all shake hands with each other once, how many handshakes will take place?

____

6–3 Class Activity

Name ______________________ Date __________

▶ Solve Real-World Problems

Use a number pattern to solve each problem.

18. One cookie costs 50¢, a bag of two cookies costs 59¢, and a bag of 3 cookies costs 68¢. If the pattern continues how much will it cost to buy a bag of 6 cookies?

____

19. This is the window pattern on a building. How many windows will be in the pattern if there are 7 floors?

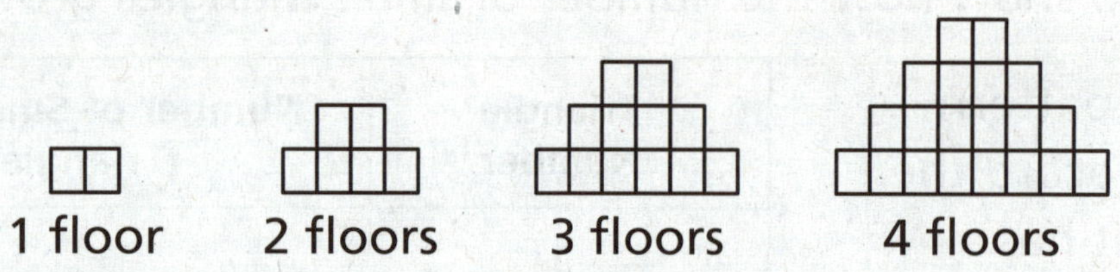

____

20. A floor has this tile pattern. If there are 4 rings around the center, how many tiles will there be in all?

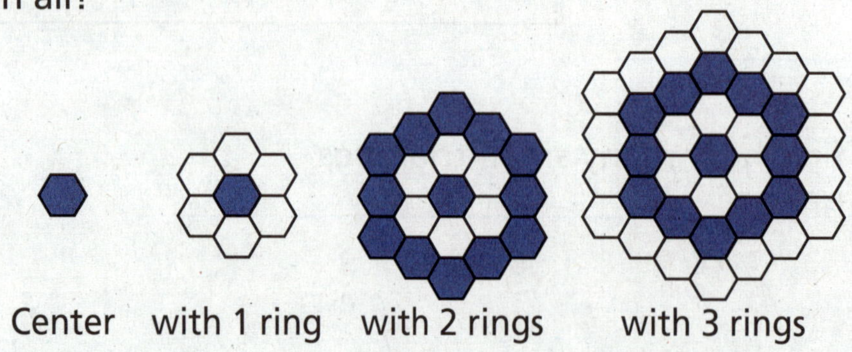

____

6
Unit Test

Name ____________ Date ____________

1. Is the second figure the result of a slide, flip, or turn?

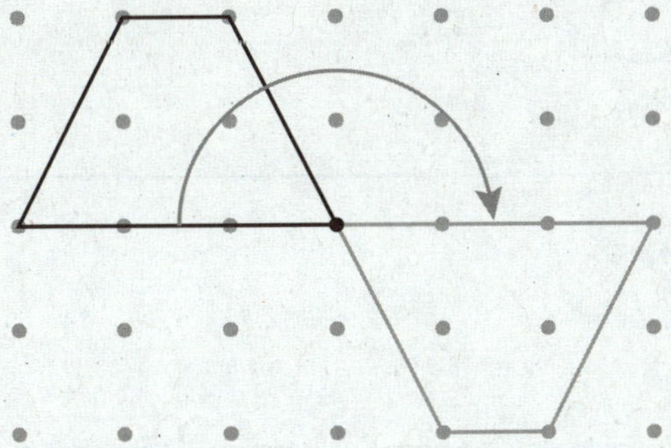

____

2. Draw the next figure in the pattern.

3. Continue the number pattern.

329329329329329 ______________________

4. Draw the next figure in the pattern.

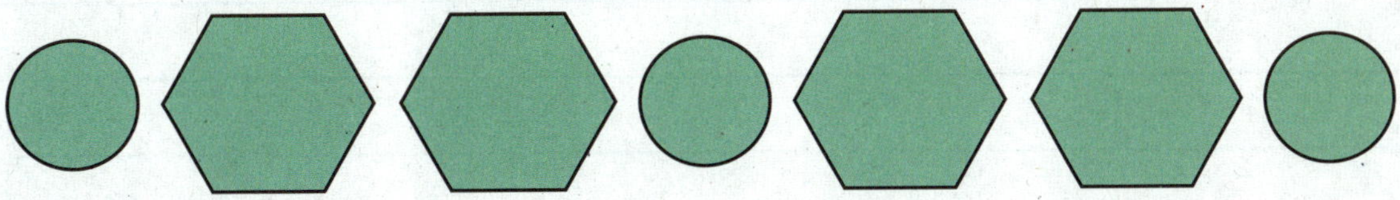

Name ______________________ Date ______________

5. Write a rule for this pattern.

□△△○□△△○

____

6. Continue this pattern.

65, 62, 59, 56, 53, 50, 47, ____ , ____ , ____ , ____ , ____

7. Continue this pattern.

12, 16, 20, 24, 28, 32, 36, ____ , ____ , ____ , ____ , ____

8. Continue this pattern.

5, 6, 8, 11, 15, 20, 26, ____ , ____ , ____ , ____ , ____

9. Write a rule for this pattern.

69, 64, 59, 54, 49, 44, 39

____

10. **Extended Response** In September, Elisa walks dogs for $1.25 per walk. In October, she charges $1.50 per walk. In November, she charges $1.75 per walk. If the pattern continues, how much will she charge per walk in December and January? Describe the pattern rule you used to solve the problem.

____

____

____

____

Name ______________________ Date ____________

► Explore Patterns with 5s

What patterns do you see below?

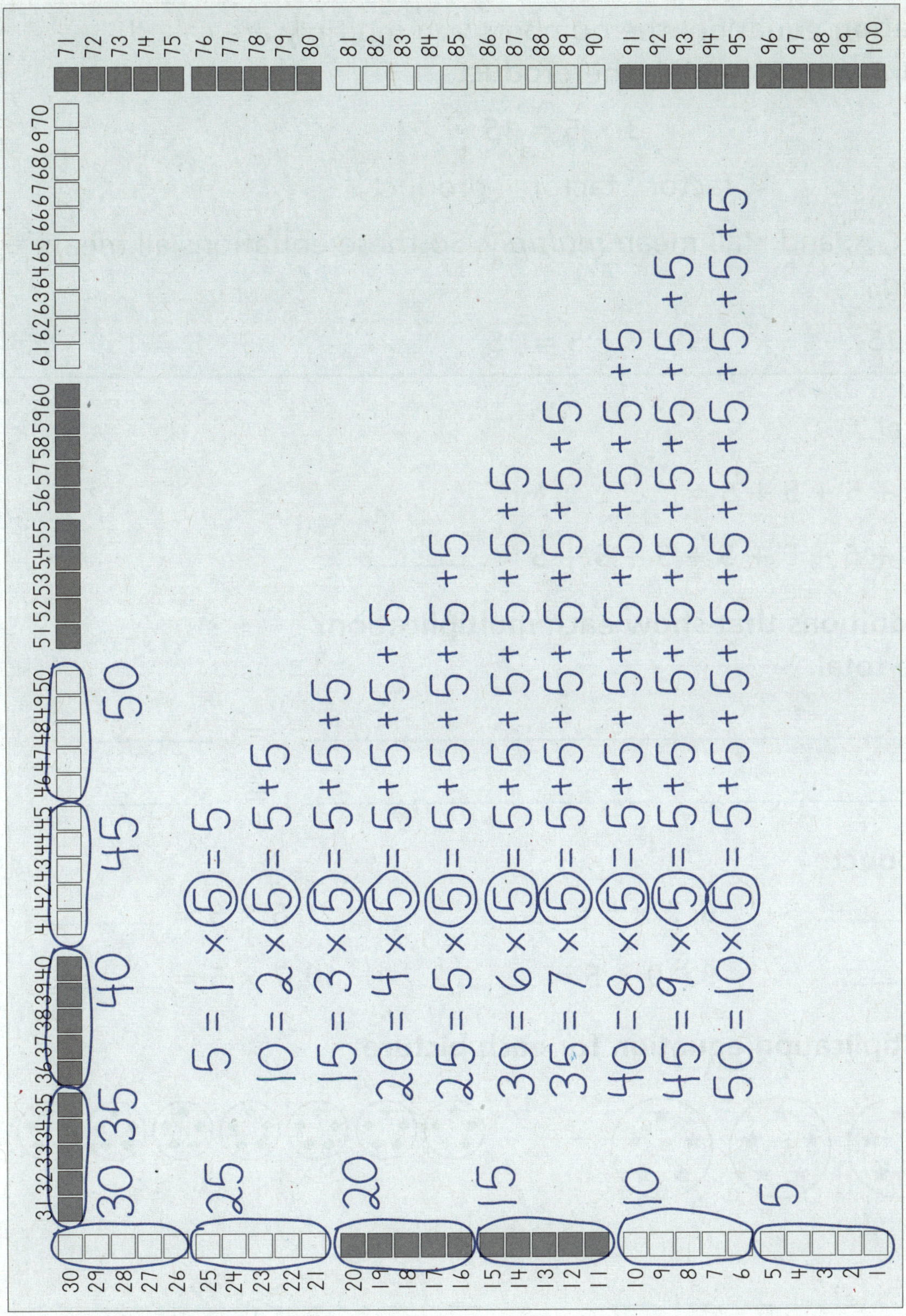

7–1 Class Activity

Name ____________________ Date ____________

Vocabulary
multiplication
factor
product

▶Practice Multiplications with 5

In a **multiplication** equation, the numbers you multiply are called **factors**. The answer, or total, is the **product**.

$$3 \times 5 = 15$$

factor (3), factor (5), product (15)

The symbols ×, *, and • all mean *multiply*. So these equations all mean the same thing.

$3 \times 5 = 15$ $3 * 5 = 15$ $3 \bullet 5 = 15$

Write each total.

1. $4 \times 5 = 5 + 5 + 5 + 5 =$ ________
2. $7 \bullet 5 = 5 + 5 + 5 + 5 + 5 + 5 + 5 =$ ________

Write the 5s additions that show each multiplication. Then write the total.

3. $6 \times 5 =$ ______________________________ = ________
4. $9 * 5 =$ ______________________________ = ________

Write each product.

5. $8 \times 5 =$ ________
6. $2 \times 5 =$ ________
7. $5 \times 5 =$ ________
8. $4 \times 5 =$ ________
9. $10 \times 5 =$ ________
10. $7 \times 5 =$ ________

Write a 5s multiplication equation for each picture.

11. 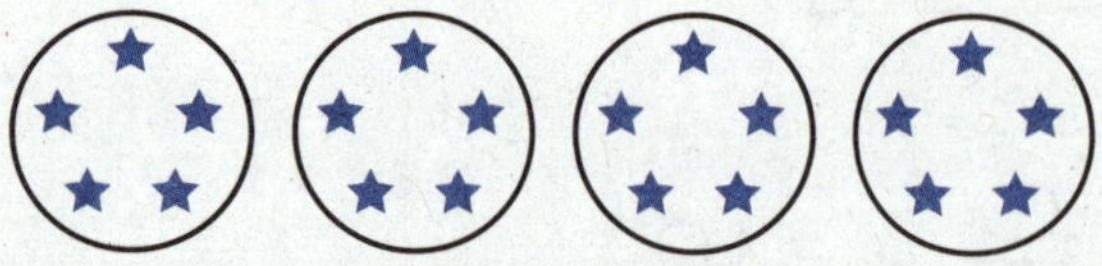

____

12. 

____

Family Letter

Dear Family,

In this unit and the next, your child will be practicing basic multiplications and divisions. *Math Expressions* incorporates studying, practicing, and testing of the basic multiplications and divisions in class. Your child is also expected to practice at home.

Study Plans Each day your child will fill out a study plan, indicating which basic multiplications and divisions he or she will study that evening. When your child has finished studying (practicing), his or her Homework Helper should sign the study plan.

4–1 Name ____ Date ____

Homework

Study Plan

5s count bys
5s multiplications

____ Homework Helper

Practice Charts Each time a new number is introduced, students' homework will include a practice chart. To practice, students can cover the products with a pencil or a strip of heavy paper. They will say the multiplications, sliding the pencil or paper down the column to see each product after saying it. Students can also start with the last problem in a column and slide up. It is important that your child studies count-bys and multiplications at least 5 minutes every night. Your child can also use these charts to practice division on the mixed up column by covering the first factor.

	In Order	Mixed Up
5s	1 × 5 = 5	9 × 5 = 45
	2 × 5 = 10	5 × 5 = 25
	3 × 5 = 15	2 × 5 = 10
	4 × 5 = 20	7 × 5 = 35
	5 × 5 = 25	4 × 5 = 20
	6 × 5 = 30	6 × 5 = 30
	7 × 5 = 35	10 × 5 = 50
	8 × 5 = 40	8 × 5 = 40
	9 × 5 = 45	1 × 5 = 5
	10 × 5 = 50	3 × 5 = 15

To help students understand the concept of multiplication, the *Math Expressions* program presents three ways to think about multiplication. They are described on the back of this letter.

Family Letter

- **Repeated groups:** Multiplication can be used to find the total in repeated groups of the same size. In early lessons, students circle the group size in repeated-groups equations to help keep track of which factor is the group size and which is the number of groups.

4 groups of bananas

$4 \times \textcircled{3} = 3 + 3 + 3 + 3 = 12$

- **Arrays:** Multiplication can be used to find the total number of items in an *array*—an arrangement of objects into rows and columns.

5 columns

2 rows  2-by-5 array

2 rows of pennies $= 2 \times 5 = 10$

- **Area:** Multiplication can be used to find the area of a rectangle.

3 units 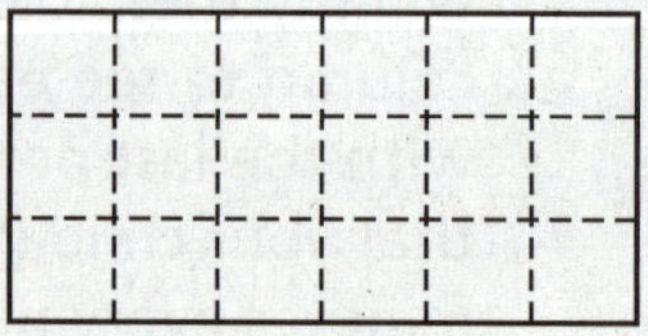

6 units

Area: 3 units × 6 units = 18 square units

Please call if you have any questions or comments.

Thank you.

Sincerely,
Your child's teacher

Carta a la familia

Estimada familia:

En esta unidad y la unidad que sigue, su niño va a practicar las multiplicaciones y divisiones básicas. *Math Expressions* incorpora en la clase el estudio, la práctica y la evaluación de las multiplicaciones y divisiones básicas. También se espera que su niño practique en casa.

Planes de estudio Todos los días su niño va a completar un plan de estudio, que indica cuáles multiplicaciones y divisiones debe estudiar esa noche. Cuando su niño haya terminado de estudiar (practicar), la persona que lo ayude debe firmar el plan de estudio.

4–1 Name ______ Date ______

Homework

Study Plan

5s count bys
5s multiplications

______
Homework Helper

Tablas de práctica Cada vez que se presente un número nuevo, la tarea de los estudiantes incluirá una tabla de práctica. Para practicar, los estudiantes pueden cubrir los productos con un lápiz o una tira de papel grueso. Los niños dicen la multiplicación y deslizan el lápiz o el papel hacia abajo para revelar el producto después de decirlo. También pueden empezar con el último problema de la columna y deslizar el lápiz o el papel hacia arriba. Es importante que su niño practique el conteo y la multiplicación por lo menos 5 minutos cada noche. Su niño también puede usar estas tablas para practicar la división en la columna de productos desordenados cubriendo el primer factor.

	En orden	Desordenados
5	1 × 5 = 5	9 × 5 = 45
	2 × 5 = 10	5 × 5 = 25
	3 × 5 = 15	2 × 5 = 10
	4 × 5 = 20	7 × 5 = 35
	5 × 5 = 25	4 × 5 = 20
	6 × 5 = 30	6 × 5 = 30
	7 × 5 = 35	10 × 5 = 50
	8 × 5 = 40	8 × 5 = 40
	9 × 5 = 45	1 × 5 = 5
	10 × 5 = 50	3 × 5 = 15

Para ayudar a los estudiantes a comprender el concepto de la multiplicación, el programa *Math Expressions* presenta tres maneras de pensar en la multiplicación. Éstas se describen a continuación.

Carta a la familia

- **Grupos repetidos:** La multiplicación se puede usar para hallar el total con grupos del mismo tamaño que se repiten. Cuando empiezan a trabajar con ecuaciones de grupos repetidos, los estudiantes rodean con un círculo el tamaño del grupo en las ecuaciones, para recordar cuál factor representa el tamaño del grupo y cuál representa el número de grupos.

4 grupos de bananas

$4 \times (3) = 3 + 3 + 3 + 3 = 12$

- **Matrices:** Se puede usar la multiplicación para hallar el número total de objetos en una *matriz,* es decir, una disposición de objetos en filas y columnas.

5 columnas

2 filas

matriz de 2 por 5

2 filas de monedas de un centavo $= 2 \times 5 = 10$

- **Área:** Se puede usar la multiplicación para hallar el área de un rectángulo.

3 unidades

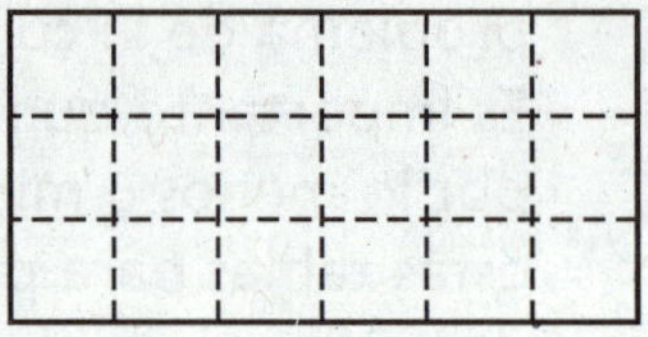

6 unidades

Área: 3 unidades $\times$ 6 unidades $=$ 18 unidades cuadradas

Si tiene alguna duda o comentario, por favor comuníquese conmigo. Gracias.

Atentamente,
El maestro de su niño

7–2 Class Activity

Name ______________________ Date ______________

Vocabulary

repeated groups

▶ Explore Repeated Groups

You can use multiplication to find the total when you have **repeated groups** of the same size.

$2 \times (5) = 5 + 5 = 10$

▶ Write Multiplication Equations

Write a multiplication equation to find the total number.

1. How many bananas?

____

2. How many toes?

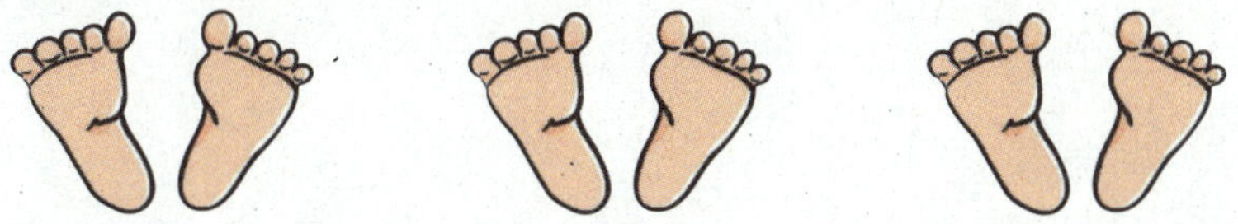

____

3. How many wheels?

____

7–2 Class Activity

Name ____________________ Date ____________

▶ Make a Math Drawing to Solve Problems

Make a drawing for each problem. Label your drawing with a multiplication equation. Then write the answer to the problem.

Show your work.

4. Sandra bought 4 bags of lemons. There were 6 lemons in each bag. How many lemons did she buy in all?

____

5. Batai baked 2 peach pies. He used 7 peaches per pie. How many peaches did he use in all?

____

6. The Fuzzy Friends pet store has 3 rabbit cages. There are 5 rabbits in each cage. How many rabbits does the store have in all?

____

7. The Paws Plus pet store has 5 rabbit cages. There are 3 rabbits in every cage. How many rabbits does the store have in all?

____

7–2 Class Activity

Name ____________________ Date ____________

Vocabulary
Equal Shares Drawing

►Explore Equal Shares Drawings

Here is a problem with repeated groups. Read the problem, and think about how you would solve it.

Ms. Thomas bought 4 bags of oranges. Each bag contained 5 oranges. How many oranges did she buy in all?

You could also find the answer to this problem by making an **Equal Shares Drawing**.

Think:

(5) (5) (5) (5)
bags of oranges
4 × (5) = ☐

Equal Shares Drawing

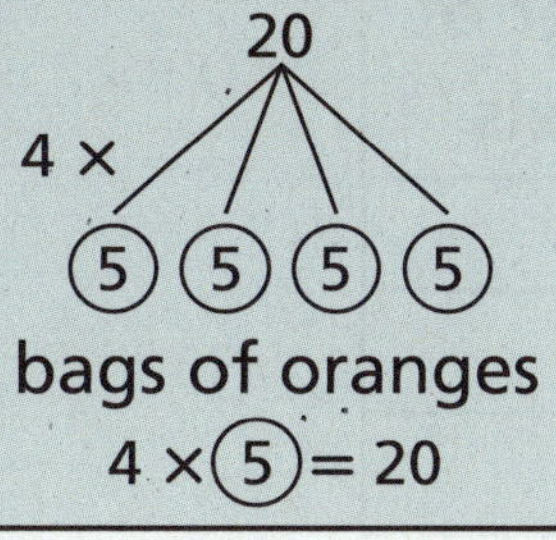

Make an Equal Shares Drawing to solve each problem.

Show your work.

8. Ms. Gonzales bought 6 boxes of pencils. There were 5 pencils in each box. How many pencils did she buy in all?

____

9. Mr. Franken made lunch for his 9 nieces and nephews. He put 5 carrot sticks on each of their plates. How many carrot sticks did he use in all?

____

7–2

Going Further

Name ______________________ Date ____________

Vocabulary
function table

▶ Function Tables

Complete each function table.

1.

Number of Tricycles	Number of Wheels
1	
2	
3	
4	
5	

2.

Number of Rabbits	Number of Ears
1	
2	
3	
4	
5	

3.

Number of Cars	Number of Wheels
1	
2	
3	
4	
5	

4.

Number of Spiders	Number of Legs
1	
2	
3	
4	
5	

7–3 Class Activity

Name Date

Signature Sheet

	Count-Bys Partner	Multiplications Partner	Divisions Partner	Multiplications Sprint	Divisions Sprint
0					
1					
2					
3					
4					
5					
6					
7					
8					
9					
10					

Name ____________ Date ____________

Study Sheet A

5s

Count-bys	Mixed Up ×	Mixed Up ÷
1 × 5 = 5	2 × 5 = 10	10 ÷ 5 = 2
2 × 5 = 10	9 × 5 = 45	35 ÷ 5 = 7
3 × 5 = 15	1 × 5 = 5	50 ÷ 5 = 10
4 × 5 = 20	5 × 5 = 25	5 ÷ 5 = 1
5 × 5 = 25	7 × 5 = 35	20 ÷ 5 = 4
6 × 5 = 30	3 × 5 = 15	15 ÷ 5 = 3
7 × 5 = 35	10 × 5 = 50	30 ÷ 5 = 6
8 × 5 = 40	6 × 5 = 30	40 ÷ 5 = 8
9 × 5 = 45	4 × 5 = 20	25 ÷ 5 = 5
10 × 5 = 50	8 × 5 = 40	45 ÷ 5 = 9

2s

Count-bys	Mixed Up ×	Mixed Up ÷
1 × 2 = 2	7 × 2 = 14	20 ÷ 2 = 10
2 × 2 = 4	1 × 2 = 2	2 ÷ 2 = 1
3 × 2 = 6	3 × 2 = 6	6 ÷ 2 = 3
4 × 2 = 8	5 × 2 = 10	16 ÷ 2 = 8
5 × 2 = 10	6 × 2 = 12	12 ÷ 2 = 6
6 × 2 = 12	8 × 2 = 16	4 ÷ 2 = 2
7 × 2 = 14	2 × 2 = 4	10 ÷ 2 = 5
8 × 2 = 16	10 × 2 = 20	8 ÷ 2 = 4
9 × 2 = 18	4 × 2 = 8	14 ÷ 2 = 7
10 × 2 = 20	9 × 2 = 18	18 ÷ 2 = 9

10s

Count-bys	Mixed Up ×	Mixed Up ÷
1 × 10 = 10	1 × 10 = 10	80 ÷ 10 = 8
2 × 10 = 20	5 × 10 = 50	10 ÷ 10 = 1
3 × 10 = 30	2 × 10 = 20	50 ÷ 10 = 5
4 × 10 = 40	8 × 10 = 80	90 ÷ 10 = 9
5 × 10 = 50	7 × 10 = 70	40 ÷ 10 = 4
6 × 10 = 60	3 × 10 = 30	100 ÷ 10 = 10
7 × 10 = 70	4 × 10 = 40	30 ÷ 10 = 3
8 × 10 = 80	6 × 10 = 60	20 ÷ 10 = 2
9 × 10 = 90	10 × 10 = 100	70 ÷ 10 = 7
10 × 10 = 100	9 × 10 = 90	60 ÷ 10 = 6

9s

Count-bys	Mixed Up ×	Mixed Up ÷
1 × 9 = 9	2 × 9 = 18	81 ÷ 9 = 9
2 × 9 = 18	4 × 9 = 36	18 ÷ 9 = 2
3 × 9 = 27	7 × 9 = 63	36 ÷ 9 = 4
4 × 9 = 36	8 × 9 = 72	9 ÷ 9 = 1
5 × 9 = 45	3 × 9 = 27	54 ÷ 9 = 6
6 × 9 = 54	10 × 9 = 90	27 ÷ 9 = 3
7 × 9 = 63	1 × 9 = 9	63 ÷ 9 = 7
8 × 9 = 72	6 × 9 = 54	72 ÷ 9 = 8
9 × 9 = 81	5 × 9 = 45	90 ÷ 9 = 10
10 × 9 = 90	9 × 9 = 81	45 ÷ 9 = 5

7–3 Class Activity

Name ________________________ Date ____________

Vocabulary
array
row
column

► Explore Arrays

An **array** is an arrangement of objects in **rows** and **columns**. You can use multiplication to find the total number of objects in an array.

2-by-5 array
5 columns

2 rows of 5 = $2 \times 5 = 10$ 2 rows 

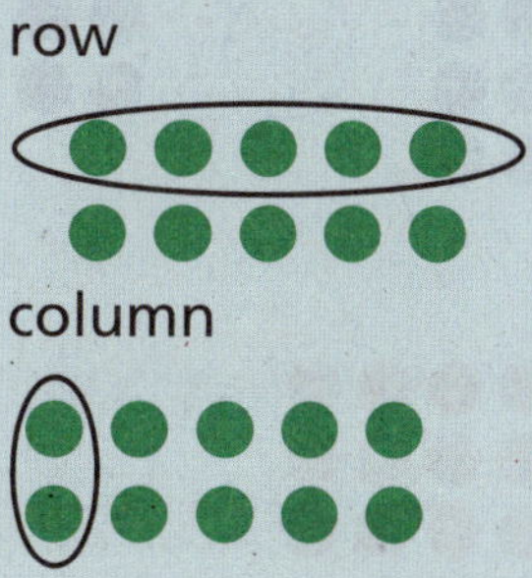

► Write Multiplication Equations

Write a multiplication equation for each array.

1. How many flowers?

____

2. How many stamps?

____

3. How many mugs?

____

4. Math Journal Write a problem that you can solve by using this array. Show how to solve your problem.

7–3 Class Activity

Name ________________________ Date ____________

▶ Compare Arrays

Without counting the dots in the array write >, < or = in the circle.

5. 

6. 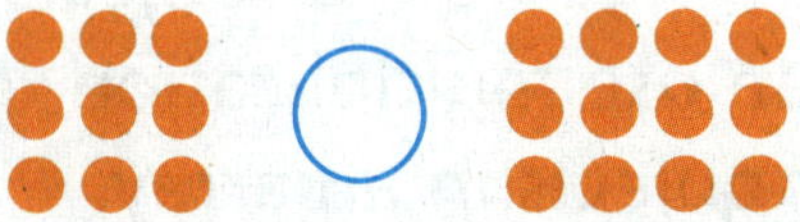

7. 

8. 

9. 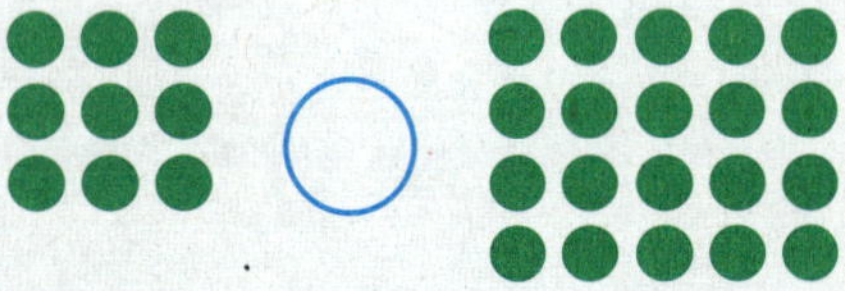

10. 

11. 

12. 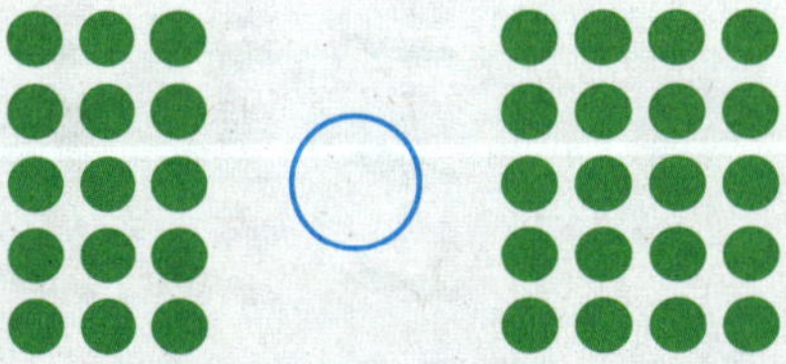

13. Create Your Own Draw two dot arrays and compare them using symbols. Then write an equation for each array to show your comparison is correct.

7–3 Class Activity

Name ______ Date ______

►Make a Math Drawing to Solve Problems

Make a drawing for each problem. Label your drawing with a multiplication equation. Then write the answer to the problem.

Show your work.

14. The clarinet section of the band marched in 6 rows, with 2 clarinet players in each row. How many clarinet players were there in all?

______

15. Mali put some crackers on a tray. She put the crackers in 3 rows, with 5 crackers per row. How many crackers did she put on the tray?

______

16. Ms. Shahin set up some chairs in 7 rows, with 5 chairs in each row. How many chairs did she set up?

______

17. Zak has a box of crayons. The crayons are arranged in 4 rows, with 6 crayons in each row. How many crayons are in the box?

______

7–3 Class Activity

Name ______________________ Date ____________

Vocabulary
Commutative Property of Multiplication

▶ Explore Commutativity

Multiplication is commutative. The **Commutative Property of Multiplication** states that you can switch the order of the factors without changing the product.

Arrays: $4 \times 5 = 5 \times 4$ **Groups:** $4 \times ⑤ = 5 \times ④$

$4 \times 5 = 20$ $5 \times 4 = 20$ $4 \times ⑤ = 20$ $5 \times ④ = 20$

▶ Solve Problems Using the Commutative Property

Make a math drawing for each problem. Write a multiplication equation and the answer to the problem.

18. Katie bought some stickers. She put the stickers on her folder in 6 rows of 2. How many stickers did she buy?

____

19. Marco also bought some stickers. He put the stickers on his folder in 2 rows of 6. How many stickers did he buy?

____

20. On Monday, Juan helped Ms. Chang clean the art cabinet. He packed jars of paint in 3 boxes, with 7 jars per box. How many jars of paint did Juan put away?

____

21. On Tuesday, Therese helped Ms. Chang. She packed jars of paint in 7 boxes, with 3 jars per box. How many jars of paint did Therese put away?

____

Family Letter

Dear Family,

In addition to practice charts for the basic multiplications and divisions for each of the numbers 1 through 10, your child will bring home a variety of other practice materials over the next several weeks.

- **Home Study Sheets:** A Home Study Sheet includes 3 or 4 practice charts on one page. Your child can use the Home Study Sheets to practice all the count-bys, multiplications, and divisions for a number or to practice just the ones he or she doesn't know for that number. The Homework Helper can then use the sheet to test (or retest) your child. The Homework Helper should check with your child to see which basic multiplications or divisions he or she is ready to be tested on. The helper should mark any missed problems lightly with a pencil.

  If your child gets all the answers in a column correct, the helper should sign that column on the Home Signature Sheet. When signatures are on all the columns of the Home Signature Sheet, your child should bring the sheet to school.

Home Study Sheet A

5s			2s		
Count-bys	Mixed Up ×	Mixed Up ÷	Count-bys	Mixed Up ×	Mixed Up ÷
1 × 5 = 5	2 × 5 = 10	10 ÷ 5 = 2	1 × 2 = 2	7 × 2 = 14	20 ÷ 2 = 10
2 × 5 = 10	9 × 5 = 45	35 ÷ 5 = 7	2 × 2 = 4	1 × 2 = 2	2 ÷ 2 = 1
3 × 5 = 15	1 × 5 = 5	50 ÷ 5 = 10	3 × 2 = 6	3 × 2 = 6	6 ÷ 2 = 3
4 × 5 = 20	5 × 5 = 25	5 ÷ 5 = 1	4 × 2 = 8	5 × 2 = 10	16 ÷ 2 = 8
5 × 5 = 25	7 × 5 = 35	20 ÷ 5 = 4	5 × 2 = 10	6 × 2 = 12	12 ÷ 2 = 6
6 × 5 = 30	3 × 5 = 15	15 ÷ 5 = 3	6 × 2 = 12	8 × 2 = 16	4 ÷ 2 = 2
7 × 5 = 35	10 × 5 = 50	30 ÷ 5 = 6	7 × 2 = 14	2 × 2 = 4	10 ÷ 2 = 5
8 × 5 = 40	6 × 5 = 30	40 ÷ 5 = 8	8 × 2 = 16	10 × 2 = 20	8 ÷ 2 = 4
9 × 5 = 45	4 × 5 = 20	25 ÷ 5 = 5	9 × 2 = 18	4 × 2 = 8	14 ÷ 2 = 7
10 × 5 = 50	8 × 5 = 40	45 ÷ 5 = 9	10 × 2 = 20	9 × 2 = 18	18 ÷ 2 = 9

4–3 **Homework** Name ______________________ Date ________

Home Signature Sheet

	Count-Bys Homework Helper	Multiplications Homework Helper	Divisions Homework Helper
0			
1			

- **Home Check Sheets:** A Home Check Sheet includes columns of 20 multiplications and divisions in mixed order. These sheets can be used as a more challenging alternative to the Home Study Sheets.

Family Letter

- **Strategy Cards:** Students use Strategy Cards in class as flashcards, to play games, and to develop multiplication and division strategies.

Sample Multiplication Card

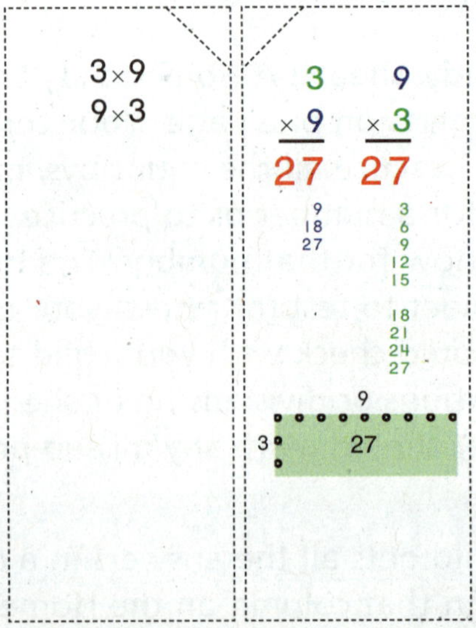

Sample Division Card

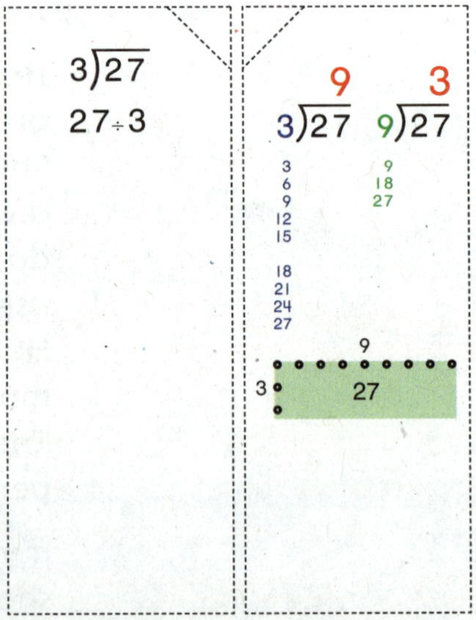

- **Games:** Near the end of this unit, students are introduced to games that provide multiplication and division practice.

Encourage your child to show you these materials and explain how they are used. Make sure your child spends time practicing multiplications and divisions every evening.

Please call if you have any questions or comments.

Thank you.

Sincerely,
Your child's teacher

Carta a la familia

Estimada familia:

Además de las tablas de práctica para las multiplicaciones y divisiones básicas para cada número del 1 al 10, su niño llevará a casa una variedad de materiales de práctica en las semanas que vienen.

- **Hojas para estudiar en casa:** Una hoja para estudiar en casa incluye 3 ó 4 tablas de práctica en una página. Su niño puede usar las hojas para practicar todos los conteos, multiplicaciones y divisiones de un número, o para practicar sólo las operaciones para ese número que no domine. La persona que ayude a su niño con la tarea puede usar la hoja para hacerle una prueba (o repetir una prueba). Esa persona debe hablar con su niño para decidir sobre qué multiplicaciones o divisiones básicas el niño puede hacer la prueba. La persona que ayude debe marcar ligeramente con un lápiz cualquier problema que conteste mal. Si su niño contesta bien todas las operaciones de una columna, la persona que ayude debe firmar esa columna de la hoja de firmas. Cuando todas las columnas de la hoja de firmas estén firmadas, su niño debe llevar la hoja a la escuela.

Home Study Sheet A

5s			2s		
Count-bys	Mixed Up ×	Mixed Up ÷	Count-bys	Mixed Up ×	Mixed Up ÷
1 × 5 = 5	2 × 5 = 10	10 ÷ 5 = 2	1 × 2 = 2	7 × 2 = 14	20 ÷ 2 = 10
2 × 5 = 10	9 × 5 = 45	35 ÷ 5 = 7	2 × 2 = 4	1 × 2 = 2	2 ÷ 2 = 1
3 × 5 = 15	1 × 5 = 5	50 ÷ 5 = 10	3 × 2 = 6	3 × 2 = 6	6 ÷ 2 = 3
4 × 5 = 20	5 × 5 = 25	5 ÷ 5 = 1	4 × 2 = 8	5 × 2 = 10	16 ÷ 2 = 8
5 × 5 = 25	7 × 5 = 35	20 ÷ 5 = 4	5 × 2 = 10	6 × 2 = 12	12 ÷ 2 = 6
6 × 5 = 30	3 × 5 = 15	15 ÷ 5 = 3	6 × 2 = 12	8 × 2 = 16	4 ÷ 2 = 2
7 × 5 = 35	10 × 5 = 50	30 ÷ 5 = 6	7 × 2 = 14	2 × 2 = 4	10 ÷ 2 = 5
8 × 5 = 40	6 × 5 = 30	40 ÷ 5 = 8	8 × 2 = 16	10 × 2 = 20	8 ÷ 2 = 4
9 × 5 = 45	4 × 5 = 20	25 ÷ 5 = 5	9 × 2 = 18	4 × 2 = 8	14 ÷ 2 = 7
10 × 5 = 50	8 × 5 = 40	45 ÷ 5 = 9	10 × 2 = 20	9 × 2 = 18	18 ÷ 2 = 9

4–3 Homework Name ______ Date ______

Home Signature Sheet

	Count-Bys Homework Helper	Multiplications Homework Helper	Divisions Homework Helper
0			
1			

- **Hojas de verificación:** Una hoja de verificación consta de columnas de 20 multiplicaciones y divisiones sin orden fijo. Estas hojas pueden usarse como alternativa de mayor desafío que las hojas para estudiar en casa.

Carta a la familia

- **Tarjetas de estrategias:** Los estudiantes usan las tarjetas de estrategias en la clase como ayuda de memoria, en juegos y para desarrollar estrategias para hacer multiplicaciones y divisións.

Ejemplo de tarjeta de multiplicación **Ejemplo de tarjeta de división**

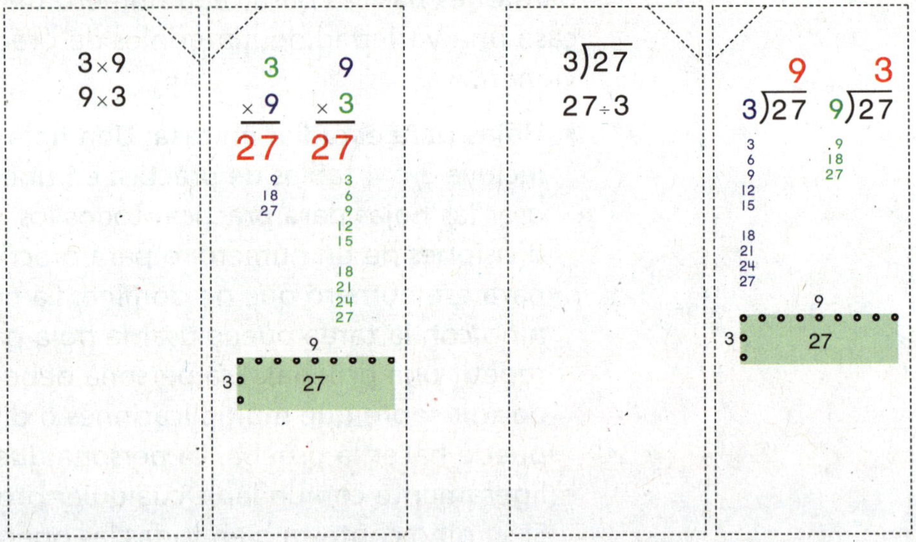

- **Juegos:** Hacia el final de esta unidad se les presentan a los estudiantes juegos para practicar la multiplicación y la división.

Anime a su niño a que le muestre a Ud. estos materiales y a que le explique cómo se usan. Asegúrese de que su niño practique la multiplicación y la división cada noche.

Si tiene alguna duda o pregunta, por favor comuníquese conmigo.

Atentamente,
El maestro de su niño

Name ______________________ Date ______________

Vocabulary
division divisor
dividend quotient

▶ Explore Division

Solve each problem.

1. Marc bought some bags of limes. There were 5 limes in each bag. He bought 15 limes altogether. How many bags did he buy?

____

2. There were 10 photographs on one wall of an art gallery. The photographs were in rows, with 5 photographs in each row. How many rows were there?

____

The problems above can be represented by multiplication equations or by **division** equations.

	Multiplication					Division				
Problem 1	□	×	(5)	=	15	15	÷	(5)	=	□
	number of groups (factor)		group size (factor)		total (product)	total (product)		group size (factor)		number of groups (factor)
Problem 2	□	×	5	=	10	10	÷	5	=	□
	number of rows (factor)		number in each row (factor)		total (product)	total (product)		number in each row (factor)		number of rows (factor)

Here are ways to write a division. The following all mean "15 divided by 5 equals 3."

$15 \div 5 = 3$ $15 / 5 = 3$ $\frac{15}{5} = 3$

$$5\overline{)15}\text{ with quotient } 3$$

3 ← quotient
5) 15 ← dividend
↑ divisor

The number you divide into is called the **dividend**. The number you divide by is called the **divisor**. The number that is the answer to a division problem is called the **quotient**.

Name ______________________ Date ______________

▶ Math Tools: Equal Shares Drawings

You can use Equal Shares Drawings to help solve division problems. Here is how you might solve problem 1 on Student Activity Book page 217.

Start with the total, 15.

$15 \div \textcircled{5} = \square$

Draw groups of 5, and connect them to the total. Count by 5s as you draw the groups. Stop when you reach 15, the total. Count how many groups you have: 3 groups.

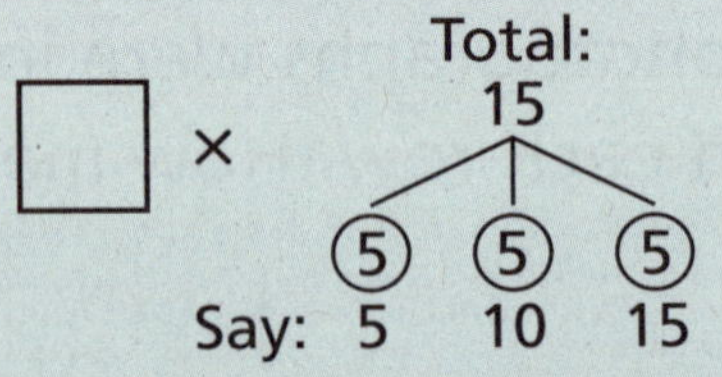

$15 \div \textcircled{5} = \boxed{3}$

You can use a similar type of drawing to find the number of rows or columns in an array. Here is how you might solve problem 2.

Start with the total, 10.

$10 \div \textcircled{5} = \square$

Draw rows of 5, and connect them to the total. Count by 5s as you draw the rows. Stop when you reach 10, the total. Count how many rows you have: 2 rows.

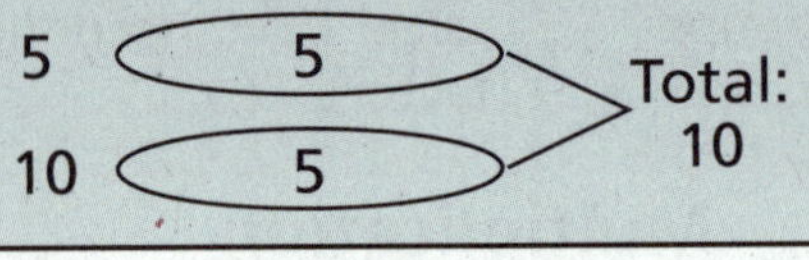

$10 \div \textcircled{5} = \boxed{2}$

Solve each problem.

3. At a bake sale, Luisa bought a lemon square for 35¢. If she paid using only nickels, how many nickels did she spend? ______________

4. Mr. Su bought a sheet of 20 stamps. There were 5 stamps in each row. How many columns of stamps were there? ______________

7–4 Class Activity

Name ______________________ Date ____________

▶ Relate Division and Multiplication Equations with 5

Find the unknown numbers.

5. $20 \div 5 = \square$ $\quad \square \times 5 = 20$ $\quad 20 \div 4 = \square$ $\quad \square \times 4 = 20$

6. $10 \div 5 = \square$ $\quad \square \times 5 = 10$ $\quad 10 \div 2 = \square$ $\quad \square \times 2 = 10$

7. $15 \div 5 = \square$ $\quad \square \times 5 = 15$ $\quad 15 \div 3 = \square$ $\quad \square \times 3 = 15$

8. $40 \div 5 = \square$ $\quad \square \times 5 = 40$ $\quad 40 \div 8 = \square$ $\quad \square \times 8 = 40$

9. $5 \div 5 = \square$ $\quad \square \times 5 = 5$ $\quad 5 \div 1 = \square$ $\quad \square \times 1 = 5$

10. $25 \div 5 = \square$ $\quad \square \times 5 = 25$ $\quad 25 \div 5 = \square$ $\quad \square \times 5 = 25$

11. $30 \div 5 = \square$ $\quad \square \times 5 = 30$ $\quad 30 \div 6 = \square$ $\quad \square \times 6 = 30$

12. $50 \div 5 = \square$ $\quad \square \times 5 = 50$ $\quad 50 \div 10 = \square$ $\quad \square \times 10 = 50$

13. $35 \div 5 = \square$ $\quad \square \times 5 = 35$ $\quad 35 \div 7 = \square$ $\quad \square \times 7 = 35$

14. $45 \div 5 = \square$ $\quad \square \times 5 = 45$ $\quad 45 \div 9 = \square$ $\quad \square \times 9 = 45$

▶ Find the Number in Each Group

Solve each problem.

15. Aziz put 15 ice cubes in 5 glasses. He put the same number of ice cubes in each glass. How many ice cubes did he put in each glass?

____

16. Lori's uncle gave her 20 stickers. She put the same number of stickers on each of 5 folders. How many stickers did she put on each folder?

____

17. **On the Back** Write a word problem for $30 \div 5$ where the 5 is the size of the group. Write another word problem where 5 is the number of groups. Explain what multiplication equations the problems relate to and why.

Name Date

7–5 Class Activity

Name ______________________ Date ______________

► Explore Patterns with 2s

What patterns do you see below?

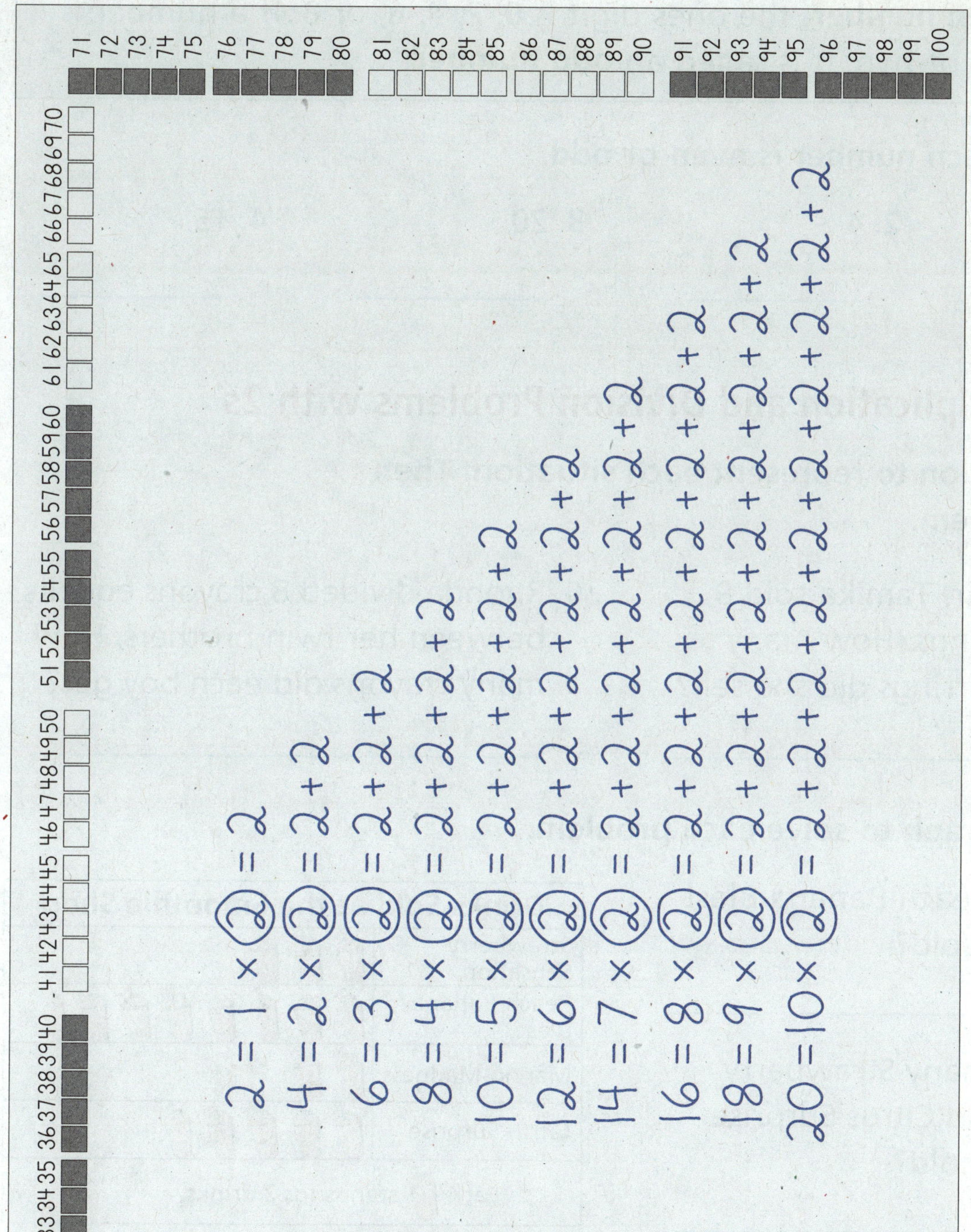

7–5 Class Activity

Name ____________________ Date ____________

Vocabulary
even number
odd number

► Even and Odd Numbers

The 2s count-bys are called *even numbers* because they are multiples of 2. In an **even number**, the ones digit is 0, 2, 4, 6, or 8. If a number is not a multiple of two, it is called an **odd number**.

Tell whether each number is even or odd.

1. 7 ________

2. 4 ________

3. 20 ________

4. 15 ________

► Solve Multiplication and Division Problems with 2s

Write an equation to represent each situation. Then solve the problem.

5. At the art fair, Tamika sold 9 pairs of earrings. How many individual earrings did she sell?

____

6. Rhonda divided 8 crayons equally between her twin brothers. How many crayons did each boy get?

____

Use the pictograph to solve each problem.

7. How many Peach-Banana Blast drinks were sold?

____

8. In all, how many Strawberry Sensation and Citrus Surprise drinks were sold?

____

9. How many more Peach-Banana Blast drinks were sold than Mango Madness drinks?

____

Name ______________________ Date ______________________

► Check Sheet 1: 5s and 2s

5s Multiplications	5s Divisions	2s Multiplications	2s Divisions
2 × 5 = 10	30 / 5 = 6	4 × 2 = 8	8 / 2 = 4
5 • 6 = 30	5 ÷ 5 = 1	2 • 8 = 16	18 ÷ 2 = 9
5 * 9 = 45	15 / 5 = 3	1 * 2 = 2	2 / 2 = 1
4 × 5 = 20	50 ÷ 5 = 10	6 × 2 = 12	16 ÷ 2 = 8
5 • 7 = 35	20 / 5 = 4	2 • 9 = 18	4 / 2 = 2
10 * 5 = 50	10 ÷ 5 = 2	2 * 2 = 4	20 ÷ 2 = 10
1 × 5 = 5	35 / 5 = 7	3 × 2 = 6	10 / 2 = 5
5 • 3 = 15	40 ÷ 5 = 8	2 • 5 = 10	12 ÷ 2 = 6
8 * 5 = 40	25 / 5 = 5	10 * 2 = 20	6 / 2 = 3
5 × 5 = 25	45 / 5 = 9	2 × 7 = 14	14 / 2 = 7
5 • 8 = 40	20 ÷ 5 = 4	2 • 10 = 20	4 ÷ 2 = 2
7 * 5 = 35	15 / 5 = 3	9 * 2 = 18	2 / 2 = 1
5 × 4 = 20	30 ÷ 5 = 6	2 × 6 = 12	8 ÷ 2 = 4
6 • 5 = 30	25 / 5 = 5	8 • 2 = 16	6 / 2 = 3
5 * 1 = 5	10 ÷ 5 = 2	2 * 3 = 6	20 ÷ 2 = 10
5 × 10 = 50	45 / 5 = 9	2 × 2 = 4	14 / 2 = 7
9 • 5 = 45	35 ÷ 5 = 7	1 • 2 = 2	10 ÷ 2 = 5
5 * 2 = 10	50 ÷ 5 = 10	2 * 4 = 8	16 ÷ 2 = 8
3 × 5 = 15	40 / 5 = 8	5 × 2 = 10	12 / 2 = 6
5 • 5 = 25	5 ÷ 5 = 1	7 • 2 = 14	18 ÷ 2 = 9

7–6 Class Activity

Name ______________________ Date ______________

▶ Sprints for 5s

As your teacher reads each multiplication or division, write your answer on the lines.

× 5	÷ 5
a. ________	a. ________
b. ________	b. ________
c. ________	c. ________
d. ________	d. ________
e. ________	e. ________
f. ________	f. ________
g. ________	g. ________
h. ________	h. ________
i. ________	i. ________
j. ________	j. ________

Name ______________________ Date ______________

▶Explore Patterns with 10s

What patterns do you see below?

7–6 Class Activity

Name ____________________ Date ____________

► Solve Problems with 10s

Solve each problem.

Show your work.

1. Raymundo has 9 dimes. How many cents does he have?

____

2. Yoko has some dimes in her pocket, and no other coins. She has a total of 70¢. How many dimes does she have?

____

3. Jonah picked 40 strawberries. He gave them to 10 of his friends. Each friend got the same number of strawberries. How many strawberries did each friend get?

____

4. There are 10 Space Command trading cards in each pack. Zoe bought 5 packs of cards. How many cards did she buy in all?

____

5. There were 80 students in the auditorium. There were 10 students in each row. How many rows of students were there?

____

6. **On the Back** Write a word problem that can be solved using the division $60 \div 10$. Then write a related multiplication word problem.

Name Date

Name Date

► Check Sheet 2: 10s and 9s

10s Multiplications	10s Divisions	9s Multiplications	9s Divisions
9 × 10 = 90	100 / 10 = 10	3 × 9 = 27	27 / 9 = 3
10 • 3 = 30	50 ÷ 10 = 5	9 • 7 = 63	9 ÷ 9 = 1
10 * 6 = 60	70 / 10 = 7	10 * 9 = 90	81 / 9 = 9
1 × 10 = 10	40 ÷ 10 = 4	5 × 9 = 45	45 ÷ 9 = 5
10 • 4 = 40	80 / 10 = 8	9 • 8 = 72	90 / 9 = 10
10 * 7 = 70	60 ÷ 10 = 6	9 * 1 = 9	36 ÷ 9 = 4
8 × 10 = 80	10 / 10 = 1	2 × 9 = 18	18 / 9 = 2
10 • 10 = 100	20 ÷ 10 = 2	9 • 9 = 81	63 ÷ 9 = 7
5 * 10 = 50	90 / 10 = 9	6 * 9 = 54	54 / 9 = 6
10 × 2 = 20	30 / 10 = 3	9 × 4 = 36	72 / 9 = 8
10 • 5 = 50	80 ÷ 10 = 8	9 • 5 = 45	27 ÷ 9 = 3
4 * 10 = 40	70 / 10 = 7	4 * 9 = 36	45 / 9 = 5
10 × 1 = 10	100 ÷ 10 = 10	9 × 1 = 9	63 ÷ 9 = 7
3 • 10 = 30	90 / 10 = 9	3 • 9 = 27	72 / 9 = 8
10 * 8 = 80	60 ÷ 10 = 6	9 * 8 = 72	54 ÷ 9 = 6
7 × 10 = 70	30 / 10 = 3	7 × 9 = 63	18 / 9 = 2
6 • 10 = 60	10 ÷ 10 = 1	6 • 9 = 54	90 ÷ 9 = 10
10 * 9 = 90	40 ÷ 10 = 4	9 * 9 = 81	9 ÷ 9 = 1
10 × 10 = 100	20 / 10 = 2	10 × 9 = 90	36 / 9 = 4
2 • 10 = 20	50 ÷ 10 = 5	2 • 9 = 18	81 ÷ 9 = 9

Name ________________ Date ________________

► Explore Patterns with 9s

What patterns do you see below?

Name ______________________ Date ______________

▶ Math Tools: Quick 9s Multiplication

You can use the Quick 9s method to help you multiply by 9. Open your hands and turn them so they are facing you. Imagine that your fingers are numbered like this.

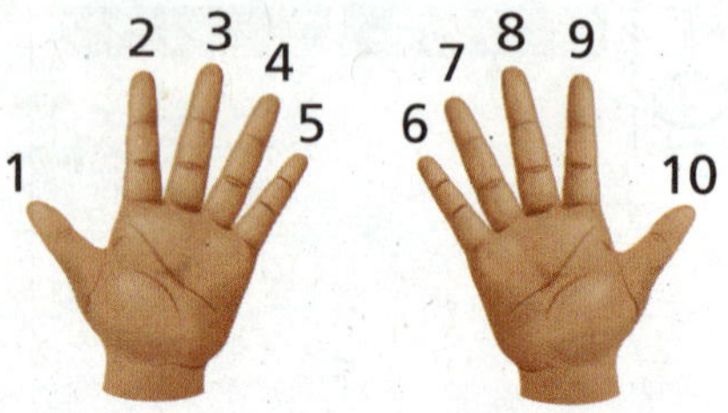

To find a number times 9, bend down the finger for that number. For example, to find 4×9, bend down your fourth finger.

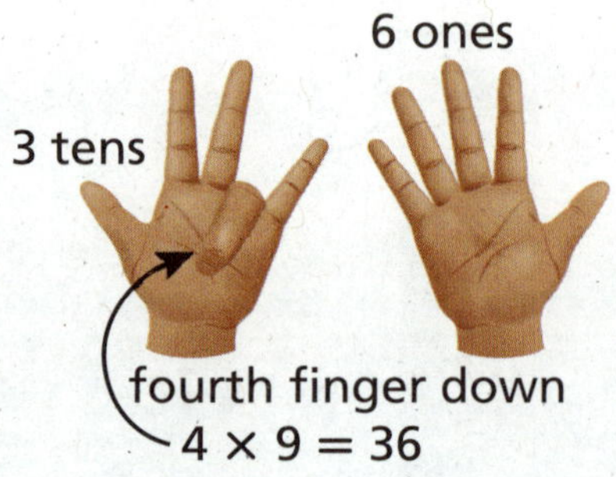

The fingers to the left of your bent finger are the tens. The fingers to the right are the ones. For this problem, there are 3 tens and 6 ones, so $4 \times 9 = 36$.

Why does this work?
Because $4 \times 9 = 4 \times (10 - 1) = 40 - 4 = 36$

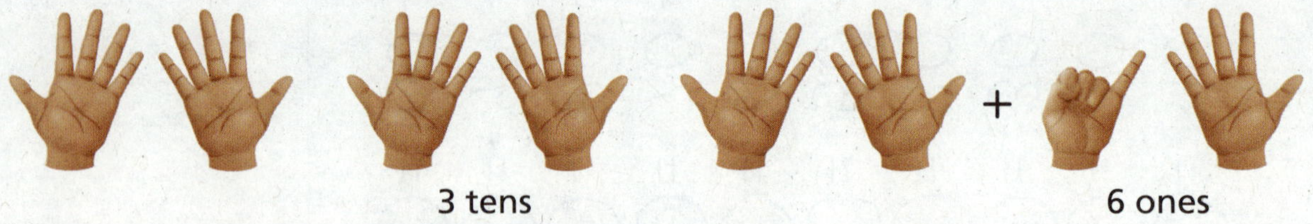

You could show 3 tens quickly by raising the first 3 fingers as shown above.

▶ Math Tools: Quick 9s Division

You can also use Quick 9s to help you divide by 9. For example, to find $72 \div 9$, show 72 on your fingers.

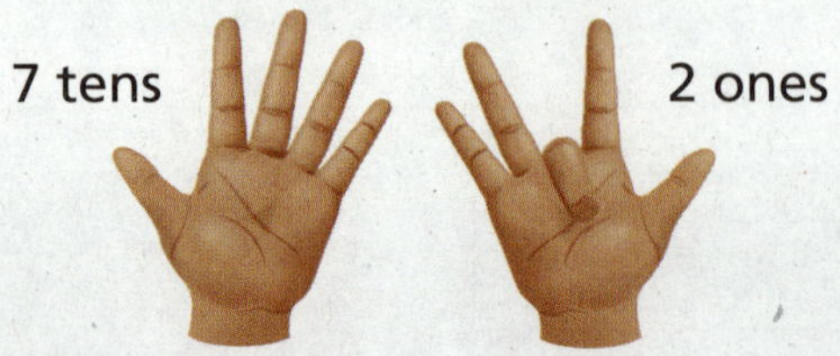

Your eighth finger is down, so $72 \div 9 = 8$.
$8 \times 9 = 80 - 8 = 72$

7–8 Class Activity

Name ____________________ Date ____________

► Sprints for 2s

As your teacher reads each multiplication or division, write your answer in the space provided.

× 2	÷ 2
a. ________	a. ________
b. ________	b. ________
c. ________	c. ________
d. ________	d. ________
e. ________	e. ________
f. ________	f. ________
g. ________	g. ________
h. ________	h. ________
i. ________	i. ________
j. ________	j. ________

Name ____________________ Date ____________________

▶ Check Sheet 3: 2s, 5s, 9s, and 10s

2s, 5s, 9s, 10s Multiplications	2s, 5s, 9s, 10s Multiplications	2s, 5s, 9s, 10s Divisions	2s, 5s, 9s, 10s Divisions
2 × 10 = 20	5 × 10 = 50	18 / 2 = 9	36 / 9 = 4
10 • 5 = 50	10 • 9 = 90	50 ÷ 5 = 10	70 ÷ 10 = 7
9 * 6 = 54	4 * 10 = 40	72 / 9 = 8	18 / 2 = 9
7 × 10 = 70	2 × 9 = 18	60 ÷ 10 = 6	45 ÷ 5 = 9
2 • 3 = 6	5 • 3 = 15	12 / 2 = 6	45 / 9 = 5
5 * 7 = 35	6 * 9 = 54	30 ÷ 5 = 6	30 ÷ 10 = 3
9 × 10 = 90	10 × 3 = 30	18 / 9 = 2	6 / 2 = 3
6 • 10 = 60	3 • 2 = 6	50 ÷ 10 = 5	50 ÷ 5 = 10
8 * 2 = 16	5 * 8 = 40	14 / 2 = 7	27 / 9 = 3
5 × 6 = 30	9 × 9 = 81	25 / 5 = 5	70 / 10 = 7
9 • 5 = 45	10 • 4 = 40	81 ÷ 9 = 9	20 ÷ 2 = 10
8 * 10 = 80	9 * 2 = 18	20 / 10 = 2	45 / 5 = 9
2 × 1 = 2	5 × 1 = 5	8 ÷ 2 = 4	54 ÷ 9 = 6
3 • 5 = 15	9 • 6 = 54	45 / 5 = 9	80 / 10 = 8
4 * 9 = 36	10 * 1 = 10	63 ÷ 9 = 7	16 ÷ 2 = 8
3 × 10 = 30	7 × 2 = 14	30 / 10 = 3	15 / 5 = 3
2 • 6 = 12	6 • 5 = 30	10 ÷ 2 = 5	90 ÷ 9 = 10
4 * 5 = 20	8 * 9 = 72	40 ÷ 5 = 8	100 ÷ 10 = 10
9 × 7 = 63	10 × 6 = 60	9 / 9 = 1	12 / 2 = 6
1 • 10 = 10	2 • 8 = 16	50 ÷ 10 = 5	35 ÷ 5 = 7

Name ____________________ Date ____________

▶ Solve Word Problems with 2s, 5s, 9s, and 10s

Write an equation to represent each problem. Then solve the problem.

1. Ian planted tulip bulbs in an array with 5 rows and 10 columns. How many bulbs did he plant?

   ____

2. Erin gave 30 basketball cards to her 5 cousins. Each cousin got the same number of cards. How many cards did each cousin get?

   ____

3. Martina bought 7 cans of racquetballs. There were 2 balls per can. How many racquetballs did she buy in all?

   ____

4. The 27 students in the orchestra stood in rows for their school picture. There were 9 students in every row. How many rows of students were there?

   ____

7–8

Class Activity

Name ______________________ Date ______________

▶ Math Tools: Fast-Array Drawings

When you solve a word problem involving an array, you can save time by making a Fast-Array drawing. This type of drawing shows the number of items in each row and column, but does not show every single item.

Here is how you might use a Fast-Array drawing for problem 1 on Student Activity Book page 235.

Show the number of rows and the number of columns. Make a box in the center to show that you don't know the total.

Here are three ways to find the total.

- Find 5 × 10.
- Use 10s count-bys to find the total in 5 rows of 10: 10, 20, 30, 40, 50.
- Use 5s count-bys to find the total in 10 rows of 5: 5, 10, 15, 20, 25, 30, 35, 40, 45, 50.

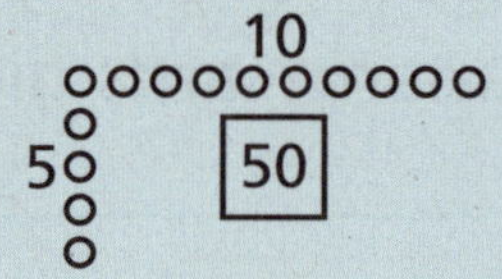

Here is how you might use a Fast-Array drawing for problem 4.

Show the number in each row and the total. Make a box to show that you don't know the number of rows.

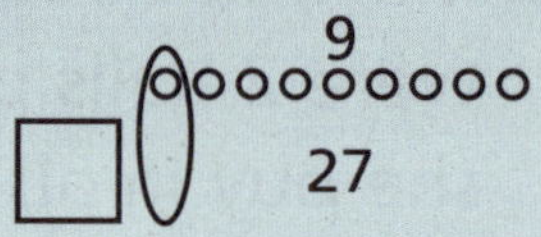

Here are two ways to find the number of rows.

- Find 27 ÷ 9 or solve □ × 9 = 27.
- Count by 9s until you reach 27: 9, 18, 27.

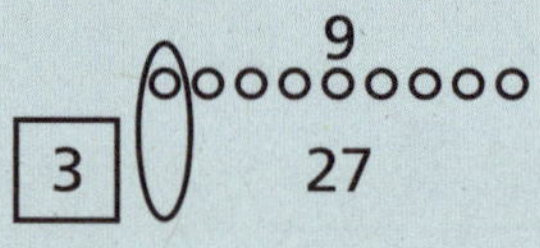

Math Journal **Make a Fast-Array Drawing to solve each problem.**

5. Beth planted tulip bulbs in an array with 9 rows and 6 columns. How many bulbs did she plant?

____

6. The 36 students in the chorus stood in 4 rows for their school picture. How many students were in each row?

____

7–9 Class Activity

Name ________________ Date ________________

▶ Sprints for 10s

As your teacher reads each multiplication or division, write your answer in the space provided.

× 10	÷ 10
a. ________	a. ________
b. ________	b. ________
c. ________	c. ________
d. ________	d. ________
e. ________	e. ________
f. ________	f. ________
g. ________	g. ________
h. ________	h. ________
i. ________	i. ________
j. ________	j. ________

7–9
Class Activity

Name ____________________ Date ____________

► Explore Patterns with 3s

What patterns do you see below?

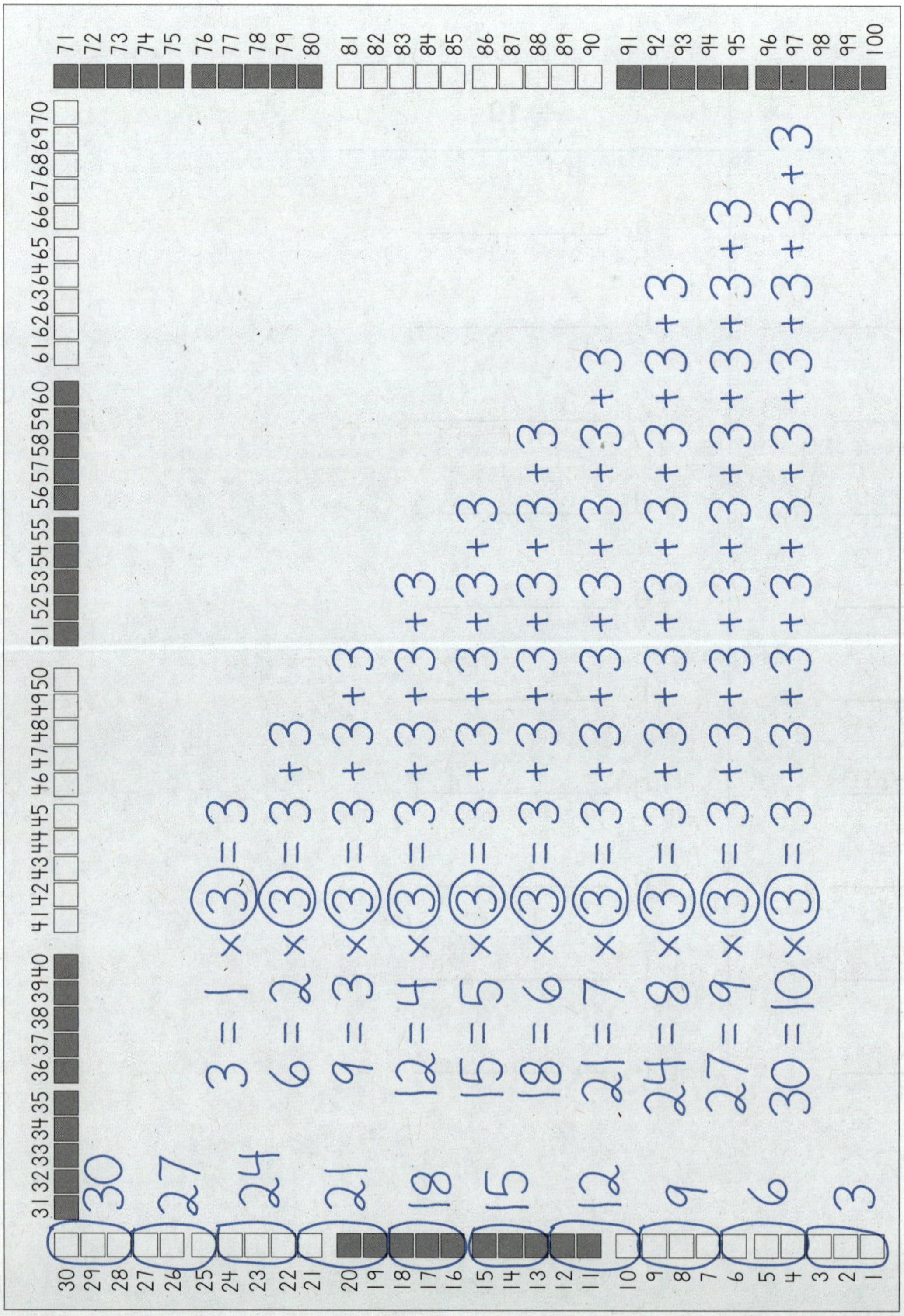

7–9 Class Activity

Name ______________________ Date ______________

▶ Use the 5s Shortcut for 3s

Write the 3s count-bys to find the total.

1. How many sides are in 8 triangles?

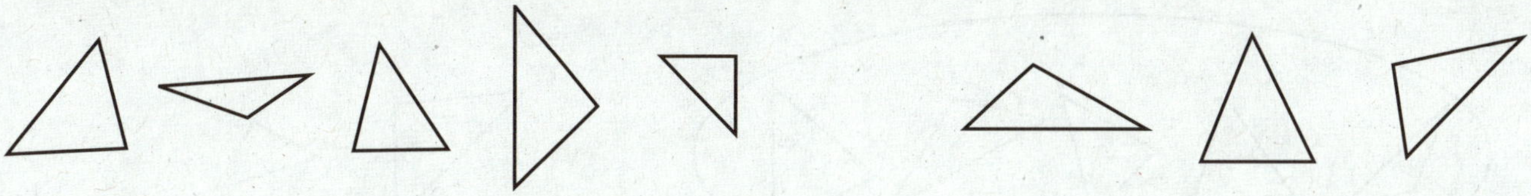

2. How many wheels are on 6 tricycles?

3. How many legs are on 7 tripods?

Name ________________________ Date ____________

Find the total by starting with the fifth count-by and counting by 3s from there.

4. How many sides are in 7 triangles?

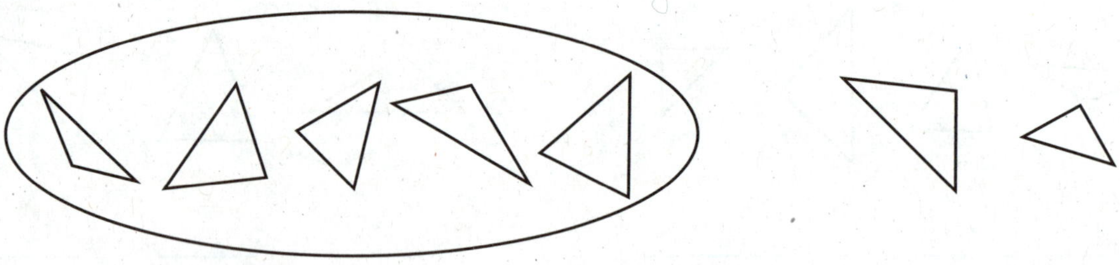

___ ___ ___

5. How many wheels are on 9 tricycles?

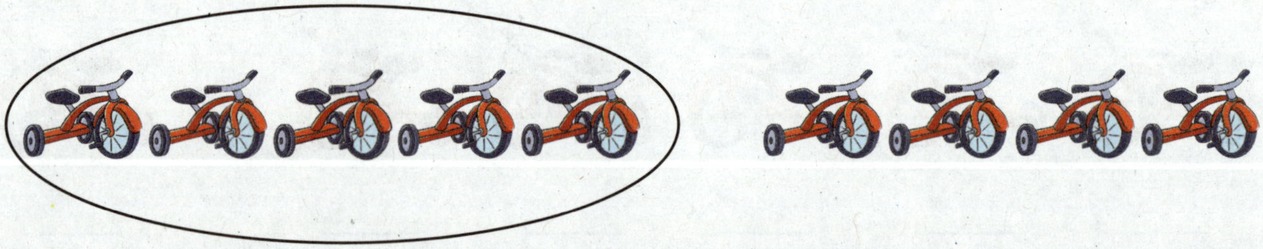

___ ___ ___ ___ ___

6. How many legs are on 8 tripods?

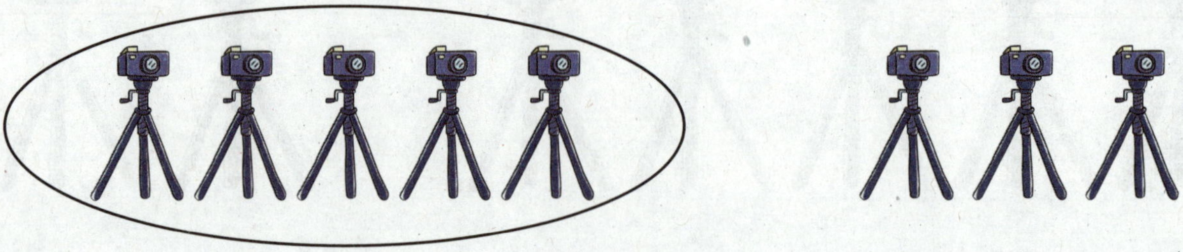

___ ___ ___ ___

Name Date

►Represent Numbers in Different Ways

You can represent numbers in different ways. Here are some equivalent expressions for 9.

3 × 3	81 ÷ 9	5 + 4	19 − 10	2 × 3 + 3
5 + 3 + 1	9 × 1	18 − 9	63 ÷ 7	3 + 6
20 − 11	4 × 2 + 1	54 ÷ 6	9 + 0	14 − 5

Circle the expression which does not represent the number given.

1. 8

   2 × 4   5 + 4   72 ÷ 9

2. 10

   2 × 5   40 ÷ 4   28 − 17

3. 18

   2 × 8   28 − 10   9 + 9

4. 30

   6 × 5   50 − 20   15 + 16

5. 35

   8 × 5   29 + 6   40 − 5

6. 40

   10 × 4   8 × 5   20 + 21

7. 54

   51 + 3   9 × 6   56 − 3

8. 72

   9 × 7   69 + 3   9 × 8

Name ______________________ Date ______________

Write 3 equivalent expressions for each number.

9. 2

____

____

____

10. 3

____

____

____

11. 5

____

____

____

12. 24

____

____

____

13. 36

____

____

____

14. 50

____

____

____

15. 63

____

____

____

16. 100

____

____

____

Name ____________________ Date ____________________

Study Sheet B

3s		
Count-bys	**Mixed Up ×**	**Mixed Up ÷**
1 × 3 = 3	5 × 3 = 15	27 ÷ 3 = 9
2 × 3 = 6	1 × 3 = 3	6 ÷ 3 = 2
3 × 3 = 9	8 × 3 = 24	18 ÷ 3 = 6
4 × 3 = 12	10 × 3 = 30	30 ÷ 3 = 10
5 × 3 = 15	3 × 3 = 9	9 ÷ 3 = 3
6 × 3 = 18	7 × 3 = 21	3 ÷ 3 = 1
7 × 3 = 21	9 × 3 = 27	12 ÷ 3 = 4
8 × 3 = 24	2 × 3 = 6	24 ÷ 3 = 8
9 × 3 = 27	4 × 3 = 12	15 ÷ 3 = 5
10 × 3 = 30	6 × 3 = 18	21 ÷ 3 = 7

4s		
Count-bys	**Mixed Up ×**	**Mixed Up ÷**
1 × 4 = 4	4 × 4 = 16	12 ÷ 4 = 3
2 × 4 = 8	1 × 4 = 4	36 ÷ 4 = 9
3 × 4 = 12	7 × 4 = 28	24 ÷ 4 = 6
4 × 4 = 16	3 × 4 = 12	4 ÷ 4 = 1
5 × 4 = 20	9 × 4 = 36	20 ÷ 4 = 5
6 × 4 = 24	10 × 4 = 40	28 ÷ 4 = 7
7 × 4 = 28	2 × 4 = 8	8 ÷ 4 = 2
8 × 4 = 32	5 × 4 = 20	40 ÷ 4 = 10
9 × 4 = 36	8 × 4 = 32	32 ÷ 4 = 8
10 × 4 = 40	6 × 4 = 24	16 ÷ 4 = 4

0s	
Count-bys	**Mixed Up ×**
1 × 0 = 0	3 × 0 = 0
2 × 0 = 0	10 × 0 = 0
3 × 0 = 0	5 × 0 = 0
4 × 0 = 0	8 × 0 = 0
5 × 0 = 0	7 × 0 = 0
6 × 0 = 0	2 × 0 = 0
7 × 0 = 0	9 × 0 = 0
8 × 0 = 0	6 × 0 = 0
9 × 0 = 0	1 × 0 = 0
10 × 0 = 0	4 × 0 = 0

1s		
Count-bys	**Mixed Up ×**	**Mixed Up ÷**
1 × 1 = 1	5 × 1 = 5	10 ÷ 1 = 10
2 × 1 = 2	7 × 1 = 7	8 ÷ 1 = 8
3 × 1 = 3	10 × 1 = 10	4 ÷ 1 = 4
4 × 1 = 4	1 × 1 = 1	9 ÷ 1 = 9
5 × 1 = 5	8 × 1 = 8	6 ÷ 1 = 6
6 × 1 = 6	4 × 1 = 4	7 ÷ 1 = 7
7 × 1 = 7	9 × 1 = 9	1 ÷ 1 = 1
8 × 1 = 8	3 × 1 = 3	2 ÷ 1 = 2
9 × 1 = 9	2 × 1 = 2	5 ÷ 1 = 5
10 × 1 = 10	6 × 1 = 6	3 ÷ 1 = 3

2×2	$\begin{array}{r} 2 \\ \times\ 3 \\ \hline \end{array}$ $\begin{array}{r} 3 \\ \times\ 2 \\ \hline \end{array}$	2×4 4×2	$\begin{array}{r} 2 \\ \times\ 5 \\ \hline \end{array}$ $\begin{array}{r} 5 \\ \times\ 2 \\ \hline \end{array}$
2×6 6×2	$\begin{array}{r} 2 \\ \times\ 7 \\ \hline \end{array}$ $\begin{array}{r} 7 \\ \times\ 2 \\ \hline \end{array}$	2×8 8×2	$\begin{array}{r} 2 \\ \times\ 9 \\ \hline \end{array}$ $\begin{array}{r} 9 \\ \times\ 2 \\ \hline \end{array}$

$10 = 2 \times 5$

$10 = 5 \times 2$

5
10

2
4
6
8
10

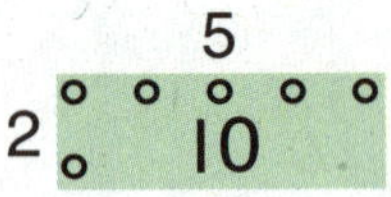

$$\begin{array}{r} 2 \\ \times\ 4 \\ \hline 8 \end{array} \qquad \begin{array}{r} 4 \\ \times\ 2 \\ \hline 8 \end{array}$$

2
4
6
8

4
8

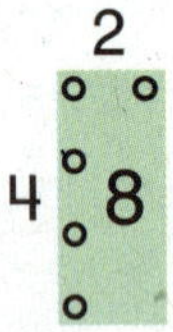

$6 = 2 \times 3$

$6 = 3 \times 2$

3
6

2
4
6

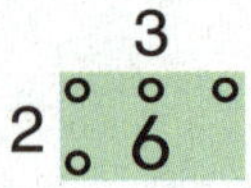

$$\begin{array}{r} 2 \\ \times\ 2 \\ \hline 4 \end{array}$$

2
4

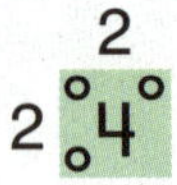

$18 = 2 \times 9$

$18 = 9 \times 2$

9
18

2
4
6
8
10

12
14
16
18

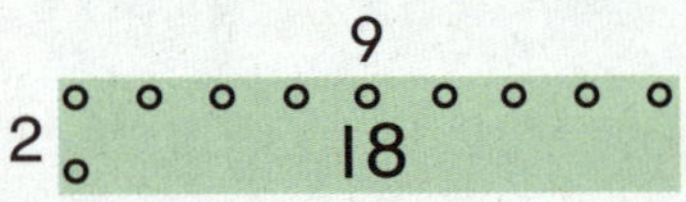

$$\begin{array}{r} 2 \\ \times\ 8 \\ \hline 16 \end{array} \qquad \begin{array}{r} 8 \\ \times\ 2 \\ \hline 16 \end{array}$$

8
16

2
4
6
8
10

12
14
16

$14 = 2 \times 7$

$14 = 7 \times 2$

7
14

2
4
6
8
10

12
14

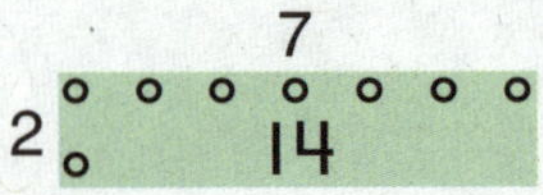

$$\begin{array}{r} 2 \\ \times\ 6 \\ \hline 12 \end{array} \qquad \begin{array}{r} 6 \\ \times\ 2 \\ \hline 12 \end{array}$$

6
12

2
4
6
8
10

12

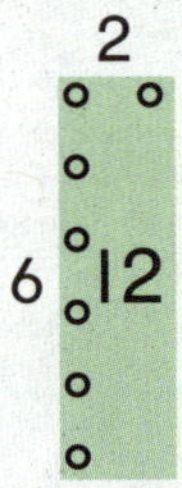

3×3	$\begin{array}{r} 3 \\ \times 4 \\ \hline \end{array}$ $\begin{array}{r} 4 \\ \times 3 \\ \hline \end{array}$	3×5 5×3	$\begin{array}{r} 3 \\ \times 6 \\ \hline \end{array}$ $\begin{array}{r} 6 \\ \times 3 \\ \hline \end{array}$
3×7 7×3	$\begin{array}{r} 3 \\ \times 8 \\ \hline \end{array}$ $\begin{array}{r} 8 \\ \times 3 \\ \hline \end{array}$	3×9 9×3	$\begin{array}{r} 4 \\ \times 4 \\ \hline \end{array}$

$18 = 3 \times 6$

$18 = 6 \times 3$

6, 12, 18

3, 6, 9, 12, 15, 18

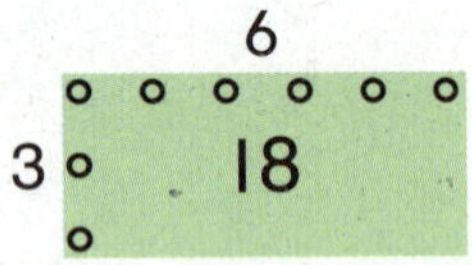

$$\begin{array}{r} 3 \\ \times\ 5 \\ \hline 15 \end{array} \qquad \begin{array}{r} 5 \\ \times\ 3 \\ \hline 15 \end{array}$$

5, 10, 15

3, 6, 9, 12, 15

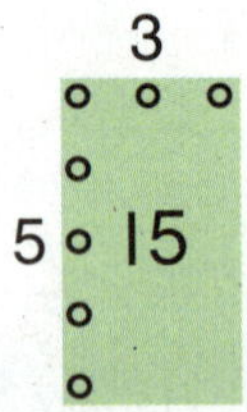

$12 = 3 \times 4$

$12 = 4 \times 3$

4, 8, 12

3, 6, 9, 12

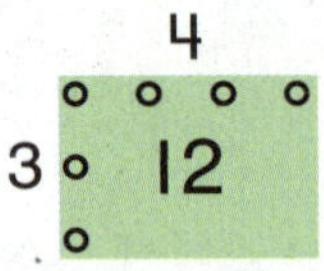

$$\begin{array}{r} 3 \\ \times\ 3 \\ \hline 9 \end{array}$$

3, 6, 9

$16 = 4 \times 4$

4, 8, 12, 16

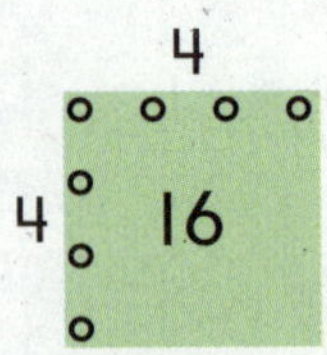

$$\begin{array}{r} 3 \\ \times\ 9 \\ \hline 27 \end{array} \qquad \begin{array}{r} 9 \\ \times\ 3 \\ \hline 27 \end{array}$$

9, 18, 27

3, 6, 9, 12, 15, 18, 21, 24, 27

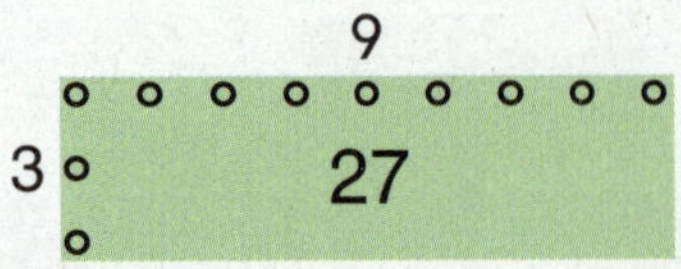

$24 = 3 \times 8$

$24 = 8 \times 3$

8, 16, 24

3, 6, 9, 12, 15, 18, 21, 24

$$\begin{array}{r} 3 \\ \times\ 7 \\ \hline 21 \end{array} \qquad \begin{array}{r} 7 \\ \times\ 3 \\ \hline 21 \end{array}$$

7, 14, 21

3, 6, 9, 12, 15, 18, 21

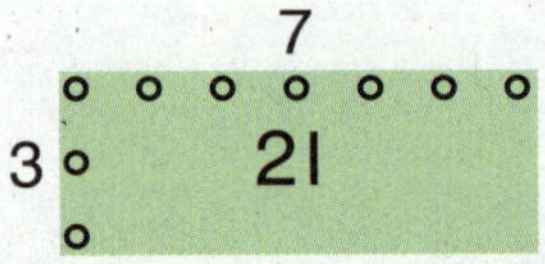

4×5 5×4	$\begin{array}{r} 4 \\ \times\ 6 \\ \hline \end{array}$ $\begin{array}{r} 6 \\ \times\ 4 \\ \hline \end{array}$	4×7 7×4	$\begin{array}{r} 4 \\ \times\ 8 \\ \hline \end{array}$ $\begin{array}{r} 8 \\ \times\ 4 \\ \hline \end{array}$
4×9 9×4	$\begin{array}{r} 5 \\ \times\ 5 \\ \hline \end{array}$	5×6 6×5	$\begin{array}{r} 5 \\ \times\ 7 \\ \hline \end{array}$ $\begin{array}{r} 7 \\ \times\ 5 \\ \hline \end{array}$

$32 = 4 \times 8$

$32 = 8 \times 4$

8	4
16	8
24	12
32	16
	20
	24
	28
	32

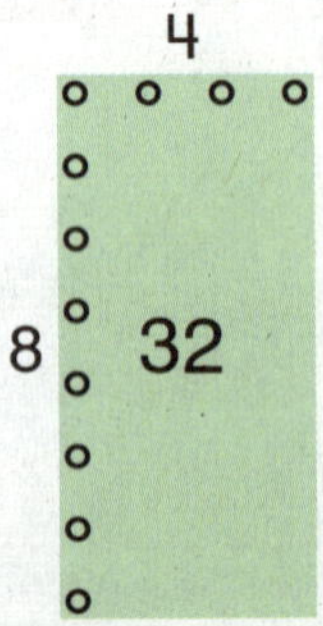

$$\begin{array}{r} 4 \\ \times\ 7 \\ \hline 28 \end{array} \qquad \begin{array}{r} 7 \\ \times\ 4 \\ \hline 28 \end{array}$$

7	4
14	8
21	12
28	16
	20
	24
	28

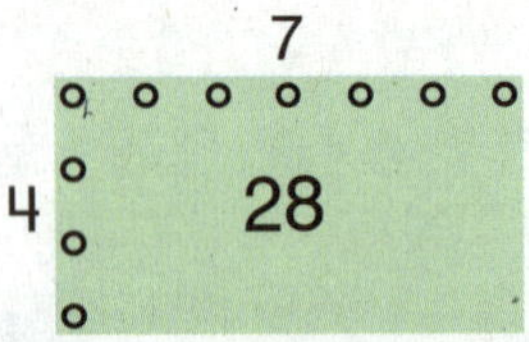

$24 = 4 \times 6$

$24 = 6 \times 4$

6	4
12	8
18	12
24	16
	20
	24

$$\begin{array}{r} 4 \\ \times\ 5 \\ \hline 20 \end{array} \qquad \begin{array}{r} 5 \\ \times\ 4 \\ \hline 20 \end{array}$$

5	4
10	8
15	12
20	16
	20

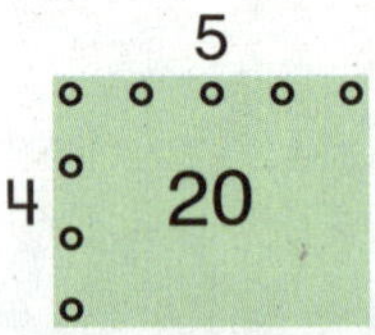

$35 = 5 \times 7$

$35 = 7 \times 5$

7	5
14	10
21	15
28	20
35	25
	30
	35

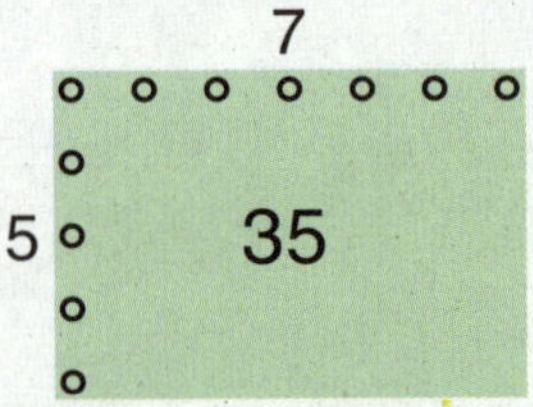

$$\begin{array}{r} 5 \\ \times\ 6 \\ \hline 30 \end{array} \qquad \begin{array}{r} 6 \\ \times\ 5 \\ \hline 30 \end{array}$$

6	5
12	10
18	15
24	20
30	25
	30

$25 = 5 \times 5$

5
10
15
20
25

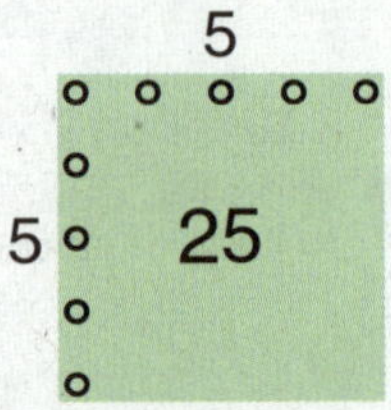

$$\begin{array}{r} 4 \\ \times 9 \\ \hline 36 \end{array} \qquad \begin{array}{r} 9 \\ \times\ 4 \\ \hline 36 \end{array}$$

9	4
18	8
27	12
36	16
	20
	24
	28
	32
	36

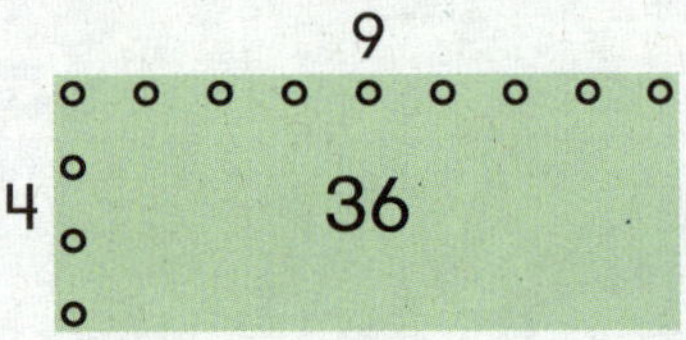

5×8 8×5	$\begin{array}{r} 5 \\ \times\ 9 \\ \hline \end{array}$ $\begin{array}{r} 9 \\ \times\ 5 \\ \hline \end{array}$	6×6	$\begin{array}{r} 6 \\ \times\ 7 \\ \hline \end{array}$ $\begin{array}{r} 7 \\ \times\ 6 \\ \hline \end{array}$
6×8 8×6	$\begin{array}{r} 6 \\ \times\ 9 \\ \hline \end{array}$ $\begin{array}{r} 9 \\ \times\ 6 \\ \hline \end{array}$	7×7	$\begin{array}{r} 7 \\ \times\ 8 \\ \hline \end{array}$ $\begin{array}{r} 8 \\ \times\ 7 \\ \hline \end{array}$

$42 = 7 \times 6$

$42 = 6 \times 7$

6	7
12	14
18	21
24	28
30	35
36	42
42	

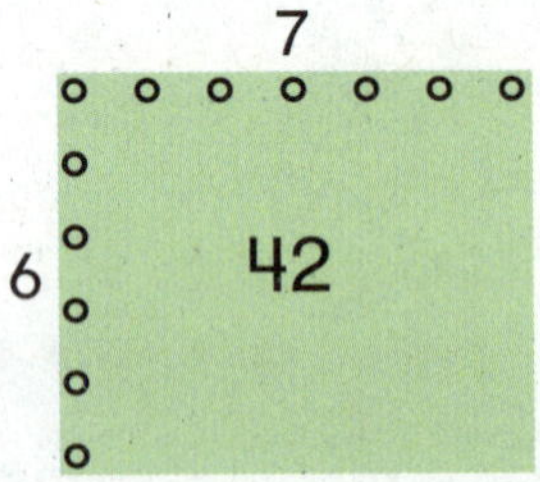

$$\begin{array}{r} 6 \\ \times\ 6 \\ \hline 36 \end{array}$$

6
12
18
24
30
36

$45 = 9 \times 5$

$45 = 5 \times 9$

5	9
10	18
15	27
20	36
25	45
30	
35	
40	
45	

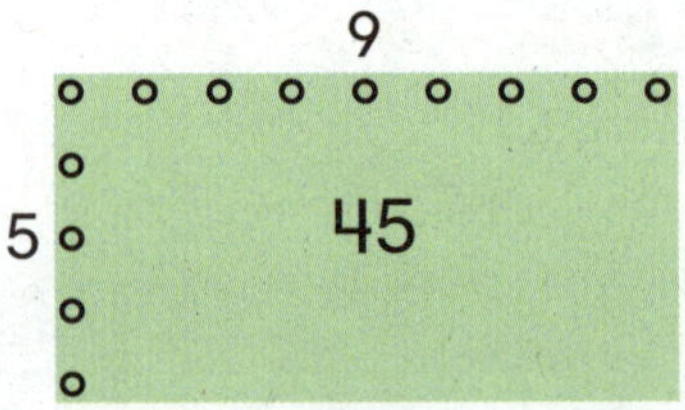

$$\begin{array}{r} 8 \\ \times\ 5 \\ \hline 40 \end{array} \qquad \begin{array}{r} 5 \\ \times\ 8 \\ \hline 40 \end{array}$$

5	8
10	16
15	24
20	32
25	40
30	
35	
40	

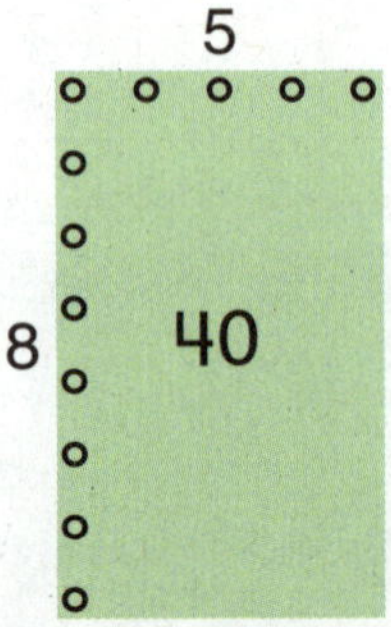

$56 = 7 \times 8$

$56 = 8 \times 7$

8	7
16	14
24	21
32	28
40	35
48	42
56	49
	56

$$\begin{array}{r} 7 \\ \times\ 7 \\ \hline 49 \end{array}$$

7
14
21
28
35
42
49

$54 = 9 \times 6$

$54 = 6 \times 9$

6	9
12	18
18	27
24	36
30	45
36	54
42	
48	
54	

$$\begin{array}{r} 6 \\ \times 8 \\ \hline 48 \end{array} \qquad \begin{array}{r} 8 \\ \times\ 6 \\ \hline 48 \end{array}$$

6	8
12	16
18	24
24	32
30	40
36	48
42	
48	

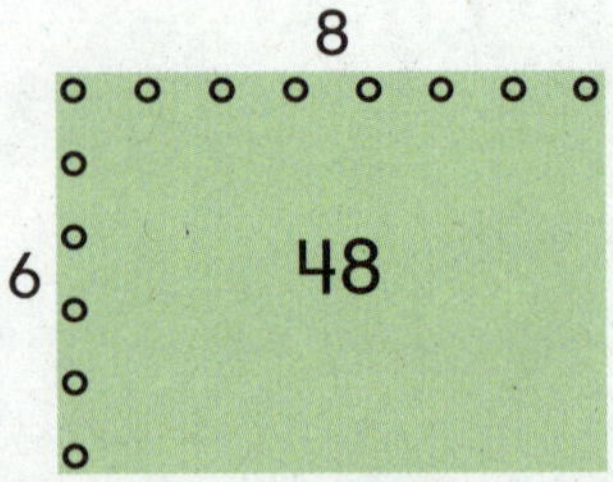

7×9 9×7	$\begin{array}{r} 8 \\ \times\ 8 \\ \hline \end{array}$	9×8 8×9	$\begin{array}{r} 9 \\ \times\ 9 \\ \hline \end{array}$

$81 = 9 \times 9$

9
18
27
36
45

54
63
72
81

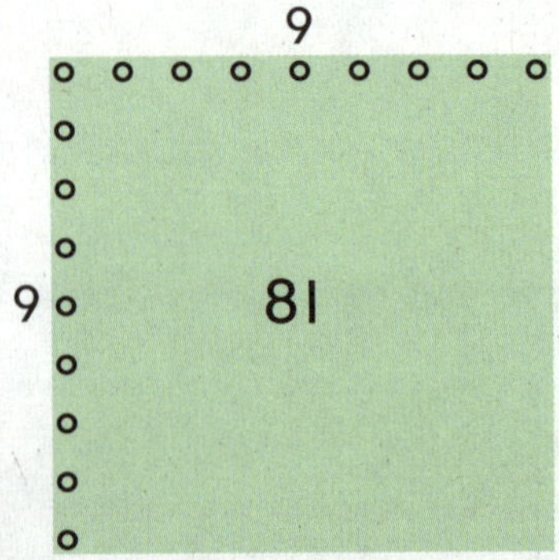

$$\begin{array}{r} 9 \\ \times\ 8 \\ \hline 72 \end{array} \qquad \begin{array}{r} 8 \\ \times\ 9 \\ \hline 72 \end{array}$$

8	9
16	18
24	27
32	36
40	45
48	54
56	63
64	72
72	

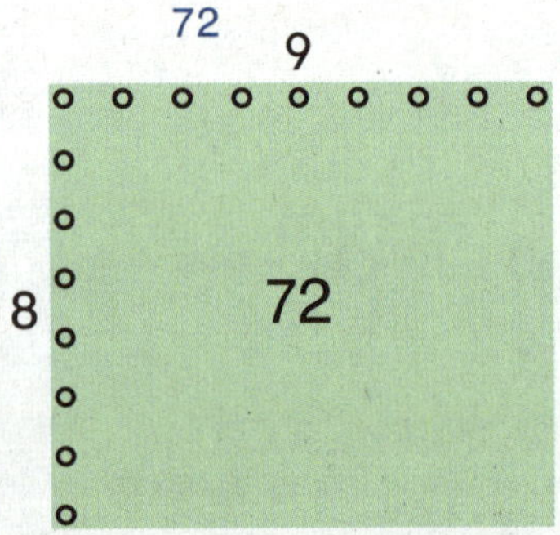

$64 = 8 \times 8$

8
16
24
32
40

48
56
64

$$\begin{array}{r} 7 \\ \times\ 9 \\ \hline 63 \end{array} \qquad \begin{array}{r} 9 \\ \times\ 7 \\ \hline 63 \end{array}$$

9	7
18	14
27	21
36	28
45	35
54	42
63	49
	56
	63

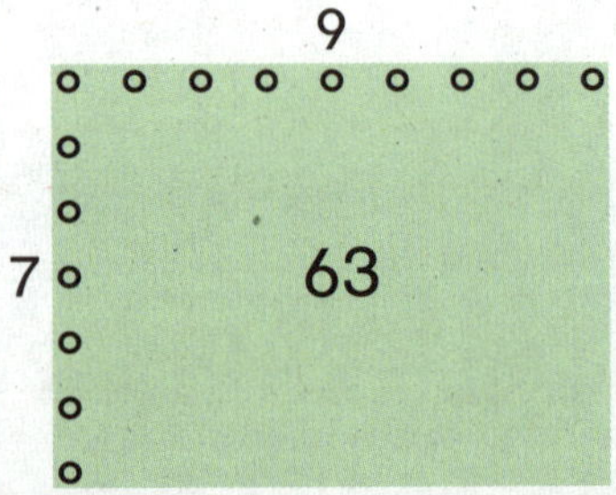

$2\overline{)4}$ $4 \div 2$	$2\overline{)6}$ $6 \div 2$	$2\overline{)8}$ $8 \div 2$	$2\overline{)10}$ $10 \div 2$
$2\overline{)12}$ $12 \div 2$	$2\overline{)14}$ $14 \div 2$	$2\overline{)16}$ $16 \div 2$	$2\overline{)18}$ $18 \div 2$

$2\overline{)10}$ = 5 $5\overline{)10}$ = 2

2, 4, 6, 8, 10

5, 10

5

2 10

$2\overline{)8}$ = 4 $4\overline{)8}$ = 2

2, 4, 6, 8

4, 8

4

2 8

$2\overline{)6}$ = 3 $3\overline{)6}$ = 2

2, 4, 6

3, 6

3

2 6

$2\overline{)4}$ = 2

2, 4

2

2 4

$2\overline{)18}$ = 9 $9\overline{)18}$ = 2

2, 4, 6, 8, 10, 12, 14, 16, 18

9, 18

9

2 18

$2\overline{)16}$ = 8 $8\overline{)16}$ = 2

2, 4, 6, 8, 10, 12, 14, 16

8, 16

8

2 16

$2\overline{)14}$ = 7 $7\overline{)14}$ = 2

2, 4, 6, 8, 10, 12, 14

7, 14

7

2 14

$2\overline{)12}$ = 6 $6\overline{)12}$ = 2

2, 4, 6, 8, 10, 12

6, 12

6

2 12

$3\overline{)6}$ $6 \div 3$	$4\overline{)8}$ $8 \div 4$	$5\overline{)10}$ $10 \div 5$	$6\overline{)12}$ $12 \div 6$
$7\overline{)14}$ $14 \div 7$	$8\overline{)16}$ $16 \div 8$	$9\overline{)18}$ $18 \div 9$	$3\overline{)9}$ $9 \div 3$

$6\overline{)12}$ = 2 $2\overline{)12}$ = 6

6
12

2
4
6
8
10
12

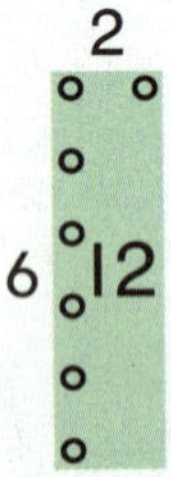

$5\overline{)10}$ = 2 $2\overline{)10}$ = 5

5
10

2
4
6
8
10

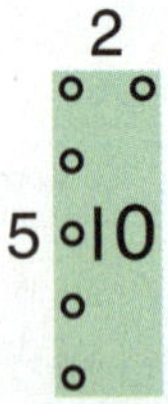

$4\overline{)8}$ = 2 $2\overline{)8}$ = 4

4
8

2
4
6
8

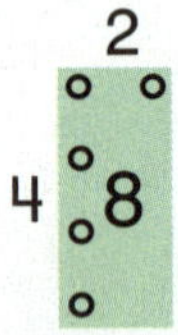

$3\overline{)6}$ = 2 $2\overline{)6}$ = 3

3
6

2
4
6

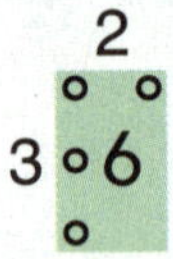

$3\overline{)9}$ = 3

3
6
9

$9\overline{)18}$ = 2 $2\overline{)18}$ = 9

9
18

2
4
6
8
10
12
14
16
18

$8\overline{)16}$ = 2 $2\overline{)16}$ = 8

8
16

2
4
6
8
10
12
14
16

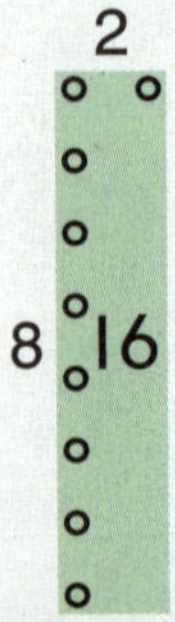

$7\overline{)14}$ = 2 $2\overline{)14}$ = 7

7
14

2
4
6
8
10
12
14

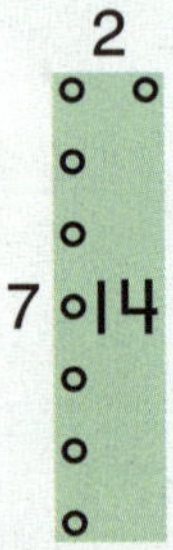

$3\overline{)12}$ $12 \div 3$	$3\overline{)15}$ $15 \div 3$	$3\overline{)18}$ $18 \div 3$	$3\overline{)21}$ $21 \div 3$
$3\overline{)24}$ $24 \div 3$	$3\overline{)27}$ $27 \div 3$	$4\overline{)12}$ $12 \div 4$	$5\overline{)15}$ $15 \div 5$

$3\overline{)21}$ = 7 $7\overline{)21}$ = 3

3, 6, 9, 12, 15, 18, 21

7, 14, 21

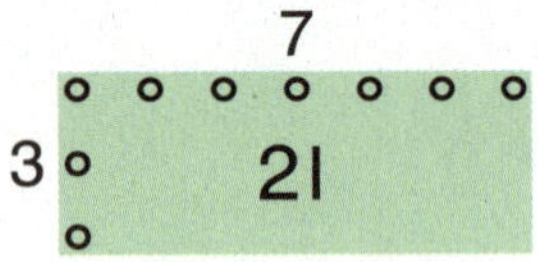

$3\overline{)18}$ = 6 $6\overline{)18}$ = 3

3, 6, 9, 12, 15, 18

6, 12, 18

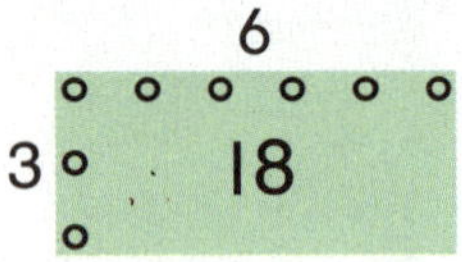

$3\overline{)15}$ = 5 $5\overline{)15}$ = 3

3, 6, 9, 12, 15

5, 10, 15

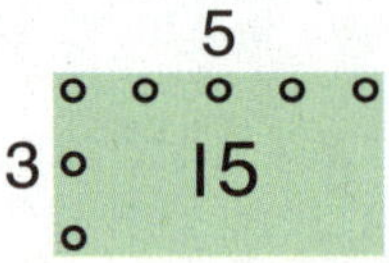

$3\overline{)12}$ = 4 $4\overline{)12}$ = 3

3, 6, 9, 12

4, 8, 12

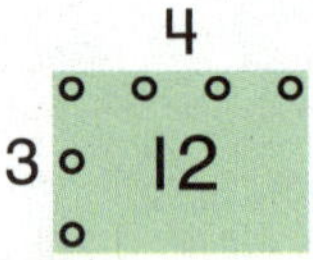

$5\overline{)15}$ = 3 $3\overline{)15}$ = 5

5, 10, 15

3, 6, 9, 12, 15

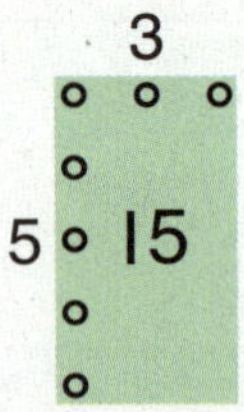

$4\overline{)12}$ = 3 $3\overline{)12}$ = 4

4, 8, 12

3, 6, 9, 12

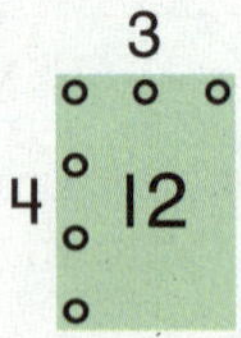

$3\overline{)27}$ = 9 $9\overline{)27}$ = 3

3, 6, 9, 12, 15, 18, 21, 24, 27

9, 18, 27

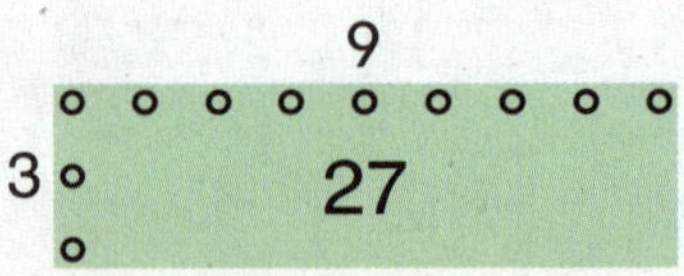

$3\overline{)24}$ = 8 $8\overline{)24}$ = 3

3, 6, 9, 12, 15, 18, 21, 24

8, 16, 24

$6\overline{)18}$ 18 ÷ 6	$7\overline{)21}$ 21 ÷ 7	$8\overline{)24}$ 24 ÷ 8	$9\overline{)27}$ 27 ÷ 9
$4\overline{)16}$ 16 ÷ 4	$4\overline{)20}$ 20 ÷ 4	$4\overline{)24}$ 24 ÷ 4	$4\overline{)28}$ 28 ÷ 4

$\begin{array}{r}3\\9\overline{)27}\end{array}$ $\begin{array}{r}9\\3\overline{)27}\end{array}$

9
18
27

3
6
9
12
15
18
21
24
27

$\begin{array}{r}3\\8\overline{)24}\end{array}$ $\begin{array}{r}8\\3\overline{)24}\end{array}$

8
16
24

3
6
9
12
15
18
21
24

$\begin{array}{r}3\\7\overline{)21}\end{array}$ $\begin{array}{r}7\\3\overline{)21}\end{array}$

7
14
21

3
6
9
12
15
18
21

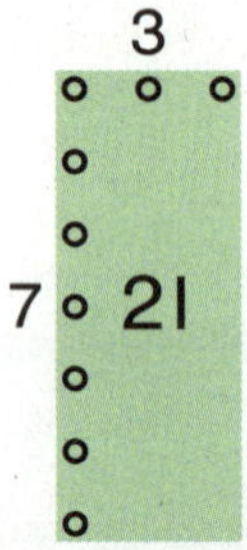

$\begin{array}{r}3\\6\overline{)18}\end{array}$ $\begin{array}{r}6\\3\overline{)18}\end{array}$

6
12
18

3
6
9
12
15
18

$\begin{array}{r}7\\4\overline{)28}\end{array}$ $\begin{array}{r}4\\7\overline{)28}\end{array}$

4
8
12
16
20
24
28

7
14
21
28

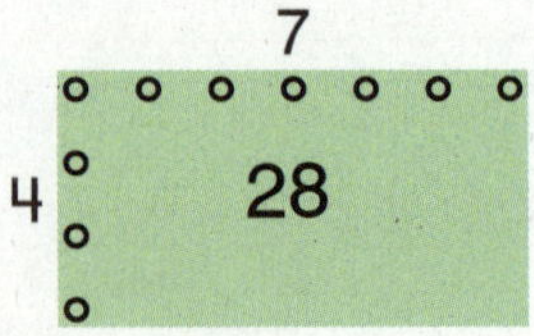

$\begin{array}{r}6\\4\overline{)24}\end{array}$ $\begin{array}{r}4\\6\overline{)24}\end{array}$

4
8
12
16
20
24

6
12
18
24

$\begin{array}{r}5\\4\overline{)20}\end{array}$ $\begin{array}{r}4\\5\overline{)20}\end{array}$

4
8
12
16
20

5
10
15
20

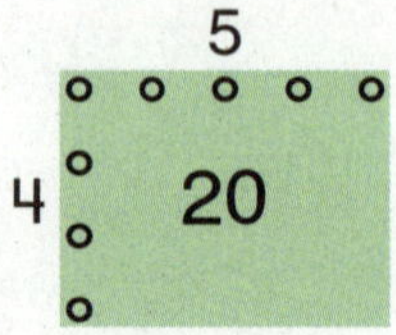

$\begin{array}{r}4\\4\overline{)16}\end{array}$

4
8
12
16

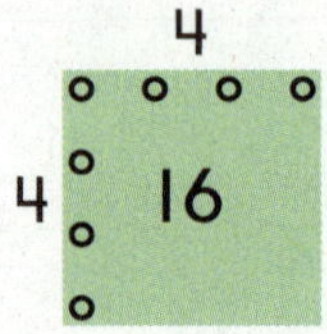

$4\overline{)32}$ $32 \div 4$	$4\overline{)36}$ $36 \div 4$	$5\overline{)20}$ $20 \div 5$	$6\overline{)24}$ $24 \div 6$
$7\overline{)28}$ $28 \div 7$	$8\overline{)32}$ $32 \div 8$	$9\overline{)36}$ $36 \div 9$	$5\overline{)25}$ $25 \div 5$

4 $\quad$ 6

$6\overline{)24}$ $\quad$ $4\overline{)24}$

6, 12, 18, 24

4, 8, 12, 16, 20, 24

4 $\quad$ 5

$5\overline{)20}$ $\quad$ $4\overline{)20}$

5, 10, 15, 20

4, 8, 12, 16, 20

9 $\quad$ 4

$4\overline{)36}$ $\quad$ $9\overline{)36}$

4, 8, 12, 16, 20, 24, 28, 32, 36

9, 18, 27, 36

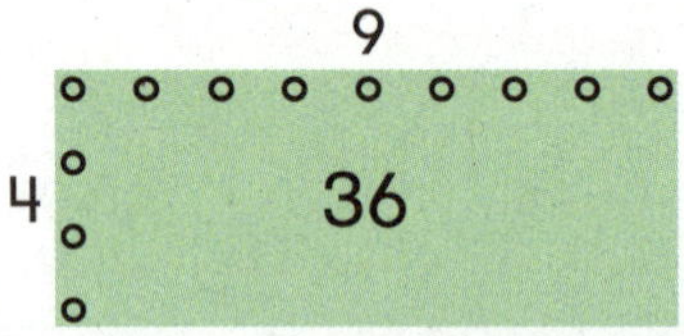

8 $\quad$ 4

$4\overline{)32}$ $\quad$ $8\overline{)32}$

4, 8, 12, 16, 20, 24, 28, 32

8, 16, 24, 32

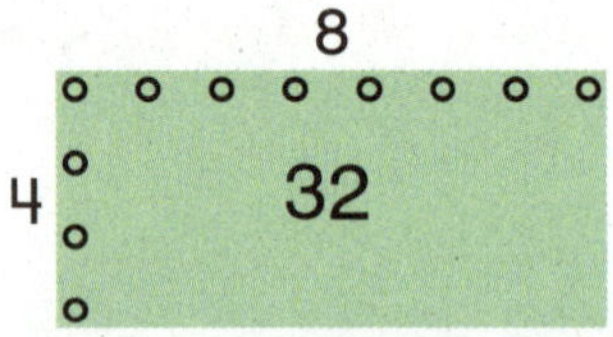

5

$5\overline{)25}$

5, 10, 15, 20, 25

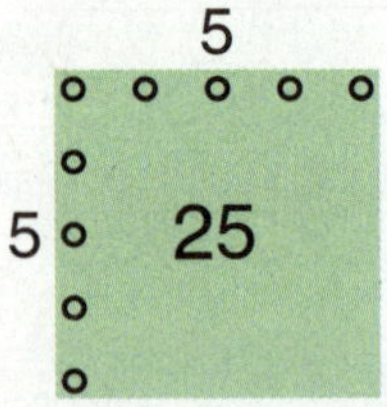

4 $\quad$ 9

$9\overline{)36}$ $\quad$ $4\overline{)36}$

9, 18, 27, 36

4, 8, 12, 16, 20, 24, 28, 32, 36

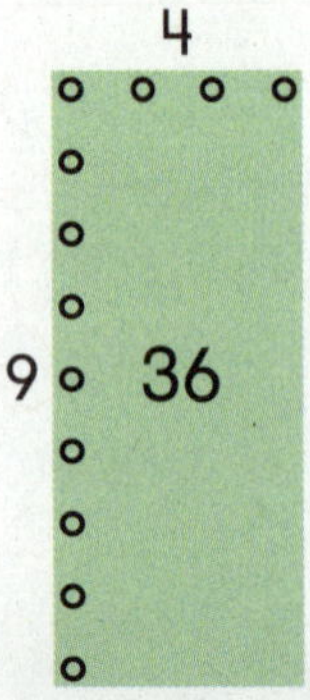

4 $\quad$ 8

$8\overline{)32}$ $\quad$ $4\overline{)32}$

8, 16, 24, 32

4, 8, 12, 16, 20, 24, 28, 32

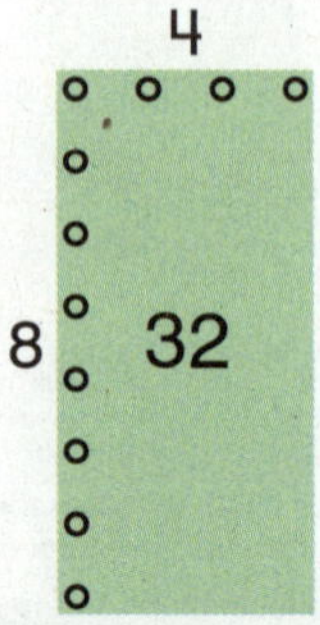

4 $\quad$ 7

$7\overline{)28}$ $\quad$ $4\overline{)28}$

7, 14, 21, 28

4, 8, 12, 16, 20, 24, 28

$5\overline{)30}$ $30 \div 5$	$5\overline{)35}$ $35 \div 5$	$5\overline{)40}$ $40 \div 5$	$5\overline{)45}$ $45 \div 5$
$6\overline{)30}$ $30 \div 6$	$7\overline{)35}$ $35 \div 7$	$8\overline{)40}$ $40 \div 8$	$9\overline{)45}$ $45 \div 9$

9	5
5)45	9)45

5
10
15
20
25
30
35
40
45

9
18
27
36
45

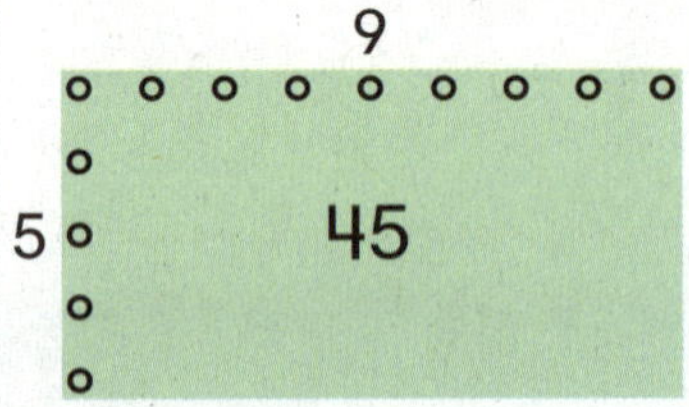

8	5
5)40	8)40

5
10
15
20
25
30
35
40

8
16
24
32
40

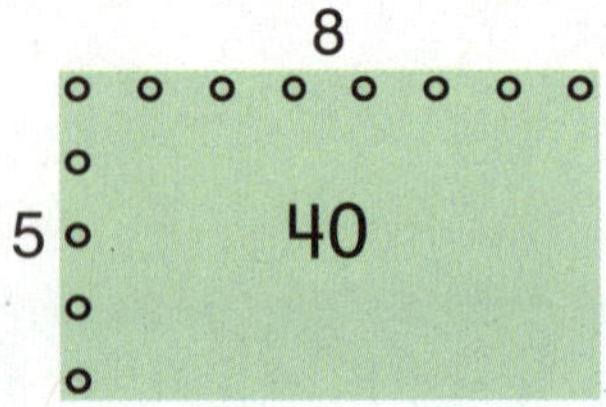

7	5
5)35	7)35

5
10
15
20
25
30
35

7
14
21
28
35

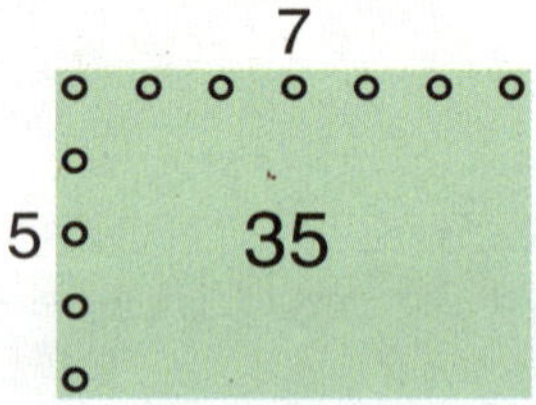

6	5
5)30	6)30

5
10
15
20
25
30

6
12
18
24
30

5	9
9)45	5)45

9
18
27
36
45

5
10
15
20
25
30
35
40
45

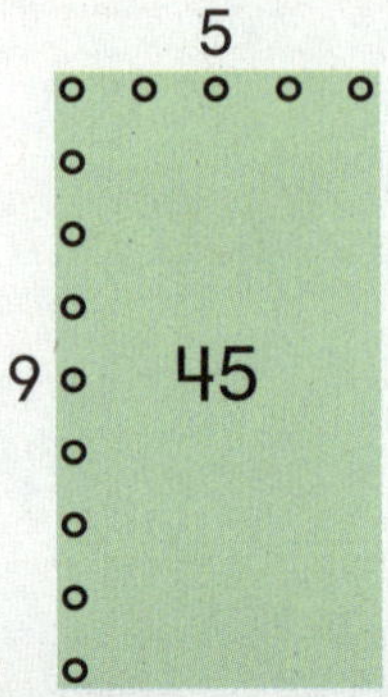

5	8
8)40	5)40

8
16
24
32
40

5
10
15
20
25
30
35
40

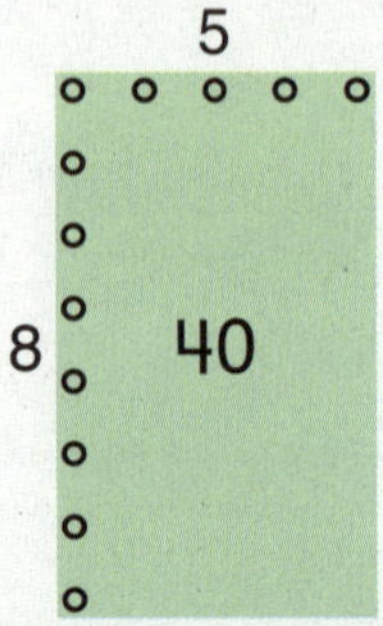

5	7
7)35	5)35

7
14
21
28
35

5
10
15
20
25
30
35

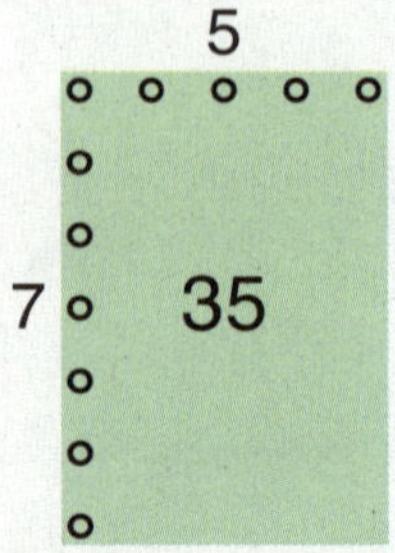

5	6
6)30	5)30

6
12
18
24
30

5
10
15
20
25
30

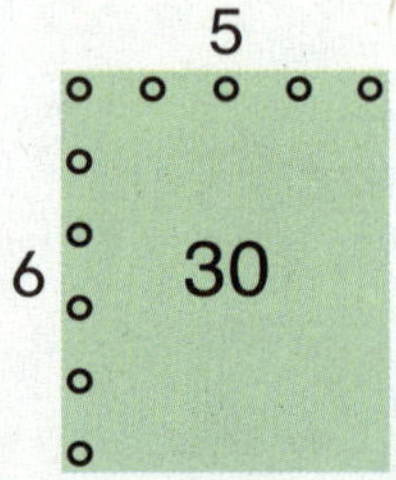

$6\overline{)36}$ $36 \div 6$	$6\overline{)42}$ $42 \div 6$	$6\overline{)48}$ $48 \div 6$	$6\overline{)54}$ $54 \div 6$
$7\overline{)42}$ $42 \div 7$	$8\overline{)48}$ $48 \div 8$	$9\overline{)54}$ $54 \div 9$	$7\overline{)49}$ $49 \div 7$

$\begin{array}{r} 9 \\ 6\overline{)54} \end{array}$ $\begin{array}{r} 6 \\ 9\overline{)54} \end{array}$

6	9
12	18
18	27
24	36
30	45
36	54
42	
48	
54	

$\begin{array}{r} 8 \\ 6\overline{)48} \end{array}$ $\begin{array}{r} 6 \\ 8\overline{)48} \end{array}$

6	8
12	16
18	24
24	32
30	40
36	48
42	
48	

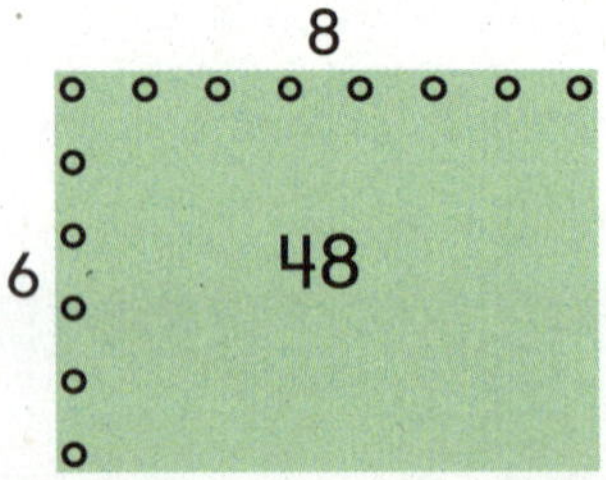

$\begin{array}{r} 7 \\ 6\overline{)42} \end{array}$ $\begin{array}{r} 6 \\ 7\overline{)42} \end{array}$

6	7
12	14
18	21
24	28
30	35
36	42
42	

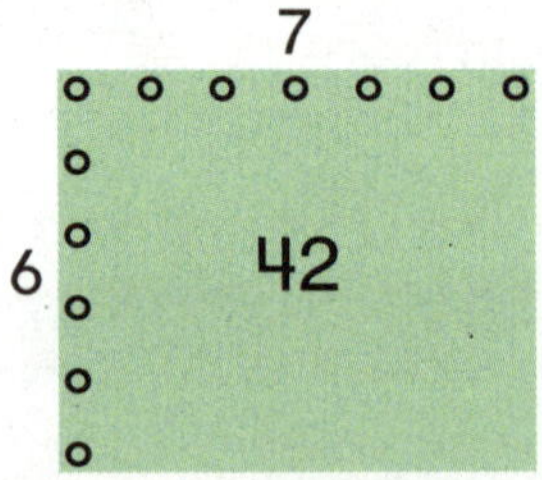

$\begin{array}{r} 6 \\ 6\overline{)36} \end{array}$

6
12
18
24
30

36

$\begin{array}{r} 7 \\ 7\overline{)49} \end{array}$

7
14
21
28
35

42
49

$\begin{array}{r} 6 \\ 9\overline{)54} \end{array}$ $\begin{array}{r} 9 \\ 6\overline{)54} \end{array}$

9	6
18	12
27	18
36	24
45	30
54	36
	42
	48
	54

$\begin{array}{r} 6 \\ 8\overline{)48} \end{array}$ $\begin{array}{r} 8 \\ 6\overline{)48} \end{array}$

8	6
16	12
24	18
32	24
40	30
48	36
	42
	48

$\begin{array}{r} 6 \\ 7\overline{)42} \end{array}$ $\begin{array}{r} 7 \\ 6\overline{)42} \end{array}$

7	6
14	12
21	18
28	24
35	30
42	36
	42

$7\overline{)56}$ $56 \div 7$	$7\overline{)63}$ $63 \div 7$	$8\overline{)56}$ $56 \div 8$	$9\overline{)63}$ $63 \div 9$
$8\overline{)64}$ $64 \div 8$	$8\overline{)72}$ $72 \div 8$	$9\overline{)72}$ $72 \div 9$	$9\overline{)81}$ $81 \div 9$

$\begin{array}{r}7\\9\overline{)63}\end{array}$ $\begin{array}{r}9\\7\overline{)63}\end{array}$

9	7
18	14
27	21
36	28
45	35
54	42
63	49
	56
	63

$\begin{array}{r}7\\8\overline{)56}\end{array}$ $\begin{array}{r}8\\7\overline{)56}\end{array}$

8	7
16	14
24	21
32	28
40	35
48	42
56	49
	56

$\begin{array}{r}9\\7\overline{)63}\end{array}$ $\begin{array}{r}7\\9\overline{)63}\end{array}$

7	9
14	18
21	27
28	36
35	45
42	54
49	63
56	
63	

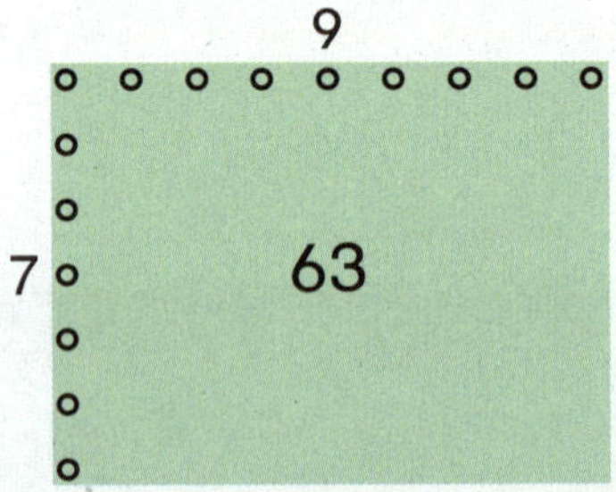

$\begin{array}{r}8\\7\overline{)56}\end{array}$ $\begin{array}{r}7\\8\overline{)56}\end{array}$

7	8
14	16
21	24
28	32
35	40
42	48
49	56
56	

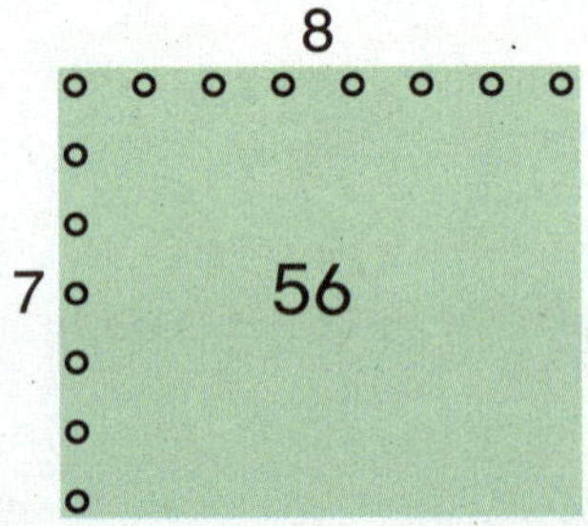

$\begin{array}{r}9\\9\overline{)81}\end{array}$

9
18
27
36
45

54
63
72
81

$\begin{array}{r}8\\9\overline{)72}\end{array}$ $\begin{array}{r}9\\8\overline{)72}\end{array}$

9	8
18	16
27	24
36	32
45	40
54	48
63	56
72	64
	72

$\begin{array}{r}9\\8\overline{)72}\end{array}$ $\begin{array}{r}8\\9\overline{)72}\end{array}$

8	9
16	18
24	27
32	36
40	45
48	54
56	63
64	72
72	

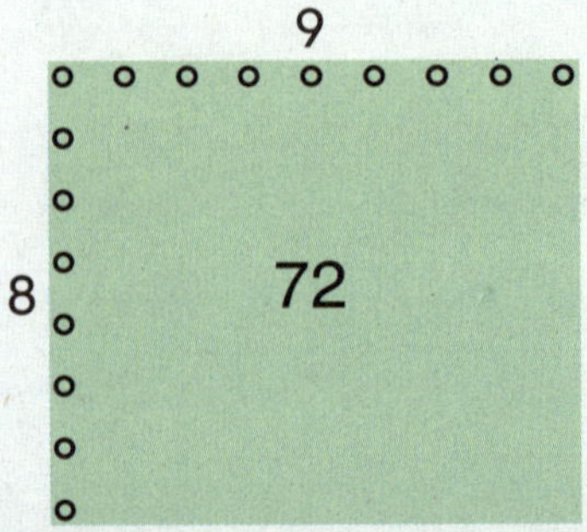

$\begin{array}{r}8\\8\overline{)64}\end{array}$

8
16
24
32
40

48
56
64

7–10 Class Activity

Name Date

▶ Find the Area

The area of a rectangle is the number of square units that fit inside of it.

Write a multiplication equation to represent the area of each rectangle.

1. 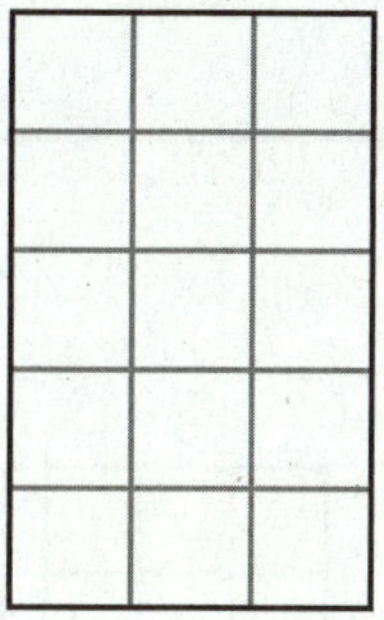

____

2. 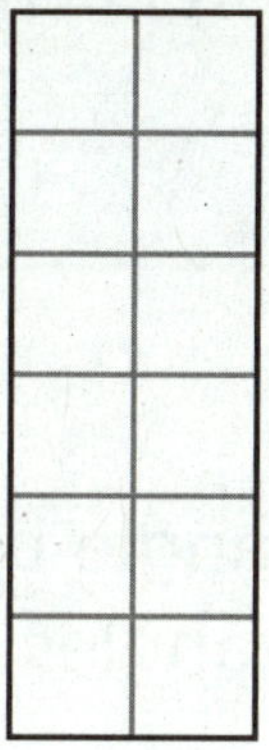

____

3. 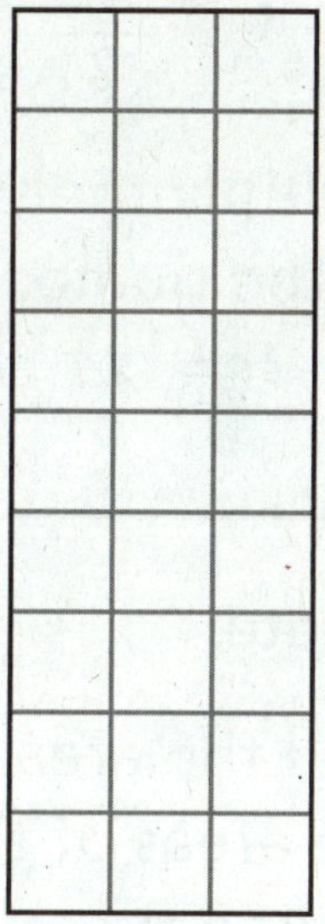

____

Make a rectangle drawing to represent each problem. Then give the product.

4. $5 \times 3 =$ _______

5. $7 * 2 =$ _______

6. $2 \bullet 9 =$ _______

7–10 Class Activity

Name ______________________ Date ______________

▶ Different Ways to Find Area

The large rectangle has been divided into two small rectangles. You can find the area of the large rectangle in two ways:

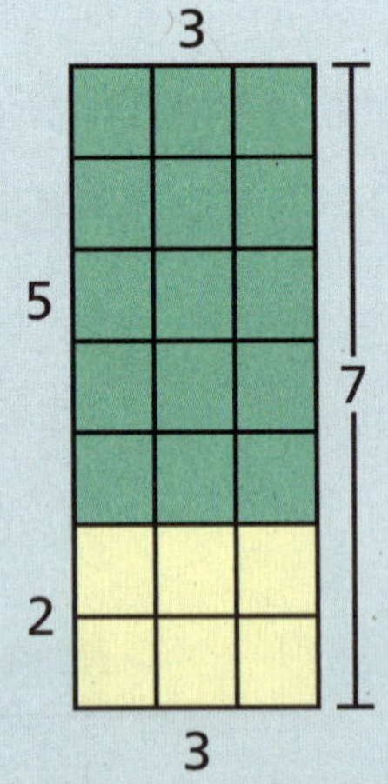

- Add the areas of the two small rectangles:

  $5 \times 3 =$ 15 square units
  $2 \times 3 =$ 6 square units
  21 square units

- Multiply the number of rows in the large rectangle by the number of square units in each row:

  $7 \times 3 =$ 21 square units

Complete.

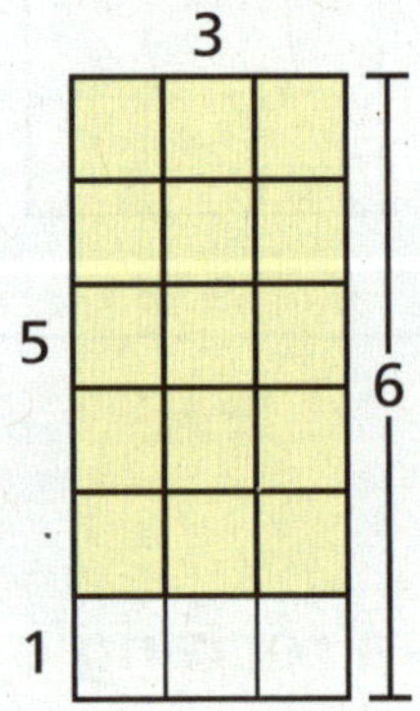

7. Find the area of the large rectangle by finding the areas of the two small rectangles and adding them.

____

____

8. Find the area of the large rectangle by multiplying the number of rows by the number of square units in each row.

____

____

9. Find this product: $5 \times 4 =$ ______

10. Find this product: $2 \times 4 =$ ______

11. Use your answers to exercises 9 and 10 to find this product: $7 \times 4 =$ ______

7–11 Class Activity

Name ______________________ Date ______________

▶ Sprints for 9s

As your teacher reads each multiplication or division, write your answer in the space provided.

× 9	÷ 9
a. ________	a. ________
b. ________	b. ________
c. ________	c. ________
d. ________	d. ________
e. ________	e. ________
f. ________	f. ________
g. ________	g. ________
h. ________	h. ________
i. ________	i. ________
j. ________	j. ________

7–11 Class Activity

Name ______________________ Date ______________________

▶ Identify Types of Problems

Read each problem and decide what type of problem it is. Write the letter from the list below. Then write an equation to solve the problem.

a. Array Multiplication

b. Array Division

c. Repeated Groups Multiplication

d. Repeated Groups Division with an Unknown Group Size

e. Repeated Groups Division with an Unknown Multiplier (number of groups)

f. None of the above

1. Mrs. Ostrega has 3 children. She wants to buy 5 juice boxes for each child. How many juice boxes does she need?

____

2. Sophie picked 15 peaches from one tree and 3 peaches from another. How many peaches did she pick in all?

____

3. Zamir brought 21 treats to the dog park. He divided the treats equally among the 7 dogs that were there. How many treats did each dog get?

____

4. Art said he could make 12 muffins in his muffin pan. The pan has space for 3 muffins in a row. How many rows does the muffin pan have?

____

5. Bia is helping with the lights for the school play. Each box of light bulbs has 6 rows, with 3 bulbs in each row. How many light bulbs are in each box?

____

6. Tryouts were held to find triplets to act in a commercial for Triple-Crunch Peanut Butter. If 24 children tried out for the commercial, how many sets of triplets tried out?

____

7–11 Going Further

Name ______ Date ______

▶ Multiply Using Patterns

Use mental math and patterns to complete.

1. $3 \times 4 =$ ______
$3 \times 40 =$ ______

2. $10 \times 2 =$ ______
$100 \times 2 =$ ______

3. $9 \times 8 =$ ______
$9 \times 80 =$ ______

4. $2 \times 9 =$ ______
$2 \times 90 =$ ______
$2 \times 900 =$ ______

5. $5 \times 5 =$ ______
$5 \times 50 =$ ______
$5 \times 500 =$ ______

6. $3 \times 4 =$ ______
$3 \times 40 =$ ______
$3 \times 400 =$ ______

7. $1 \times 1 =$ ______
$10 \times 1 =$ ______
$100 \times 1 =$ ______

8. $2 \times 3 =$ ______
$20 \times 3 =$ ______
$200 \times 30 =$ ______

9. $5 \times 6 =$ ______
$5 \times 60 =$ ______
$5 \times 600 =$ ______

10. $2 \times 4 =$ ______
$2 \times 40 =$ ______
$2 \times 400 =$ ______

11. $5 \times 3 =$ ______
$5 \times 30 =$ ______
$5 \times 300 =$ ______

12. $9 \times 2 =$ ______
$9 \times 20 =$ ______
$9 \times 200 =$ ______

13. $2 \times 30 =$ ______

14. $5 \times 40 =$ ______

15. $9 \times 60 =$ ______

16. $3 \times 80 =$ ______

17. $2 \times 70 =$ ______

18. $5 \times 90 =$ ______

19. $9 \times 500 =$ ______

20. $5 \times 200 =$ ______

21. $3 \times 300 =$ ______

22. $5 \times 800 =$ ______

23. $9 \times 900 =$ ______

24. $5 \times 600 =$ ______

25. **On the Back** Describe a pattern you can use to find 4×200.

Name Date

Name ____________________ Date ____________________

►Check Sheet 4: 3s and 4s

3s Multiplications	3s Divisions	4s Multiplications	4s Divisions
8 × 3 = 24	9 / 3 = 3	1 × 4 = 4	40 / 4 = 10
3 • 2 = 6	21 ÷ 3 = 7	4 • 5 = 20	12 ÷ 4 = 3
3 * 5 = 15	27 / 3 = 9	8 * 4 = 32	24 / 4 = 6
10 × 3 = 30	3 ÷ 3 = 1	3 × 4 = 12	8 ÷ 4 = 2
3 • 3 = 9	18 / 3 = 6	4 • 6 = 24	4 / 4 = 1
3 * 6 = 18	12 ÷ 3 = 4	4 * 9 = 36	28 ÷ 4 = 7
7 × 3 = 21	30 / 3 = 10	10 × 4 = 40	32 / 4 = 8
3 • 9 = 27	6 ÷ 3 = 2	4 • 7 = 28	16 ÷ 4 = 4
4 * 3 = 12	24 / 3 = 8	4 * 4 = 16	36 / 4 = 9
3 × 1 = 3	15 / 3 = 5	2 × 4 = 8	20 / 4 = 5
3 • 4 = 12	21 ÷ 3 = 7	4 • 3 = 12	4 ÷ 4 = 1
3 * 3 = 9	3 / 3 = 1	4 * 2 = 8	32 / 4 = 8
3 × 10 = 30	9 ÷ 3 = 3	9 × 4 = 36	8 ÷ 4 = 2
2 • 3 = 6	27 / 3 = 9	1 • 4 = 4	16 / 4 = 4
3 * 7 = 21	30 ÷ 3 = 10	4 * 6 = 24	36 ÷ 4 = 9
6 × 3 = 18	18 / 3 = 6	5 × 4 = 20	12 / 4 = 3
5 • 3 = 15	6 ÷ 3 = 2	4 • 4 = 16	40 ÷ 4 = 10
3 * 8 = 24	15 ÷ 3 = 5	7 * 4 = 28	20 ÷ 4 = 5
9 × 3 = 27	12 / 3 = 4	8 × 4 = 32	24 / 4 = 6
2 • 3 = 6	24 ÷ 3 = 8	10 • 4 = 40	28 ÷ 4 = 7

7–12 Class Activity

Name ____________________ Date ____________

►Explore Patterns with 4s

What patterns do you see below?

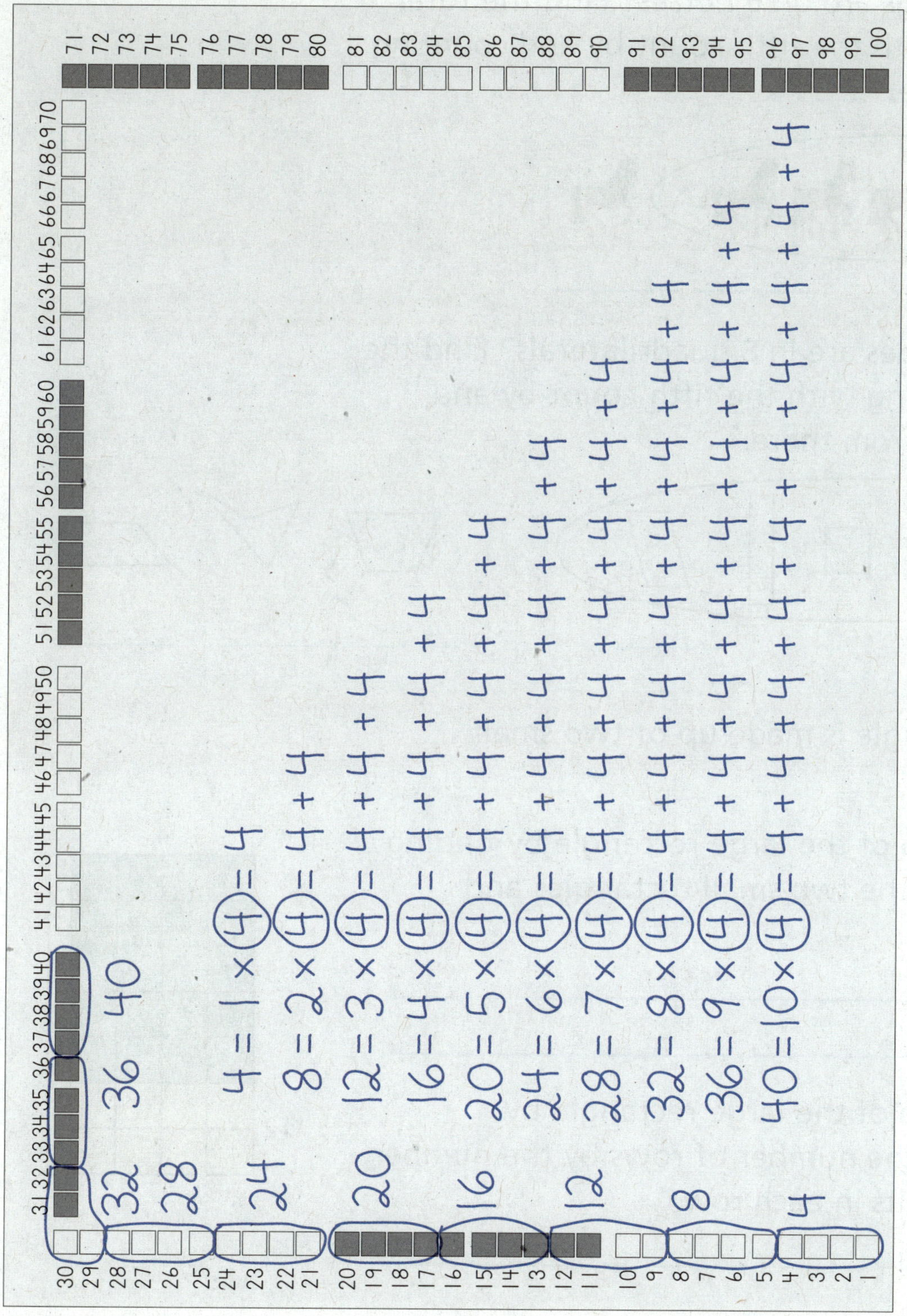

Name ____________________ Date ____________

▶Use the 5s Shortcut for 4s

Solve each problem.

1. How many legs are on 6 horses? Find the total by starting with the fifth count-by and counting up from there.

______ ______

2. How many sides are in 8 quadrilaterals? Find the total by starting with the fifth count-by and counting up from there.

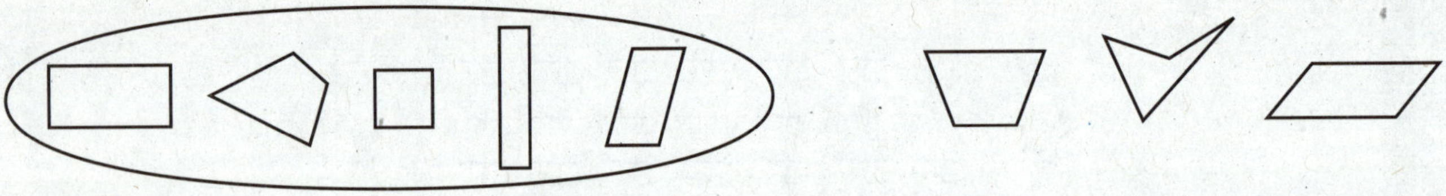

______ ______ ______ ______

This large rectangle is made up of two small rectangles.

3. Find the area of the large rectangle by finding the areas of the two small rectangles and adding them.

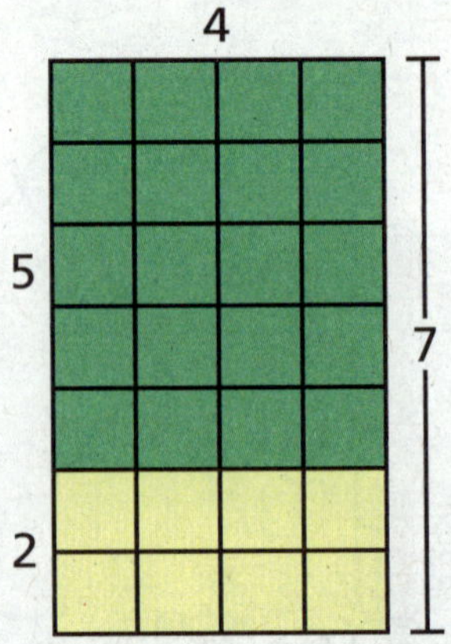

____

____

4. Find the area of the large rectangle by multiplying the number of rows by the number of square units in each row.

____

7–12 **Class Activity**

Name ______________________________ Date ____________

▶ Use Multiplications You Know

You can combine multiplications to find other multiplications.

This Equal-Shares Drawing shows that 7 groups of 4 is the same as 5 groups of 4 plus 2 groups of 4.

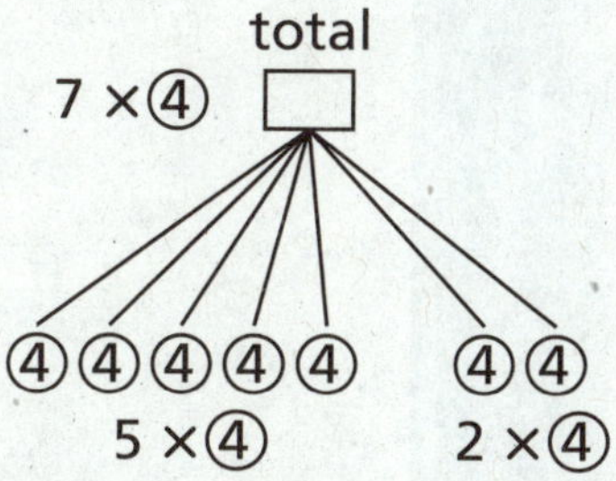

5. Find 5 ×④ and 2 ×④ and add the answers.

____

6. Find 7 ×④. Did you get the same answer as in exercise 5?

____

7. Find this product: $5 \times 4 =$ ________

8. Find this product: $4 \times 4 =$ ________

9. Use your answers to exercises 7 and 8 to find this product: $9 \times 4 =$ ________.

▶ The Puzzled Penguin

Dear Math Students:

Today I had to find 8 x 4. I didn't know the answer, but I figured it out by combining two multiplications I did know:

$$\begin{array}{r} 5 \times 2 = 10 \\ 3 \times 2 = 6 \\ \hline 8 \times 4 = 16 \end{array}$$

Is my answer right? If not, please help me understand why it is wrong.

Thank you,
The Puzzled Penguin

10. On the Back Make a drawing to show that your answers to exercises 7–9 are correct.

Name Date

7–13 Class Activity

Name ____________________ Date ____________

► Sprints for 3s

As your teacher reads each multiplication or division, write your answer in the space provided.

$\times 3$	$\div 3$
a. ________	a. ________
b. ________	b. ________
c. ________	c. ________
d. ________	d. ________
e. ________	e. ________
f. ________	f. ________
g. ________	g. ________
h. ________	h. ________
i. ________	i. ________
j. ________	j. ________

Use the Strategy Cards

Name Date

► Play *Solve the Stack*

Read the rules for playing *Solve the Stack*. Then play the game with your group.

Rules for *Solve the Stack*

Number of players: 2–4
What you will need: 1 set of multiplication and division Strategy Cards

1. Shuffle the cards. Place them exercise side up in the center of the table.
2. Players take turns. On each turn, a player finds the answer to the multiplication or division on the top card and then turns the card over to check the answer.
3. If a player's answer is correct, he or she takes the card. If it is incorrect, the card is placed at the bottom of the stack.
4. Play ends when there are no more cards in the stack. The player with the most cards wins.

Name ____________________ Date ____________

►Explore Patterns with 1s

What patterns do you see below?

1.

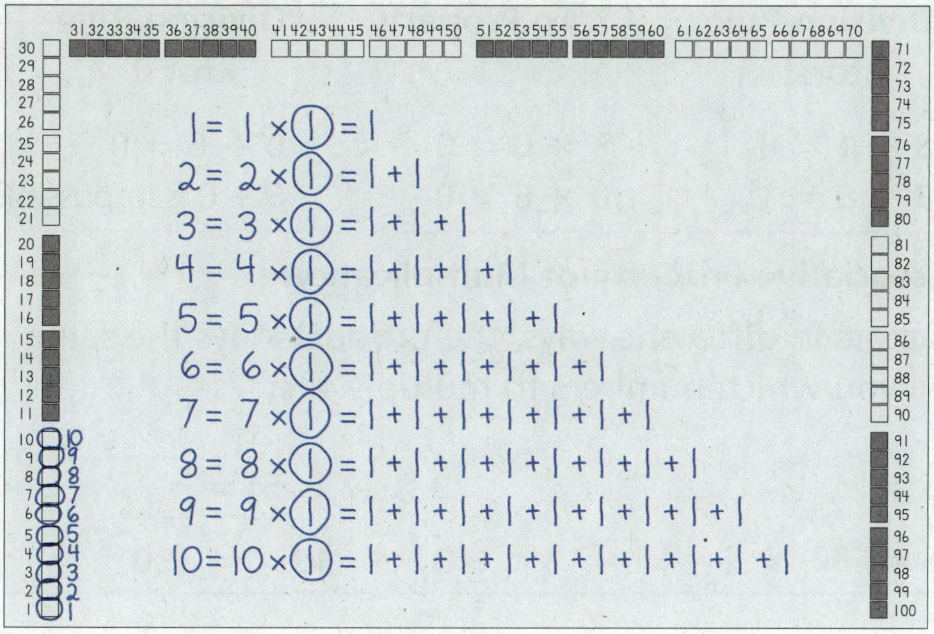

►Explore Patterns with 0s

What patterns do you see below?

2.

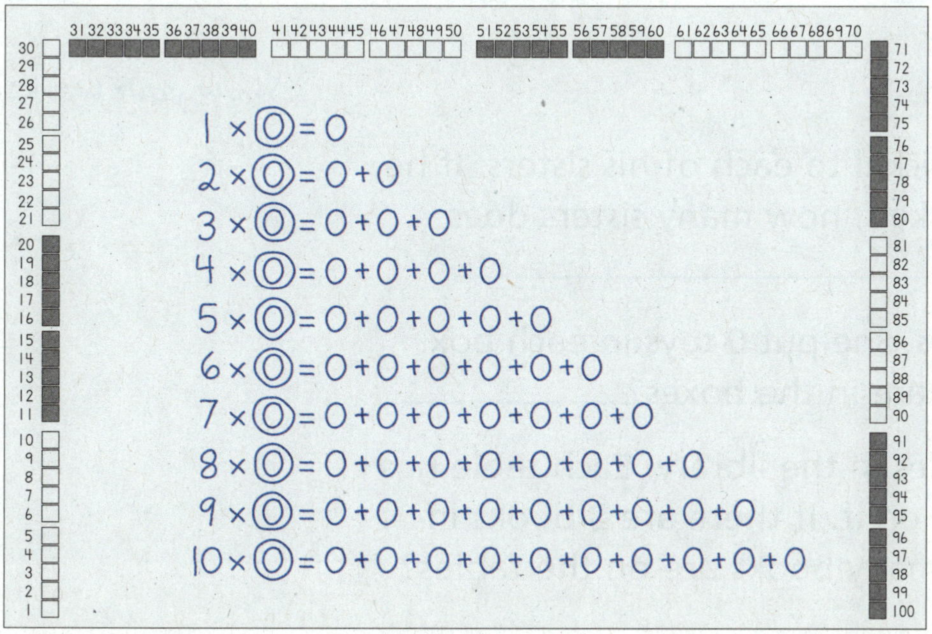

7–14 Class Activity

Name ______ Date ______

▶ Multiplication Properties and Division Rules

Properties and Rules

Property for 1	Division Rule for 1	Zero Property	Division Rule for 0
$1 \times 6 = 6$ $6 \times 1 = 6$	$8 \div 1 = 8$ $8 \div 8 = 1$	$6 \times 0 = 0$ $0 \times 6 = 0$	$0 \div 6 = 0$ $6 \div 0$ is impossible.

Associative Property of Multiplication

When you group factors in different ways, the product stays the same. The parentheses tell you which numbers to multiply first.

$(3 \times 2) \times 5 = \square$

$6 \times 5 = 30$

$3 \times (2 \times 5) = \square$

$3 \times 10 = 30$

Find each product.

3. $2 \times (6 \times 1) = \square$ **4.** $(4 \times 2) \times 2 = \square$ **5.** $7 \times (1 \times 5) = \square$

6. $(9 \times 8) \times 0 = \square$ **7.** $3 \times (2 \times 3) = \square$ **8.** $6 \times (0 \times 7) = \square$

Solve each problem.

Show your work.

9. Shawn gave 1 nickel to each of his sisters. If he gave away 3 nickels, how many sisters does Shawn have? ______

10. Kara has 3 boxes. She put 0 toys in each box. How many toys are in the boxes? ______

11. There are 3 tables in the library. Each table has 2 piles of books on it. If there are 3 books in each pile, how many books are on the tables?

______

7–14 Class Activity

Name ______ Date ______

► Identify Addition and Multiplication Properties

Addition Properties	Multiplication Properties
A. Commutative Property of Addition The order in which numbers are added does not change their sum. $3 + 5 = 5 + 3$	**D. Commutative Property of Multiplication** The order in which numbers are multiplied does not change their product. $3 \times 5 = 5 \times 3$
B. Associative Property of Addition The way in which numbers are grouped does not change their sum. $(3 + 2) + 5 = 3 + (2 + 5)$	**E. Associative Property of Multiplication** The way in which numbers are grouped does not change their product. $(3 \times 2) \times 5 = 3 \times (2 \times 5)$
C. Identity Property of Addition If 0 is added to a number, the sum equals that number. $3 + 0 = 3$	**F. Identity Property of Multiplication** The product of 1 and any number is that number. $3 \times 1 = 3$
	G. Zero Property of Multiplication If 0 is multiplied by a number, the product is 0. $3 \times 0 = 0$

Write the letter of the property that is shown.

12. $1 \times 9 = 9$ ____

13. $5 + (6 + 7) = (5 + 6) + 7$ ____

14. $5 \times 0 = 0$ ____

15. $8 + 0 = 8$ ____

16. $3 \times 9 = \square \times 3$ ____

17. $(2 \times 1) \times 3 = 2 \times (\square \times 3)$ ____

7–14 Class Activity

Name ______ Date ______

►Use Properties to Solve Equations

Use properties and rules to find the unknown numbers.

18. $5 \times 8 = \square \times 5$
19. $4 + 3 = \square + 4$
20. $0 \div 8 = \square$
21. $4 \div 4 = \square$
22. $(3 \times 2) \times 4 = 3 \times (\square \times 4)$
23. $6 \times 2 = 2 \times \square$
24. $5 \times 3 = \square \times 5$
25. $(6 + 2) + 2 = 6 + (\square + 2)$
26. $11 + 0 = \square$
27. $65 \times 1 = \square$
28. $5 \times (2 \times 6) = (5 \times 2) \times \square$
29. $17 \times 0 = \square$

►Use Equations to Demonstrate Properties

Write your own equation that shows the property.

30. Commutative Property of Multiplication

______

31. Associative Property of Addition

______

32. Identity Property of Addition

______

33. Identity Property of Multiplication

______

34. Associative Property of Multiplication

______

35. Zero Property of Multiplication

______

36. Commutative Property of Addition

______

Name ______________________ Date ______________

▶ Sprints for 4s

As your teacher reads each multiplication or division, write your answer in the space provided.

× 4	÷ 4
a. ________	a. ________
b. ________	b. ________
c. ________	c. ________
d. ________	d. ________
e. ________	e. ________
f. ________	f. ________
g. ________	g. ________
h. ________	h. ________
i. ________	i. ________
j. ________	j. ________

Name _______________ Date _______________

▶Check Sheet 5: 1s and 0s

1s Multiplications	1s Divisions	0s Multiplications
1 × 4 = 4	10 / 1 = 10	4 × 0 = 0
5 • 1 = 5	5 ÷ 1 = 5	2 • 0 = 0
7 * 1 = 7	7 / 1 = 7	0 * 8 = 0
1 × 8 = 8	9 ÷ 1 = 9	0 × 5 = 0
1 • 6 = 6	3 / 1 = 3	6 • 0 = 0
10 * 1 = 10	10 ÷ 1 = 10	0 * 7 = 0
1 × 9 = 9	2 / 1 = 2	0 × 2 = 0
3 • 1 = 3	8 ÷ 1 = 8	0 • 9 = 0
1 * 2 = 2	6 / 1 = 6	10 * 0 = 0
1 × 1 = 1	9 / 1 = 9	1 × 0 = 0
8 • 1 = 8	1 ÷ 1 = 1	0 • 6 = 0
1 * 7 = 7	5 / 1 = 5	9 * 0 = 0
1 × 5 = 5	3 ÷ 1 = 3	0 × 4 = 0
6 • 1 = 6	4 / 1 = 4	3 • 0 = 0
1 * 1 = 1	2 ÷ 1 = 2	0 * 3 = 0
1 × 10 = 10	8 / 1 = 8	8 × 0 = 0
9 • 1 = 9	4 ÷ 1 = 4	0 • 10 = 0
4 * 1 = 4	7 ÷ 1 = 7	0 * 1 = 0
2 × 1 = 2	1 / 1 = 1	5 × 0 = 0
1 • 3 = 3	6 ÷ 1 = 6	7 • 0 = 0

Name ______________________ Date ______________________

►Check Sheet 6: Mixed 3s, 4s, 0s and 1s

3s, 4s, 0s, 1s Multiplications	3s, 4s, 0s, 1s Multiplications	3s, 4s, 1s Divisions	3s, 4s, 1s Divisions
5 × 3 = 15	0 × 5 = 0	18 / 3 = 6	4 / 1 = 4
6 • 4 = 24	10 • 1 = 10	20 ÷ 4 = 5	21 ÷ 3 = 7
9 * 0 = 0	6 * 3 = 18	1 / 1 = 1	16 / 4 = 4
7 × 1 = 7	2 × 4 = 8	21 ÷ 3 = 7	9 ÷ 1 = 9
3 • 3 = 9	5 • 0 = 0	12 / 4 = 3	15 / 3 = 5
4 * 7 = 28	1 * 2 = 2	5 ÷ 1 = 5	8 ÷ 4 = 2
0 × 10 = 0	10 × 3 = 30	15 / 3 = 5	5 / 1 = 5
1 • 6 = 6	5 • 4 = 20	24 ÷ 4 = 6	30 ÷ 3 = 10
3 * 4 = 12	0 * 8 = 0	7 / 1 = 7	12 / 4 = 3
5 × 4 = 20	9 × 2 = 18	12 / 3 = 4	8 / 1 = 8
0 • 5 = 0	10 • 3 = 30	36 ÷ 4 = 9	27 ÷ 3 = 9
9 * 1 = 9	9 * 4 = 36	6 / 1 = 6	40 / 4 = 10
2 × 3 = 6	1 × 0 = 0	12 ÷ 3 = 4	4 ÷ 1 = 4
3 • 4 = 12	1 • 6 = 6	16 / 4 = 4	9 / 3 = 3
0 * 9 = 0	3 * 6 = 18	7 ÷ 1 = 7	16 ÷ 4 = 4
1 × 5 = 5	7 × 4 = 28	9 / 3 = 3	10 / 1 = 10
2 • 3 = 6	6 • 0 = 0	8 ÷ 4 = 2	9 ÷ 3 = 3
4 * 4 = 16	8 * 1 = 8	2 ÷ 1 = 2	20 ÷ 4 = 5
9 × 0 = 0	3 × 9 = 27	6 / 3 = 2	6 / 1 = 6
1 • 1 = 1	1 • 4 = 4	32 ÷ 4 = 8	24 ÷ 3 = 8

Name ________________________ Date ____________

▶Play *Multiplication Three-in-a-Row*

Read the rules for playing *Multiplication Three-in-a-Row*. Then play the game with a partner.

Rules for *Multiplication Three-in-a-Row*

Number of players: 2
What You Will Need: A set of multiplication Strategy Cards, *Three-in-a-Row* Game Grids for each player (see page 271)

1. Each player looks through the cards and writes any nine of the products in the squares of a Game Grid. A player may write the same product more than once.
2. Shuffle the cards and place them exercise side up in the center of the table.
3. Players take turns. On each turn, a player finds the answer to the multiplication on the top card and then turns the card over to check the answer.
4. If the answer is correct, the player looks to see if the product is on the game grid. If it is, the player puts an X through that grid square. If the answer is wrong, or if the product is not on the grid, the player does not mark anything. The player then puts the card problem side up on the bottom of the stack.
5. The first player to mark three squares in a row (horizontally, vertically, or diagonally) wins.

Name Date

▶Play *Division Race*

Read the rules for playing *Division Race*. Then play the game with a partner.

Rules for *Division Race*

Number of Players: 2
What You Will Need: a set of division Strategy Cards, the *Division Race* game board (see page 272), a different game piece for each player

1. Shuffle the cards and then place them exercise side up on the table.
2. Both players put their game pieces on "START."
3. Players take turns. On each turn, a player finds the answer to the division on the top card and then turns the card over to check the answer.
4. If the answer is correct, the player moves *forward* that number of spaces. If a player's answer is wrong, the player moves *back* a number of spaces equal to the *correct* answer. Players cannot move back beyond the "START" square. The player puts the card on the bottom of the stack.
5. If a player lands on a space with special instructions, he or she should follow those instructions.
6. The first player to reach "END" wins.

Name Date

Name ________________________ Date ________________

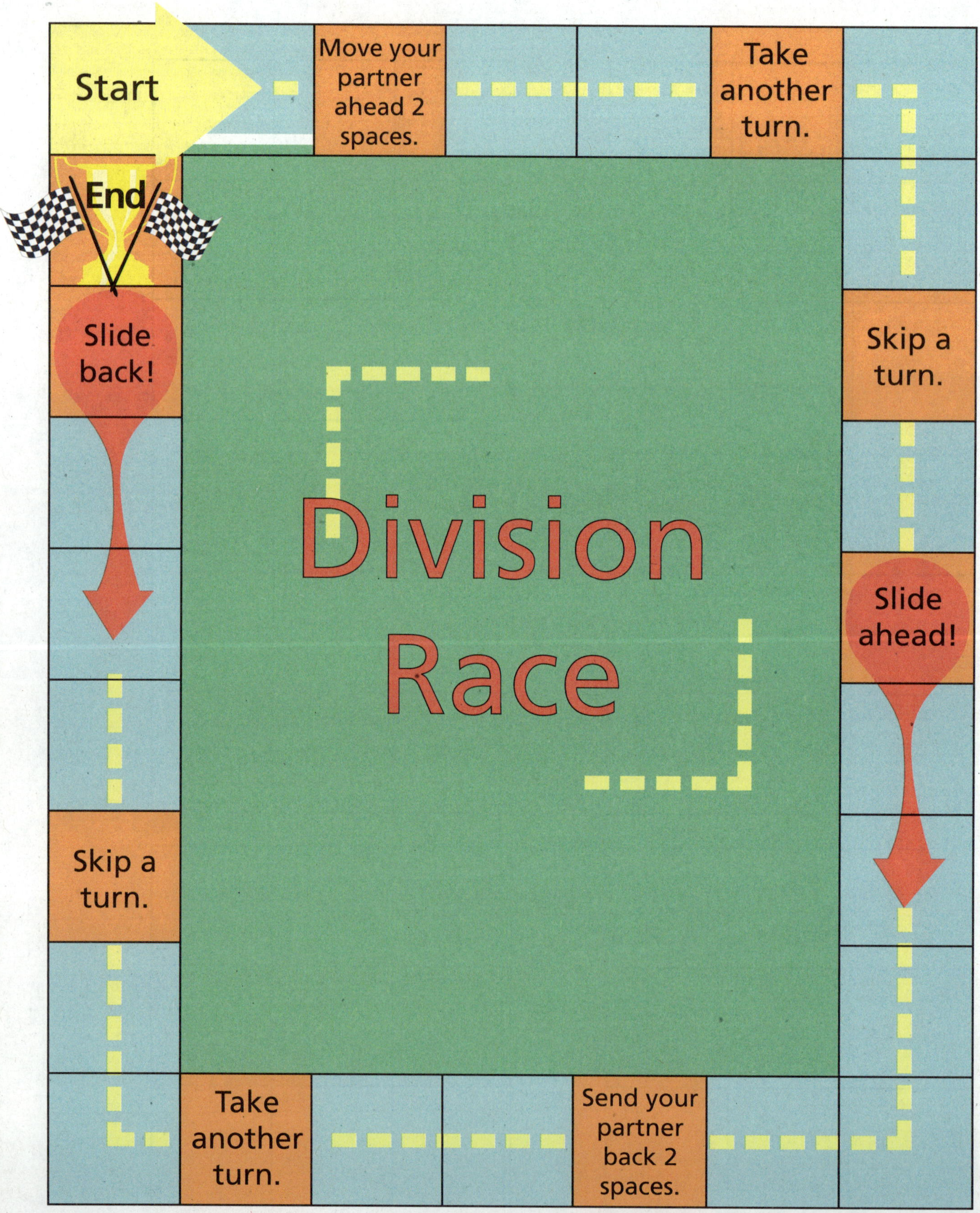
Start
Move your partner ahead 2 spaces.
Take another turn.
Skip a turn.
Slide ahead!
Send your partner back 2 spaces.
Take another turn.
Skip a turn.
Slide back!
End
Division Race

Name ____________________ Date ____________________

▶ Check Sheet 7: 0s, 1s, 2s, 3s, 4s, 5s, 9s and 10s

0s, 1s, 2s, 3s, 4s, 5s, 9s, 10s Multiplications	0s, 1s, 2s, 3s, 4s, 5s, 9s, 10s Multiplications	1s, 2s, 3s, 4s, 5s, 9s, 10s Divisions	1s, 2s, 3s, 4s, 5s, 9s, 10s Divisions
3 × 0 = 0	0 × 4 = 0	9 / 1 = 9	40 / 10 = 4
7 • 1 = 7	5 • 1 = 5	4 ÷ 2 = 2	7 ÷ 1 = 7
2 * 2 = 4	6 * 7 = 42	9 / 3 = 3	16 / 2 = 8
1 × 3 = 3	2 × 3 = 6	20 ÷ 4 = 5	18 ÷ 3 = 6
4 • 4 = 16	5 • 0 = 0	15 / 5 = 3	16 / 4 = 4
6 * 5 = 30	1 * 1 = 1	45 ÷ 9 = 5	50 ÷ 5 = 10
5 × 9 = 45	10 × 2 = 20	50 / 10 = 5	81 / 9 = 9
0 • 10 = 0	5 • 3 = 15	10 ÷ 1 = 10	30 ÷ 10 = 3
0 * 4 = 0	4 * 5 = 20	8 / 2 = 4	10 / 1 = 10
1 × 8 = 8	5 × 6 = 30	12 / 3 = 4	8 / 2 = 4
2 • 5 = 10	9 • 7 = 63	16 ÷ 4 = 4	27 ÷ 3 = 9
3 * 2 = 6	4 * 10 = 40	35 / 5 = 7	36 / 4 = 9
4 × 3 = 12	6 × 0 = 0	27 ÷ 9 = 3	30 ÷ 5 = 6
5 • 4 = 20	1 • 6 = 6	60 / 10 = 6	9 / 9 = 1
9 * 6 = 54	3 * 2 = 6	7 ÷ 1 = 7	80 ÷ 10 = 8
10 × 7 = 70	7 × 3 = 21	8 / 2 = 4	10 / 1 = 10
0 • 8 = 0	4 • 0 = 0	18 ÷ 3 = 6	4 ÷ 2 = 2
4 * 9 = 36	9 * 5 = 40	12 ÷ 4 = 3	21 ÷ 3 = 7
2 × 0 = 0	4 × 9 = 36	40 / 5 = 8	8 / 4 = 2
1 • 3 = 3	10 • 5 = 50	36 ÷ 9 = 4	25 ÷ 5 = 5

Name ______________________ Date ______________________

▶Dashes 1–4

Complete each Dash. Check your answers on page 277.

Dash 1 2s, 5s, 9s, 10s Multiplications	Dash 2 2s, 5s, 9s, 10s Divisions	Dash 3 3s, 4s, 0s, 1s Multiplications	Dash 4 3s, 4s, 1s Divisions
a. 4 × 5 = __	a. 8 / 2 = __	a. 3 × 0 = __	a. 12 / 4 = __
b. 10 • 3 = __	b. 50 ÷ 10 = __	b. 4 • 6 = __	b. 5 ÷ 1 = __
c. 8 * 9 = __	c. 15 / 5 = __	c. 9 * 1 = __	c. 21 / 3 = __
d. 6 × 2 = __	d. 63 ÷ 9 = __	d. 3 × 3 = __	d. 1 ÷ 1 = __
e. 5 • 7 = __	e. 90 / 10 = __	e. 8 • 4 = __	e. 16 / 4 = __
f. 10 * 5 = __	f. 90 ÷ 9 = __	f. 0 * 5 = __	f. 9 ÷ 3 = __
g. 8 × 2 = __	g. 35 / 5 = __	g. 1 × 6 = __	g. 32 / 4 = __
h. 6 • 10 = __	h. 14 ÷ 2 = __	h. 4 • 3 = __	h. 8 ÷ 1 = __
i. 9 * 3 = __	i. 27 / 9 = __	i. 7 * 4 = __	i. 24 / 4 = __
j. 2 × 9 = __	j. 45 / 5 = __	j. 3 × 7 = __	j. 18 / 3 = __
k. 5 • 8 = __	k. 10 ÷ 10 = __	k. 0 • 1 = __	k. 10 ÷ 1 = __
l. 10 * 7 = __	l. 25 / 5 = __	l. 10 * 1 = __	l. 40 / 4 = __
m. 5 × 5 = __	m. 54 ÷ 9 = __	m. 4 × 4 = __	m. 12 ÷ 3 = __
n. 1 • 5 = __	n. 6 / 2 = __	n. 9 • 3 = __	n. 6 / 3 = __
o. 9 * 6 = __	o. 72 ÷ 9 = __	o. 8 * 0 = __	o. 4 ÷ 4 = __
p. 10 × 10 = __	p. 40 / 5 = __	p. 5 × 4 = __	p. 7 / 1 = __
q. 4 • 2 = __	q. 80 ÷ 10 = __	q. 1 • 6 = __	q. 28 ÷ 4 = __
r. 10 * 8 = __	r. 18 ÷ 2 = __	r. 3 * 8 = __	r. 24 ÷ 3 = __
s. 3 × 9 = __	s. 36 / 9 = __	s. 4 × 9 = __	s. 20 / 4 = __
t. 9 • 9 = __	t. 30 ÷ 5 = __	t. 0 • 4 = __	t. 27 ÷ 3 = __

Name ____________________ Date ____________________

▶ Dashes 1–4

Complete each Dash. Check your answers on page 277.

Dash 1 2s, 5s, 9s, 10s Multiplications	Dash 2 2s, 5s, 9s, 10s Divisions	Dash 3 3s, 4s, 0s, 1s Multiplications	Dash 4 3s, 4s, 1s Divisions
a. 4 × 5 = __	a. 8 / 2 = __	a. 3 × 0 = __	a. 12 / 4 = __
b. 10 • 3 = __	b. 50 ÷ 10 = __	b. 4 • 6 = __	b. 5 ÷ 1 = __
c. 8 * 9 = __	c. 15 / 5 = __	c. 9 * 1 = __	c. 21 / 3 = __
d. 6 × 2 = __	d. 63 ÷ 9 = __	d. 3 × 3 = __	d. 1 ÷ 1 = __
e. 5 • 7 = __	e. 90 / 10 = __	e. 8 • 4 = __	e. 16 / 4 = __
f. 10 * 5 = __	f. 90 ÷ 9 = __	f. 0 * 5 = __	f. 9 ÷ 3 = __
g. 8 × 2 = __	g. 35 / 5 = __	g. 1 × 6 = __	g. 32 / 4 = __
h. 6 • 10 = __	h. 14 ÷ 2 = __	h. 4 • 3 = __	h. 8 ÷ 1 = __
i. 9 * 3 = __	i. 27 / 9 = __	i. 7 * 4 = __	i. 24 / 4 = __
j. 2 × 9 = __	j. 45 / 5 = __	j. 3 × 7 = __	j. 18 / 3 = __
k. 5 • 8 = __	k. 10 ÷ 10 = __	k. 0 • 1 = __	k. 10 ÷ 1 = __
l. 10 * 7 = __	l. 25 / 5 = __	l. 10 * 1 = __	l. 40 / 4 = __
m. 5 × 5 = __	m. 54 ÷ 9 = __	m. 4 × 4 = __	m. 12 ÷ 3 = __
n. 1 • 5 = __	n. 6 / 2 = __	n. 9 • 3 = __	n. 6 / 3 = __
o. 9 * 6 = __	o. 72 ÷ 9 = __	o. 8 * 0 = __	o. 4 ÷ 4 = __
p. 10 × 10 = __	p. 40 / 5 = __	p. 5 × 4 = __	p. 7 / 1 = __
q. 4 • 2 = __	q. 80 ÷ 10 = __	q. 1 • 6 = __	q. 28 ÷ 4 = __
r. 10 * 8 = __	r. 18 ÷ 2 = __	r. 3 * 8 = __	r. 24 ÷ 3 = __
s. 3 × 9 = __	s. 36 / 9 = __	s. 4 × 9 = __	s. 20 / 4 = __
t. 9 • 9 = __	t. 30 ÷ 5 = __	t. 0 • 4 = __	t. 27 ÷ 3 = __

Name Date

►Answers to Dashes 1–4

Use this sheet to check your answers to the Dashes on page 275.

Dash 1 2s, 5s, 9s, 10s Multiplications	Dash 2 2s, 5s, 9s, 10s Divisions	Dash 3 3s, 4s, 0s, 1s Multiplications	Dash 4 3s, 4s, 1s Divisions
a. 4 × 5 = 20	a. 8 / 2 = 4	a. 3 × 0 = 0	a. 12 / 4 = 3
b. 10 • 3 = 30	b. 50 ÷ 10 = 5	b. 4 • 6 = 24	b. 5 ÷ 1 = 5
c. 8 * 9 = 72	c. 15 / 5 = 3	c. 9 * 1 = 9	c. 21 / 3 = 7
d. 6 × 2 = 12	d. 63 ÷ 9 = 7	d. 3 × 3 = 9	d. 1 ÷ 1 = 1
e. 5 • 7 = 35	e. 90 / 10 = 9	e. 8 • 4 = 32	e. 16 / 4 = 4
f. 10 * 5 = 50	f. 90 ÷ 9 = 10	f. 0 * 5 = 0	f. 9 ÷ 3 = 3
g. 8 × 2 = 16	g. 35 / 5 = 7	g. 1 × 6 = 6	g. 32 / 4 = 8
h. 6 • 10 = 60	h. 14 ÷ 2 = 7	h. 4 • 3 = 12	h. 8 ÷ 1 = 8
i. 9 * 3 = 27	i. 27 / 9 = 3	i. 7 * 4 = 28	i. 24 / 4 = 6
j. 2 × 9 = 18	j. 45 / 5 = 9	j. 3 × 7 = 21	j. 18 / 3 = 6
k. 5 • 8 = 40	k. 10 ÷ 10 = 1	k. 0 • 1 = 0	k. 10 ÷ 1 = 10
l. 10 * 7 = 70	l. 25 / 5 = 5	l. 10 * 1 = 10	l. 40 / 4 = 10
m. 5 × 5 = 25	m. 54 ÷ 9 = 6	m. 4 × 4 = 16	m. 12 ÷ 3 = 4
n. 1 • 5 = 5	n. 6 / 2 = 3	n. 9 • 3 = 27	n. 6 / 3 = 2
o. 9 * 6 = 54	o. 72 ÷ 9 = 8	o. 8 * 0 = 0	o. 4 ÷ 4 = 1
p. 10 × 10 = 100	p. 40 / 5 = 8	p. 5 × 4 = 20	p. 7 / 1 = 7
q. 4 • 2 = 8	q. 80 ÷ 10 = 8	q. 1 • 6 = 6	q. 28 ÷ 4 = 7
r. 10 * 8 = 80	r. 18 ÷ 2 = 9	r. 3 * 8 = 24	r. 24 ÷ 3 = 8
s. 3 × 9 = 27	s. 36 / 9 = 4	s. 4 × 9 = 36	s. 20 / 4 = 5
t. 9 • 9 = 81	t. 30 ÷ 5 = 6	t. 0 • 4 = 0	t. 27 ÷ 3 = 9

7–16 Class Activity

Name ____________________ Date __________

▶ Solve Word Problems with 2s, 3s, 4s, 5s, 6s, 7s, and 9s

Solve each problem.

1. Toni counted 36 legs in the lion house at the zoo. How many lions were there?

____

2. One wall of an art gallery has a row of 5 paintings and a row of 9 paintings. How many paintings are on the wall?

____

3. Josh's muffin pan is an array with 4 rows and 6 columns. How many muffins can Josh make in the pan?

____

4. To get ready for the school spelling bee, Tanya studied 3 hours each night for an entire week. How many hours did she study?

____

5. The 14 trumpet players in the marching band lined up in 2 equal rows. How many trumpet players were in each row?

____

6. The Sunnyside Riding Stable has 9 horses. The owners are going to buy new horseshoes for all the horses. How many horseshoes are needed?

____

Name _______________ Date _______________

►Use Patterns to Divide 2- and 3-Digit Numbers

Find each quotient.

1. $8 \div 2 =$ 8 ones $\div 2 =$ 4 ones or ______

$80 \div 2 =$ 8 tens $\div 2 =$ 4 tens or ______

$800 \div 2 =$ 8 hundreds $\div 2 =$ 4 hundreds or ______

2. $9 \div 3 =$ 9 ones $\div 3 =$ ______ ones or ______

$90 \div 3 =$ 9 tens $\div 3 =$ ______ tens or ______

$900 \div 3 =$ 9 hundreds $\div 3 =$ ______ hundreds or ______

3. $8 \div 4 =$ ______

$80 \div 4 =$ ______

$800 \div 4 =$ ______

4. $6 \div 2 =$ ______

$60 \div 2 =$ ______

$600 \div 2 =$ ______

5. $6 \div 3 =$ ______

$60 \div 3 =$ ______

$600 \div 3 =$ ______

6. $4 \div 2 =$ ______

$40 \div 2 =$ ______

$400 \div 2 =$ ______

7. $9 \div 3 =$ ______

$90 \div 3 =$ ______

$900 \div 3 =$ ______

8. $25 \div 5 =$ ______

$250 \div 5 =$ ______

$2{,}500 \div 5 =$ ______

9. $36 \div 4 =$ ______

$360 \div 4 =$ ______

$3{,}600 \div 4 =$ ______

10. $72 \div 9 =$ ______

$720 \div 9 =$ ______

$7{,}200 \div 9 =$ ______

11. $54 \div 9 =$ ______

$540 \div 9 =$ ______

$5{,}400 \div 9 =$ ______

Name ______________________ Date ______________

▶ Math and Science

Apatosaurus Triceratops Stegosaurus

Take a survey. Find out which dinosaur is the favorite.

1. What question will you ask?

____

2. How many people will you ask?

____

3. Take the survey. Record your results in the tally chart below.

	Tally	Total
Apatosaurus		
Triceratops		
Stegosaurus		

4. Which dinosaur is the favorite? How do you know?

____

____

____

5. What is the difference between the number of votes for the most popular dinosaur and the number of votes for the least popular dinosaur?

____

7–17

Class Activity

Name ____________________ Date ____________

▶ Take a Survey

6. What question would you like to ask in a survey?

____

____

____

7. What answer choices will you have in your survey?

____

____

____

8. How many people will you survey?

____

9. Take the survey. Record your results in the tally chart below.

	Tally	Total

10. Show the results of the survey in a bar graph. Use grid paper to make the graph.

11. Make 3 statements about the results of your survey.

____

____

____

7 Unit Test

Name ______________________ Date ______________

Multiply or divide.

1. $8 \times 2 = \square$ 2. $5 \bullet 7 = \square$ 3. $10 \div 1 = \square$

4. $81 \div 9 = \square$ 5. $4 \times 0 = \square$ 6. $63 / 9 = \square$

7. $6 \bullet 4 = \square$ 8. $45 / 5 = \square$ 9. $9 \times 3 = \square$

10. $3\overline{)24}$ $\square$ 11. $28 \div 4 = \square$ 12. $10 * 8 = \square$

Write a multiplication equation to find the total number.

13. ______________________

Without counting the oranges, compare the arrays. Write >, <, or = in the ◯. Then write an equation for each array to show your comparison is correct.

14.

 ◯ 

______________________ ______________________

Write a multiplication equation to represent the area of the rectangle.

15.

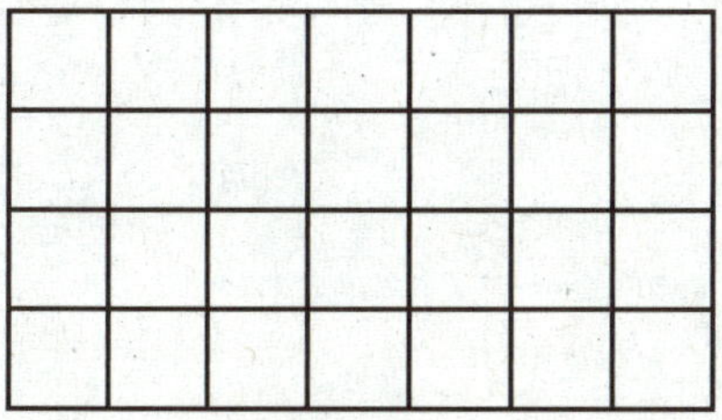

____

7 Unit Test

Name ____________________ Date ________

Complete.

16. $9 + 9 + 9 + 9 + 9 + 9 + 9 + 9 = \_\_\_\_\_ \times 9 = \_\_\_\_\_$

Write a related division equation.

17. $8 \times 5 = 40$ ____________________

Write a related multiplication equation.

18. $18 \div 2 = 9$ ____________________

Write an equation to solve each problem. Then write the answer.

19. Olivia's CD rack has 4 shelves. It holds 8 CDs on a shelf. How many CDs will fit in the rack altogether?

____

20. **Extended Response** Paco set up 7 tables to seat 28 children at his birthday party. The same number of children will sit at each table. How many children will sit at each table? Explain how you found your answer. Make a math drawing to help explain.

____

____

____

____

Glossary

A

acute angle An angle whose measure is less than 90°.

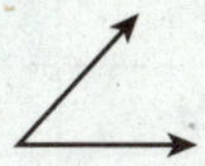

acute triangle A triangle in which the measure of each angle is less than 90°.

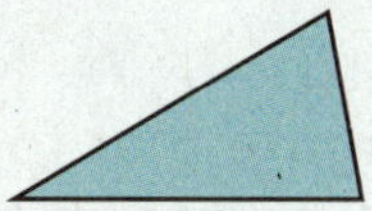

addend A number to be added.

Example: $8 + 4 = 12$

addend (8), addend (4)

addition A mathematical operation that combines two or more numbers.

Example: $23 + 52 = 75$

addend (23), addend (52), sum (75)

adjacent (sides) Two sides that meet at a point.

Example: Sides *a* and *b* are adjacent.

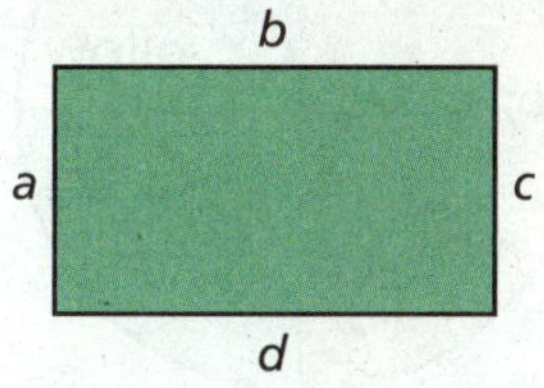

A.M. The time period between midnight and noon.

angle A figure formed by two rays or two line segments that meet at an endpoint.

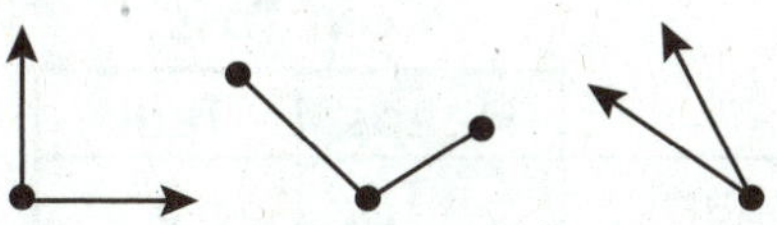

area The number of square units in a region

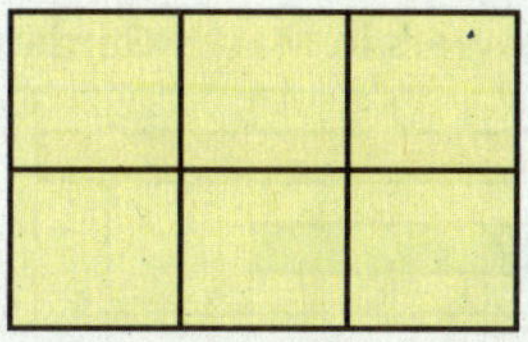

The area of the rectangle is 6 square units.

array An arrangement of objects, pictures, or numbers in columns and rows.

Associative Property of Addition (Grouping Property of Addition) The property which states that changing the way in which addends are grouped does not change the sum.

Example: $(2 + 3) + 1 = 2 + (3 + 1)$

$5 + 1 = 2 + 4$

$6 = 6$

Associative Property of Multiplication (Grouping Property of Multiplication) The property which states that changing the way in which factors are grouped does not change the product.

Example: $(2 \times 3) \times 4 = 2 \times (3 \times 4)$

$6 \times 4 = 2 \times 12$

$24 = 24$

axis (plural: **axes**) A reference line for a graph. A bar graph has 2 axes; one is horizontal and the other is vertical.

Flowers in Mary's Garden

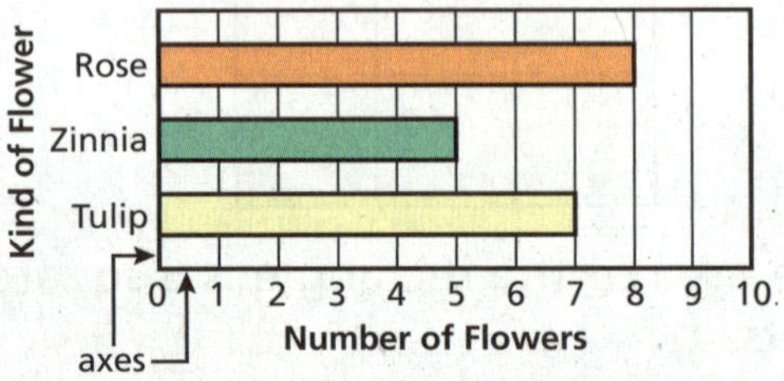

B

bar graph A graph that uses bars to show data. The bars may be horizontal or vertical.

Canned Goods at Turner's Market

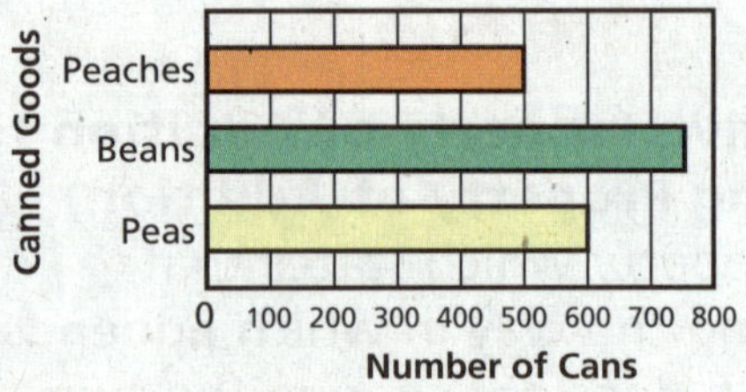

base (of a geometric figure) The bottom side of a 2-D figure or the bottom face of a 3-D figure.

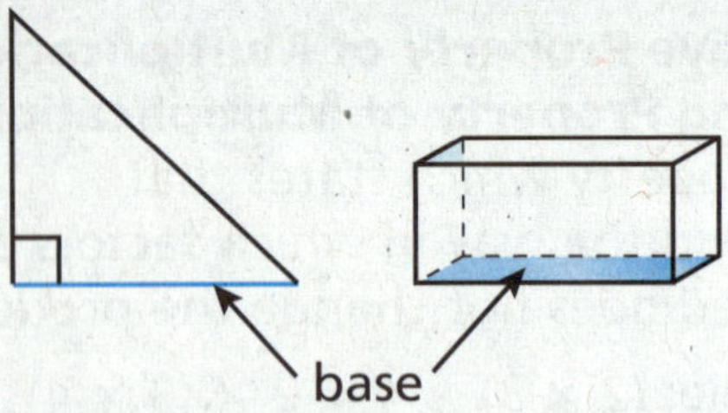

C

calculator A tool used to perform mathematical operations.

capacity The amount a container can hold.

cell A rectangle in a table where a column and row meet.

Coin Toss

	Heads	Tails
Sam	11	6
Zoe	9	10

} cell

centimeter (cm) A metric unit used to measure length.

100 cm = 1 m

circle A plane figure that forms a closed path so that all points on the path are the same distance from a point called the center.

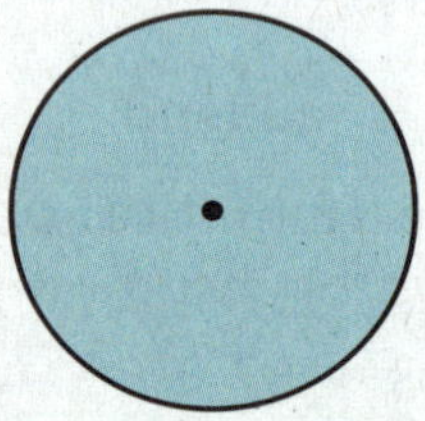

circle graph A graph that represents data as parts of a whole.

Jacket Colors in Ms. Timmer's Class

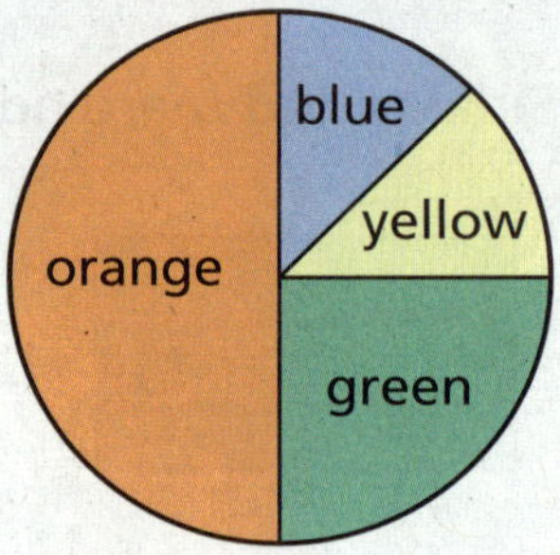

circumference The distance around a circle, about $3\frac{1}{7}$ times the diameter.

column A vertical group of cells in a table.

Coin Toss

	Heads	Tails
Sam	11	6
Zoe	9	10

column

Commutative Property of Addition (Order Property of Addition) The property which states that changing the order of addends does not change the sum.

Example: $3 + 7 = 7 + 3$

$10 = 10$

Commutative Property of Multiplication (Order Property of Multiplication) The property which states that changing the order of factors does not change the product.

Example: $5 \times 4 = 4 \times 5$

$20 = 20$

comparison bars Bars that represent the larger amount, smaller amount, and difference in a comparison problem.

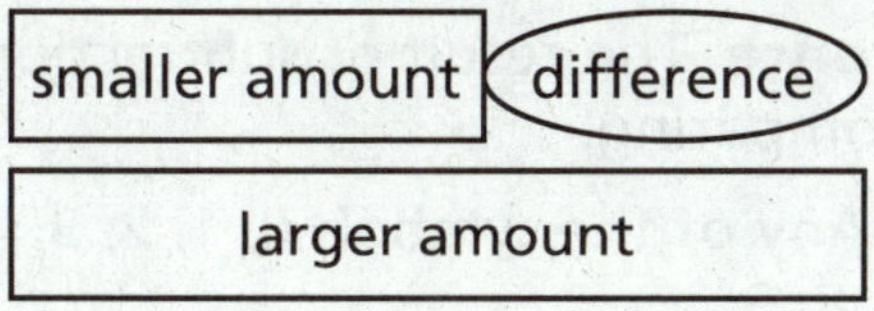

In Volume 2, we use comparison bars for multiplication.

cone A solid figure that has a circular base and comes to a point called the vertex.

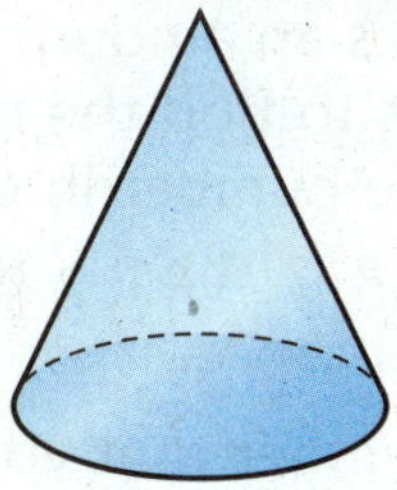

congruent figures Figures that have the same size and shape.

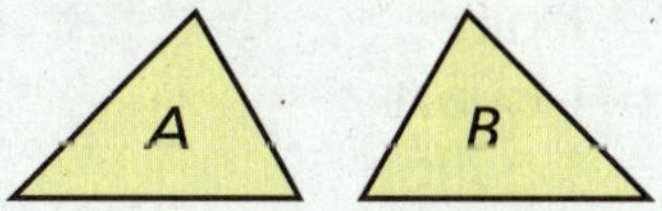

Triangles A and B are congruent.

coordinates The numbers in an ordered pair that locate a point on a coordinate grid. The first number is the distance across and the second number is the distance up.

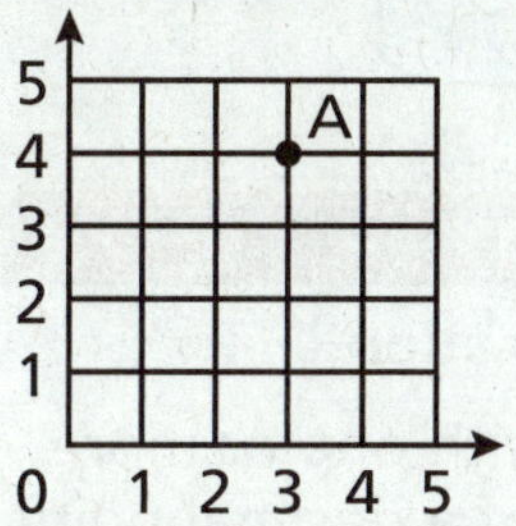

The coordinates 3 and 4 in the ordered pair (3, 4) locate Point *A* on the coordinate grid.

coordinate grid A grid formed by two perpendicular number lines in which every point is assigned an ordered pair of numbers.

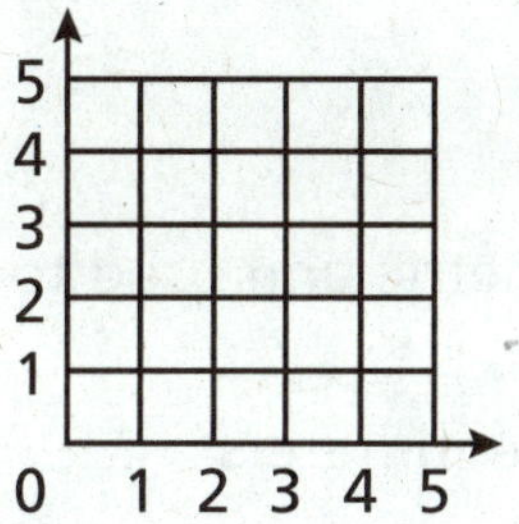

cube A solid figure that has six square faces of equal size.

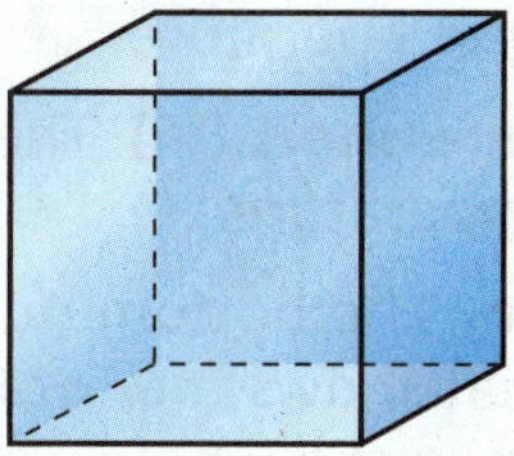

cup (c) A customary unit of measurement used to measure capacity.

2 cups = 1 pint
4 cups = 1 quart
16 cups = 1 gallon

cylinder A solid figure with two congruent circular or elliptical faces and one curved surface.

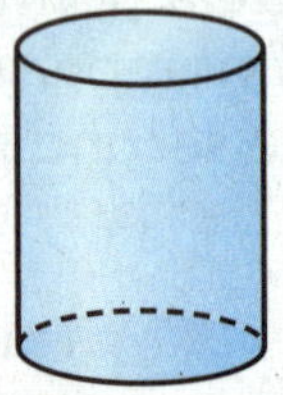

D

data Pieces of information.

decimal A number with one or more digits to the right of a decimal point.

Examples: 1.23 and 0.3

decimal point The dot that separates the whole number from the decimal part.

1.23
↑
decimal point

decimeter (dm) A metric unit used to measure length

1 decimeter = 10 centimeters

degree (°) A unit for measuring angles or temperature.

degrees Celsius (°C) The metric unit for measuring temperature.

degrees Fahrenheit (°F) The customary unit of temperature.

denominator The bottom number in a fraction that shows the total number of equal parts in the whole.

Example: $\frac{1}{3}$ ← denominator

diagonal A line segment that connects two corners of a figure and is not a side of the figure.

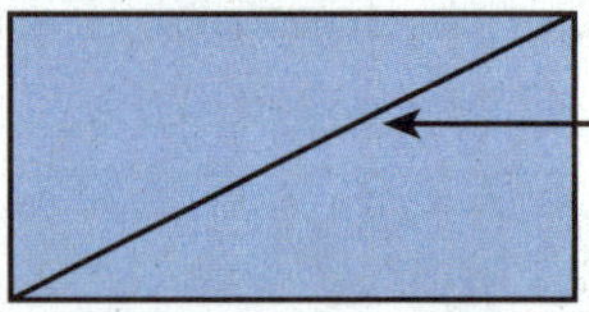

diameter A line segment that connects two points on a circle and also passes through the center of the circle. The term is also used to describe the length of such a line segment.

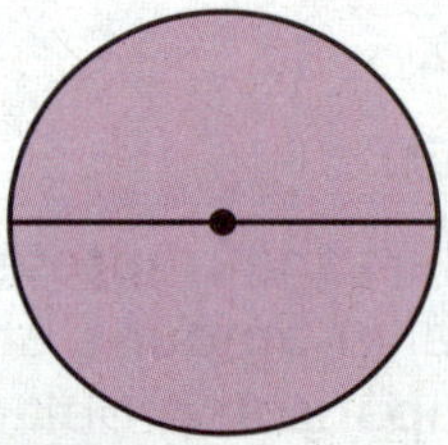

difference The result of subtraction or of comparing.

digit Any of the symbols 0, 1, 2, 3, 4, 5, 6, 7, 8, 9.

dividend The number that is divided in division.

Examples:

$12 \div 3 = 4$ (↑ dividend: 12)

$3\overline{)12}$ with quotient 4 (↑ dividend: 12)

division The mathematical operation that separates an amount into smaller equal groups to find the number of groups or the number in each group.

Example: 12 ÷ 3 = 4 is a division number sentence.

divisor The number that you divide by in division.

Example: $12 \div 3 = 4$ (↑ divisor: 3) $3\overline{)12}$ with quotient 4 (↑ divisor: 3)

E

edge The line segment where two faces of a solid figure meet.

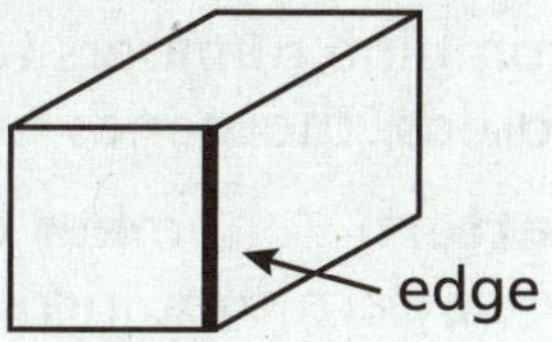

elapsed time The time that passes between the beginning and the end of an activity.

endpoint The point at either end of a line segment or the beginning point of a ray.

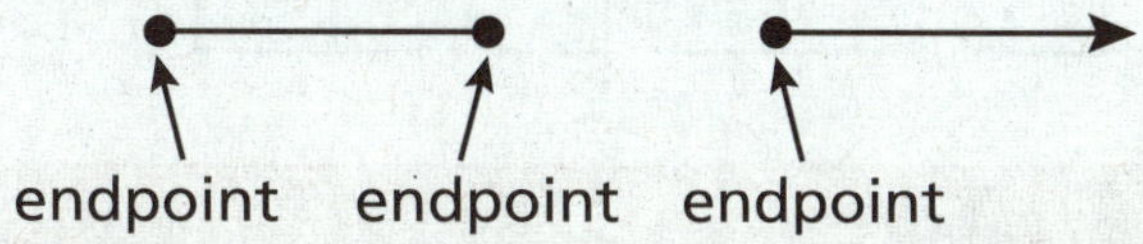

equation A mathematical sentence with an equals sign.

Examples: $11 + 22 = 33$
$75 - 25 = 50$

equilateral triangle A triangle whose sides are all the same length.

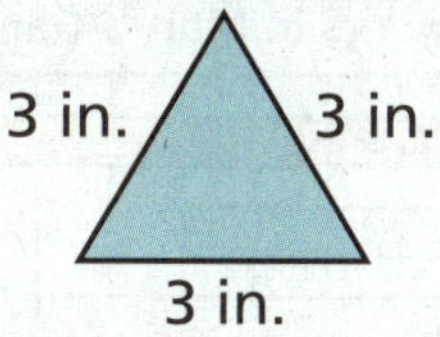

equivalent Equal, or naming the same amount.

equivalent fractions Fractions that name the same amount.

Example: $\frac{1}{2}$ and $\frac{2}{4}$

equivalent fractions

estimate About how many or about how much.

even number A whole number that is a multiple of 2. The ones digit in an even number is 0, 2, 4, 6, or 8.

event In probability, a possible outcome.

expanded form A number written to show the value of each of its digits.

Examples:
$347 = 300 + 40 + 7$
$347 = 3$ hundreds $+ 4$ tens $+ 7$ ones

expression A combination of numbers, variables, and/or operation signs. An expression does not have an equals sign.

Examples: $4 + 7$ $\quad a - 3$

F

face A flat surface of a solid figure.

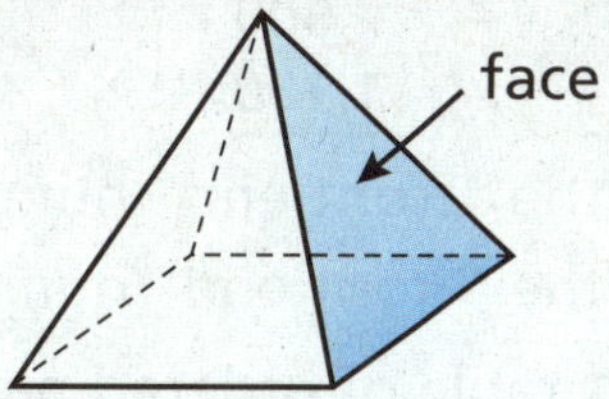

factors Numbers that are multiplied to give a product.

Example: $4 \times 5 = 20$

factor factor product

flip To reflect a figure over a line. The size and shape of the figure remain the same.

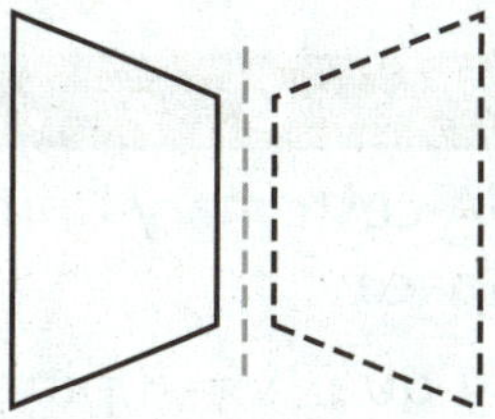

foot (ft) A customary unit used to measure length.

1 foot = 12 inches

formula An equation with variables that describes a rule.

The formula for the area of a rectangle is:

$A = l \times w$

where A is the area, l is the length, and w is the width.

fraction A number that names part of a whole or part of a set.

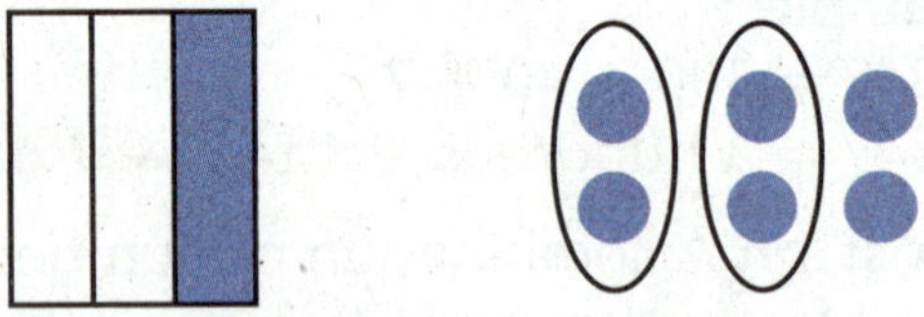

$\frac{1}{3}$ ← fraction → $\frac{2}{3}$

front-end estimation A method of estimating that keeps the largest place value in a number and drops the rest.

Example:

527	→	500
+ 673	→	+ 600
		1,100

The 5 in 527 is the "front end" number

The 6 in 673 is the "front end" number

function table A table of ordered pairs that shows a function.

For every input number, there is only one possible output number.

Rule: add 2	
Input	Output
1	3
2	4
3	5
4	6

G

gallon (gal) A customary unit used to measure capacity.

1 gallon = 4 quarts = 8 pints = 16 cups

gram (g) A metric unit of mass, about 1 paper clip.

1,000 grams = 1 kilogram

greater than (>) A symbol used to compare two numbers.

Example: $6 > 5$

6 is greater than 5.

group To combine numbers to form new tens, hundreds, thousands, and so on.

growing pattern A number or geometric pattern that increases.

Examples: 2, 4, 6, 8, 10…

1, 2, 5, 10, 17…

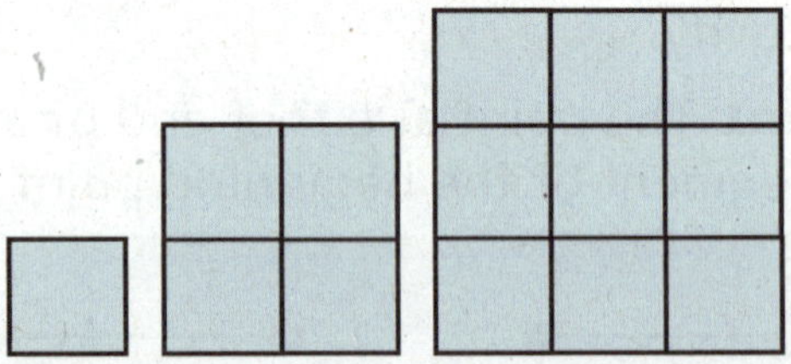

H

height A measurement of vertical length, or how tall something is.

horizontal Extending in two directions, left and right.

horizontal bar graph A bar graph with horizontal bars.

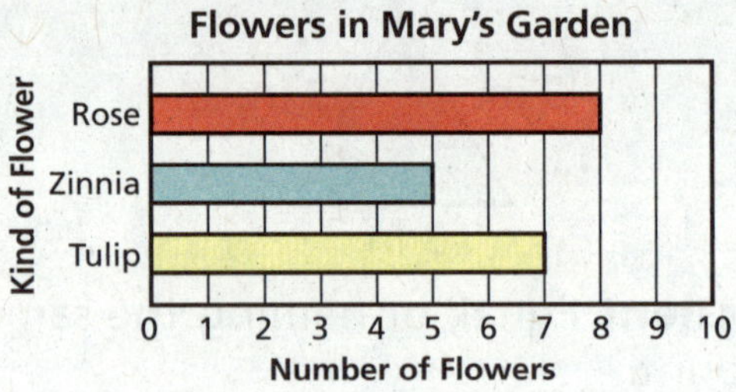

hundredth One of the equal parts when a whole is divided into 100 equal parts.

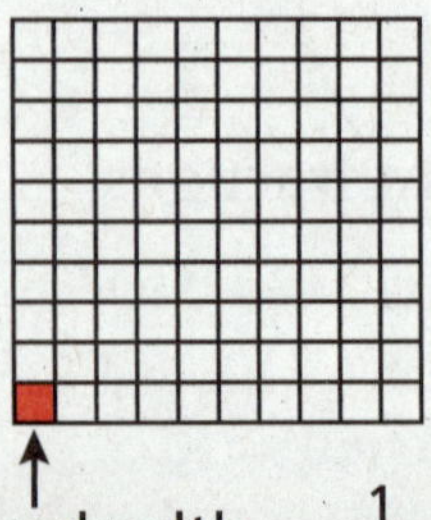

one hundredth = $\frac{1}{100}$ = 0.01

I

improper fraction A fraction in which the numerator is equal to or is greater than the denominator. Improper fractions are equal to or greater than 1.

$\frac{5}{5}$ and $\frac{8}{3}$ are improper fractions.

inch (in.) A customary unit used to measure length.

12 inches = 1 foot

isosceles triangle A triangle that has at least two sides of the same length.

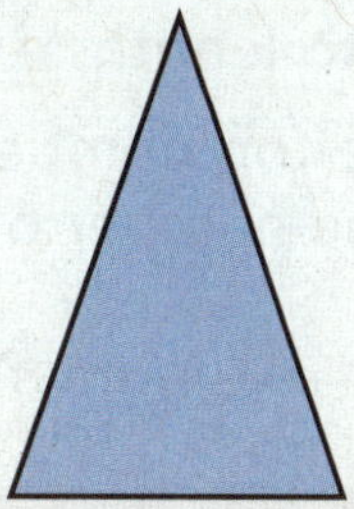

K

key A part of a map, graph, or chart that explains what symbols mean.

kilogram (kg) A metric unit of mass.

1 kilogram = 1,000 grams

kilometer (km) A metric unit of length.

1 kilometer = 1,000 meters

L

less than (<) A symbol used to compare numbers.

Example: $5 < 6$

5 *is less than* 6.

line A straight path that goes on forever in opposite directions.

line graph A graph that uses a straight line or a broken line to show changes in data.

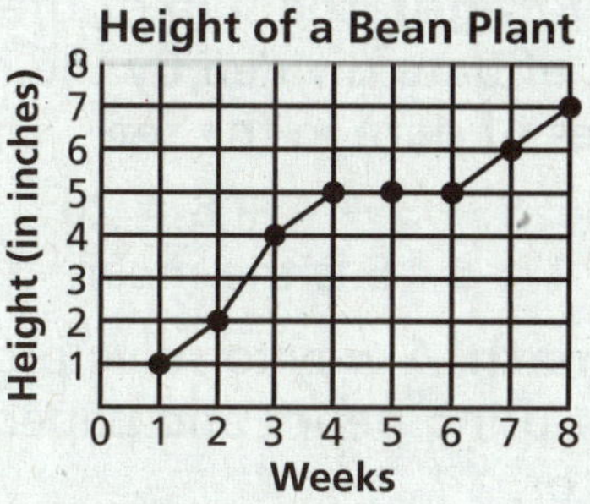

line of symmetry A line on which a figure can be folded so that the two halves match exactly.

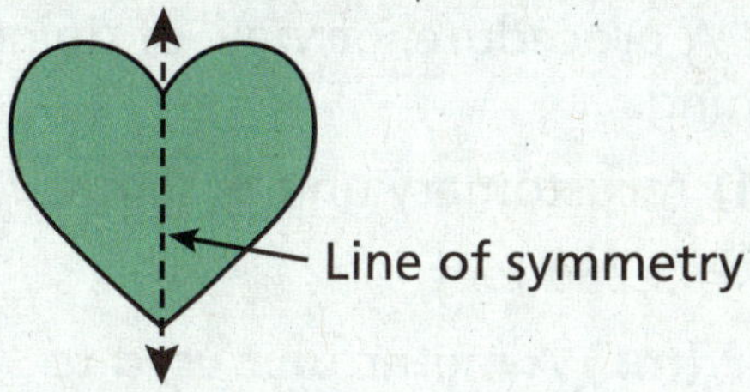

line plot A way to show data using a number line.

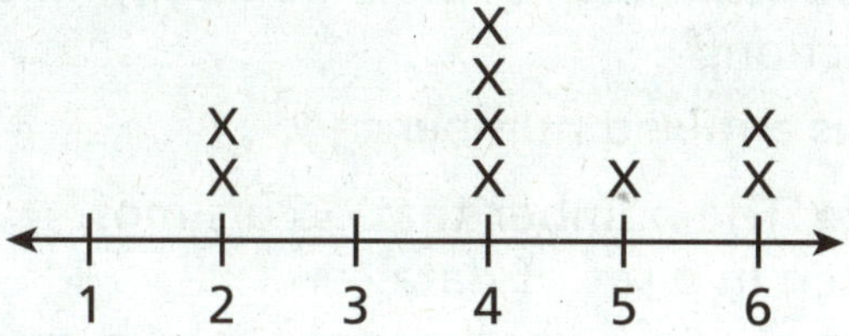

line segment A part of a line. A line segment has two endpoints.

liter (L) A metric unit used to measure capacity.

1 liter = 1,000 milliliters

M

mass The amount of matter in an object.

mean (average) The sum of the values in a set of data divided by the number of pieces of data in the set.

Example: $3 + 5 + 4 + 8 = 20$
$20 \div 4 = 5$ 5 is the mean

mental math A way to solve problems without using pencil and paper, or a calculator.

meter (m) A metric unit used to measure length.

1 meter = 100 centimeters

method A procedure, or way, of doing something.

mile (mi) A customary unit of length.

1 mile = 5,280 feet

milliliter (mL) A metric unit used to measure capacity.

1,000 milliliters = 1 liter

mixed number A whole number and a fraction.

$1\frac{3}{4}$ is a mixed number.

mode The number that occurs most often in a set of data.

In this set of numbers {3, 4, 5, 5, 5, 7, 8}, 5 is the mode.

multiple A number that is the product of the given number and another number.

multiplication A mathematical operation that combines equal groups.

Example: $4 \times 3 = 12$

factor factor product

$\underbrace{3 + 3 + 3 + 3}_{\text{4 times}} = 12$

N

net A flat pattern that can be folded to make a solid figure.

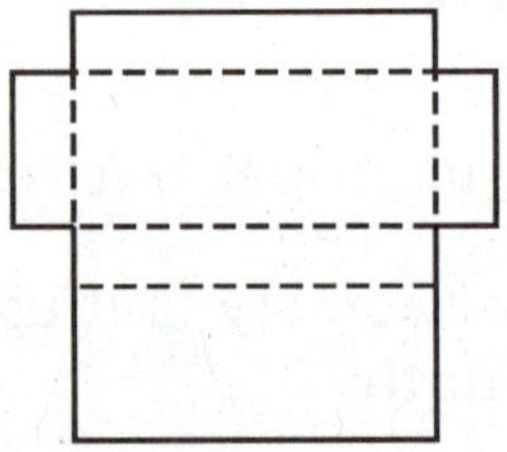

This net can be folded into a rectangular prism.

number line A line on which numbers are assigned to lengths.

numerator The top number in a fraction that shows the number of equal parts counted.

Example: $\frac{1}{3}$ ← numerator

O

obtuse angle An angle that measures more than 90° but less than 180°.

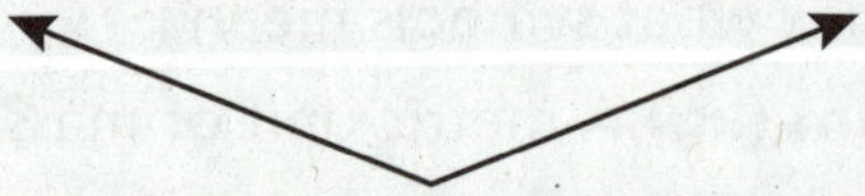

obtuse triangle A triangle with one angle that measures more than 90°.

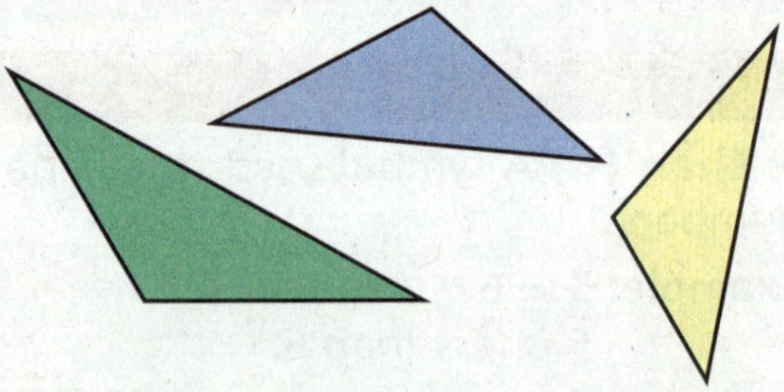

odd number A whole number that is not a multiple of 2. The ones digit in an odd number is 1, 3, 5, 7, or 9.

opposite sides Sides that are across from each other; they do not meet at a point.

Example: Sides *a* and *c* are opposite.

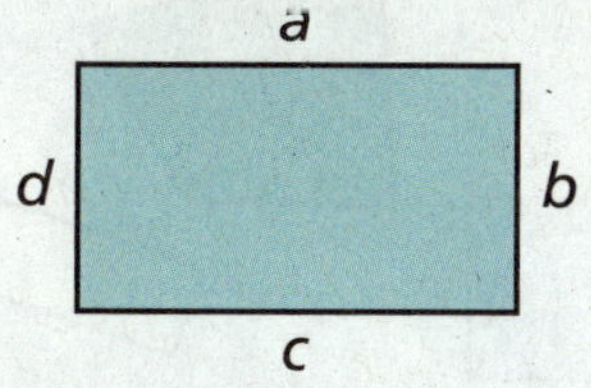

ordered pair A pair of numbers such as (3, 4) in which one number is considered to be first and the other number second. They can name a point on a coordinate grid.

ordinal numbers Numbers used to show order or position.

Example: first, second, fifth

ounce (oz) A customary unit used to measure weight.

16 ounces = 1 pound

P

parallel lines Two lines that are everywhere the same distance apart.

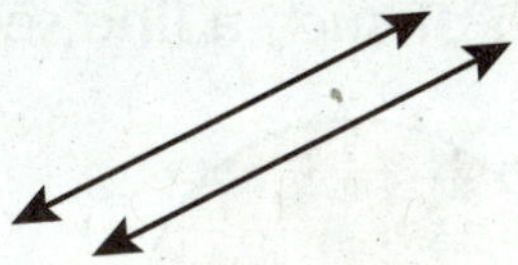

parallelogram A quadrilateral with both pairs of opposite sides parallel.

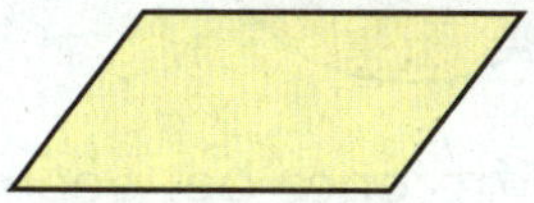

partner One of two numbers that add to make a total.

Example: 9 + 7 = 16 ← total *sum*

partner *addend* (9), partner *addend* (7)

perimeter The distance around the outside of a figure.

perpendicular Two lines or line segments that cross or meet to form right angles.

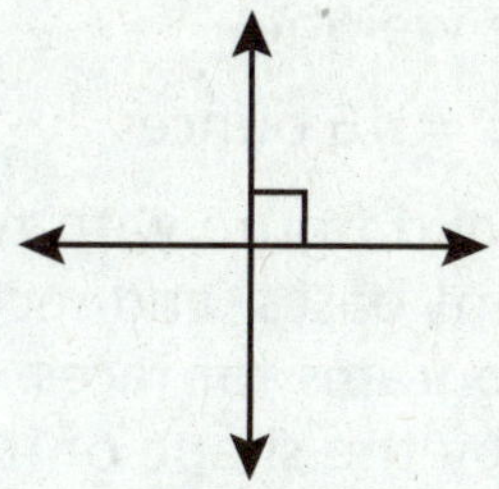

pictograph A graph that uses pictures or symbols to represent data.

pint (pt) A customary unit used to measure capacity.

1 pint = 2 cups

place value The value assigned to the place that a digit occupies in a number.

9 6 2

↑ hundreds ↑ tens ↑ ones

place value drawing A drawing that represents a number. Hundreds are represented by boxes, tens by vertical lines, and ones by small circles.

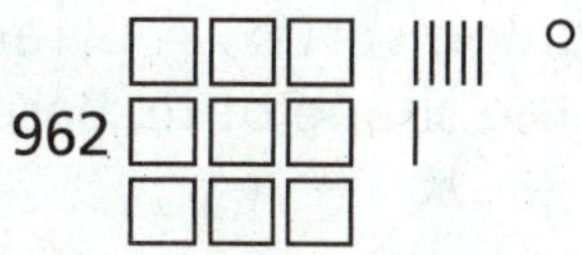

plane figure A closed figure that has two dimensions.

P.M. The time period between noon and midnight.

pound (lb) A customary unit used to measure weight.

1 pound = 16 ounces

prism A solid figure with two parallel congruent bases, and rectangles or parallelograms for faces. A prism is named by the shape of its bases.

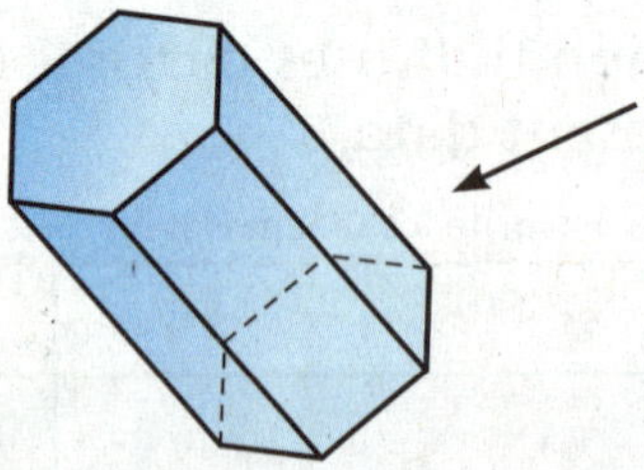

hexagonal prism

probability The chance of an event occurring.

product The answer when you multiply numbers.

Example: 4 × 7 = 28

factor factor product

proof drawing A drawing used to show that an answer is correct.

$$\begin{array}{r} 249 \\ +\ 386 \\ \hline 635 \end{array}$$

(regrouping marks: 11)

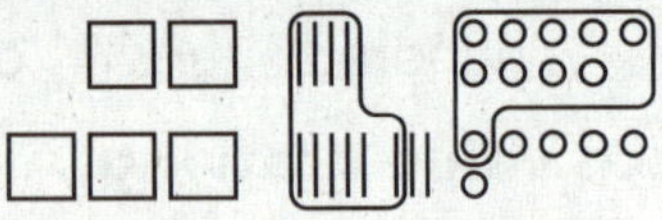

pyramid A solid figure with one base and whose other faces are triangles with a common vertex. A pyramid is named by the shape of its base.

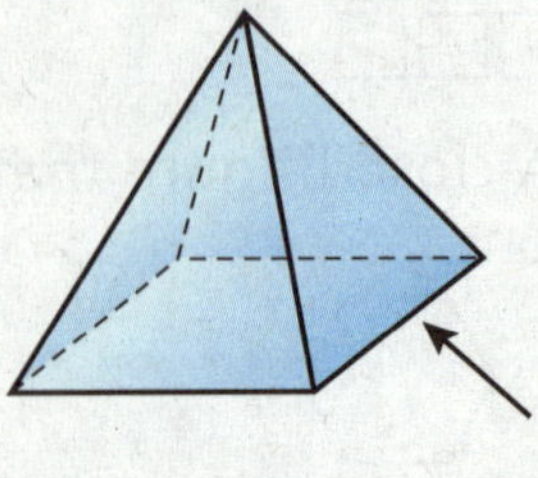

square pyramid

Q

quadrilateral A figure with four sides.

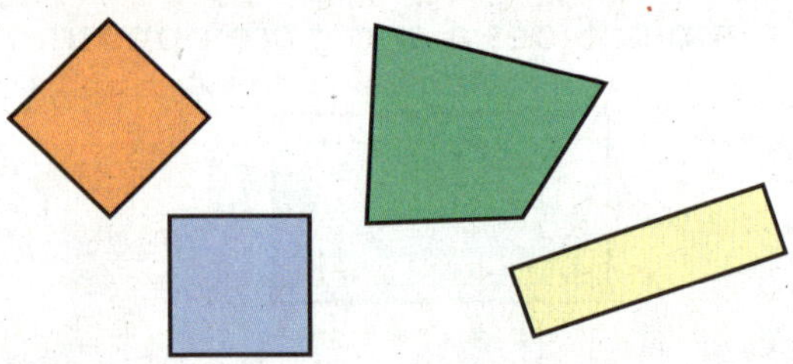

quart (qt) A customary unit used to measure capacity.

1 quart = 4 cups

quotient The answer when you divide numbers.

Examples:

35 ÷ 7 = 5 ← quotient (5)

$7\overline{)35}$ with 5 on top ← quotient

R

radius A line segment that connects the center of a circle to any point on the circle. The term is also used to describe the length of such a line segment.

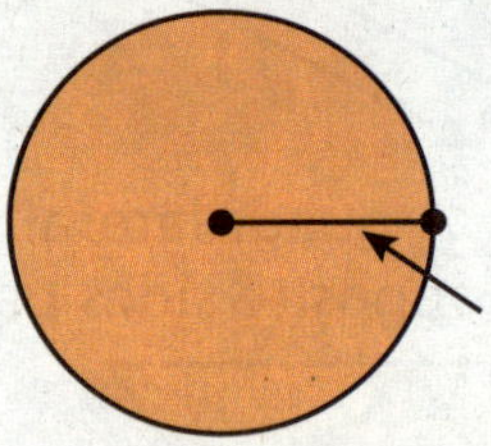

radius

range The difference between the greatest number and the least number in a set of data.

In this set of numbers {12, 15, 18, 19, 20}, the range is 20 − 12 or 8

ray A part of a line that has one endpoint and goes on forever in one direction.

rectangle A parallelogram that has 4 right angles.

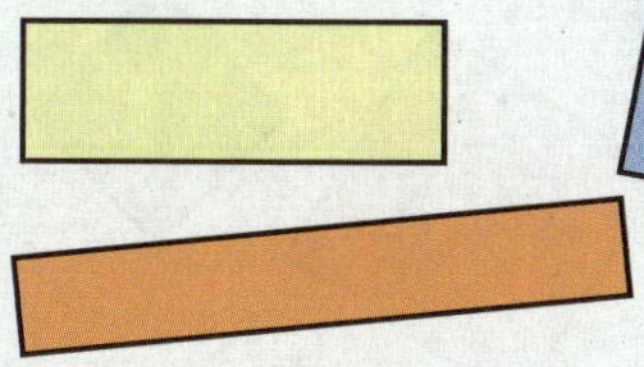

rectangular prism A prism with six rectangular faces.

rectangular pyramid A pyramid with a rectangular base and four triangular faces.

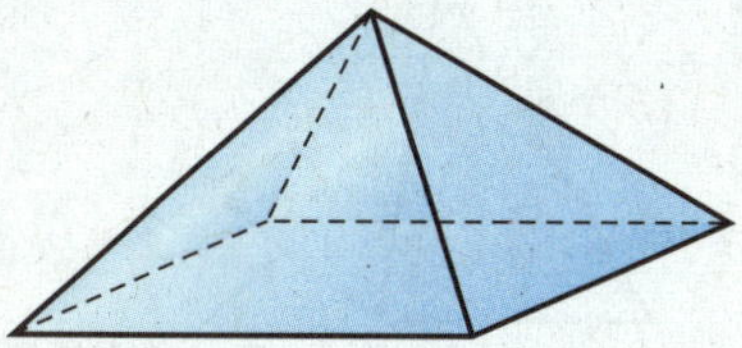

repeating pattern A pattern consisting of a group of numbers, letters, or figures that repeat.

Examples: 1, 2, 1, 2, ...
A, B, C, A, B, C, ...

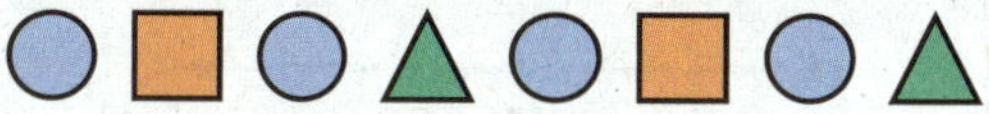

rhombus A parallelogram with congruent sides.

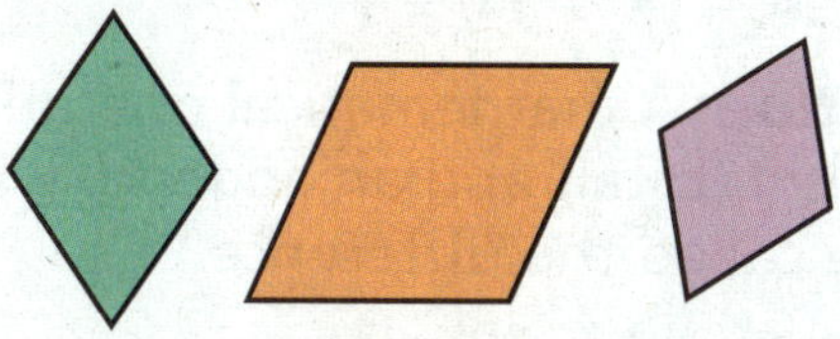

right angle An angle that measures 90°.

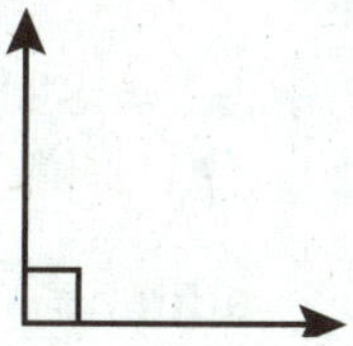

right triangle A triangle with one right angle.

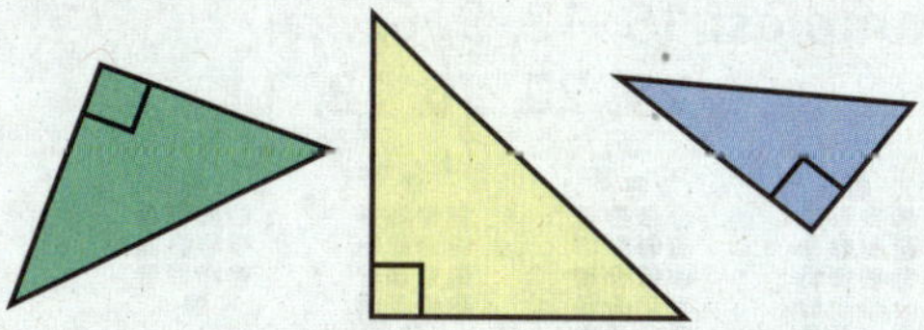

round To find about how many or how much by expressing a number to the nearest ten, hundred, thousand, and so on.

route The path taken to get to a location.

row A horizontal group of cells in a table.

Coin Toss

	Heads	Tails	
Sam	11	6	
Zoe	9	10	} row

S

scale An arrangement of numbers in order with equal intervals.

scalene triangle A triangle with sides of three different lengths.

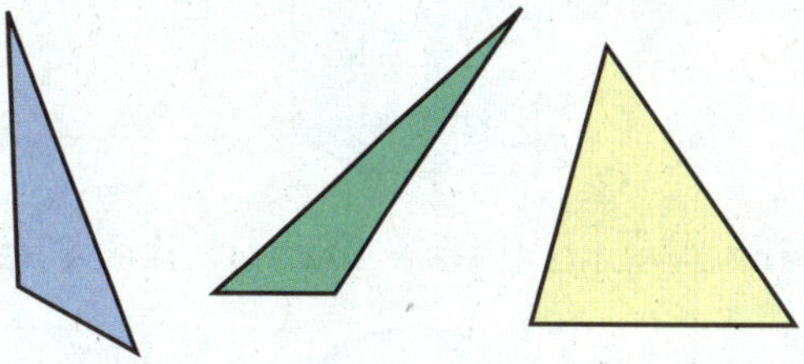

shrinking pattern A number or geometric pattern that decreases.

Examples: 15, 12, 9, 6, 3,...
25, 20, 16, 13, 11,...

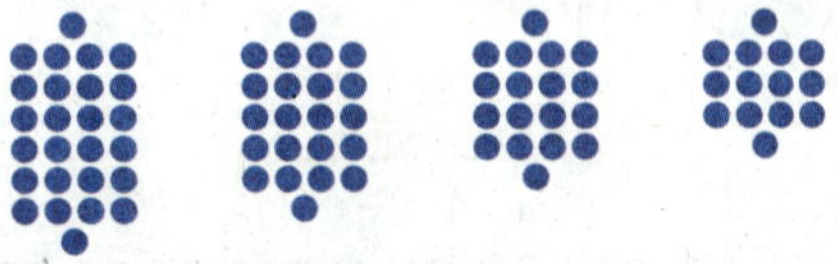

side (of a figure) A line segment that makes up a figure.

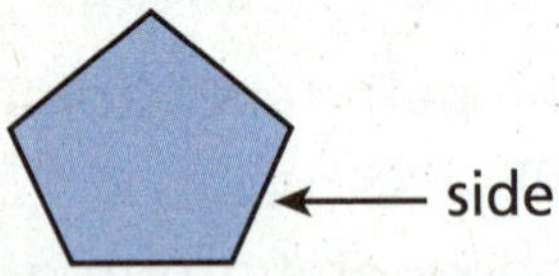

simplify To write an equivalent fraction with a smaller numerator and denominator.

slide To move a figure along a line in any direction. The size and shape of the figure remain the same.

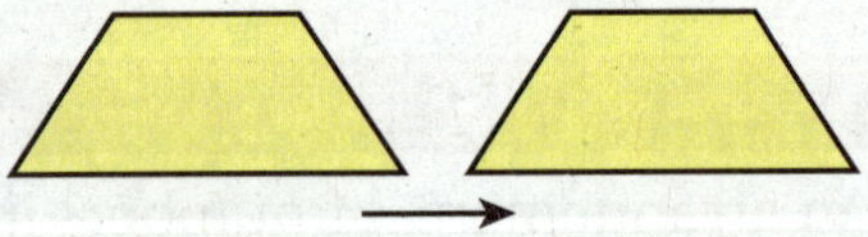

solid figure A figure that has three dimensions.

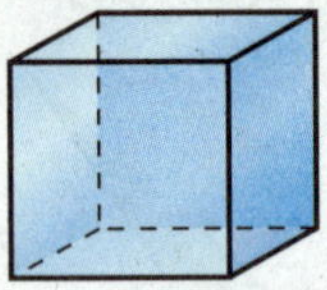

sphere A solid figure shaped like a ball.

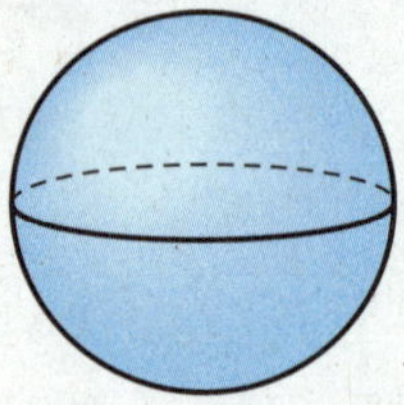

square A rectangle with four sides of the same length.

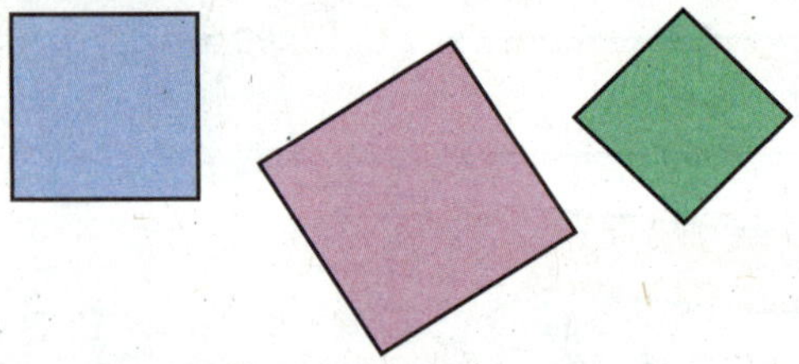

square number A product of a whole number and itself.

Example: $4 \times 4 = 16$

↑ square number

square pyramid A pyramid with a square base and four triangular faces.

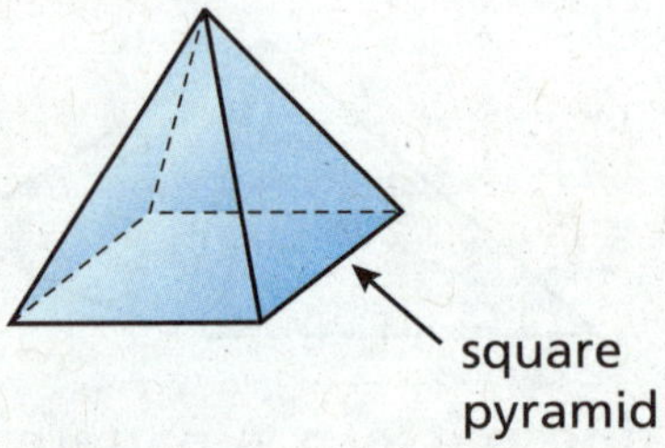

standard form The name of a number written using digits.

Example: 1,829

straight angle An angle that measures 180°.

subtract To find the difference of two numbers.

Example: $18 - 11 = 7$

subtraction A mathematical operation on a sum (total) and an addend, which can be called the difference.

Example: $43 - 40 = 3$

sum The answer when adding two or more addends.

Example: $37 + 52 = 89$

addend *partner* — addend *partner* — sum *total*

survey A method of collecting information.

symmetry A figure has symmetry if it can be folded along a line so that the two halves match exactly.

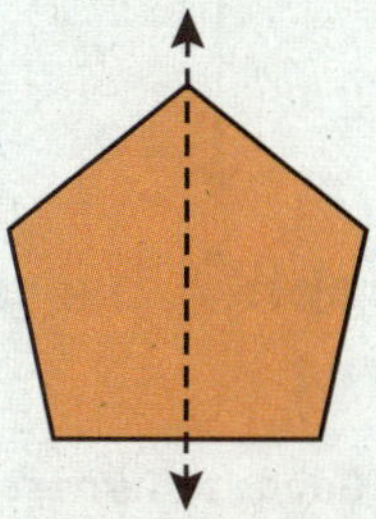

T

table An easy to read arrangement of data, usually in rows and columns.

Coin Toss

	Heads	Tails
Sam	11	6
Zoe	9	10

tally marks Short line segments drawn in groups of 5. Each mark including the slanted marks stands for 1 unit.

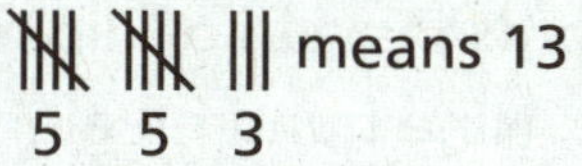

tenth One of the equal parts when a whole is divided into ten equal parts.

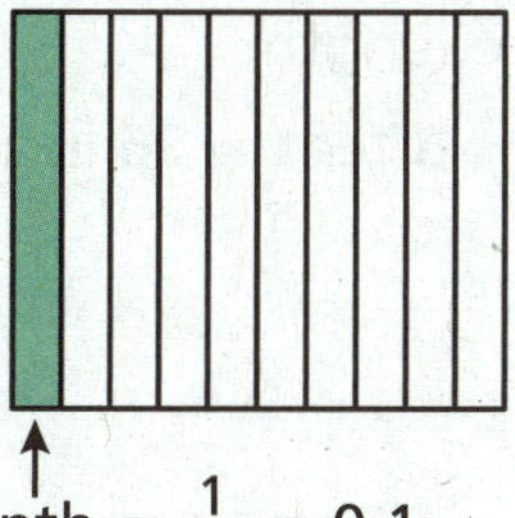

one tenth = $\frac{1}{10}$ = 0.1

thermometer A tool for measuring temperature.

total The answer when adding two or more addends. The sum of two or more numbers.

Example: 672 + 228 = 900

partner *addend* (672), partner *addend* (228), total *sum* (900)

trapezoid A quadrilateral with exactly one pair of parallel sides.

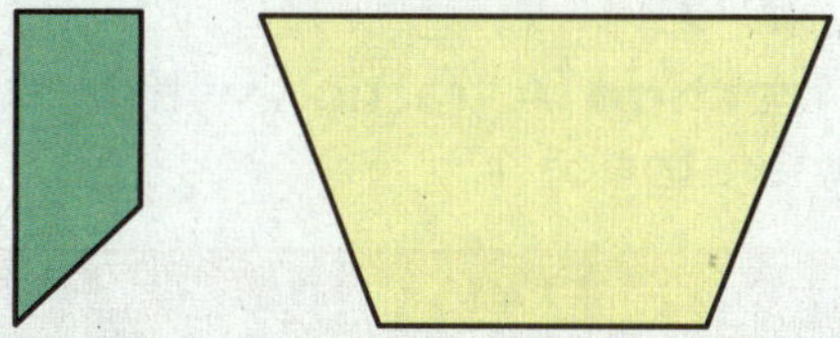

triangular prism A solid figure with two triangular faces and three rectangular faces.

Example:

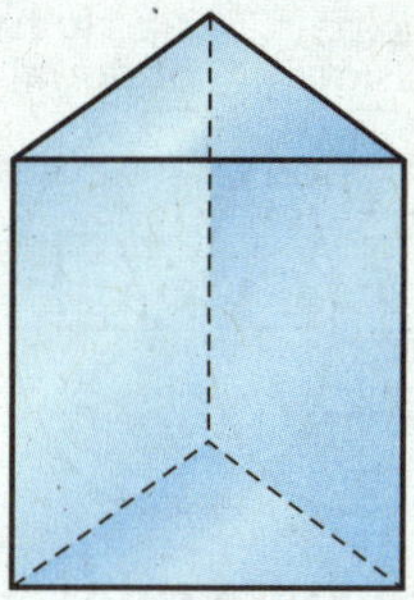

triangular pyramid A pyramid whose base is a triangle.

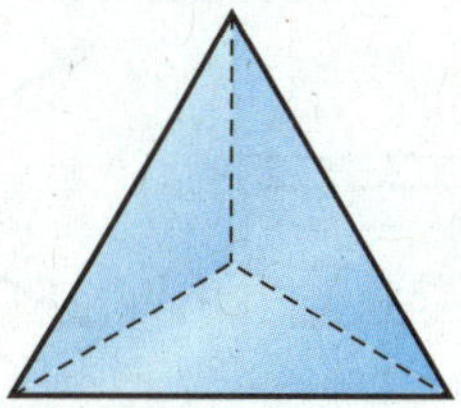

turn To rotate a figure around a point. The size and shape of the figure remains the same.

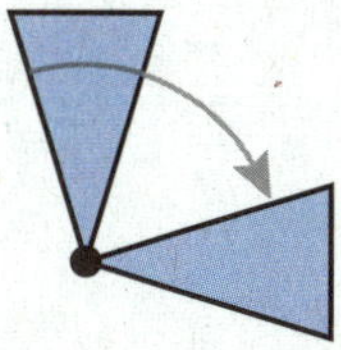

U

ungroup To open up 1 in a given place to make 10 of the next smaller place value in order to subtract.

unit fraction A fraction with a numerator of 1.

V

Venn diagram A diagram that uses circles to show the relationship among sets of objects.

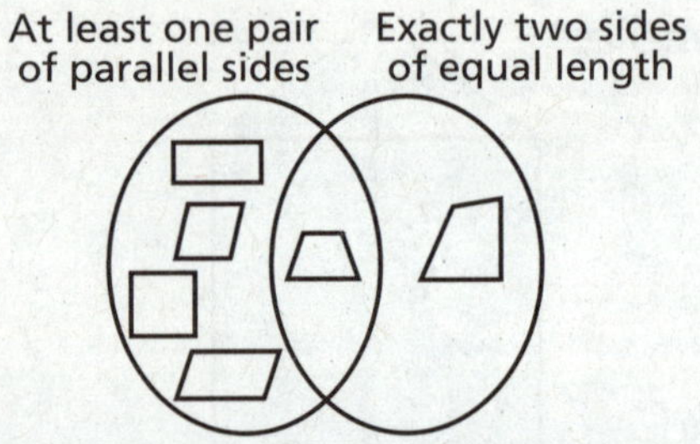

vertex A point where sides, rays, or edges meet.

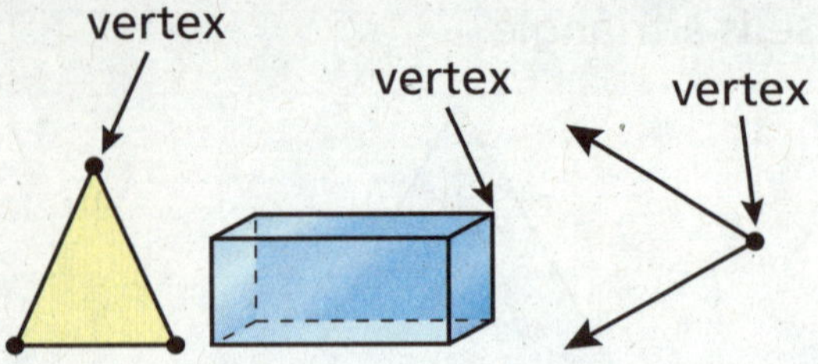

vertical Extending in two directions, up and down.

vertical bar graph A bar graph with vertical bars.

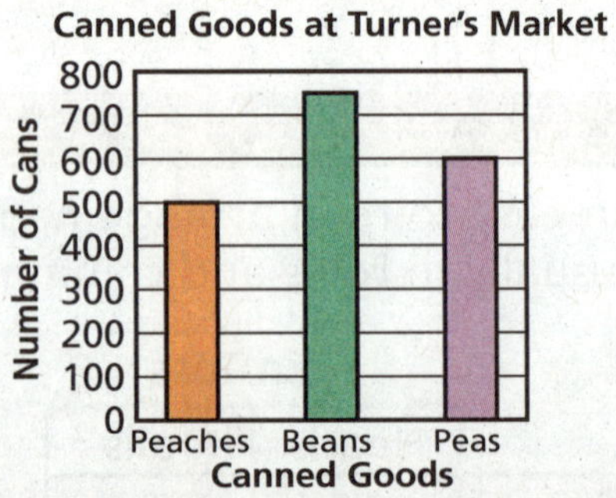

W

weight The measure of how heavy something is.

word form A name of a number written using words instead of digits.

Example: Nine hundred eighty-four

Y

yard (yd) A customary unit used to measure length.

1 yard = 3 feet = 36 inches